THE WINE OF CERTITUDE

DAVID ROONEY

The Wine of Certitude

A Literary Biography of Ronald Knox

IGNATIUS PRESS SAN FRANCISCO

Cover photograph of Ronald Arbuthnott Knox
by
Howard Coster
Half plate film negative, 1938
National Portrait Gallery, London

Cover design by Roxanne Mei Lum

ISBN 978-1-58617-232-9
Library of Congress Control Number 2008926723
Printed in the United States of America ♾

CONTENTS

PREFACE

The English Catholic literary revival had already been thriving for almost three-quarters of a century when Ronald Knox, fourth son of the Anglican Bishop of Manchester, was received into the Roman communion on September 22, 1917. It had begun with the conversions of the clergymen John Henry Newman and Henry Edward Manning, both later to become cardinals, and the layman William George Ward, whose son and granddaughter would carry on the apostolate of the pen, the former through books and essays, and the latter primarily as cofounder with her husband of the most famous Catholic publishing house of the twentieth century.[1]

In the early 1900s, that world of letters was the domain of Hilaire Belloc and G.K. Chesterton (though Chesterton's formal entry into the Church wouldn't come until 1922), and of the prolific but short-lived novelist Robert Hugh Benson, himself the convert son of an Archbishop of Canterbury. It was a world in which many well-educated men and women had come to see the Church of England as insufficiently countercultural in the face of materialism, agnosticism, and alternating moods of self-pride and despair, and who then saw in Rome a constancy and a consistency betokening a sure guide to the meaning of the Gospel message. There were converts among scientists, among historians, among novelists, even among actors, and the impression they produced, especially during the decades of Knox's prominence (the 1910s through the 1950s) was fortifying to those already in the Church, encouraging to those thinking about conversion, and vaguely alarming to those who retained the prejudice against Rome so thoroughly inbred in the nominally tolerant, vestigially Protestant culture that dominated the printed and spoken media.

[1] Technically W. G. Ward too had been a clergyman, but he had become convinced that Anglican orders were invalid and was engaged to be married even before he was stripped of his Oxford degrees for his advanced Roman-leaning views. He subsequently entered the Catholic Church a vociferous member of the laity.

Two fairly recent books have chronicled that world through an examination of many of the figures who experienced conversion to Catholicism. Patrick Allitt's *Catholic Converts* surveys both sides of the Atlantic Ocean for writers to profile and consequently includes sketches of figures such as Theodore Maynard, Dorothy Day, and Carlton Hayes along with the British intellectuals whose works were likely to be found on the Sheed and Ward book list.[2] Joseph Pearce's *Literary Converts* focuses solely on the British writers but illustrates well the web of contacts that continued to breathe life into the movement up to the days when Alec Guinness converted.[3] Not surprisingly both historians accord Knox a respectable chapter or so, but in such comprehensive overviews one would not anticipate finding more than a brief analysis of some of his signature works.

In a way, Knox was blessed in his choice of biographer and literary executor. Evelyn Waugh was certainly one of the most celebrated novelists in mid-twentieth-century England, and he was a friend who genuinely admired Knox for what he wrote and how he crafted what he wrote. Waugh had access to Knox's private papers, and with Waugh being only fifteen years Knox's junior, Waugh's circle of friends intersected enough with Knox's to allow him to mine reminiscences fairly effortlessly while working on his biography. Yet the formidable shadow of Waugh, coupled with the temporary eclipse Knox suffered during the postconciliar years, may have deflected later historians from producing another biography in the near half century since Knox's death. Waugh had assumed, incorrectly as time was to show, that in the years after Knox's death, scholars would pore over Knox's writings, dissertation following dissertation in theology faculties much as they have on, say, Newman or Thomas Merton. Knox's niece, the gifted writer Penelope Fitzgerald, did write a highly acclaimed (and recently reissued) composite biography in the 1970s of the four Knox brothers: Edmund (her father), Dillwyn, Wilfred, and Ronald. The reader interested in Knox's life will find in her book some personal touches that supplement what Waugh provides in his more formal biography. In the mid-1960s, Robert Speaight, an accomplished actor and biogra-

[2] Patrick Allitt, *Catholic Converts: British and American Intellectuals Turn to Rome* (Ithaca, N.Y.: Cornell University Press, 1997).

[3] Joseph Pearce, *Literary Converts: Spiritual Inspiration in an Age of Unbelief* (San Francisco: Ignatius Press, 1999).

pher of personages as disparate as Belloc and Teilhard de Chardin, wrote a lengthy essay on Knox's contributions to apologetics, detective fiction, satire, and other genres. This was then bound in hardcover by Sheed and Ward (ever obliging to Knox's memory) to an equally long essay by Father Thomas Corbishley on Knox's spiritual writings. Much time has passed since then, and more than one commentator has noted some slips of the pen in Speaight's essay. Twenty years later, Father Milton Walsh wrote a doctoral dissertation for the Pontifical Gregorian University that concentrates primarily on Knox's apologetics, though it also notably presents some previously unpublished sermons Walsh discovered on a visit to Knox's final resting place in Mells, home to the Earl of Oxford and Asquith. Father Walsh kindly sent me a copy some years ago, and its scholarly merit is evident. It has now happily been made available in updated form for the reading public as *Ronald Knox as Apologist*.[4]

The time then may be auspicious for an overview of the full range of the mind of Ronald Knox, a fifty-year-later retrospective of a fifty-year career in letters, which commenced at Eton College in 1906 and was stilled only when death from liver cancer overtook him on August 24, 1957. The present work is an intellectual portrait of the kind that I flatter myself might have qualified for the English Men of Letters series of a century ago. The following pages do not attempt to add anything to the story of Knox's life. The first chapter is included merely to provide the reader who has not read either Waugh or Fitzgerald with a framework within which to peg chronologically Knox's literary endeavors, which are segregated largely by subject matter in the remaining chapters. Likewise, it does not purport to address his place in modern theology, a subject Father Walsh is far better equipped to analyze than I am. It is instead a purely armchair survey of what Knox wrote in a variety of genres, with the attendant advantages and disadvantages of such an exercise. The seasoned historian, and even more so the student of theology, who scans the footnotes will no doubt find too frequently the reference to a less-definitive study on some topic, read and cited merely because it happened to occupy a more convenient place on a home or institutional bookshelf. On the other hand,

[4] Milton Walsh, *Ronald Knox as Apologist: Wit, Laughter and the Popish Creed* (San Francisco: Ignatius Press, 2007).

armchair readers will find that most of the references are to books available in reasonably large university libraries, and none to manuscripts or letters rendered practically inaccessible to them because they repose in out-of-the-way archives, or for that matter to books written in tongues the author is insufficiently conversant in to read more rapidly than at the pace *d'un escargot.*[5]

As with all writers, Knox was influenced by other writers, yet neither Waugh nor Fitzgerald was particularly interested in charting those influences; it was enough for them simply to write their biographies with the occasional nod toward Knox's literary achievements. This book too was initially planned as a portrait of his mind and no one else's. But others necessarily found their way onto the canvas. Some, like W. H. Mallock and Father Maturin, entered by invitation lest the portrait be missing something; some entered by brute force of personality, like Arnold Lunn; others, like Samuel Butler, wandered in unexpectedly, while yet others, like Bertrand Russell and Julian Huxley, were ushered in to provide some needed chiaroscuro. As a result, the final portrait differs from those of Allitt and Pearce, not only in the far greater attention devoted to but one Catholic convert, but also in being more inclusive (even if at times only in the footnotes) of Catholic-from-birth thinkers like Fathers Martin D'Arcy and Herbert Thurston, as well as of various symposiasts, BBC Brains Trust commentators, and others to whom Knox had to react in his public ministry as apologist for Catholicism.

The reader will observe too that around one-quarter of this book was actually written by Knox himself, so frequent and so lengthy are the quotes included in the text. Indeed, in writing and assembling it, I have often considered the work in light of the "mosaic" approach used by the great contemporary historian Emmet Larkin, who so skillfully has patched together extensive extracts from Irish bishops and other personages to make the period from 1850 to the early twentieth century in Irish ecclesiastical history emerge so vividly from the printed page in his multivolume series.[6]

At the same time, when as in the present work the quotes are so predominantly issuing from the writings of one person, the author/

[5] "Of a snail".

[6] See, for example, Emmet Larkin, *The Making of the Roman Catholic Church in Ireland, 1850–1860* (Chapel Hill, N.C.: University of North Carolina Press, 1980).

arranger must often guard against the inclination to present the reader with too much of the best of what the subject has written, thereby inadvertently fostering the impression in the reader's mind that there is no need to go back to the originals, since the purest gold has already been extracted from the ore of commonplace writing, and so any expenditure of energy directed to sifting through the rest would be superfluous. Let the reader be assured that such is not the case with Knox's writing. In editing and reviewing the quotes used, I am frequently tempted to employ far more material; how much more edifying, indeed, it would be, just to reprint whole sermons rather than paragraphs from them. When Philip Caraman edited Knox's sermons and Oxford conferences alone, he ended up with three volumes of small print, each running to well over four hundred pages.

There are over forty thousand words taken from Knox's writings in the present book, but they represent well under 1 percent of his published output. The other 99 percent is of the same quality. The reader need only randomly consult any of his books to verify that assertion. He was a consummate writer: every word in its place, every sentence carrying forward an argument or an image, every thought intelligible and, far more often than not, compellingly persuasive. If the present work does not encourage the reader to seek out and read a book written *by* Knox, and not just a book *about* Knox, it will have failed in its intent.

It should also be mentioned in passing that a little over a decade ago, the publisher of this book brought out a volume called *The Quotable Knox*.[7] No doubt it is a good introduction to its subject, but with a deliberateness bordering on scrupulosity, I have avoided ever seeing it, not to mention perusing it. That is simply because I did not want to be influenced in any way by what its estimable editors considered quotable in his writings while I was selecting what I found useful to quote. If there is an overlap, it may then be attributed to the overwhelming effect certain Knoxian paragraphs produce on whoever reads them. The same probability of overlap might have been presumed to exist vis-à-vis Father Walsh's study, but in actuality the overlap is not at all great, so quotable is our common quarry.

[7] George Marlin, Richard Rabatin, and John Swan, *The Quotable Knox: A Topical Compendium of the Wit and Wisdom of Ronald Knox* (San Francisco: Ignatius Press, 1996).

Finally, the reader will, I hope, excuse a personal note, which a preface seems to demand. As was mentioned above, this study is of the armchair variety and was cobbled together outside normal duties, which revolve around teaching university students in such noncongruent subject matter to literature and theology as aerodynamics and structural analysis. The staff of Hofstra University Library, especially its interlibrary loan office, has been very helpful in tracking down whatever books I needed so that I could follow through on a line of investigation.

I should admit that I was already well into my adult years when I first became familiar with Ronald Knox's writings, even though I had read continental writers like Jacques Maritain, Josef Pieper, and Karl Adam a long time earlier. Around 1990, I was serving in a very part-time capacity as literary editor for a small Midwestern Catholic monthly journal of opinion when I received a batch of potential review books containing, among other items, a new printing of *A Retreat for Lay People*. I owned at the time only a copy of *Enthusiasm* among Knox's titles, and I regret now to say that it had remained unread because its scope and its subject seemed a bit too peripheral to my reviewing interests in modern American and British Church history. In any case, I read the retreat book and was henceforth a Knox admirer.

Which brings me to my largest debt of gratitude. I deeply appreciate the patience of my wife Mary and of my five children, Mary Therese, Margaret, Bernadette, Claire, and Robert, during the years I have worked on this project in the hope of introducing a new generation of readers to a remarkable writer and expositor of philosophical and theological truth. My children can no longer be unaware of Ronald Knox: his books cover a fair number of shelves and will increasingly invite inspection as adulthood rapidly approaches. May they and other children grow into full womanhood and manhood appreciating them and achieving a deeper faith with their assistance.

CHAPTER ONE

A PRIESTLY LIFE

Ronald Arbuthnott Knox was born into a family whose circumstances guaranteed a certain predisposition to the clerical life. Both his grandfathers were clergymen, though of widely different outlook and careers, and his father rose to some eminence as an Evangelical Bishop of Manchester. George Knox, the paternal grandfather, was by all accounts a dour man, whose mother died in 1818 when he was four and whose father bore him little affection. After an undistinguished record at Cambridge gained him a pass degree, he took ministerial orders and went to Wales as a curate in 1837. Two years later, he sailed to India as a chaplain to the East India Company and in 1844 married a pious Quaker named Frances Reynolds. (Frances' younger sister soon afterward married David Arbuthnott, which gave occasion for that name to crop up in future generations but also brought about a schism in the family, because the Arbuthnotts converted to Catholicism and henceforth the Knoxes could not in good conscience communicate with them.) George and Frances eventually had four sons and four daughters, most of whom were born in India before the family's return to England in 1855. The second of their children was Ronald's father, Edmund Arbuthnott Knox, whose lively memoirs published in 1934 at the age of 87 provide much of the source material for the Knox family history.[1]

Filial piety precluded Edmund from direct criticism of his father's regimen, but his recounting of a youthful life marked by spartan meals, isolation from other families, and a wardrobe of indestructible clothing that each child inherited regardless of changing fashions, suggests

[1] Edmund A. Knox, *Reminiscences of an Octogenarian, 1847–1934* (London: Hutchinson and Co., 1935). They are truly personal reminiscences, with almost no attention directed toward the careers of his by-then-illustrious children.

a home stifled by parsimony and Puritanism. In England, George functioned as secretary to a missionary society and rector of a parish in Waddon. His sermons were held up as a model of literary style to his children, whose choices for recreational reading were carefully monitored.

Of the eight children, the eldest son became a judge, Edmund and his brother Lindsey became clerics, and none of the sisters married, though one achieved distinction as an educator in Canada. Fortunately, Edmund grew into a decidedly different type of man from his father. He attended Saint Paul's, a day school in London, his academic performance earning him free tuition, and in 1865 won a full scholarship to Oxford, to the satisfaction of his father who as a result did not have to pay anything for Edmund's entire education. After securing a first-class honors degree, he won a clerical fellowship to Merton College in 1869, where he pursued studies in modern history and was ordained the next year. The fellowship guaranteed him three hundred pounds a year and the life of a scholar, which he led for fifteen years while taking on various administrative duties and ministering to several parishes. In 1876, the Reverend Thomas Valpy French briefly settled in a nearby parish, and the eldest of his eight children, Ellen, was courted by Edmund. They married in 1878.

Thomas French, who was thereby to become Ronald Knox's maternal grandfather, was a far more zealous seeker of souls than George Knox had been. A man with a natural gift for languages, he followed the call to India in 1850 at the age of twenty-seven, married a young woman from a well-to-do mercantile family, and proceeded to evangelize in the marketplace with the fearlessness of Saint Paul. While George Knox never returned to foreign fields after settling in at Waddon, Thomas French was forever beckoned by the prospect of converting Hindus and Muslims, whose languages and cultures he thoroughly assimilated. His presence at Oxford in the mid-1870s was occasioned only by the need to recover from an illness acquired while working on a Pushtu translation of the Bible. By the time of Ellen's marriage, he was serving as bishop of Lahore in what is now Pakistan. He would die in 1891 wandering through Muscat still preaching to the occasional Muslim who would deign to listen to a messenger of the Gospel.

Ellen, whose health was never robust, had four children with Edmund during their Oxford years. Ethel, the eldest, was born in 1879 and although long-lived was mildly retarded. The first son was born in 1881: Edmund Jr., who would later achieve fame as a writer and editor for *Punch*. Winifred, born the next year, became a successful novelist. Dillwyn followed in 1883 and later in life gained repute first as a classicist at Cambridge and then as a cryptographer in government service.

In 1884, the growing young Knox family moved to Kibworth in Leicestershire, where an opening in a country parsonage offered what seemed to be an excellent opportunity for Ellen to regain her health, which had suffered at Oxford. A more picturesque homestead could hardly be imagined. The solid brick rectory house built in the late eighteenth century still resonated in Bishop Knox's mind fifty years later:

> . . . its bay windows looking out on the rectory garden and fields, its shrubbery with a marvelous wealth of aconites, primroses of all shades of colour, and wild violets—its spacious walled kitchen garden, its sunny flower garden sheltered from north and east winds. Nowhere have I seen finer strawberries, raspberries, and Victoria plums than those we grew in the rectory garden. We had a well-built stable between us and the churchyard, a snug rookery, and rook-pies in their season—we had our cowshed, and fields, and like Herrick, our cows and a few sheep disporting themselves in our own fields. What more could we wish?[2]

It was here that Wilfred, later to become an Anglican priest and an accomplished New Testament scholar, was born in 1886, and that on February 17, 1888, the last of the six Knox children, Ronald, entered the world.

Unfortunately, Ellen did not thrive in Leicestershire and was weakened further during an influenza epidemic in 1889. By 1891, the Evangelically minded trustees of Aston-juxta-Birmingham sought out Knox to take charge of their massive parish, which had mushroomed to some forty thousand souls as industrial expansion created a metropolis around it. Since his Oxford days, Edmund Sr. had always been associated with the Evangelical wing of the Anglican Church. He did not sympathize with the Oxford Movement and was unyielding when Edward Pusey

[2] Ibid., p. 127.

tried to convince him to accept the Real Presence according to the Catholic understanding of the Sacrament.

The Aston church itself was a beautiful structure in the Gothic style, one of the finest, in Edmund Sr.'s estimate, in England. But the vicarage, dwarfed by a brewery in a soot-laden street and overlooking a graveyard overrun with gaudy memorials, was not an ideal home for his family. Nevertheless, both he and Ellen gave themselves wholly to the building up of parish life, and the family's first Christmas in Aston in 1891 was their happiest in years because everyone was healthy. By the beginning of 1892, however, Ellen had fallen ill again, and although she was transported to various sites in the hope of convalescence, she died in August.

In accordance with the custom of the time, the young children were parceled out to relatives because Edmund Knox's duties to the parish rendered it impossible for him to oversee their upbringing. Ronald and Wilfred were sent to lodge with Edmund's brother Lindsey, a bachelor cleric who was vicar of Edmundthorpe in Lincolnshire and who shared a home with his widowed mother Frances and three unmarried sisters. He was a benevolent influence, and the two young brothers savored the warm Evangelical atmosphere, spending much time out of doors but also beginning their acquaintance with the Greek and Latin languages.

The diaspora was limited in duration, because by the time Edmund Knox was consecrated a bishop in December 1894, preliminary to his appointment as rector of Saint Philip's, archdeacon of Birmingham, and suffragan bishop of the Diocese of Coventry, he was engaged, this time to Ethel Newton, the eldest daughter of the vicar of Ridditch. Ethel, twenty years younger than the now portly bishop, brimmed with self-confidence: she was very intelligent, cultured, and undaunted by the prospect of being stepmother to six unruly children. Ronald's niece Penelope, also a successful novelist, who wrote a book about her father (Edmund Jr.) and her three uncles, described the first visit of the Knoxes to Holmwood, the Newton estate:

> The Knox children looked like scarecrows, or remnants from a jumble sale, the girls in all-purpose black frocks, two sizes too large to allow for growth, Ronnie and Wilfred in grotesque black suits, hand-sewn by their grandmother's maid at Edmundthorpe. The six of

> them clung together awkwardly, too shy to find the right words. They had known them at Kibworth, but had forgotten them since. For their part, they stared almost in disbelief at the house to which they had been brought. Holmwood was in the highest style of the Arts and Crafts movement, with stone-framed lattice windows and steep slate roofs, the haunt of doves in summer, now deep in snow. Once inside the white-painted hall they saw shining floors, Gimson furniture, Morris chintzes, and a staircase sweeping upwards to the glass dome of the house. A blazing wood fire drew out the scent of hot-house plants. And where did the light come from? None of the children had ever seen electric light in a house before. When Wilfred and Ronnie were put to bed they sat in their nightgowns, taking strict turns, as they always did, to turn it on and off, and nobody told them to stop.[3]

Ethel brought order to the Knox household after her 1895 marriage to the bishop. Despite Edmund's preference for sending his children to day schools, she convinced him that boarding schools would provide the discipline they needed. So Ronald was sent at age eight to Summer Fields for four years of study preparatory to entering Eton in September 1900.

In his later years, Ronald Knox unabashedly referred to his six years at Eton as the happiest in his life. His biographer, Evelyn Waugh, explained why:

> Eton was the scene of Ronald's brilliant intellectual development and of his ardent and undying friendships. Most candid Englishmen recognize it as a school *sui generis* [altogether unique] which marks the majority of its sons with a peculiar Englishry, genial, confident, humorous, and reticent; which gives to each as little or as much learning as his abilities and tastes demand; which while correcting affectation allows the genuine eccentric to go his own way unmolested; which nourishes its rare favourites—among whom Ronald was immediately numbered—in a rich and humane traditional culture which admits no rival. The fact that it was the training ground of Edwardian plutocracy, that it afforded early intimacy

[3] Penelope Fitzgerald, *The Knox Brothers* (New York: Coward, McCann and Geoghegan, 1977), pp. 43–44. Writing almost two decades later, Fitzgerald, as Edmund Jr.'s daughter and a successful author herself, supplements Evelyn Waugh's biography with valuable insights about her uncle and the rest of the Knoxes.

with the sons of the powerful and opened the ranks of privilege to the ambitious, meant nothing to Ronald.[4]

The bishop was not well-to-do, and Ronald, along with his brothers and his sister Winifred, could aspire to pursue studies at the most elite institutions in the country solely on the basis of scholarships earned, not on wealth or family connections. However, many of Ronald's friends were from aristocratic families, such as the Grenfell brothers, Charles Lister, and Edward Horner. In a class-conscious society, Knox was nevertheless easily accepted among them because of his intelligence, wit, and affability.

Midway through Ronald's Eton years came the final translation of his father's career, to the bishopric of Manchester, where he had oversight of more than six hundred parishes but could count on a better supply of clergymen (virtually none of them advanced Ritualists) and a stronger base of financial support than he had had to grapple with in Birmingham. Here he would carry on his campaigns for church schools, which a secularized government was undermining through legislation promoting state schools devoid of religious education, and also do battle against the Romeward-tinged wing of the hierarchy over the Anglican Prayer Book revision and the toleration of symbols redolent of the Sacrifice of the Mass.

The bishop's immersion in diocesan and national affairs left little time to keep track of each of his children's intellectual and religious progress. Of the former, he need have had little worry, although his eldest son required stern admonitions from a professor of logic to avoid being sent down from Oxford for inattention to his studies. But adhesion to Evangelical forms of piety was weak: the elder sons drifted toward agnosticism, while Ronald, supported by his sister Winifred, inclined toward Ritualism.

Meanwhile, Ronald was writing for the *Eton Chronicle*, where his precocious literary skills were gaining polish, and he published a slim volume of his cleverest poetry at the age of eighteen. The title of the

[4] Evelyn Waugh, *Ronald Knox* (Boston: Little, Brown and Co., 1959), p. 54. Waugh knew Knox well in the last decade of Knox's life, and his book remains the only full-scale biography to date. Despite an enormous amount of information culled from firsthand sources woven into an engrossing portrait, given the force of Waugh's own personality and opinions, the appearance of a comprehensive biographical study by a more dispassionate hand is overdue.

book, *Signa Severa* (A severe sign), was deliberately obscure, but the subject matter of the verses was drawn largely from school life. The effects of a youthful devotion to W. S. Gilbert's *Bab Ballads* are to be seen in poems such as "A Prospective Epithalamium", composed in February 1904 to herald the marriage of Reverend Cyril Alington, the master of the college. It begins:

> Let the fiat of joy to man and to boy to the points of the
> compass go forth,
> Which chiefly consist, as you know, of the west and the
> east and the south and the north;
> For he, who to College in absence of knowledge
> devoted a part of his life,
> Will now be consoled, as was Adam of old, by the comfort
> and care of a wife.[5]

It goes on in the same vein for another four verses. Almost all the contributions are sprinkled liberally with classical allusions, and some with lines rendered in Greek. That encumbrance, compounded by their peculiarly Etonian topicality, leaves many of them as opaque to the modern reader as the title of the book. While one can appreciate the rhyming of

> Eton, didst thou think that Canon Lyttleton would turn a lissom
> Ear to the remonstrances of silly-season journalism?

what is one to make of further lines in the same poem about the accession of the new headmaster?

> Still thy wonted thiasus its lustre to the scene adds,
> Lyssades and Bacchanals, and Bassarids and Maenads,
> Pop and Upper Sixpenny and Colleger and Sap
> Famously walking up and down in front of Tap.[6]

When Ronald entered Balliol College in Oxford in September 1906, one among a large contingent of highly talented Etonians, much was expected of him as a scholar, and he lived up to those expectations

[5] Ronald Knox, *Signa Severa* (Eton College: Spottiswoode and Co., 1906), p. 7.
[6] Ibid., pp. 42–43.

without seeming to tax himself inordinately. While he accrued various scholarships and prizes, he participated in countless social, political, and religious clubs and, despite his unprepossessing frame and subdued voice, won renown as a public speaker and debater. His crystallizing theological opinions led him to frequent Pusey House over Balliol Chapel for religious services. He became friendly with Francis Urquhart, the junior dean of Balliol, who was a Roman Catholic, and who invited him on one of his annual reading parties to Chamonix in 1908. Ronald also visited the Anglican Benedictines at Caldey Island in 1909. And while old friendships perdured, his rooms became a magnet for new acquaintances who shared his Anglo-Catholic beliefs. A summer trip to Bruges in 1910 in the company of Reverend Maurice Child and Samuel Gurney afforded him the opportunity to experience a Catholic culture for the first time as an adult. He had already decided to prepare himself for Anglican orders, and the offer of a fellowship at Trinity College fitted in well with his plans.

That year, Knox also published his second book, *Juxta Salices* (By the side of the willow trees). The preface, in explanation of the title, directs the reader to Psalm 137 (or 136 in the Catholic numbering), which tells of the captives from Zion weeping by the willow trees of Babylon. The material within its covers, however, is hardly melancholic, except for some farewell verses to Eton (written in July 1906 and therefore too late to show up in *Signa Severa*) that employ the exilic imagery of the above-cited psalm. Prose mingles with poetry in the new volume. An early jab at the pedants appears in a parody of the methodology of *The Golden Bough* to explain away Guy Fawkes Day as a primitive sun myth. A symposium on the nature of love—in which Socrates, Aristotle, the March Hare, George Bernard Shaw, Mrs. Malaprop, Sherlock Holmes, and Samuel Johnson spar with enough other participants to allow speaking roles for the nineteen members of one Oxford club to which Knox belonged—was performed prior to being committed to print.[7]

While he tutored in logic and the great Greek and Latin epics, Knox followed his own course of readings in theology. He also counseled a new generation of Oxford undergraduates, including Harold

[7] Ronald Knox, *Juxta Salices* (London: Alden and Co., 1910). The author owns Julian Huxley's annotated copy of this book, which reveals that Huxley was assigned the role of Mrs. Malaprop in the play, a symbolically appropriate casting for a scientist who would later betray difficulty in using religious terminology properly in his own writings.

Macmillan, the future prime minister, who inclined toward Catholicism. Macmillan's parents, who were stout Protestants, relieved Knox of his private tutorship of their son because they feared his loss to idolatrous worship. The break was short-lived, however, and although Macmillan did not follow Knox on his spiritual journey, the two remained lifelong friends.

Knox was ordained on September 22, 1912. Meanwhile, his friends Child and Gurney had established the Society of Saints Peter and Paul as a publishing house to dispense tracts expounding the Anglo-Catholic message. It soon provided a vehicle for Knox's most famous satirical swipes at liberal Protestantism, reprinting *Absolute and Abitofhell*, after its initial appearance in the *Oxford Magazine*, and also *Reunion All Round*. In addition, the publishing house printed his sermons summoning the Anglican faithful to a more sacramental religion; this at the very time his father was writing a book called *Sacrifice or Sacrament?* which urged his episcopal brethren "not to betray that form of Liturgy to which they have declared their allegiance, and not to corrupt it by meretricious ornaments which belong to a distinct and wholly alien teaching." [8]

Father and son had by now become the leading spokesmen for two mutually exclusive branches of the same church. Ronald thought then that a closer adhesion to Roman Catholic belief and usage would save the Anglican Church from dissolution in relativism; Edmund looked to continental Protestantism to invigorate the church against the idolatry he believed Rome countenanced, and even championed. Ronald wrote *Some Loose Stones* to expose the logical errors of the Modernist theologians; Edmund saw Modernists simply as the outgrowth of Anglo-Catholicism, whose chief fault lay in their dismissal of Scriptural inerrancy as the bedrock of faith.

Despite his growing reputation as a thorn in the side of mainstream Anglicanism, Ronald spent the prewar years from 1910 to 1914 secure in his station. "His prayers", Evelyn Waugh notes in his biography, "were so easy and his association with his friends so congenial that he was able to live for some years in a hallowed world of his own." [9] But then the reading parties ended, and Oxford became depopulated, as

[8] E. Knox, *Reminiscences*, p. 310.

[9] Waugh, *Knox*, p. 111.

enthusiasm for war broke out over England. Virtually all his friends from his own generation—Julian Grenfell, Edward Horner, Charles Lister, Patrick Shaw-Stewart—enlisted, as did the younger men he knew as a tutor. Knox himself, who as a youth had celebrated British victories in the Boer War with painfully jingoistic verse, was among the few not caught up in war fever in 1914.

Knox would, however, have gone to the front as a chaplain, but his theological views were too sacramental for the authorities, who wanted hearty, bluff clerics who would administer cigarettes rather than last rites to dying soldiers, and so he was not selected for service. He was finally wavering in his adherence to Anglicanism. Several friends, facing the immolation that awaited enlistees at the front, had opted to become Catholics. Uncertain himself about the validity of his priestly orders after he attended his brother Wilfred's first service in May 1915, he was loath to counsel others whether or not to convert. With little to do at Oxford, he volunteered as a replacement classics instructor at Shrewsbury. By all accounts, he was a creative teacher, and he did not allow his inner turmoil to be perceived by the VI Form boys. During the summer vacation in 1916, he left the school to work alongside his brother Dillwyn in the section of naval intelligence devoted to code breaking. He had confided his doubts about his religious position to the Jesuit C. C. Martindale, whom he had met at the home of Lord Halifax, the great promoter of Anglican rapprochement with Rome. Father Martindale advised him against converting merely out of dissatisfaction but rather to wait until positive reasons drew him to the Catholic Church. The next spring they spoke again, and Martindale, himself a convert, urged him to proceed. In September 1917, Knox resigned his Trinity fellowship, went on retreat to the Benedictine abbey at Farnborough, and was received into the Catholic Church on September 22, five years to the day after his ordination as an Anglican priest. To the last, his father had entreated him not to convert; from his perspective, Ronald would be throwing away his talents on an unworthy cause. The letters back and forth between father and son in 1917 were truly anguished. All the controversial points were rehashed, and the elder Knox did not disdain overtly emotional appeals, claiming for example that Ronald's decision would force him to resign the See of Manchester. In the event, of course, he did not, but the rupture between the two was so deep that when Bishop Knox died in 1937, Ronald's name was not to be found in his will.

Other bonds of friendship were also being severed, but not because of his conversion. Julian Grenfell had died in action in May 1915, Charles Lister in August 1915, Edward Horner in November 1917, Patrick Shaw-Stewart in December 1917, and Guy Lawrence, who had preceded Knox into the Catholic Church and hoped to become a priest when the war was over, was killed in August 1918. Lawrence had been especially close to Knox, and to Harold Macmillan, whose hesitancy about converting in the midst of the war proved permanent. Charles Lister's sister Laura had converted prior to marrying Lord Lovat, a landed Scottish aristocrat, and her residence at Beaufort Castle was to become a mainstay of Knox's vacations in the 1920s. Edward Horner's sister Katharine, who married Raymond Asquith, son of the prewar prime minister, would also play an important role in his future life. Her husband was killed in the Battle of the Somme in July 1916, leaving her with two daughters and a son, and she later converted to Catholicism. Their home at Mells Park in Somerset, a one-time monastery that had been owned by the Horners for four centuries and boasted a substantial Pre-Raphaelite collection, was to be Ronald's residence the last ten years of his life.[10]

The hecatomb left families and friends groping for ways to alleviate their sorrow. The writing of memoirs of foreshortened lives that had promised brilliance was one outlet for those possessed of sufficient correspondence and testimonials to flesh out a story of which the final pages read the same for millions of dead soldiers across Europe and the Near East.

[10] Knox's friendships with the Grenfells, Listers, Horners, and other families, which together constituted the clique known as the Souls (of whom Arthur Balfour and George Wyndham were also noteworthy members) ought not to give the impression that the Knox family was part of the group. Knox knew them through his years at Eton and Balliol: as the son of a bishop in an industrial city, he was not of the aristocratic sector of society. It is worth noting that a history of the two generations that constitute the Souls and their children (the generation that included his close friends who were largely obliterated by World War I) does not mention him even once. See Angela Lambert, *Unquiet Souls* (New York: Harper and Row, 1984). Likewise Jeanne Mackenzie in *The Children of the Souls* (London: Chatto and Windus, 1986) mentions him only tangentially as the sharpest mind of the lot, but not in the context of habitué of country houses.

Charles Lister's account of one such battleground was compiled by his father, Lord Ribblesdale.[11] Lister had been in the diplomatic corps in Rome and Constantinople before the war and resigned a post in the headquarters staff to seek combat duty in the Mediterranean. His battalion landed at Gallipoli, where it executed fruitless charges against machine guns, suffered desultory shelling from Turkish strongholds, and endured the tedium of trench life amid heat, flies, and the stench of partly buried corpses. Lister was wounded on his first day ashore, was sent to Malta to recover, and then went back into action, where he was wounded a second time by stray shrapnel and then a third time by a shelling. These last wounds proved fatal some days after shipboard surgery.

Knox had contributed a chapter on Lister's Eton and Balliol days to help frame Lord Ribblesdale's memoir. Patrick Shaw-Stewart's parents, on the other hand, had predeceased their son, and the task of sifting through his letters to family and friends to preserve a record of his wit as well as his gallantry fell to Knox. Shaw-Stewart was a Scotsman who followed a career in banking with Baring Brothers after excelling at Oxford in ancient history. He spent six months on business in the United States just before the war and then signed up with the Royal Naval Division. He shared passage through the Mediterranean with Charles Lister and the poet Rupert Brooke. Brooke contracted sun poisoning and pneumonia before they reached the Dardanelles, and when he died he was interred on an island in the Aegean Sea. Shaw-Stewart wrote to Knox of Charles Lister "constantly doing the most reckless things, walking between the lines with his arms waving under a hot fire from *both* sides; but his last wound, like his others, was from a shell in a trench, and no blame could attach."[12] As liaison between French and British troops, Shaw-Stewart survived many tedious months of intermittent warfare before the British evacuation of the peninsula in January 1916. The insanity of the conflict was not lost on him:

> It's pretty sad when you think of what it has cost us, but since they got German ammunition through, the shelling has been very tire-

[11] Lord Ribblesdale, *Charles Lister: Letters and Recollections* (London: T. Fisher Unwin, 1917).

[12] Ronald Knox, *Patrick Shaw-Stewart* (Glasgow: William Collins and Co., 1920), p. 148.

> some, and I am quite persuaded that it's the only thing to do. Only the French guns remain (of the French), and the French C.O. and I have been walking up and down looking unconcerned and smelling the breeze (in case it should develop), and burning anything we think the Turks would enjoy or be able to use. I have burnt some queer things, including a bowler hat.... But, on the whole, it's nothing to be proud of for the British Army or the French either—nine months here, and pretty heavy losses, and now nothing for it but to clear out.[13]

From the Dardanelles, Shaw-Stewart went to inaction in Macedonia and then took a short leave in England, only to return to the front in France in 1917. While in command of a battalion, he was killed in a barrage of German fire on December 30, 1917. He was an agnostic who found no consolation in a life after death. But culture and civility and a shared intellectual life endeared him to Knox. All the more poignant then is an untitled poem Shaw-Stewart composed and scribbled on the blank sheet of a book he owned:

> I saw a man this morning
> Who did not wish to die:
> I ask, and cannot answer,
> If otherwise wish I.
>
> Fair broke the day this morning
> Against the Dardanelles;
> The breeze blew soft, the morn's cheeks
> Were cold as cold sea-shells.
>
> But other shells are waiting
> Across the Aegean sea,
> Shrapnel and high explosive,
> Shells and hells for me.
>
> O hell of ships and cities,
> Hell of men like me,
> Fatal second Helen,
> Why must I follow thee?

[13] Ibid., pp. 157–58.

The penultimate verse is particularly haunting as the classicist, reflecting on the fate of the Homeric hero who fought similar battles in similar places, ponders over his own temporary reprieve, one which he no doubt surmised would be only temporary:

> Was it so hard, Achilles,
> So very hard to die?
> Thou knowest and I know not—
> So much the happier I.[14]

It may seem disproportionate in an abbreviated sketch of Knox's life to dilate at such length on the wartime experiences and reflections of the old Etonians. But their deaths in combat one by one affected him grievously, leaving him bereft of the spiritual and intellectual stimulus bred by deep friendship and impelled instead along a solitary path toward, and then within, a new and still unfamiliar Church.[15]

The end of hostilities meant that Knox could pursue ordination as a Catholic priest. While still a layman, he had written *A Spiritual Aeneid* during spare hours after his naval intelligence work. Now Cardinal Bourne assigned Knox to teaching duties at Saint Edmund's College in Hertfordshire, a combination preparatory school for boys and seminary for young men studying for the secular priesthood. He was ordained on October 5, 1919, a priest of the Westminster diocese, after following a self-directed course of study in lieu of being sent to a seminary in Rome.

No doubt the appointment to a Catholic school that did not even have the éclat of the Jesuit Stonyhurst College sustained Bishop Knox in his conviction that the Roman Catholic hierarchy would squander his son's talents in second-rate work. Even Ronald Knox's biographer cannot suppress an invidious comparison between the quality of Edmundians and Etonians. And yet he had several intellectual equals and friends

[14] Ibid., pp. 159–60.

[15] Many of Knox's friends did not share his religious outlook at all. A letter from Raymond Asquith, a somewhat older contemporary, to Diana Manners is representative of the viewpoint of men like Shaw-Stewart as well: "After all death is only a solution of the problem of life ... to be killed in action would gracefully set at rest many urgent and recurring anxieties. It has seemed to me of late that my only point was being a potential corpse. Without the glamour of the winding sheet I have no *locus standi* in the world." Quoted in Mackenzie, *Children of the Souls*, p. 218.

on the faculty (Laurence Eyres and Canon George Smith in particular), and he threw himself into teaching Latin and New Testament studies to the boys in his forms with gusto. Waugh perceptively notes another major outgrowth of the seven years from 1919 to 1926 Knox spent on the staff at Saint Edmund's:

> The lessons he learned and the friendships he made there were as formative as those of Eton, Balliol, and Trinity. During his time some sixty or seventy priests passed through the seminary as students and lecturers, some of them on the way to bishoprics, and these formed a solid company who in his later years never failed him in respect and affection, welcoming and supporting him in his vicissitudes, accepting him without reservation as one of themselves, and, in very many cases, taking him as their model. He was never to be, as R.H. Benson had been, an exotic; at St. Edmund's he was given a view deep into the human heart of the Church and an intimation of how he could best serve her.[16]

With a salary of under a hundred pounds per year and teaching duties that did not tax him excessively, Knox had both the incentive and the time to write. To these years belong his futuristic satire *Memories of the Future* (1923); a selection of word puzzles with the self-explanatory title *A Book of Acrostics* (1924), which he culled from a weekly feature he provided for a magazine; his W.H. Mallock–inspired weekend party symposium *Sanctions* (1924); the first of his mystery novels, *The Viaduct Murder* (1925); and a novel tweaking Spiritualist gullibility called *Other Eyes Than Ours* (1926). Several more purely scholarly works also date from this period. His annotated translation of part of *The Aeneid* was published by the Clarendon Press, and he teamed up with Shane Leslie to bring to public attention *The Miracles of King Henry VI*. These were compiled in a Latin manuscript (itself a translation from an English original) in the British Museum dating from 1500, which records the accounts, by some 174 pilgrims to his shrine in Windsor, of cures attributable to the intercession of the Lancastrian king, the founder of Eton and King's College, Cambridge. The manuscript even bears the annotations of a later investigator into their authenticity. In an introductory essay consonant with

[16] Waugh, *Knox*, p. 177.

the highest historiography, Knox deduced that the authentication, which is incomplete, was undertaken and then halted in the reign of Henry VIII as the religious climate changed. Twenty-three of the miracles, nevertheless, were regarded by the annotator as proven, based on multiple living witnesses. Knox and Leslie, both Etonians, hoped that their historical discoveries might prompt further interest in reopening the king's cause for canonization; in the event, however, no one else followed up on it, and his cause still languishes for lack of a promoter.[17]

These were also the years when Laura Lovat's home at Beaufort Castle was a favorite vacation retreat for Knox. There he made the acquaintance of Maurice Baring, novelist and linguist and madcap bachelor "uncle" to the Lovat children.[18] Knox could also hardly avoid meeting Hilaire Belloc, who welcomed him into the Catholic camp with the anticipation that he would play a key role in the revitalizing of the faith in England and in Europe. Belloc was one of those who thought Saint Edmund's was an entirely inappropriate vehicle for Knox's talents. Knox also corresponded with G.K. Chesterton and seems to have had some part in the crystallization of the latter's decision to formally enter in 1922 the Church he had long championed. And Knox caught the attention of Arnold Lunn, then in the throes of agnosticism and eager to expose the frail underpinnings of its alternatives, who included a critical essay on Knox alongside Chesterton and Cardinal Manning and other prominent Catholic personages in *Roman Converts*, published in 1924.

When due note is also taken of the weekend excursions to parishes across England to preach on special occasions (many of these sermons appear in Philip Caraman's three-volume collection published in the early 1960s) and of Knox's first forays as a retreat master at schools, clearly he was not hiding his light under a barrel. He was exercising his role foremost as a Catholic priest and as an educator but also as a man of letters with a distinct but subtle apologetics informing books meant for a general readership.

[17] Ronald Knox and Shane Leslie, *The Miracles of King Henry VI* (London: Cambridge University Press, 1923).

[18] On Maurice Baring, see the biography by Emma Letley, *Maurice Baring: A Citizen of Europe* (London: Constable, 1991), and the much briefer memoir by Laura Lovat, *Maurice Baring: A Postscript with Some Letters and Verse* (New York: Sheed and Ward, 1948), which includes a short appreciation of Baring's literary talents by Knox on pp. 107–12.

But internal problems in Saint Edmund's administration caused Knox discomfort. So when the Catholic chaplaincy of Oxford emerged as a possible post with the imminent retirement of its longtime incumbent, Knox did not discourage his friend Francis Urquhart from politicking for him. Urquhart was a consummate insider, both among Oxford dons and among Catholic bishops.[19] He soothed feelings among some board members who suspected that Knox was too flippant and secured a favorable vote.

With no experience as a pastor, Knox inherited a flock of about 150 undergraduates to sustain with the sacraments and with regular conferences in apologetics, as stipulated among the duties of the Catholic chaplain. He never supposed that the task of keeping university students on the straight and narrow would be easy, especially since Oxford had long since ceased to provide anything approaching a Christian ambiance. He was perhaps handicapped by his constitutional recoiling from intruding on people: rather than seek out new Catholic arrivals, he would patiently await their calling on him in his lodgings in the Old Palace, which also housed a chapel, rooms for a few lodgers, and a lecture room. He could count on possibly a dozen daily Mass attendees. Sunday mornings he said the early Mass, which was followed by the Jesuit Mass at 9 A.M. and the Dominican Mass at 10:30 A.M., at which he sometimes gave the conference. Sunday evenings he would host outside lecturers in the Newman Room. The rest of the week he would practice the art of being available for students in need of spiritual advice while working away on his writing commitments.

A new chapel and lecture room were completed in 1931, the former accommodating 140 people and the latter about 180. His bishop, Cardinal Bourne, expected Knox to give a series of talks to the students on apologetics, and he did so in three-year cycles, corresponding to the normal term of an undergraduate's residence. Much of his time was devoted to crafting these talks carefully, to the point where even though he followed a written text, he did not have to refer to it often during the course of the lecture. He preferred this type of communication to the one-on-one talk with an undergraduate. In 1936 the Jesuit Oxford house, Campion Hall, relocated next door to the

[19] On Urquhart's life as an Oxford institution, see Cyril Bailey, *Francis Fortescue Urquhart* (London: Oxford University Press, 1936).

chaplaincy, and Knox consequently became neighbor to the brilliant philosopher Father Martin D'Arcy, who attracted to his dinners the likes of Graham Greene, C. S. Lewis, Isaiah Berlin, and other intellectuals along with the more retiring Knox.[20]

It was not a very exciting life, and if Evelyn Waugh did not have Knox's *The Whole Art of Chaplaincraft* at hand (a document written for the benefit of Father Alfonso de Zulueta, his successor in 1939), that section of his biography devoted to these years would have been considerably thinner. Father Thomas Corbishley sees not the monotony of the task but a sense of not having succeeded in it as inducing Knox to find a chaplain's life increasingly uncongenial over the years:

> For the first time in his life, he had direct and permanent responsibility for the spiritual welfare of a group of young men at what is notoriously the most difficult and challenging period of their lives. Miserably aware of their failures, he attributed these to some lack in himself. He tried everything he could think of to interest, attract and encourage the young men in fidelity to their religion. But, having done all that was required of him, he still felt an unprofitable servant. Their relatively infrequent lapses were patent and, as he felt, a reflection on his guidance. Success in this department was supremely important; it was the only kind of success that seemed to elude him.[21]

And yet, perhaps not. The historian of the Oxford Catholic chaplaincy has noted that this assignment "was his longest period of pastoral responsibility and it may well be that his greatest influence for good was exercised on the congregation and the Oxford friends of those years".[22]

[20] Fr. D'Arcy's biographer notes a remark that also made its way into Evelyn Waugh's life of Knox, to the effect that Knox would be happy to go for a walk every afternoon with D'Arcy to converse with this luminous thinker. However, when Waugh transmitted the remark to D'Arcy, he was surprised: "He replied: 'I had an affection for him & a great admiration for his gifts, but I never realised, while he was living, that the affection was mutual. That made me rather slow in inviting myself to, for instance, the Old Palace.'" See H. J. A. Sire, *Father Martin D'Arcy: Philosopher of Christian Love* (Leominster: Gracewing, 1997), p. 95.

[21] Thomas Corbishley, S.J., *Ronald Knox: The Priest* (New York: Sheed and Ward, 1965), p. 28.

[22] Walter Drumm, *The Old Palace: A History of the Oxford University Catholic Chaplaincy* (Dublin: Veritas, 1991), p. 70.

The literary side of the ledger was far more estimable. *The Belief of Catholics*, a concise explanation of the faith for believers and inquirers, was published in 1927. That same year, Knox wrote *The Three Taps*, the second of his mystery novels, and the first to be written as a pure puzzler. Four more would appear at regular intervals through 1937. They are distinguished by intricacy of plot and richness of scenic description, although the detective hero he invented to solve the crimes was not very memorable. He also edited an anthology of short stories of crime and sleuthing and was a founding member of the Detection Club, along with Dorothy Sayers, Agatha Christie, G.K. Chesterton, and others.

Essays in Satire collected articles and talks going back to *Absolute and Abitofhell* and other pastiches, along with more recent efforts such as the script Knox wrote for a BBC radio broadcast in 1926 describing a fictional proletarian uprising in London, which fooled many listeners into believing such a revolution was actually taking place. It was this incident, more than any other, that had occasioned the resistance to his appointment to the chaplaincy that Urquhart had to overcome.

Two books from this period confront popular views of religion as expounded by journalists, writers, and scientists. *Caliban in Grub Street* (1930) exposes to searching logical scrutiny the sentimental vague Deism of an assortment of pundits, including Rebecca West and Arnold Bennett. *Broadcast Minds*, published two years later, deals with writers who had developed a far more coherent and more militantly anti-Christian philosophy, chief of whom are Julian Huxley, Knox's old Balliol contemporary now renowned biologist, and the mathematician and philosopher Bertrand Russell.

Barchester Pilgrimage, appearing in 1935, marks a return to lighter topics. Knox was a devoted admirer of Anthony Trollope's mid-Victorian era novels centered around Church of England clergy in the fictional see of Barsetshire. The characters Trollope created were so appealing that Knox decided they could not remain without further issue, so his narrative follows the fortunes of the succeeding generation of Grantlys and Arabins in a respectfully imitative prose style.

In the meantime, the combative Arnold Lunn entered into correspondence with Knox to debate the tenets of the Catholic faith and to probe historical events deemed embarrassing to the Church's claim to supernatural guidance. The back-and-forth epistolary debate appeared in book form under the title *Difficulties* in 1930. Less than two years later, Lunn had satisfied himself intellectually that Knox's position was indeed the only truly tenable one and became a Catholic. His subsequent career in letters was devoted in part to spirited championing of Catholicism against opponents such as the biologist J. B. S. Haldane and the historian G. G. Coulton, using the same format of debate by post.

Several shorter books were also published during these years. Most noteworthy are two books of sermons focusing on specific themes. *The Mystery of the Kingdom* is a profound examination of the parables of Jesus, particularly on their bearing on the meaning of the oft-misused phrase "the kingdom of God". *Heaven and Charing Cross* is a series of sermons on the Eucharist and ranks among his most beautifully crafted spiritual writings. Knox also headed a committee that revised the *Westminster Hymnal*, and he was commissioned to do the same for the *Manual of Prayers* until criticisms mounted from individual bishops and the project became bogged down.

The final product of Knox's Oxford years was the critically acclaimed *Let Dons Delight*, a witty and wistful chronicle of likely dialogues among university dons in fifty-year intervals from 1588 to 1938 (the year of its publication), faithfully transcribed in the idiomatic English of each period. It served as an appropriate farewell to a milieu he had first experienced in 1906 but which he needed to leave in order to concentrate fully on his next major task, the translation of the Bible for the English hierarchy.

The opportunity to leave had arisen in 1937 when Knox made the acquaintance of a prospective convert, Daphne Lady Acton, a granddaughter of the great nineteenth-century physicist Lord Rayleigh, and wife of the grandson of the famous Cambridge historian John Emmerich Dalberg Acton. She had been referred to Knox by her sister-in-law Mia, who was married to his friend Douglas Woodruff, the editor of the London *Tablet*. Back in 1931, when she was nineteen, Daphne's parents had been upset by her marriage to Lord Acton simply because he was a Catholic, and her parents had consented to the match only on the grounds that any children not be brought up in the faith. But when her second daughter contracted pneumonia in 1935 when only a few months old, she had the baby baptized at the point of death, and the tragedy set Lady Acton on the road to a more mature inquiry into the tenets of the religion of her husband. Hence the Woodruffs plied her with theological and spiritual classics, which she read with avidity. Knox's tuition was therefore on a higher plane than he was used to dispensing to the Catholic undergraduates in his care, and a strong friendship based on mutual admiration arose between these two converts, the one a middle-aged priest, and the other a young married mother whose household would eventually expand to ten surviving children and who would end up managing a farm in Africa.

Evelyn Waugh had access to the correspondence that passed between them in the early years of their friendship and suggested that if published someday they would constitute "a charming and unconventional book" of spiritual letters.[23] Waugh's own biographer, Martin Stannard, more frankly states that Waugh was disconcerted by them and, in the course of writing his life of Knox, traveled to the Actons' farm in Rhodesia (where they had moved in 1947 because of the difficulties of keeping up an estate in England) to elicit Mrs. Acton's memories of those years. He also interviewed Dom Hubert van Zeller, the Benedictine spiritual writer from Downside Abbey, who knew them both. Lady Acton impressed Waugh as a devout and forthright person, and she confided to him that she had fallen in love with Knox. Knox himself valued her friendship immensely but was so imbued with the priestly ideal of disinterested love that he apparently remained unaware of her quandary. In any case, Dom Hubert counseled them wisely about the gift of friendship, and from the years 1939 to 1947, Knox served as chaplain at the Acton estate in Aldenham, where he could write and study without the distractions that the Oxford chaplaincy necessarily entailed.[24]

Knox's desire to work on a modern translation of the New Testament was gratified by the formal approval of his initiative by the English hierarchy in November 1938. But he settled into Aldenham just as war broke out, and the planned evacuation of children to the British countryside brought fifteen Assumption nuns, several lay teachers, and over fifty schoolgirls from Kensington Square to the estate for the duration of hostilities. As it was, the estate was far from grand, since

[23] Waugh, *Knox*, p. 250.

[24] Martin Stannard, *Evelyn Waugh: The Later Years, 1939–1966* (New York: W. W. Norton and Co., 1992), pp. 401–8.

the Actons were not well off financially, and the letting out of most of the rooms to the evacuees cramped living conditions even more.

Nominally, Knox was to consult with a committee of advisors, which included the formidable C. C. Martindale,[25] submitting drafts to each member and responding point by point to criticisms of his choice of wording. Differences not only on particulars, but more ominously over the nature of the translation, immediately arose: Should it be a revision of the time-hallowed Douay-Challoner, as at least one committee member argued, or a new translation of the Latin Vulgate, as Knox wanted? Should it be in his "timeless English" or should it convey the inherent differences between Mark and Luke, as Father Martindale desired? The bishops decided in favor of Knox's approach in 1940, and despite grumblings from individual prelates, he continued to follow his own plan.

In the meantime, Knox performed his unanticipated duties as chaplain to the school with assiduity. The sermons he preached to the girls on the meaning of the Mass and the Creed, although crafted to appeal particularly to the age group he was addressing, were deep and lucid. They were published in the years after the war as *The Mass in Slow Motion* (1948) and *The Creed in Slow Motion* (1949). Other published works too owe their origin to his interaction with the nuns and schoolgirls, and he also contributed short weekly essays to the *Sunday Times*, which were duly collected in book form.

Knox completed his New Testament translation appropriately enough on the Feast of Saint Jerome, September 30, 1942. The first printing "for private use"—not widely advertised because the new version had not yet received official authorization—was approved by the cardinal archbishop of Westminster and met with resounding success. The inevitable wartime restrictions on print held back its issuance until April 1944, and the bishops did not get around to approving it formally

[25] For the life of this prolific writer, who lived from 1879 to 1963, see Philip Caraman, S.J., *C. C. Martindale* (London: Longmans, Green and Co., 1967). Fr. Martindale's forced stay in Denmark after its occupation by Hitler's army in 1940 prevented him from having any influence on Knox's work of translation. That they disagreed on methodology is evident from a letter of Martindale to his father claiming that "all he wants me to do is to make a paraphrase of the more obscure passages in St. Paul and St. John, which really means guessing how their minds really worked and what thoughts occurred to them which they did not write down." Quoted on pp. 198–99.

until the next year, so it was not until October 1945 that the Knox version of the New Testament finally appeared in bookstores.

By then the war was over. Knox, who had turned down an offer to return to Oxford in 1942, where the archbishop of Birmingham thought he could do useful public service "by counteracting some of the confounded left-wingers and pro-Russians", had studiously avoided making any political statements throughout the conflict.[26] But the dropping of the atomic bombs on Hiroshima and Nagasaki elicited from Knox a lengthy reflection published as *God and the Atom* in the immediate aftermath of the carnage. The book was not a success. It invited soul searching in a time when euphoria was rampant and when secular panaceas such as the United Nations promised to meet the hunger for peace.

Knox did not earn much money during the years he spent on his translation. As a successful author in various genres, however, his savings accrued to respectable amounts, but he was prodigious in his gifts to Catholic charitable societies and to needy people, who often did not know who their benefactor was. One touching story is related by Penelope Fitzgerald, in connection with the funds left by his stepmother to all surviving Knox children on her death in 1946. "What was the best thing to do with the legacy? A characteristic idea, at the same time romantic and reserved, struck Ronnie. The cousin who, fifty years before, had courted Mrs. K. had fallen on hard times, and Ronnie had always believed 'that there might have been something in it' if the Bishop had not come along; so he arranged, in total secrecy, to make over the money to the old man he had never met."[27]

With Lord Acton's return from service and the departure of the schoolgirls and their teachers, the Acton family tried to make a living farming their acreage, but it was a failure. They decided to move to Rhodesia, so in 1947 Knox closed down the chapel, as Aldenham was transferred to Lady Acton's non-Catholic brother. She and her large family remained in Rhodesia until the 1970s as cattle farmers and horse breeders, building a church on their extensive properties in the early 1960s and creating a strong biracial Catholic community at M'bebi. Eventually, when her children were grown, she and her husband

[26] Waugh, *Knox*, p. 288.

[27] Fitzgerald, *Knox Brothers*, pp. 261–62.

migrated to Majorca and finally back to England, where she could be in contact with many of her children and grandchildren.[28]

Meanwhile, another old friend, Katharine Asquith, invited Knox to take over the chaplaincy at her home in Mells Manor, near Downside Abbey. There, in a serene and stately home replete with Old Masters paintings and several formidable libraries, he completed his translation of the Old Testament in 1948 (finally released in 1955) and his magisterial historical study of emotional religious movements called *Enthusiasm* in 1950. His sociability, enervated by the cramped and somewhat chaotic existence at Aldenham in the war years, revived, and he even took two trips abroad: one to Germany in 1953 and one to Africa in 1954, where he visited Mrs. Asquith's son and his family for a few weeks in Zanzibar and spent a month with the Actons in Rhodesia.

The conferences on the Catholic faith that Knox had given to Oxford undergraduates during his tenure as chaplain had been published in 1942 under the title *In Soft Garments*. He had followed with a second series of conferences years later, which appeared in 1952 as *The Hidden Stream*. Out of his cornucopia of sermons, retreat talks, newspaper articles, and even letters to questioners seeking guidance, more volumes were fashioned throughout the decade he spent at Mells. One major achievement was his three-volume *New Testament Commentary*, which appeared in installments between 1952 and 1956. With a daily life consisting of prayer, celebrating Mass, writing, correspondence, and conversation with genial friends, his "great work of the pen—apostolate" (as Cardinal Hinsley had once characterized his contribution to the Church) throve.

In his late sixties, Knox still had many projects ahead of him. He translated Saint Thérèse of Lisieux's unabridged autobiography into English in 1956 and had begun working on a new book of apologetics as well. But at the end of the year, he began to fail in health. He was operated on for colon cancer in January 1957, but the cancer had spread to his liver. The latter malignancy was inoperable, but he was not told about it and attempted to return to work. Evelyn Waugh and his wife took Knox to a seaside resort in March, to no avail. Food

[28] Lord Acton died in 1989, and Lady Acton lived on until 2003. Their eldest son, born in 1941, inherited the title Fourth Baron Acton of Aldenham. For a brief account of the life of Daphne Lady Acton, see her obituary in the London *Daily Telegraph* issue of March 21, 2003.

became intolerable to him. Only at the end of May was he informed of the nature of the illness from which he suffered.

And yet he had one literary commitment still to fulfill. Knox had been invited to give a talk, the distinguished Romanes Lecture, at Oxford on June 11, the title being "On English Translation". Father Thomas Corbishley was in the audience that evening and, several years later, recollected the shock of seeing Knox in such a disease-ravaged state, his face yellow from the cancer.

> We held our breath for the first paragraph, wondering if we should be disappointed—disappointed in the quality of the work, disappointed in the delivery, which might fail to do justice to the text. We need not have feared. The voice, gentle as ever, yet clear and strong, began. All the old magic was there. Ripple after ripple of laughter ran through the theatre, to be hushed to silence as his argument developed. Few knew, and those who did not know could hardly suspect, the nature of the difficulties under which he had laboured to produce this superb analysis of the task of the translator. The range of knowledge seemed inexhaustible, the precision of memory so astonishing, the penetration of judgment so accurate. It was a triumph of literary criticism; still more was it a triumph of simple human courage.[29]

The next day, Knox visited with his old pupil, Harold Macmillan, at 10 Downing Street. The prime minister's doctor confirmed the diagnosis of liver cancer. On the train ride back to Mells, Knox admitted to Dom Hubert his reluctance to die. "One clings and I can't think why", he mused. "You would have thought anyone would prefer heaven to fruit juice." Weakness confined him to his room in July. He and Dom Hubert heard each other's confessions on July 19, just before the latter had to leave for the United States, and they discussed their humanly opposite feelings about facing death.[30]

On August 11, Knox received Communion for the last time. He fell into a coma on August 20 and died on August 24. Father Martin D'Arcy, the Jesuit theologian whose company Knox valued so highly in Oxford when D'Arcy was his counterpart in Campion Hall, preached

[29] Corbishley, *Knox: The Priest*, p. 63.

[30] Hubert van Zeller, *One Foot in the Cradle: An Autobiography* (New York: Holt, Rinehart and Winston, 1966), p. 242.

at his funeral Mass at Westminster Cathedral. Knox's body was buried in the cemetery at Mells a few days later.

Evelyn Waugh had assumed the task of literary executor, as well as biographer, and under his watchful eye, several new volumes of collected sermons and talks were published posthumously. Among the most important were *Literary Distractions* (1958), a compilation of papers and articles chiefly on authors Knox admired; *The Priestly Life* (1958), a second set of retreat conferences for priests following an initial 1946 book intended for the same audience; and *The Layman and His Conscience* (1961), a companion volume to *A Retreat for Lay People*, which had been published in 1955.

That his literary output should reach its coda in retreat books was highly appropriate. Knox was first and foremost a priest. His classical scholarship and his felicity with the English language dazzled several generations of readers, but the sparer prose of the retreat talks, like the readable English of his Bible, is evidence that his life's overriding mission was simply to bring modern people to the practice of the presence of God.

How successful he was in that endeavor obviously cannot be gauged by book sales or royalties. Perhaps a turn of phrase here or there arrested an auditor's attention or nudged a reader's mind from its complacent agnosticism. The train of events unleashed by that encounter with Knox's spoken or written words might then be highly consequential, though imperceptible in the mere chronicling of his literary accomplishments. It is, in any case, the task of succeeding chapters merely to elaborate on those accomplishments.

CHAPTER TWO

THE JOURNEY HOME

Hindsight renders incongruous the image of Ronald Knox as an Evangelical. It is difficult to believe that the author of *Enthusiasm* could ever have been immersed in a religious world view that exalts the apprehension of communion with a personal Savior to the detriment of the mediating influence of a Church established by that Savior. And the innate logician in Knox seems irreconcilable with the emotion-laden, hymn-drenched spirituality cultivated by Wesleyanism.

But Ronald was the son of Edmund Knox, who held to a distinctly Low Church theology. Consequently, it was but natural for the son to imbibe Protestant piety unquestioningly, because the environment in which he grew up was so thoroughly suffused with it. Not only was it so in his father's home but also in that of his relatives, with whom he lived after his mother's early death. The Evangelical ideal was upheld, and its uncomplicated tenets were impressed on the young Knox.

Indeed, its vitality can be ascribed to its simplicity. "It has external marks", Knox recollects in *A Spiritual Aeneid*, "a strong devotion to and belief in Scripture; a careful observance of Sunday; framed texts, family prayers, and something indefinably patriarchal about the ordering of the household." Even writing after his conversion, he found no grounds to inveigh against any repressiveness in his upbringing, not yielding to a temptation already common in autobiographical writing. Eminent literary figures, then no less than in later times, frequently cast about for childhood influences upon which to lay the blame for whatever personality deficiencies their humility could summon forward for censure, or their complacency give thanks for having overcome. Knox could not remember such an atmosphere, instead noting that

> candour compels me to admit that I neither then found, nor have since managed to persuade myself that I found, anything repulsive or frightening in such a religious atmosphere. Hell was part of those beliefs, like death; neither death nor hell dwells with any morbid fixity in the mind of a normal child. Rather, the personal love which God devotes to us, the ever-surprising miracle of His Redemption, the permanent ease of access to the glorified Saviour—these are the central characteristics of Evangelical devotion, and these its formative influences.[1]

A sense of piety toward his home causes Knox to stop short of reviewing in any greater detail the religious influences of his youth, save for the formal practices encountered at Eton. It is sufficient to extract one more quote from his reminiscences to convey the spirit of public school religion: "a religion without 'enthusiasm' in the old sense, reserved in its self-expression, calculated to reinforce morality, chivalry, and the sense of truth, providing comfort in times of distress and a glow of contentment in declining years; supernatural in its nominal doctrines, yet on the whole rationalistic in its mode of approaching God".[2]

One must look elsewhere than the institutionalized common religion bred into boys at Eton for a key to what Knox believed in while growing to maturity. Fortunately, his father was not solely a practitioner of Evangelical beliefs but a man who was committed enough to the propagation of his theological views that he wrote a book defending them against the corrosive onslaught of modern Broad Church criticism. Appropriately enough, he titled his work of apologetics *On What Authority?* and although he wrote it late in life (it was published three years after his son's conversion story), it may be presumed to convey quite adequately the intellectual underpinnings informing Ronald Knox's religious outlook throughout his early years.

For Bishop Knox, the authority in question is of course that of the Bible. The Holy Spirit teaches people how to use the Bible properly, while the Church with her bishops and other officials exists primarily as a facilitator of that direct communication between God and the believer, most emphatically not as a mediator or channel of sacramental grace. Hence much of his argument is given over to an analysis of

[1] Ronald Knox, *A Spiritual Aeneid* (London: Longmans, Green and Co., 1918), pp. 5–6.
[2] Ibid., p. 19.

how the seemingly inexorable conclusions of higher criticism can be reconciled with a sturdy belief in the efficacy of the Word of God. He cuts a path midway between Fundamentalist literalism and dogmatically diffuse Modernism so that readers might retain the Bible as the anchor to their faith. For example, during one disquisition on a Cambridge conference at which speakers were etherealizing the Bible away, he inserts an aside that goes a long way to explain his creed:

> The debt which the world owes to the uncriticised Bible is too often overlooked, the great release from sacerdotal tyranny, the purging of the official Church from open and unblushing immorality, the bringing of lofty ideals of Christian life into the homes of the people, as a life that laymen ought to live, the recognition of the value of each several man in the sight of God, the message of restoration to the profligate, the outcast, the harlot, the reformation of prisons, the bursting of the bonds of slavery, the proclamation of the glad tidings of reconciliation to the whole world, these are but a portion of the blessings that the modern world owes to the uncriticised Bible, placed in the hands of the unlearned, as God's message to them.[3]

An inspiriting creed to be sure, but certainly not a sacramental one. Bishop Knox's view of the Church is of a robust national brotherhood, which he would be the first to distinguish from the kingdom of heaven. Its one mission is to proclaim that kingdom, which would come into existence only at the Second Coming of Christ. That concept is essential to Protestantism and is different from the Catholic view that the Church established by Christ and ruled by Peter and his successors is herself the kingdom. Bishop Knox naturally refuses to acknowledge any testimony to Peter's primacy in the Gospel texts, and likewise any record of an organized Church. The apostles, he asserts, were given no special gifts; rather, each Christian was endowed with the necessary charisms to carry on the message of Jesus. Hence he is even mistrustful of the early Church Councils, which are deprecated for being at the mercy of majority opinion, and that opinion manipulable by political pressure. Particularly abhorrent to him is anything savoring of the Roman Catholic view of authority:

[3] Edmund A. Knox, *On What Authority?* (London: Longmans, Green and Co., 1923), p. 223.

> For the Roman Catholic the question of Councils, and indeed, of tradition itself, has become unimportant since the last great Vatican Council of 1870 declared that the infallibility of the Church resided in the Pope decreeing *ex Cathedra*. Councils and Tradition are both swallowed up by the Papacy: "I am Tradition," said Pio Nono. The basis of authority in the Church of Rome is no longer Scripture, nor tradition, nor history, but an act of dogmatic self-assertion.[4]

If the Pope is a false authority set up by a misreading of Scripture, so too are the priesthood and the episcopate, if they are construed as possessing any sacramental powers of effecting transubstantiation or absolving sins. Of the latter power, Bishop Knox waxes eloquent in denunciation of the confessional as a channel of grace:

> Theoretically, the whole of human life in all its manifold relations, political, commercial, professional, industrial, theatrical, sporting, educational, even to the very games of boys and girls, the most intimate relation of husband and wife, of father and child, all pass under the surveillance of the priesthood, from which there can be no secret, since no human act or thought is wholly free from sin. The Christian world is subjected to a priestly class which, after all, is drawn from sinful humanity and subject to the temptations of the world, the flesh, and the Spirit of Evil. Angels might be expected to fall if they were subjected to such a burthen. For human nature it is wholly intolerable.[5]

If a note of lubriciousness has crept into the description of the scope of the confessional, it is not to be imputed to any unsalutary habit of Bishop Knox's mind. He is merely heir to a long tradition of Protestant invective against sacramental confession, which welled up in especially virulent form whenever no-Popery movements flourished and abated only moderately during more tranquil times. What is of more significance is that he is declaiming against a practice that for at least two decades prior to his writing had become commonplace in an ascendant wing of his own church. How could a bishop of the Anglican Church hold in utter horror auricular confession when some of his fellow bishops encouraged it? What principle of unity could bind two such ecclesiastics who differed so fundamentally over the

[4] Ibid., p. 236.
[5] Ibid., pp. 243–44.

sacramental system? The elder Knox, perceiving the problem, is content to identify unity with the presence of the Spirit in the Church and to state (without ever attempting to prove his point) that the Spirit manifests himself in national churches, or more surprisingly still, through a divergence of beliefs: "[T]he Baptists, Independents, the Society of Friends, and in some sense the Wesleyans, to say nothing here of the Societies of Continental Protestants, have manifested the truest of all signs of Church life, that is, the Presence of Christ."[6] He appeals to Bishop Westcott for support in defining this unity. "The true unity of believers," the latter says, "like the Unity of Persons in the Holy Trinity with which it is compared, is offered as something far more than a mere moral unity of purpose, feeling, affection: it is in some mysterious mode which we cannot distinctly apprehend a vital unity."[7]

Needless to say, these are not helpful words to a budding logician. But then, since classic Reformed theology defers the Mystical Church to the afterlife, it is relieved of the need to explain to its adherents why God looks benignly on earthly creedal disunion. However, in the face of the serene doctrinal unity possible under a common authority that Rome so clearly presents at all times, regardless of the turmoil engendered by disaffected segments within its ranks, some nod toward external unity has to be made. Bishop Knox points to a recent Anglican initiative as a hopeful sign:

> The Lambeth appeal for unity was a genuine recognition of the desire for unity and a memorable attempt by the Anglican Bishops assembled in 1920 to give embodiment to the desire. A vision or ideal was held out to the Christian world of a Church with a common ministry commissioning the ministers of the various Churches to exercise their ministry throughout the whole Society. Federation of churches was not contemplated. Interference with the doctrine or discipline of churches was not contemplated. But all churches who responded to the ideal were invited to commission ministers of such churches to exercise their ministry in each several church.[8]

[6] Ibid., p. 247.
[7] Quoted in ibid., pp. 248–49.
[8] Ibid., p. 250.

Whether the elder Knox really thought this ecumenical effort would augur well for the future is debatable, because no sooner does he suggest it than he sets about clearing the way for a face-saving retreat. He recognizes the objection that superficial unity is attained in Protestantism only at the risk of diluting doctrinal content to a level consonant with only a bland form of Unitarianism. So he likens the current discord to the travails of the universe in the early stages of creation. That an omnipotent God formed a very specific universe by a supreme act of creative design satisfies him that the disharmony apparent in the religious realm must equally veil a deeper unity. Again the logician may balk at the implied minor premise in the syllogism, namely, that mankind's designs are necessarily as perfect as God's. But Bishop Knox is grappling with the basis of authority, which is the Achilles' heel of his argument, and logic must defer to hopeful thinking:

> To such criticisms our answer is that while we admit that human imperfections, and especially attempts of fallible men to state in precise definitions such inscrutable mysteries as predestination, election, assurance of salvation, indefectibility, and the like, have created divisions which ought not to have existed: while there are sins to lament which must grieve the Holy Spirit of God, yet for all that it does not follow that there is not under these differences a stronger unity than any that external bonds can fashion, a unity of growth not of manufacture. That unity we believe is being wrought out by the Spirit of Truth in spite of the impatience and unbelief of men.[9]

In the concrete world inhabited by a multiplicity of churches, some claimants to fealty were offering the undiluted Calvinist doctrine of predestination as reality, while others were extolling the Catholic notion of free will accepting the grace offered by God to find the path that leads to salvation. The difference in outlook is so fundamental, and the importance of the believer's choice so critical to how life is to be lived, that the supposititious growth toward unity proffered by the bishop could offer little solace to the earnest seeker.

The court of final appeal, then, for Bishop Knox is the Bible, which if read in the proper spirit becomes the medium of a personal communication from God, fostering the theological virtues and thwarting

[9] Ibid., pp. 252, 253.

sin. But even here, trouble lurks: he cites the Anabaptists and other sects that have used Scripture to justify immoral practices. On the other hand, he will have none of the appeal to tradition that Roman Catholicism uses to interpret the Bible, for that way lies "the confessional, indulgences and the temporal power of the Popes".[10] The Church's innate fallibility must be recognized, and the medieval Church is dismissed for being too authoritative while insufficiently spiritual. Ultimately, one's guide must be a Christian conscience. But finally the question must be asked, how is that conscience to be properly formed? Appeal is once more made to the Church Mystical: "We shall not go far wrong if we call the Church Mystical the conscience of the Church Visible, a conscience which works with the authority of Christ. It is this conscience which, with convincing authority, authenticates the Word of God to us in the Scriptures and the formulae of the Church."[11]

In the bishop's continued fear of having "doctrines externally imposed", he accepts that there will always be disagreements over the truth, because the consciences of different individuals will lead them to different conclusions, and yet he holds out the hope that a Christian conscience purged of unbalanced judgment will be a sure, though never infallible, guide. As an Evangelical Christian, he must ultimately choose in favor of direct illumination of individual consciences rather than accept the idea that Christ founded a Church that would be a faithful repository of his message throughout the ages. A religion of experience displaces a religion of sacraments; a religion of the Spirit supplants a religion of authority.

This, then, is the religion Ronald Knox was brought up in, and if undue attention appears to have been devoted to a system of beliefs he was to shed before reaching full maturity, excuse may be sought through appeal to two observations. First, he lived in a country where a very large number of people continued to believe with Bishop Knox that the unfettered Bible was the sole guide to truth, and when the younger Knox saw the insufficiency of so subjective an authority, he devoted a good part of his apologetic writing to showing how Catholicism offers a surer and fuller knowledge about Christ and his message than Evangelicalism does. Second, his father's religion, reliant as it was

[10] Ibid., p. 265.
[11] Ibid., p. 269.

on the emotions, engendered a subjectivity that ill accords with a logician's mind. The Ritualist wing of Anglicanism, and ultimately the Roman Catholic Church, offered an alternative view of the world and how God communicates with individuals. Both took their cue from the Church of the apostolic and postapostolic era and were Sacramentalist. They held that the sacraments, including the much-maligned auricular confession, were the channels established by Christ to draw people to himself.

Knox himself pinpoints exactly when the sacramental idea took hold of him. It was on Christmas Day 1903 when he read Robert Hugh Benson's *The Light Invisible*, just after having argued against the use of Catholic practices in the Church of England. Reference will be made later to Benson's influence on Knox during the period prior to the latter's conversion. For now it is sufficient to note that this small collection of stories had been written while Benson was still an Anglican priest living at the Community of the Resurrection at Mirfield. Purporting to be the experiences of an old wise priest, they lead the reader to a keen appreciation of the intersection of the natural and the supernatural in the affairs of the world. "It was the setting of the book—the little chapel in which the priest celebrated, the description of confessions heard in an old parish church—that riveted me even more than the psychological interest. All that Catholic system which I had hitherto known only distantly, felt as something wicked and felt attracted to only because it seemed wicked, now for the first time entered my horizon." [12]

One story in particular must have arrested his attention. In "Consolatrix Afflictorum" (Consoler of the afflicted), a correspondent is emboldened to reveal a secret to the priest after hearing his Christmas Day sermon reminding the congregation how "the Creation, the Incarnation, and the Sacramental System alike, in various degrees are the manifestations of God ... [and] that the 'spiritual' world and the personages that inhabit it sometimes express themselves in the same manner as their Maker". The hearer recalls that when he was seven years old, his mother died and he was devastated: "Night after night I used to lie awake, with the firelight in the room, remembering how she would look in on her way to bed; when at last I slept it seems to me

[12] Knox, *Spiritual Aeneid*, p. 36.

now as if I never did anything but dream of her; and it was only to wake again to that desolate emptiness." [13]

After weeks of disconsolateness, the boy awakens to the sound of his door opening and his mother silently beckoning him to a gentle embrace. The experience was repeated, not nightly, but only on those nights when he fell into despair. One night in particular while lying with his head on her shoulder, he hears a soft murmuring of a vast crowd before falling off to sleep. Only when he has recovered fully, a year later, does she visit him a last time, and then he finally sees her face in the light of dawn and finds out that she is not the mother he presumed she was: "[M]y little soul dimly saw that my own mother for some reason could not at that time come to me who needed her so sorely, and that another great Mother had taken her place.... I have never seen her since, but I have never needed to see her, for I know who she is; and, please God, I shall see her again; and next time I hope my mother and I will be together; and perhaps it will not be very long; and perhaps she will allow me to kiss her hand again." [14]

This story deserves mention here not solely for the unabashed homage it offers to the Mother of Jesus, startling enough as that would have been to an Evangelical youth of fifteen. It will be recalled that Knox's mother died when he was four years old, so the circumstances of Benson's story must have resonated with him. In an essay in *On Getting There*, Knox lets fall a remark that has been taken to be humorous but may have had a more somber origin. "I am assured", he comments, "that once, when I was only four years of age, being asked what I did when I couldn't get to sleep at night, I replied: 'I lie awake and think of the past.'" [15] Only someone who has long since ceased to be in contact with young children will doubt their capacity for storing away memories at an early age. Maturity erodes most of those memories, but at four they are precise and many. It is not too far-fetched to suppose that it was of his own mother that he was thinking then. There survives an old photograph of him, aged possibly eighteen months, nestled as contentedly on his mother's shoulder as the young boy in Benson's story is on Mary's.

[13] Robert Hugh Benson, *The Light Invisible* (London: Burns, Oates and Washbourne, n.d.), pp. 88–89.

[14] Ibid., pp. 99–100.

[15] Ronald Knox, *On Getting There* (London: Methuen, 1929), p. 2.

Interestingly, Benson himself deprecated *The Light Invisible* in subsequent years, largely because of the sentimentality it mixed in with the evocation of the supernatural. Nevertheless, and somewhat paradoxically, it remains true that it was instrumental in lifting Knox out of a religion of feeling and toward a deeper appreciation of Catholicism. His is just one instance of many where an acquaintance with Robert Hugh Benson proved decisive in an individual's life.

It would be outside the scope of the present chapter to retail the steps by which Knox gradually moved toward the Anglo-Catholic camp. They are sketched in *A Spiritual Aeneid* and were largely the result of reading and the establishing of congenial friendships at Eton, then at Balliol, and finally as a teaching fellow at Trinity College in Oxford, where ordination brought him a chaplaincy in 1911. By then he could say of the circle of friends to which he belonged:

> We all believed in (Roman) Catholicism as a system which worked, which held the ordinary man and attracted the poor where Anglicanism did not; we all agreed that the Roman system—the preaching of Penance and attendance at Mass as obligatory, the preference for short and business-like services, the attempt to stimulate devotion by means of the rosary, benediction, etc.—was the right way of going about things: our only difference between ourselves was how much of it could be done prudently, and how much of it an intelligent theory of Anglicanism would carry.[16]

But Knox was also an Oxford don and, as such, privy to much theological conversation that sprang from entirely different roots than the orthodoxy to which he was acclimating himself. Of especial importance to his future career was an informal Friday luncheon group to which he was attached, which featured many of the young theologians who were steeped in the speculations of German exegetes. These men believed that the time had come to formulate a restatement of Christian belief in light of the findings of modern science and Biblical criticism, and so they produced a multiauthored volume called *Foundations*.[17]

[16] Knox, *Spiritual Aeneid*, p. 92.

[17] B. H. Streeter et al., *Foundations: A Statement of Christian Belief in Terms of Modern Thought: By Seven Oxford Men* (1912; reprint, Freeport, N.Y.: Books for Libraries Press, 1971).

If there is a unifying theme to their contributions, it is the notion that not only can no orthodox doctrine be *presumed* to be correct but even that no orthodox doctrine can be accepted, after analysis, without major qualifications. For example, William Temple, the future archbishop of Canterbury, writing an essay entitled "The Church", argues that while received doctrine has the weight of tradition behind it, "the synthesis already made is bound to be inadequate, and progress is won through the perception of this inadequacy by the individual man of genius." Yet his formula for discerning the truth is hardly an exemplar of clarity of thought, appealing as it does "to the general principle that, as a rule, men are right when they assert and wrong when they deny".[18] Reference to the wind blowing where it listeth is made, the better to brace readers for excursions down theological paths that lead to radically new interpretations of old beliefs.

Such latitude allows the authors to abandon tradition whenever it seems too difficult to maintain in the face of a nonbelieving public. Their goal is to engage that public on its own theologically minimalist plane. Burdening them with the miraculous or with assertions of Jesus' two natures in one Person is to them unfruitful and an exercise in archaisms.

Burnett Hillman Streeter's task is to examine the historic Christ. Streeter is certain Jesus only gradually came to know who he was: "The moment of Baptism, the rite of mystic initiation into the kingdom proclaimed so near at hand, would not unnaturally be to our Lord the moment of illumination as to His own position in that kingdom." The temptation in the desert cannot be interpreted as literally having occurred, though one may accept as much as "that the effects of a long hunger combined with the nervous reaction of the stirring experience of His call actually caused His inner conflict to become visualized in the form related".[19] Streeter reserves his strongest criticism,

[18] Ibid., p. 352. William Temple (1881–1944) was the son of Frederick Temple, who was archbishop of Canterbury from 1897 to his death in 1902. The younger Temple was a theologian and philosopher and followed a career path similar to his father, finally being appointed archbishop of Canterbury, after a long tenure as archbishop of York, in 1942. A highly sympathetic account of his life and thought, especially his "process theology", is found in Joseph Fletcher, *William Temple: Churchman* (New York: Seabury, 1963). Temple's view of the Church's incompleteness is illustrated by the quote: "I believe in the Holy Catholic Church, and sincerely regret that it does not exist." Fletcher, *William Temple*, pp. 40–41.

[19] Streeter et al., *Foundations*, pp. 98–100.

however, for the theological position that the Resurrection and Ascension are historical events, a position, as he notes, that is clearly stated in the Thirty-nine Articles defining the Anglican faith:

> [T]he theory that the actual physical body laid in the tomb was raised up seems to involve (as indeed Article IV baldly states) that it was subsequently taken up, "flesh and bones," into heaven—a very difficult conception if we no longer regard the earth as flat and the centre of the solar system, and heaven as a definite region locally fixed above the solid bowl of the skies.... I know of no living theologian who would maintain a physical Ascension in this crude form, yet so long as emphasis is laid on the physical character of the Resurrection it is not obvious how any refinement of the conception "physical" really removes the difficulty.[20]

Streeter's difficulty is with miracles as divine interventions in the physical world, and he dismisses their possibility without any hesitancy: "The scientific, metaphysical, and historical difficulties which arise if this element in the conception of miracle is insisted upon are too well known to be worth repeating." He would, however, allow miracles in some restricted sense to occur, for example, God's answering of prayers or seeing progress issue from evolutionary processes, but nothing as upsetting to a Deist as a suspension of the laws of the natural world. He concludes:

> There are some, I know, to whom such an interpretation of them seems lacking in reality and substance, but for myself I feel I am on firmer ground than if I were to rest all on a view of miracle which the lapse of time and the growth of knowledge seems ever to be making less secure, and which in the last resort appears to mean that God did things in Palestine nineteen hundred years ago which He will not or cannot do for us today, and that Christ was raised from the dead in a way that we shall not be.[21]

It virtually follows from these presuppositions that Jesus can be considered divine in only a subsidiary sense. Temple asserts that "what we are forced to by the work of Christ in the world is not the belief that He is the Absolute God in all His fulness of Being ... but the belief

[20] Ibid., p. 132.
[21] Ibid., pp. 138–40.

that in all which directly concerns the spiritual relation of Man to God, Christ is identically one with the Father in the content of His Being".[22] In reviewing historical Christology, he cites no authority more recent than Abelard, pointedly implying that the scholastics had nothing to add to the discussion of the two natures in Christ. He then sums up his argument: "The wise question is not, 'Is Jesus Divine?' but, 'What is God like?' And the answer to that is 'Christ.' So, too, we must not form a conception of Humanity and either ask if Christ is Human or insist on reducing Him to the limits of our conception; we must ask, 'What is Humanity?' and look at Christ to find the answer." And if pressed for clarification, Temple responds by asserting simply that human thought is incapable of defining terms like *Deity* and *humanity* and must go on "with repeated efforts to restate and understand as far as may be ... because all our language and mental apparatus is constructed to deal with a different class of data".[23]

The *Foundations* authors' innate mistrust of the power of reason to apprehend theological truth impels them time and again to reject dogmatic statements of orthodoxy as too beholden to the framework of Greek philosophy and Roman jurisprudence to convey correctly a properly nuanced image of God. Conversely, they freely employ the language of the mystics and manifest a sincere piety toward Christ, but that piety stops short of worshipping him as truly the Father's Son, the Second Person of the Trinity.

Knox, it will be recalled, knew these young clerics well. Needless to say, he was not disposed to join them in their foray into print. But sensing that a major challenge to traditional belief was in the offing, his first inclination was to subject it to parody. It was a habit he admits to having entertained often in the course of his life, and in this case, it brought him some—largely favorable—notoriety. He wrote his rejoinder during the summer of 1912, before *Foundations* appeared in print, casting it in the form of a poem in the manner of John Dryden, and published it in the *Oxford Magazine*. *Absolute and Abitofhell, or Noah's Ark Put in Commission, and Set Adrift (with No Walls or Roof to Catch the Force of Those Dangerous Seas) on a New Voyage of Discovery* has been reprinted many times since and occupies no more than seven pages in

[22] Ibid., p. 250.
[23] Ibid., pp. 259–60.

Knox's 1928 compilation *Essays in Satire*.[24] It is a disarming lampoon, gauged to sink the pretensions of the modern theologians, and it cannot be denied that it found its target, even though launched when that target was yet in port.

It begins with a paean to the Henrician schism, which opened the way for religious speculation unfettered by Roman authority:

> In former Times, when Israel's ancient Creed
> Took Root so widely that it ran to Seed
> When Saints were more accounted of than Soap
> and Men in happy Blindness serv'd the Pope;
> Uxorious Jeroboam, waxen bold,
> Tore the Ten Tribes from David's falt'ring Hold.
> And, spurning Threats from Salem's Vatican
> Set gaiter'd Calves in Bethel and in Dan.

Freedom reigns for three hundred years

> Till men began for some Account to call,
> What we believ'd, or why believ'd at all?

The higher criticism then comes to the rescue, first to demythologize the Old Testament:

> First, Adam fell; then Noah's Ark was drown'd,
> And Samson under close inspection bound;
> For Daniel's Blood the Critick Lions roar'd,
> And trembling Hands threw Jonah overboard.

Eventually the seven authors of *Foundations* band together to confect a palatable theological synthesis for the man in the street. They are presented as sturdy mariners commissioned to undergird the vessel of Anglicanism. The modern theologian will declare:

> What I believe is what the Church believes:
> Yet some might find it matter for Research,
> Whether the Church taught him, or he the Church.

[24] Ronald Knox, "Absolute and Abitofhell", in *Essays in Satire* (1928; reprint, New York: Sheed and Ward, 1955), pp. 55–61.

Of course, mistrust of purely intellectual argumentation would be a mark of theirs:

> What difference, whether black be black or white,
> If no officious Hand turn on the Light?
> Whether our Fact be Fact, no Man can know,
> But, Heav'n preserve us, we will treat it so.

Knox ends the poem, which is replete with unmistakable allusions to each of the authors, with a warm dedication:

> Praying that Providence this Wind may use
> To puff your Sales, and to confound your Views.

As might be expected, it was the sales of the parody that took off, but clearly the theological tome needed an equally serious response if its conclusions were to be refuted.

The authors of *Foundations* breathed the same air of accommodation to the spirit of the age as did the Modernists who had flourished only a decade earlier in the Catholic Church. The latter had had their speculations condemned by Pope Pius X in 1907, but the young Church of England theologians could confidently assume that no similar fate awaited them from any authority in their communion. Knox knew that as well, and in *Some Loose Stones*, he acknowledges repeatedly that the arguments he puts forward will be labeled obscurantist by forward-looking thinkers. As always, however, he will not tolerate lack of clarity in language and suggests that theologians who would suppress hard truths in order to make religion more palatable to a wider audience are obscurers, whereas the orthodox theologian, who broadcasts the difficult truths because they come from what he believes to be an unimpeachable authority, is the more open of the two. In one important sense, he accepts the characterization:

> But if obscurantism is simply to believe, that there are limits defined by authority, within which theorizing is unnecessary and speculation forbidden; that there are some religious principles of such a priori certainty, that any evidence which appears to conflict with them does not destroy them, as it would destroy a mere hypothesis, but by conflicting with them proves itself to have been erroneously or inadequately interpreted, then I would welcome the title, contenting myself with the remark, firstly that all of us, except

> the blankest agnostics, do in fact hold such a priori principles on certain questions, and secondly that if we did not religion could never be a practical thing, because a continual flux of first principles is (as a matter of observation) necessarily incompatible with any stable development of the spiritual life.[25]

The problem with the modern theologians, according to Knox, is that they start with a hypothesis, for example, that miracles are impossible. Then they make deductions from it, such as that Jesus could not really have multiplied the loaves and fishes to feed the multitudes. The orthodox theologian starts instead with a priori beliefs such as God's not being circumscribed by the laws of nature, so therefore the miracles of Jesus are explicable by his divinity. It is not true that the moderns adopt a purely objective viewpoint about the documentary evidence: they start with a conviction Knox characterizes as "at least arbitrary and unnatural. The conviction is briefly put, that Man is not meant to have a complete ready-made Revelation from God: he is meant to work out his own theology, as he works out his own salvation."[26]

Knox quotes A. E. J. Rawlinson's dismissal of the notion of infallibility as a prime example of the flights of emotion-laden rhetoric to which the moderns are given when hard logic cannot be summoned to dispatch an uncomfortable tenet. Rawlinson proclaims that we should no more seek infallibility in the Church than impeccability in her rulers. But even though each member of the Church be sinful, and yet the Church strives to emulate Jesus' ideals, by the same token "we may believe, in spite of Robber Councils and Erastian Confessions, and the chaos of sects and parties in modern Christendom, that the Church has been, and is being, guided into an ever-deepening apprehension of divine truth."[27]

This elicits a brief rejoinder from Knox: "[I]t is perfectly possible for one's heart to beat true to a moral ideal when one's own conduct, through imperfection of the will, belies it; but it is hard to see how anyone could entertain an intellectual theory as true, and yet maintain positions contrary to it."[28]

[25] Ronald Knox, *Some Loose Stones* (London: Longmans, Green and Co., 1913), p. x.
[26] Ibid., p. 36.
[27] Streeter et al., *Foundations*, p. 368.
[28] Knox, *Some Loose Stones*, p. 37.

Knox readily admits that not all the contributors to *Foundations* held equally to a minimizing theological outlook, but the overall impression they leave is one of a begrudging admission of some, but not many, of the prerogatives traditional Christians ascribed to God and the Church. Streeter in one chapter suggests that God would rather employ confluences of natural events in special providences to effect his will than resort to true miracles that would puncture the normal working of the laws of nature. The impression he leaves is that miracles are a bit embarrassing to the modern mind and also that if one admitted that Jesus used them for evidentiary purposes, it would reflect ill on the faith of the apostles; they should instead have been convinced by intellectual arguments alone, like twentieth-century theologians. The same commentator is queasy about the evidence of the empty tomb and believes the modern mind would prefer that the apostles saw Jesus "spiritually" after the Resurrection, not Jesus in the same body that had just been crucified days earlier. It follows that Streeter does not believe that the Ascension took place either. Temple proclaims his disbelief in the omniscience and omnipotence of Jesus, claiming to find evidence in the Gospels for his redefinition of "divine" as something more limited than orthodox theologians understand it to mean. If, Temple says,

> the word Divine suggests omniscience; then where is the evidence that Jesus of Nazareth was omniscient? He suffered surprise and disappointment and openly stated that He did not know the hour of the Judgment. The word suggests Omnipresence; what can be meant by saying that Jesus of Nazareth was omnipresent? It suggests Omnipotence; where is the evidence that He was omnipotent? He "could do no mighty work" in face of unbelief.[29]

Knox's counter to this challenge is first to observe that proving positive qualities, for instance, omnipotence, is impossible because the Gospel accounts report only a limited number of actions performed by Jesus, so no argument from the texts can be comprehensive. But reliance on the quote that Jesus "could not do" suggests a tendentious reading of a phrase that in the Greek means "could not bring himself to do", the obvious interpretation being that even miracles would not convince the Galileans. Knox sums up:

[29] Streeter et al., *Foundations*, pp. 213–14.

> Now, this being so far as I know the only instance in which the language of the Evangelists suggests a physical limitation of our Lord's powers, and this being susceptible of a different interpretation, is it not at least arguable that the man whom the winds and the sea obeyed, the man who could multiply matter and raise the dead, possessed, whether he cared to use them or not, powers absolutely unlimited? It may, of course, be suggested that it detracts somewhat from the completeness of his Humanity; how could he experience the last depths of despair and disappointment, if he knew that he could at any moment lift a finger, and have everything his own way? But I confess that to my thinking there is a sort of tragic irony about the old-fashioned view from which we can gain more, devotionally, than from the view which supposes him to have been subject to complete human helplessness. He did allow a handful of soldiers to overpower him, though he might at any moment have summoned ten legions of his Angels to his succour; he did listen to the Jews crying, "If Christ be the King of Israel, let him now come down from the Cross, and we will believe him"; and knew all the time that he could—and he did not do it. I should say that our conception of the sacrifice of the Cross gains, instead of losing, if we believe that the death was voluntary in the sense, not merely that he brought it on himself by opposition to the unfaithful shepherds of Israel, but that he might, up to the last moment, have saved himself: there was no point at which his sacrifice did not demand a continuous act of the will on his own part.[30]

It almost goes without saying that the young Anglican theologians likewise doubt Jesus' consciousness of his divine mission, or rather, would depict it as a slow and somewhat hazy unfolding of a desire to be a conduit for God's will. A lingering piety bids Rawlinson to uphold Jesus' sinlessness but only with the proviso that he maintained it at the cost of a heroic moral struggle. But surely, a reading of the Gospels does not lend any support to that presupposition, and so once again, the theologians' dependence on a priori beliefs shines out clearly against a backdrop of evidence calling for one of two conclusions. As Knox observes:

> [I]f the Evangelists did not think that Jesus realized his Divinity, they have put on record what ought, from their point of view, to be classed as sinful actions. Even the destruction of property involved

[30] Knox, *Some Loose Stones*, pp. 94–95.

> in cleansing the Temple can only be justified with confidence if we think of Jesus as the conscious heir of his Father's house.... It is only if our Lord knew *exactly what he was doing*, only if he judged, and knew that he judged, his age in the light of full Divine knowledge, that I can feel perfectly confident in saying that he was sinless.[31]

Predictably, too, the *Foundations* authors discredit the Infancy Narratives of Matthew and Luke, because if Jesus is to be the figure they want him to be, he could not have been born of a virgin. They argue the priority of Mark's Gospel because it omits that part of his life and then suggest that these narratives are merely embellishments of a later date. But one event recorded in all four Gospels undermines that argument. When Jesus' opponents attempt to discredit him by pointing to his ordinary antecedents, in Matthew they say, "Is not this the carpenter's son?" Luke and John similarly have, "Is not this the son of Joseph?" But Mark puts the question as, "Is not this the carpenter, the son of Mary?" If Matthew and Luke wanted to accentuate a later accretion to the life of Jesus, they should be the ones to cast the question in a form congruent with their early chapters; and if Mark, as the modern theologians hypothesize, wrote without any knowledge of the Virgin Birth, why would he use the phrase he did? There are other reasons—the unity of style in language between the Infancy Narratives and subsequent chapters of Matthew and Luke, for example—that compel one to conclude that ignoring them as evidence is a purely arbitrary stance to adopt.

> If all you know of the origin of Jesus of Nazareth is the bare names of his family, as recorded by S. Mark; if he springs, full-armed, on to the stage of his Life's Work as a man who has been "converted" by a strange psychical experience following on his baptism; then I suppose it is the right, if not the duty, of the critic to estimate the influences on such a man's character of his environment, his times, his acquaintance with the Hebrew Prophets, his sympathy with Messianic ideals. But IF it is true that the birth of this man was foretold by the visit of an Angel, that his Mother was hailed by her cousin as blessed among women, and the Mother of her Lord; if the birth itself was beyond the use of nature, since the Mother remained a virgin in her childbearing; if his coming into the world was of such

[31] Ibid., pp. 106–7.

> moment, that the stars in heaven could not keep the secret, and the Angels burst into song over the fields of Bethlehem; if his infancy was protected by continual divine warnings and visions of the night; then it does seem to me that any sense of the fitness of things forbids such an analytical treatment. . . . You cannot think of the mind of such a man as "looking at life" or "interpreting his office" in this way or in that; and to say that God was ever present to his mind as the one great reality, is something akin to describing the Judgment Day as a fine sight.[32]

Likewise Canon W. H. Moberly finds the orthodox interpretation of the atonement too all-encompassing, so when he speaks of Christ saving mankind by his suffering and death, Moberly feels compelled to use quotes around the word "save", as if to underline the fact that he defines atonement in a different sense from its traditional meaning. The idea of suffering to satisfy divine justice offended by the accumulated sins of mankind is abhorrent to him. Instead he holds that the most Jesus could do was to inspire people to shun sin through his noble example. And yet Moberly also maintains that we are incapable of transforming ourselves into sinless creatures. He is consequently left with a conundrum: either accept the vicarious suffering and atonement (the orthodox view) or admit the perfectibility of our species under our own power:

> Either there was something in the work of our salvation which was quite outside of and apart from ourselves, call it Love, or Sorrow, or Penitence, if you will; a measure of it which we could never have felt, and can to the end of all time never feel, though the gift of tears were granted us beyond the experience of the holiest of God's Saints; something which, not by way of quickening our hearts or altering our state of mind, but in its own right contributed to the achievement of our deliverance—and then you have what the moderns call an "immoral" transaction; someone doing for others what they could not do for themselves; you are forced back on the Conservative view. Or you may say that the example of Calvary, and not merely the example, but the direct influence of the Divine Love therein made manifest, is a stimulus on which our own souls react, and thereby develop themselves into something fit for the presence of God; our sins not condoned, but left behind us by the mere fact

[32] Ibid., pp. 134–35.

> of our having travelled so far from our original position—and then you have broken away from historic doctrine and the experience of the saints, and from the common-sense reading of innumerable texts of Scripture.[33]

In challenge after challenge to the theologians of *Foundations*, Knox appeals to "historic doctrine" or a received tradition. The mere "corporate witness" on which they would anchor belief is far too fragile a base—indeed, it is only some loose stones—to support anything more than a religion of experience. And "experience", he notes, is a word they often seek repose in, because it is a catchword associated with the contemporary interest in psychology. Canvass the populace to find out what their experience is and cobble together statements of belief from the emerging consensus. Hence the doctrinal trimming to avoid offending a large bloc of self-proclaimed Christians. The vapidity of the resulting popularly acclaimed set of dogmas is witheringly exposed by Knox throughout his book.

But when Knox anticipates his critics' objection that he justify his own doctrinal beliefs by appeal to some authority, he must already have felt his own footing to be a little uncertain. He points to an apostolic tradition and avers that when local traditions conflicted, the Holy Spirit would guide bishops in Council to choose the right tradition. But when he poses the question *Which Councils does one accept?*—because, of course, there were some early Councils, such as the Latrocinium of the fifth century, that were rejected by the Church—Knox uncharacteristically bypasses the opportunity to answer it in detail. Acknowledging wistfully that "the Roman Catholic has a very simple ready-made answer, Those which are recognized by the See of Peter", he as an Anglican adheres to the decisions of those Councils "which were subsequently ratified by acceptance on the part of the faithful". But then he says, "It is not relevant to our point here to consider the very difficult objection, Yes, but how do you know whether the Nestorians or their opponents were the faithful?"[34] And he doesn't consider it. Yet in a final peroration, he advocates that the seeker of truth follow a straight path made visible by "the two headlights of Scripture and Tradition". He describes that path as "[s]traight, because it is the

[33] Ibid., p. 169.
[34] Ibid., p. 193.

simplest way of accomplishing your journey; straight, because the whole business of faith is not picking and choosing your way, or looking out for sign-posts, but having the pertinacity to follow your nose; straight, because after all the road is very largely Roman".[35]

A reader aware of Knox's subsequent actions might be pardoned for assuming that he was already eyeing submission to Rome as the only credible response to the capture of Anglican theology by Modernism. But he asserts unequivocally in *A Spiritual Aeneid* that such was not the case in 1913, when he wrote *Some Loose Stones*. Instead he was possessed of the idea of a future corporate reunion between a failing Anglican branch and a more vigorous, but still, to his mind, somewhat diseased, Roman tree.[36] The same summer that he was composing his response to the theological liberals, he preached in Plymouth a series of sermons that boldly put forward his views on the Church

[35] Ibid., p. 217.

[36] Several times in his autobiography, Knox alludes to a historical novel, *John Inglesant: A Romance*, which impressed him greatly for its evocation of a time when Roman Catholicism and Anglicanism seemed reconcilable. Living in mid-seventeenth-century England, the fictional hero, John Inglesant, is a page in the household of King Charles I, where he is stationed by his calculating mentor, the Jesuit Fr. St. Clare, to be a bridge helping effect a reunion. Of course, Charles is beheaded by the Cromwellians, and so the half-Anglican, half-Catholic Inglesant wanders on to Rome, where he is repelled by the combination of baseness and credulity of Italian Catholicism. The one shining light in the city is Fr. Miguel de Molinos, whose condemnation by Church authorities is portrayed in lurid color, calculated to suggest to readers the horrors popularly associated with the Spanish rather than the Roman Inquisition. Knox notes that the novel is little known in Catholic circles though very popular among Anglicans. The following extract, in which the mature Inglesant, returned to the groves of Oxford and the pure light of Anglicanism, explains his reasons for abandoning Roman Catholicism, may suggest why: "It has based its system upon the profoundest truths, and upon this platform it has raised a power which has, whether foreseen by its authors or not, played the part of human tyranny, greed, and cruelty. To support this system it has habitually set itself to suppress knowledge and freedom of thought. . . . It has, therefore, for the sake of preserving intact its dogma, risked the growth and welfare of humanity, and has, in the eyes of all except those who value this dogma above all other things, constituted itself the enemy of the human race." Conversely, he goes on, the English church respects spirituality without giving in to the gross superstition of Catholicism, and reason without succumbing to infidelity, and is therefore the safest haven for the seeker of truth. See J. Henry Shorthouse, *John Inglesant: A Romance*, 8th ed. (New York: Macmillan Company, 1903), p. 442. Shorthouse (1834–1903) was a Quaker who converted with his wife to Anglicanism in 1861; ironically, he was a near neighbor to John Henry Newman in Edgbaston but never seems to have met him. The ten years of labor devoted to his magnum opus were rewarded with sales of over eighty thousand in its first twenty years, but none of his other works became famous. See Andrew Drummond, *The Churches in English Fiction* (Leicester: Edgar Backus, 1950), pp. 86–93.

in England past, present, and future. Those sermons, published in booklet form under the title of the first of them, *Naboth's Vineyard in Pawn*, clearly show that for all his distaste for what had become of the national religion, he had not yet given up hope of its eventual renaissance. He begins by asserting that loyalty to the Church of England is a virtue only for those who are not complacent about its defects. He proceeds to describe its evolution in terms starkly contrasting with the patriotic stories imbibed by generations of English youth but in line with the conclusions of modern historians: "As Ahab coveted the vineyard of Naboth, in spite of his own broad possessions, so King Henry VIII, not content with the temporal power he could claim over his subjects, determined to be their spiritual master as well. Blessed Thomas More, Blessed John Fisher, and many others, refused, like Naboth, to give up the inheritance of their fathers, and met with Naboth's end." [37]

And yet Knox later castigates the Catholic reading of Henry's usurpation and More's martyrdom as equally unhistorical, denying that Henry founded a new church or that More died in defense of the old Church. Rather, Henry tyrannized over the one Church, and More resisted his tyranny. So too Elizabeth patched up a settlement meant to satisfy Catholics and Protestants sufficiently to keep the realm together. Knox proposes that that settlement was not meant to be permanent but that the force of legal sanctions against dissidents made it so over the next few centuries. Authority had come to mean the impress of a hobnailed boot rather than a double commission:

> Elizabeth's bishops were her henchmen; they did the work, and, if necessary, had the responsibility shifted on to them. The Caroline bishops ruled the Church, but they ruled it in virtue of the Court of Star Chamber and the Court of High Commission. They had authority, but it came straight from the Crown. They never pretended to be primitive bishops, each a pope in his own diocese. The jurisdiction which had been taken away from the Naboth of the Vatican, had been vested, for all practical purposes, in the Crown.... The bishops were meant to be a kind of ecclesiastical

[37] Ronald Knox, "Naboth's Vineyard in Pawn", reprinted in *University and Anglican Sermons of Ronald A. Knox*, ed. Philip Caraman, S.J. (New York: Sheed and Ward, 1963), p. 450.

> body of policy, spying on their clergy and handing over delinquents to the arm of the law.[38]

But the Oxford Movement provided a glimmer of hope, and, despite what Knox characterizes as Newman's despair at the movement's slowness to catch fire in the Anglican community (leading to his individual submission to Rome), Knox would have his listeners stand fast through persecution and derision until that corporate reunion could take place, perhaps fifty years hence. The appeal for constancy in faith within his present communion is heavily tinged with emotion. There is an undercurrent of the quixotic about his call for loyalty to seemingly lost causes and doing penance for the corporate sins of the standard-bearers of the state religion rather than opting for the more logical route of directly embracing Roman Catholicism: "It is not for us, the glamour of the Seven Hills, and the confidence of membership, living and actual, in the Church of the Ages; we cannot set our feet upon the rock of Peter, but only watch the shadow of Peter passing by, and hope that it may fall on us and heal us. We shall bear the reproach of the Catholic name, without enjoying the full privileges of the Catholic heritage."[39] Here the logician has abandoned his ramparts for the refuge of an unwholesome sentimentality. While this characterization may seem unduly harsh given the innumerable ties of family, friendship, ordination, and culture that bound him to the religion of his forefathers, there can be little doubt that he was more aware of the insupportability of the via media he was proposing to Catholic-oriented Anglicans than his pleas for dutiful guardianship of orthodoxy within the fold would suggest.

In the second of the three Plymouth sermons, Knox addresses the increasingly hospitable climate for the growth of heresy within Anglicanism, the climate that was educing from him his book-length response

[38] Ibid., p. 453.

[39] Ibid., p. 466. There is a strong resemblance to Newman's melancholy mood voiced in Tract 90, when he was still years away from joining Rome but thought that corporate unity was attainable: "Till we, her children, are stirred up to this religious course, let the Church, our Mother, sit still; let her children be content to be in bondage; let us work in chains; let us submit to our imperfections as a punishment; let us go on teaching with the stammering lips of ambiguous formularies, and inconsistent precedents, and principles but partially developed." Quoted in Ian Ker, *John Henry Newman: A Biography* (Oxford: Oxford University Press, 1988), p. 217.

to its manifestations among his Oxford colleagues. Heresy, he concludes, will be fostered in this environment:

> [T]he old Evangelicals could appeal to the Bible as their authority; and the Roman Catholics have always been able to appeal to the traditions of our holy Mother the Church. But the Church of England, as such, has nothing to appeal to. How can we pretend to appeal to Church tradition, when we have cut ourselves off from the main stream of it, and any exposition of it must needs be a raking up of old dead documents, instead of obedience to a living voice? And how can we pretend to appeal to the Bible, when the Bible is for every man's private interpretation, and not expounded by authority? The Reformation compromise was based on an infallible certainty, that of the literal inspiration of the Bible; but the new compromise does not claim to believe in that, and is therefore powerless in the face of modernist theology.[40]

Sermons do not call for footnotes, and Knox himself later recalled that these sermons in particular were composed in something of a white heat, but the ascription of the ideas behind the above paragraph is unmistakable. They represent a synopsis of the arguments of William Hurrell Mallock, put forward in a book published at the turn of the century called *Doctrine and Doctrinal Disruption*. Knox was a staunch admirer of Mallock's work, and a later chapter will discuss the debt he acknowledges to the older writer's *The New Republic* when he published *Sanctions* in 1922. But Mallock's book on the crisis in Anglican theology struck at the very root of the difficulties Knox was facing in 1913 and left little doubt what course a reasonable person must follow to escape from the morass engulfing the established church. Mallock's premise is that the old consensus on the theology of the Reformers, with their literalist interpretation of the Bible, has long since eroded, so that questions of authority must now come to the fore. Already Anglicanism had its Ritualist, High Church, Low Church, and Broad Church wings, each with its own distinctive doctrine about where its authority lies but none of them willing to test the internal logic of their respective cornerstones:

[40] Knox, *University and Anglican Sermons*, p. 458.

> Each party, in building up its own system of theology, assumes its premises, instead of analysing and defending them, and remains content with the task of arguing that, these premises being assumed, its own special doctrines follow from them. Indeed, this task so completely absorbs its attention that it practically forgets, when controverting the conclusions of its opponents, that the premises from which its opponents start are not the same as its own, and that if their conclusions are to be disproved, it is their premises that must be dealt with first. I do not say that any party is forgetful of this theoretically. They all remember it, but they remember it inadequately; or, in other words, they forget it practically. They forget it to such good purpose that in the Anglican controversy of to-day the question of authority, of proofs, and of first premises hardly makes its appearance as a disputed point at all.[41]

The Ritualist postulates a consensus between the presently disunited branches of Eastern and Western Christendom as to what constitutes the irreformable truths of Christianity. But who, besides the Ritualists themselves, adheres to this viewpoint? As Mallock unflinchingly asserts:

> Now it is plain, from its own terms, that if this theory is to have any weight at all, it must itself be ratified by a consensus of the mass of those who are referred to in it. But is such the case? On the contrary, by an overwhelming majority of them it is absolutely denied and repudiated. It is absolutely denied and repudiated by the whole of the Church of Rome, which is twice as numerous as all the Protestant Communions in the world: and this is not all, for, what is still more striking, it is similarly denied and repudiated by the majority of Protestants themselves.[42]

The High Churchman looks to the primitive Church for direction but must assign a cutoff date to the divine guidance of the Church; and the Low Churchman simply trusts the individual illumination granted to the reader of the Word of God but is at a loss to explain why different people are illuminated in different ways. And the Bible also suffers as an infallible guide because, without an authoritative voice

[41] W. H. Mallock, *Doctrine and Doctrinal Disruption* (London: Adam and Charles Black, 1900), p. 34.

[42] Ibid., p. 90.

to interpret it, the passages imbued with doctrinal content cannot be sifted from the passages reflecting ephemeral local color. Individuals thereby become their own oracles of doctrine and will appeal to subjective feelings to justify their theological stances. Whatever the believer's persuasions, then, "the three theories which the Anglican Church offers us of the basis and test of the doctrines of doctrinal Christianity, have not even the merit of an internal consistency with themselves; but involve, when stated clearly, the same kind of absurdity to which Euclid reduces certain false hypotheses in geometry." [43]

The collapse of the consensus theory is devastating to the entire panoply of the Ritualists' doctrinal system. Much as he might have disliked the label, Knox was a Ritualist. (He preferred the term *Sacramentalist* because of its emphasis on the essentials as opposed to the accessories of religion.) The whole argument of *Some Loose Stones* rests on there being an a priori consensus about the cornerstones of the faith, which both a Wesleyan chapel and a Roman cathedral would resound with, alongside Saint James' in Plymouth. Mallock cut through to the frail props underlying that presumption:

> If the Anglican doctrine of consensus cannot establish *itself*, by what possible means is it capable of establishing any others? We do not ask that it should establish itself by ordinary historical evidences. We invoke it, in order that it may corroborate and supplement them, not because we imagine it rests on them: and if we accept it at all, we must accept it by an act of faith. But in order to accept an authority by an act of faith, what we do require is that there shall be some authority to accept. We require that it shall have some identifiable organ of utterance; and if we are to believe what it tells us, we must be able to distinguish what it tells us.[44]

What a coherent belief system needs is logical consistency, so that if one makes an act of faith in it, argues Mallock, it can provide all the necessary foundations to buttress securely the initial acceptance of it. Surveying the different churches, Mallock saw only one meeting that stringent requirement, the Roman Catholic Church. She held the consensus theory but was possessed of a historical continuity and universality, not present in Anglicanism, that allowed her to limit the consensus

[43] Ibid., p. 92.
[44] Ibid., p. 129.

to members of her own fold. She could appeal to the beliefs of the primitive Church, because she was one and the same Church. Even the interior witness of her vast membership, as demonstrated so often through history by the popular devotion to the Mother of Jesus and to the saints, and the tenacious hold of the laity to the true faith even when bishops would lead them astray, clearly satisfies the criterion for right belief held up by the Low Churchman.

Just as important in Mallock's eyes as the credentials it supplies is the promise Roman Catholicism holds to meet the new intellectual challenges of the present and the future. Anglicanism of whatever orientation holds at best that the past, whether the end be at the Reformation or the sixth century, can supply the believer's theological needs. But not so Rome:

> The fact, therefore, that Rome is provided by the Roman theory with a teaching authority, which it never has lost or can lose, which is as living to-day as on the day of the first Council; which is as ready to meet the scientific discoveries of the future as it ever was to meet the philosophic thought of the past; and which is destined, perhaps, to unfold to us a body of Christian doctrine wider and deeper even than that which it has unfolded and defined already—the fact that Rome is provided with an authority of this indestructible kind, is the feature by which that Church is most clearly shown to be the one Christian body still possessing the means of presenting Christian doctrine to the modern world as a body of truths supported by a system of definite proofs, and destined, like other truths, to develop as knowledge widens.[45]

So where did Knox's appreciation of these arguments leave him intellectually? In *A Spiritual Aeneid*, he chronicles closely his state of mind during the critical years from his emergence as a voice of orthodoxy in the Anglican communion up to his conversion to Rome. After he published *Some Loose Stones*, he believed Anglicanism had no future save in corporate reunion with Rome. "And yet I had no intention of becoming a Catholic. Since my conversion, people have said to me, 'Of course we knew you were on the way to becoming a Catholic.' To which (humanly speaking) I have a quite simple reply 'I wasn't.' "[46]

[45] Ibid., p. 153.
[46] Knox, *Spiritual Aeneid*, p. 157.

It is ironic, if irony can appropriately be summoned to judge in matters of faith, that Knox ultimately converted before Mallock, who left the casting of his lot with the Church until his deathbed in 1923. Mallock had had his faith undermined while still a university student, and the climb back was via the arid path of pure logic. Knox had surety of belief as he progressed on his Aeneid and could build on the spiritual comforts still afforded him by the national church.

But in order to feel comfortable in the church of his birth, Knox had to stretch the envelope of its hospitality to mutually immiscible beliefs. He did so by proclaiming that Anglican formularies were designed merely to include minimalists like Puritans within the fold but were not thereby meant to exclude maximalists like the Romanizers:

> The disloyalty of believing less than the fixed minimum was patent, but if anybody said to us, "You are exceeding the maximum," we had a right to inquire how he knew. This point of view I still think historically sound so far as the later revisions of the Prayer Book are concerned—I mean, that it was always the minimizers and not the maximizers who were being considered. Nor can I accuse myself of paradox for having suggested that there was nothing in Anglican formularies which either deliberately forbade the reservation of the Sacrament, or explicitly made Confession optional rather than obligatory: the effort to establish the contrary by reference to Prayer Book rubrics which were not designed to meet the case has always seemed to me mere special pleading.[47]

The preoccupation of the country with the world war by then raging prompted a voluntary cessation of controversy on the part of Knox and his clerical allies. But the daily mounting toll of dead from among comrades of Oxford and Eton days also impelled them to initiate religious practices throughout the nation, such as Forty Hours' Devotion, that had never been allowed previously. It goes without saying that these devotions were encouraged simply to petition God to be merciful during a time of acute crisis; they were not introduced to gain a strategic advantage for a party position. They fulfilled a major spiritual need of the congregations, and Knox's preaching sought to heighten people's awareness of the value of impetrative prayer. A series of sermons given during Holy Week 1915 in London was published

[47] Ibid., pp. 177–78.

under the title *Bread or Stone*. They unfold the doctrine of the efficacy of prayer against those who declaim its futility in the name of materialistic determinism or of cold Deism, by emphasizing the spiritual treasures built up with a God who loves all persons far more even than they love themselves. Some of the difficulty experienced in prayer is precisely because the prayers offered are not like the unceasing prayer Jesus offered up to the Father. The ordinary prayer

> is not a continuous state, but an occasional exercise, demanding of us the setting apart of special time, the putting out of special spiritual energy. And, just as the poor man, because he is poor, is anxious to make certain that he is getting full value for his money, so we, in our spiritual poverty, like to be assured that there is some return for our grudging expenditure, and want to be informed how that expenditure can be most profitably laid out.[48]

Obviously the mind of God cannot be read by the petitioner, but when the meaning of omnipotence is reflected on, it must be accepted that even the most untoward outcomes of petitions (for example, the battlefield death of a loved one) are part of his overarching plan for the best possible outcomes in people's lives. And those prayers for that person's safety, were they then without effect?

> Do you ever think of the people who have very few to pray for them, few friends, few acquaintances, few friends or acquaintances who use the habit of prayer? I sometimes wonder if our unanswered prayers (as we think them) are not placed to the credit of such forgotten soldiers in the battle of life: you will remember that the talent bestowed on the unworthy servant, who could make no use of it, was at the Lord's disposal to give to another. Suppose that you are praying for the soul of one now dead, who secretly, unknown to you, spent his whole life in deliberate revolt against God, and refusal of his inspirations—one whom your prayers cannot avail to help. It may be—I say, it may be—that your prayers are winning refreshment, light, and peace, for some poor misjudged penitent who was thought to have cut himself off from God in life, and died by his own hand, who now, in the place of waiting, remembers

[48] Ronald Knox, *Bread or Stone: Four Conferences on Impetrative Prayer* (London: Society of SS. Peter and Paul, 1915), p. 35.

gratefully the prayers you, who never knew him, are offering for his sake.[49]

Controversy is absent from *Bread or Stone*, but the small tract could certainly have passed for a Roman Catholic work of devotion. Each chapter is preceded by a devotional picture, and the cover and title page display an idealization of a ciborium with IHS at its center.

Satisfaction with his status as a catholicizing Anglican working sedulously for the inevitable reunion with Rome once the war was over was short-lived, however. When Knox's brother Wilfred was ordained and celebrated his first Anglican Mass at Saint Mary's, Graham Street in London, doubts began to assail Ronald's mind whether the service he was witnessing was what it purported to be:

> If this doubt, this shadow of a scruple which had grown up in my mind, were justifiable—only suppose it were justifiable, then neither he nor I was a priest, nor was this the mass, nor was the host the Saving Host; the accessories of the service—the bright vestments, the fresh flowers, the mysterious candle-light, were all settings to a sham jewel.... [M]y intellect, thus peeping down the vista of a mere doubt, forced my eyes open to the whole mockery it involved—and all the time I was supposed to be worshipping. So far was I, in this agony of realization, from any holy thoughts, that at the last Gospel I found only a curse framing itself in my mind; a curse directed against Henry the Eighth.[50]

Rereading *Naboth's Vineyard in Pawn* that summer only heightened Knox's sense of unease with his publicly proclaimed stance: "With the best will in the world I searched for a strictly logical flaw in it, and failed to find one; but, somehow, the whole attitude now seemed unreal. It was not that there was anything wrong with the book, there was simply nothing right; it was like an ingenious mathematical proof deduced from unreal premisses." [51] Dissatisfaction with his past arguments did not lead him Romeward quickly. He had to pass through two more years of spiritual torpor, during which he gave up preaching and hearing confessions. Oxford had become sufficiently depopulated that his services as chaplain at Trinity were not needed,

[49] Ibid., pp. 39–40.
[50] Knox, *Spiritual Aeneid*, p. 197.
[51] Ibid., pp. 202–3.

so he took up a post teaching boys at Shrewsbury while their lay faculty were off at the front. Anglican controversial literature was ineffectual in steadying him, so sympathetic advisors recommended a dose of early Church history to test his growing suspicion that the Papacy was of the essence, rather than just the well-being, of Christianity. Reading the sturdily Protestant Dean Milman's account of the rise of the Latin Church proved an epiphany because of its unintended reinforcing of the very doctrine distinguishing Roman Catholicism from Anglicanism:

> [H]e comments upon the extraordinary precision with which, time after time, the Bishops of Rome managed to foresee which side the Church would eventually take in a controversy, and "plumped" for it beforehand. The Church fixes the date of Easter, the Church decides that heretics need not be rebaptized, the Church decides that the Incarnate combined two Natures in one Person; but each time Rome (like Lancashire) thinks to-day what the world will think to-morrow. This uncanny capacity for taking the pulse of the Church is ascribed by Milman partly to their geographically central position, and so on. And then it occurred to me that there was another explanation. I could have laughed aloud.[52]

It should also be mentioned that there were before Knox during this period of doubt two English converts who exercised a gentle, sometimes imperceptible, influence over him. One was Robert Hugh Benson, whom Knox had met just once and who had died prematurely in 1914 at the height of his literary powers. The other was Basil Maturin, the Catholic chaplain at Oxford who died aboard the *Lusitania* in 1915.

It is difficult today to appreciate the totally different perspective Benson provided on the English Reformation to a wide readership through his historical novels. Centuries of primers, official histories, church handbooks, and pious political oratory had obliterated every other than the official outlook among the populace, i.e., that the Reformation freed England from the shackles of priestcraft and Rome. There was, of course, Lingard to offer a more sober academic-style history, but he was a Catholic priest writing at a time when that

[52] Ibid., p. 220.

was sufficient reason to cause him to be dismissed as a biased partisan.[53] Benson wrote for a popular audience and could evoke the sixteenth-century milieu with the skill of an artist, vividly depicting the overturn of a hallowed societal order (in *The King's Achievement*) or the persecution of priests in Elizabethan times (in *Come Rack! Come Rope!*). Knox mentions the latter novel among the books occupying his attention during his time of indecision, along with Father Martindale's just-published biography of Benson.[54] But it is equally Benson's own pilgrimage from ordained Anglican priest, and son of an Anglican bishop—indeed, son of the archbishop of Canterbury—to Catholic priest that intrigued Knox. Although the similarities in their cases could not be pressed too far, for Benson was not a logician but rather an artist, and with his predilection for mystical theology was sometimes preliminarily open to Modernist restatements of traditional Catholic theology, nevertheless he had gone through precisely the same agony of doubt and indecision that Knox was now experiencing. For Benson, the disturbance to his equilibrium began in 1902, when he was 31 and ordained one year, and culminated in his reception into the Roman Catholic Church in September 1903.[55]

Knox mentions in *A Spiritual Aeneid* that Benson had been praying for Knox's conversion, obviously at a time when he was not even considering such a move. The esteem in which he holds Benson is thereby all the more understandable, even if Evelyn Waugh is

[53] John Lingard (1771–1851) was a Catholic priest who wrote a multivolume history of England that was far more scientific in its use of sources than any earlier historian's work. For his life, see Martin Haile and Edward Bonney, *Life and Letters of John Lingard, 1771–1851* (St. Louis, Mo.: B. Herder, 1911), and for an appreciation of his work see Donald F. Shea, *The English Ranke: John Lingard* (New York: Humanities Press, 1969), who notes: "In the discovery and critical use of manuscript and printed, domestic and foreign primary documents, Lingard's work on the sixteenth century was novel in his day and remained so for at least two generations.... [H]e stands immeasurably above his contemporaries Turner, Hallam, and Macaulay; in fact, only James Anthony Froude, almost fifty years later, rivals him—and his scholarship was marred by his chronic and proverbial inaccuracy" (pp. 94–95).

[54] C. C. Martindale, *The Life of Monsignor Robert Hugh Benson*, 2 vols. (London: Longmans, Green and Co., 1916).

[55] Interestingly, his biographer records one letter of May 1903 that describes the effect of one book on Benson's religious outlook: "I have just been reading today an *irresistible* book—Mallock's *Doctrine and Doctrinal Disruption*. My word! It is a *masterpiece*. Really, honestly, I have no further doubts." Quoted in Martindale, *Benson*, 1:230.

somewhat baffled by it. Waugh regards Benson as "an exotic"[56] and, in comparing the two writers, states unequivocally that "their differences of temperament and of accomplishment seem enormously wider than their similarities."[57] But a spiritual bond had been formed back in 1903 when the youthful Knox discovered sacramentality in *The Light Invisible*, and it did not end with Benson's death.

Father Maturin was a Catholic priest Knox associated with more frequently since he was stationed at Oxford, and he too had not only converted after a long stint as an Anglican missionary priest with the Cowley Fathers, but also had written probably the most incisive psychological study of the difficulties facing a High Anglican in *The Price of Unity*, which was published in 1912. Having endured a four-year struggle himself prior to entering the Catholic communion in 1897, he was keenly aware of the debilitating effect of controversial literature and overt proselytizing—hence Knox's willingness to let down his own combativeness when confronted with this most genuine counterpart in the chaplaincy who "always treated you with the openness of a friend".[58] Here was a man whose own conversion had stung the young Benson but who was present years later to guide the latter shortly after his reception into the Church.

Every attraction the Sacramentalist movement in the Church of England presented to Benson and then to Knox had previously been experienced by Maturin and had been found ultimately deficient:

> You spoke of it, thought of it, dreamed of it as the Church of the Fathers, of the Martyrs and Confessors, the Home of the Saints, that could face the world and conquer it, and could part with multitudes of those who had been her own children rather than tamper with the faith. What cared you for the Anglican Church, except as it represented the ancient Church? You endowed her with an authority which she repudiated; you gave her titles of honour and respect which made her awkward and nervous; you put upon her lips words which she never uttered, and gave a meaning and emphasis to her words which she disowned. You were indeed at times startled and shocked when for a moment some more glaring inconsistency than common, or some more flagrant betrayal of trust, brought into relief

[56] Evelyn Waugh, *Ronald Knox* (Boston: Little, Brown and Co., 1959), p. 177.
[57] Ibid., p. 146.
[58] Knox, *Spiritual Aeneid*, p. 169.

> the contrast between the reality and the ideal with which you had clothed it. But you felt such a thought to be treachery. You distinguished between the Church and its official representatives and their utterances, sometimes individual and sometimes collective. You said, "the Church is not compromised by what this Bishop or that Priest may do or say." You tried to pacify the anxiety that sometimes would not be quieted, when you realized that you were individually under the spiritual charge of a man who openly preached what you knew to be heresy. But you argued that there have always been unfaithful Priests in the Church, and that it is merely the anomalous condition of the present relations between Church and State, and the temporary loss of discipline, that makes such things possible.[59]

How truly this picture applies to the zealous young author of *Naboth's Vineyard in Pawn*. Maturin goes on to portray the revivifying experience of the Anglo-Catholic movement, with its reintroduction of the sacrament of penance, its adoration of the Sacrament of the Altar, and revival of monastic communities:

> You breathed in the Catholic atmosphere that was sweeping over the dried and barren plains, and brought with it the refreshing rains so long withheld, and you saw in very truth the wilderness blossoming like a rose. How could you doubt? How could you doubt the reality of your own spiritual experiences? You were not brought up perhaps in the narrow and chilling school of a hard and frost-bound Protestantism. You did not know your Church could give you such great things, but you sought it and you found it. And it was to you like passing from winter to a glorious spring, fresh with life and light and hope, and recovered youth, and movement and conscious growth. And if there was opposition and difficulty, aye, and persecution, was not that but another witness to the continuity of the Church's life and her claim to be the Church of the ages? Was there ever a time when she had not to face opposition? You felt like an early Christian.[60]

Yes, the very boorishness of the authorities who tried to snuff out the revival of Catholic practices only stiffened the resolve of young

[59] B. W. Maturin, *The Price of Unity* (London: Longmans, Green and Co., 1912), pp. 40–42.
[60] Ibid.

clerics to press forward in full confidence that they were breathing life into a moribund religious body. It was the spirit of the early Church building up communities in the face of Roman and Jewish opposition.

Then the doubts begin to enter, singly at first, and consequently answerable by some responsible cleric who has himself faced down the allurements of Rome. But they return, and they reach such a force that they threaten not merely a change of communion but seem at times to presage a wholesale abandonment of faith. Whatever the outcome of grappling with these doubts, one thing at least is certain. Those who experience them can never again feel secure in the Anglican faith. They have become privy to the root cause of the disunity within their church:

> It seems to them ever more and more clear, that ever since the English Church began her separate existence, she not only tolerated, but authoritatively permitted, different and conflicting schools of thought within her fold. That she knowingly and deliberately commissions a clergy who teach doctrines that are irreconcilable. That however great the revival, the different parties are as strong and mutually antagonistic as ever. That the existence of the English Church in any place is synonymous with difference of teaching. That as a member of the body you are dependent, in the ultimate issue, upon yourself for what you believe. That in fact you may believe what you like, and pass from one school of thought to the other. And that the poor, being necessarily dependent for their beliefs upon the teaching of their parish clergy, are at the mercy of the chance that sends them a High Churchman or a Low Churchman. There is, it seems, to them no sign of the diminishing of these differences. There is no doubt a wider toleration, but that may be rather the result of a growing indifference to doctrine, than of a deepening of doctrinal orthodoxy. But the fundamental differences are as great as ever. No doubt the present state of things can be traced to the past, but not merely to past neglect or indifference, but to the position of compromise which the English Church assumed on her separation from Rome. She is herself the fountain and source of the differences in her Communion. Wherever she is she carries them with her, as truly as where Rome is she carries the sources of her unity. Ignore it as we may, explain it as we may, idealize as we may, when we are brought face to face with the official Church, we feel and understand that diversity—not unity, compromise—not

> authority, is too deeply rooted in her whole conception of her office ever to be dislodged.[61]

Rome offers an authoritative voice, something the English Church, with its habitual toleration of dissonant theologies, cannot. That is the crux of the issues driving the would-be convert Romeward. But searching self-criticism lays the seeds of doubt. Is conversion justifiable?

> Will it be his marring or his making? He knows some to whom it has brought a new life, whom it has made saints, and he knows others whom it has made all that he dislikes. What will it be to him? After all is not the spiritual life everything? What is the use of any religion except to deepen the spiritual life and bring a person nearer to God? Has he any right to risk that? And he cannot doubt that it is a risk to a man of his temperament, a very serious risk. Perhaps he has made too much of the controversial aspect of the question. Has he sufficiently considered it from the spiritual point of view? He has certainly grown and deepened where he is. Why should he not be content with that? What more does he want? Why should not he stay where God has put him? Those who know him best, and whose judgment he most trusts, tell him that the Roman Church has become an obsession to him, that he has idealized it and dwelt upon it, till his judgment has become warped, and he is incapable of seeing it really as it is. That he is unfair to his own Church and refuses to see its advantages and is always on the lookout for its defects. That he admires in Rome what many of her own more thoughtful children regret, and thinks everything she does is right, everything the English Church does is wrong, and that all he has been through has certainly not improved him. It has interfered with everything, and made him unfair, critical, bitter, disloyal, controversial.[62]

[61] Ibid., pp. 208–9. As Knox put it in a series of sermons delivered in 1927 on the specious hold of the national church on the potential English convert: "It is the Church of the country; as an Englishman, I feel that I have a right to go there, whatever my views are; it does not commit me to anything. There can be no harm in stopping here until I am absolutely convinced, until I have absolutely made up my mind. For an Englishman, after all, the national Church is the natural Church. Well, I will not stop to consider whether you are really paying a great compliment to the Church of England, when you look upon it as a sort of lost luggage office for insufficiently addressed parcels." Ronald Knox, *Anglican Cobwebs* (London: Sheed and Ward, 1927), p. 21.

[62] Ibid., pp. 77–78.

This was indeed the state of Knox's mind when he was at Shrewsbury. He had seceded from his leadership role in the battle for orthodoxy and relapsed into a lethargic state of mind, which allowed him to feel a benevolent tolerance for all shades of opinion because he was too exhausted to prosecute his own struggle to its ultimate conclusion. And yet the prospect of remaining in this inertial condition filled him with fear. He could not reassure himself that his indecision was not a culpable terminus achieved by spurning God's provisions of grace: "It seemed to me that the loss of faith, and even the loss of moral standards, would neither be an unnatural result of my hesitation, nor, if it were culpable, an inappropriate punishment for it."[63]

Finally Knox decided to give up his teaching post at Shrewsbury, resign his fellowship at Trinity, and place himself in a Catholic atmosphere for a retreat in September 1917. There is no reason to suppose that he thought of the two-week stay at the Benedictine abbey at Farnborough as merely the necessary preliminary to his formal admission to the Catholic Church. He went there still uncertain about the outcome. Certainty was what his logician's mind craved, but it was elusive. Authority was what the Anglican Church decidedly could not give him, but authority alone could validate the beliefs he had come to cherish as a High Churchman, which had been left unnourished during two years of doubts.

> For authority played a large part in my belief, and I could not now find that any certain source of authority was available outside the pale of the Roman Catholic Church. Once inside, I should not care how the authority came to me; I did not crave for infallible decrees; I wanted to be certain I belonged to that Church of which Saint Paul said proudly, "We have the Mind of Christ." I was by this time unable to believe that I was already in the Church—it was not that I had ceased to believe anything, but that I had a more exacting idea of what "being inside the Church" meant. Now, either I must accept this fuller idea, with all the corollaries it involved in the way of spiritual submission and worldly resignation, or I must give up all positive basis for my religion.[64]

[63] Knox, *Spiritual Aeneid*, p. 234.

[64] Ibid., pp. 240–41.

In the end, all obstacles were overcome, and Knox was received into the Church on September 22 at the abbey. He recalls in *A Spiritual Aeneid* succumbing to lassitude during the ceremony, a not entirely surprising feeling to someone who had just endured a protracted mental struggle. Writing about his own experiences was not a congenial task for Knox, so recourse to the insights of Father Maturin may be pardoned for filling in the details of what would have gone through his mind as he approached the momentous step. Again, it must be emphasized that conversion in those days, no less than in Newman's time, signaled almost an act of treason to many of one's compatriots, for it was a national religion that was being discarded in favor of one that had been successfully portrayed to the people of England for over three hundred years as a baneful foreign influence. Writing to an unnamed person around 1914, Father Maturin speaks of the feelings experienced by the new convert:

> I have never been able to understand the mental attitude of people who speak of their reception in a state of exaltation. The more real the English Church has been to you, and all your past experiences in it, the more terrible the wrench. And there is added a kind of uncertainty as to what you will find after you are received, the fear of the unknown—and with me, and probably with you, moments of mental agony, lest through some unknown act of your own you are, after all, making a mistake and doing wrong. I had such feelings up to the last moment, and went through the reception like a stone. ... At such a moment one feels utterly alone, and how little help one can get from anyone else! But be assured that no agony of regret for what you are leaving, or shrinking from the unknown future, or mental recoil of any kind, need lead you to any uncertainty that you are right.[65]

Both writers concur, however, in experiencing ultimately a liberating effect with their decision to become Catholics. As Anglicans, they had supposed that submission to Rome would inevitably entail some restriction of mental freedom, that the price of unity was a

[65] Maisie Ward, *Father Maturin: A Memoir* (London: Longmans, Green and Co., 1920), pp. 38–39. Basil Maturin (1849–1915) died on board the *Lusitania*; he was last seen handing a baby to people on a lifeboat, with the admonition that the child's mother be found, and then calmly going about his priestly duties of administering last rites to some of the passengers who remained on the ship's deck.

narrowness of outlook that would dampen individual creativity. One could be adventurous as an Anglican because of its latitudinarianism; surely dogmatic intolerance would stultify self-expression as a Catholic. Knox had factored that presumption in before taking the step and was prepared to endure it. However, within a year, he had found otherwise:

> [T]he curious thing is that my experience has been exactly the opposite. I have been overwhelmed with the feeling of liberty—the glorious liberty of the sons of God. I am speaking for myself when I say that as an Anglican I was for ever bothering about this and that detail of correctness—was this doctrine one that an Anglican could assert as of faith? Was this scruple of conscience one to be encouraged or one to be fought? And, above all, was I right? Were we all doing God's Will? or merely playing at it? Now, this perpetual Is-my-hat-straight sort of feeling is one that had become so inveterate with me as an Anglican that I had ceased to be fully conscious of it; just in the same way you can carry a weight so long that you cease to feel it; instead, you feel an outburst of positive relief when it is withdrawn.[66]

And Father Maturin, with many more years to reflect on life as an Anglican and as a Catholic (for he wrote fifteen years after a conversion that he had undergone at the age of fifty), exults in the realization of having arrived at a secure destination, "in which your own weak faith is braced and strengthened by the faith of a vast multitude, and is supported by an authority upon which you can rest". He continues, in language that suggests the traveler's theme:

> You feel indeed like an exile who has returned to his Fatherland. There is a strange sense of coming to a land, and amongst a people, to whom you always belonged, though you did not know it. The surprises that meet you are surprises that seem to awaken memories of some long-forgotten past. It takes but a short time for a newcomer to feel as if he had always been there. All that was true in his former beliefs find their home and their place in the atmosphere to which they belong and from which they had been taken. They are

[66] Knox, *Spiritual Aeneid*, pp. 247–48.

like strains from some great symphony, whose full beauty is only recognized when the whole is heard.[67]

Ronald Knox placed the emphasis only slightly differently in his autobiographical work, which was composed when he was also deeply immersed in the Virgilian poem, quotations from which introduce each chapter. Aeneas' journey culminated in the eventual establishment of the new city of Rome, and likewise the convert's journey "involves not merely coming home, but coming home to a place you have never been in before—one that combines in itself all that you valued in the old home with added promises of a future that is new".[68]

Knox indeed found himself at home in the Roman Catholic communion in 1917, and in the forty years of life and writing remaining to him he was to become the most prominent spokesman in its behalf in England.

[67] Maturin, *Price of Unity*, pp. 282–83.
[68] Knox, *Spiritual Aeneid*, p. 1.

CHAPTER THREE

TRACTS FOR THE TWENTIES

Evelyn Waugh insisted on seeing in Knox's career many similarities to that of John Henry Cardinal Newman, but Knox himself seems to have regarded the life of Robert Hugh Benson as a more suitable template for his own. Yet whichever of these convert priests is chosen as a yardstick, one is at a loss to find a parallel in the writings of either of them with Knox's use of the light novel as a literary vehicle. The historical novel, to be sure, was Benson's staple, and Newman composed a few of them himself, but such works as *Loss and Gain* were written with an evident apologetic aim.[1] Of the three novels Knox wrote in the 1920s (not counting the detective fiction he would soon become an adept at writing), two of them appear at first glance to be pure fantasy, while the third is a conscious imitation of a nineteenth-century classic. The fantasies revolve around subjects of topical interest in that decade and no doubt were read simply as such by some devotees of the imaginative novel. But they are all in fact expressions of Knox's willingness to use any genre, however popular, to nudge even the casual novel reader to serious reflection.

[1] This was Newman's first book written and published after his conversion. It is a rather cerebral novel, most of it being composed of theological conversations between Charles Reding, an Oxford undergraduate, and various friends and tutors who become increasingly alarmed at his Romeward-moving thoughts. It is not, however, without humor, and Newman's portrayal of a latitudinarian preacher is no less piquant than Knox's or Mallock's: "He concluded with one word in favour of Nestorius, two for Abelard, three for Luther, 'that great mind,' as he worded it, 'who saw that churches, creeds, rites, persons, were nought in religion, and that inward spirit, *faith*,' as he himself expressed it, 'was all in all;' and with a hint that nothing would go well in the University till this great principle was so far admitted, as to lead its members—not, indeed, to give up their own distinctive formularies, no—but to consider the direct contradictories of them equally pleasing to the divine Author of Christianity." J. H. Newman, *Loss and Gain: The Story of a Convert* (London: James Burns, 1848), pp. 63–64.

MEMORIES OF THE FUTURE

Memories of the Future was published in 1923 in the middle of Knox's years on the faculty of Saint Edmund's.[2] It was his first effort at full-length fiction and could be considered "science fiction" since it purports to describe events taking place during the fifty years beyond the date of authorship. However, the science is so indifferently alluded to, and the whole composition so decidedly tongue-in-cheek, that it might instead be viewed simply as a riposte to the popular nonfictional works of H. G. Wells, which charted the benign influence of an ascendant science on the future course of history. It bears some resemblance to Edward Bellamy's *Looking Backward*, the very earnest and very popular American novel published in the year of Knox's birth, which tells the story of a proper Bostonian who is awakened from slumber in September 2000 to a world that has solved all social problems and now guarantees the fulfillment of all noble human desires.[3] *Memories of the Future* suggests, to the contrary, that the future will be all too recognizable in its continuity with the past.

The temptation on reading any futuristic novel from an earlier generation is of course to compare the author's fancies with what has in the meantime come to fruition. Some instances of Knox's relative prescience will be duly recorded in the following pages, but it was certainly not his intent to establish himself as a seer, even if he did intend his extrapolations of certain uncongenial trends of the 1920s into the future to serve as warnings to contemporary readers to be more respectful of traditional patterns of life. *Memories* is also reminiscent (though

[2] The full title of the novel is *Memories of the Future: Being Memoirs of the Years 1915–1972 Written in the Year of Grace 1988 by Opal, Lady Porstock* (London: Methuen, 1923).

[3] Edward Bellamy (1850–1898) was trained as a lawyer and worked as a newspaperman, writing editorials and book reviews for newspapers in Springfield, Massachusetts. *Looking Backward* was his most successful novel by far, but he was also instrumental in establishing the People's Party, which received over one million votes in the 1892 U.S. presidential election. A well-read student of utopian and socialist literature, he was an implacable foe of the inequalities wrought by industrial plutocracy and wrote his famous futurist novel to describe a humanitarian, vaguely Christian, state-controlled alternative to unrestrained capitalism. In England, the novel sold over one hundred thousand copies by March 1890, strongly influenced the early Fabians, including George Bernard Shaw, and even influenced urban planners. For Bellamy's impact on England, see Peter Marshall, "A British Sensation", in *Edward Bellamy Abroad: An American Prophet's Influence* (New York: Twayne Publishers, 1962), pp. 86–118.

not in its conclusions) of *Erewhon*, Samuel Butler's satire from the 1870s, which is relatively discreet on the externals of a newfound people's civilization but considerably more voluble on their philosophy of life.

Opal, Lady Porstock, actually commits her memories to print in the year 1988 (coincidentally one hundred years after Knox's birth) when at the mature age of seventy-three she is able to survey the social, cultural, religious, and political events of the years from her birth to a second world war, which Knox places in the year 1972. Like the war during which she was born, this second conflagration proves just as inconsequential for the betterment of human nature, and so her memoirs end with its inception.

Robert Speaight has suggested that the doings of the heroine would make sense only to those familiar with the habits of the British aristocracy, but the passage through life of Opal Winterhead, to use her maiden name, is generic enough in its encounters with types of mankind to bridge any social gap between memoirist and reader. Opal is the only child of an industrialist and a socialite mother. While her father was content to play golf and "direct his financial schemes from a distance", her mother followed a diurnal schedule no more pressing: "The hundred little domestic duties of the day—in those days, the mistress of the house would order the dinner, go through the books, supervise the work of the servants, and altogether behave as a sort of unpaid agent—would occupy her till eleven or half-past eleven in the morning: only then would she put her season ticket in her reticule and set out for the mystery of the shops and the repose of her club." [4]

[4] Knox, *Memories*, p. 25. Perhaps Mrs. Winterhead's workload was inspired by that of some of the women who ran the social life of the Souls. One of Mary Elcho's daughters recalls her demanding schedule as follows: "Whilst Mamma organised the transport [of guests], sleeping and eating arrangements for those visitors already within her gates, a large fraction of her mind would be simultaneously engaged in planning ahead exactly how next week's party should be occupied during every hour of their stay: 'But Cynthia, if you and your friends go to the dance Saturday evening, who will make a fourth at Bridge with Papa and the This and That's?' ... Then, there's Sunday evening when I've promised to hear Professor L. read his lecture, and the D's want to listen too, but poor Mrs. B. is much too deaf for either reading aloud or for charades. Who is to talk to her? I *believe* she plays Bezique. Can you think of anyone in the neighborhood who plays Bezique?" Quoted in Angela Lambert, *Unquiet Souls* (New York: Harper and Row, 1984), p. 133.

Opal grows up at a time "when no privilege of the governing classes was more tenaciously preserved than their exemption from education", but as the British government had begun giving a subsidy to every child who attended school, she shuffles off to a girls' school at fifteen. The youngest children in the school of the 1930s are about ten or eleven years of age; Knox rather wildly misjudged future social and governmental pressures on that score. In any case, she proceeds on to Oxford, blissfully devoid of any store of knowledge. Fortunately, she is able to circumvent the rigors of the university's classical curriculum by substituting for it a heterogeneous mixture of subjects, thanks to Oxford's succumbing to the American bachelor of arts elective system. She settles on a dual major in geography and Byzantine architecture, following the lectures of a scholar who inspired her by declaiming on "The Whence as an Aspect of the Whither" and then proposing marriage to her. After her stern aunt interviews the prospective groom, their "engagement was broken off, but I promised that I would always be a sister to him, and when he married his typist a few months later, suggested that I would be a sister-in-law to his wife."

Of greater import for Opal is her meeting with Canon Amphibolus Dives, who becomes her mentor, advising her to take holy orders when her employment outlook appeared predictably bleak on completing her degree. Forecasting the ordination of women in the Church of England is perhaps prescient for 1922, though Knox allows for its gradual introduction: Opal has the option of becoming a deaconess in 1938, but it would only be around 1958 that full priestly rank would be made available to her and other women. She feels somewhat abashed about following his advice, so she travels abroad instead. But after her father's early demise, she inherits his estate and makes the acquaintance of the Reverends Didymus and Agapé Rowlands, the local clergy couple, the former a vicar and the latter a curate. The husband is a social progressive: "Another fixed principle of his was that all these movements of our time would work themselves out right in the long run: whatever was best, he used to say, would remain, while everything else would disappear. The only occasion on which this conviction is known to have deserted him was one night when his house was broken into by burglars." His wife is militant in her feminism and in her opposition to all the remnants of tradition still encumbering theology and liturgy. Anything modern or American catches her fancy, and she scans the dailies for evidence to debunk an old axiom. Opal, even though indifferent to religion, chafes under her preaching. When Mrs. Rowlands informs her "that it was now proved, from a skull discovered near Letchworth, that man had existed three hundred million years before Adam; it was no good my suggesting that Eve's appearance must in that case have been welcomed with relief; she would be off on a fresh tangent before I had finished my sentence." [5]

Years later, when one of Opal's sons fell ill, his older brother sought the clergywoman's advice, asking "'[i]f it would be right to pray that his brother might get well.' Mrs. Rowlands, who had her views on this as on most other points, said perhaps it would be safer to pray to God that His will might be done. The first time he met her again after Gervase's recovery he said to her very seriously, 'Now, Mrs. Rowlands, ought I to thank God for doing His will?' For once, Mrs. Rowlands had to admit defeat." [6]

Business takes Opal to America, a country Knox never visited, so her recollections of her transcontinental travels are suitably misty. But the trip gives Knox the opportunity to indulge in some more guesswork. He imagines Britain paying off its war debt by selling peerages by lottery (at one thousand pounds or more per ticket) to interested American citizens. Hence among the more prominent Americans Opal meets are Lord and Lady Massachusetts and Lord Poughkeepsie.[7] And

[5] Knox, *Memories*, pp. 86–87.

[6] Ibid., p. 158. These circumlocutions recall a conversation between Samuel Butler's characters Rev. Theobald Pontifex and his fiancée Christina Allaby, who yearns for martyrdom either as a missionary or fighting Romanism: "'We, dearest Theobald,' she exclaimed, 'will be ever faithful. We will stand firm and support one another even in the hour of death itself. God in His mercy may spare us from being burnt alive. He may or may not do so. Oh Lord' (and she turned her eyes prayerfully to Heaven), 'spare my Theobald, or grant that he may be beheaded.'

"'My dearest,' said Theobald gravely, 'do not let us agitate ourselves unduly. If the hour of trial comes we shall be best prepared to meet it by having led a quiet unobtrusive life of self-denial and devotion to God's glory. Such a life let us pray God that it may please Him to enable us to pray that we may lead.'" Samuel Butler, *The Way of All Flesh* (London: Collins, 1903; reprint, London: Collins, 1953), p. 68.

[7] The notion was not far-fetched in the early 1920s. As a prominent critic of British culture has noted: "By the time Lloyd George was a triumphant warlord and prime minister, there was a recognized tariff: £10,000 for a knighthood, £30,000 for a baronetcy, and £50,000 upwards for a peerage. As Lloyd George's election funds dwindled in 1921–2 creations reached higher and higher levels, with 26 peerages, 74 baronetcies and

an enterprising young man from Connecticut who bought eighty-six tickets on one title lands the distinction of being proclaimed Lord Porstock. He then woos Opal Winterhead, conveying her about in his "helico". Of course, when Knox wrote, helicopters were yet to be perfected (Sikorsky produced a workable one in 1937); airplanes were in use, but not commercially; and dirigibles were the luxury liners of the air. To suppose that helicopters would, in the 1940s, be the favored mode of transportation for short trips is an interesting conjecture. He also fancies that trains would continue to carry most land traffic, betraying that fondness for the railways he often displayed.

The ensuing nuptials with Lord Porstock offer an occasion for the Reverend Mrs. Rowlands to suggest a ceremony utilizing the Book of Modern Prayer, in which the bride promises fidelity "till death, permanent insanity, cruelty, infidelity, or incompatibility of temperament us did part." Canon Dives' contribution to the event is a hortatory letter extolling the deeper meaning modern society has accorded matrimony:

> Marriage, besides being a Sacrament, is a contract. A contract holds good so long, and only so long, as the essential facts of the situation, in consideration of which the contracting parties bound themselves, remain unaltered. Thus, if I am under contract to water a particular plant, my obligation ceases if the plant dies, or (to put the case more strongly) if a friend of mine hands me an egg, and promised to put it under a hen and give it, when hatched, the freedom of my fowl-run, my contract automatically ceases if the egg proves to be that of a crocodile. Now, the marriage contract is made between two persons each of whom is to the other, and therefore philosophically speaking *is*, the most beautiful creature in the world. They are married, a shadow grows up between them, there are scenes, difficulties—suddenly they wake up to find that they are no longer in love with one another.[8]

Since change has taken place, the man and woman are different from the original consenting parties, and therefore the contract is automatically voided, a formal divorce only recognizing that fact. The epistle

214 knighthoods." A. N. Wilson, *After the Victorians: The Decline of Britain in the World* (New York: Farrar, Straus and Giroux, 2005), p. 119.

[8] Knox, *Memories*, p. 121.

closes with his wishes for a blessed marriage, and the hope that all will discern meaning in the disturbing signs of the times.

Despite this encouraging advice, the marriage does take place, and Opal soon relinquishes control of her nebulous company and becomes immersed in London society. The vicissitudes of fashion in art, couture, and literature are chronicled in more detail than a reader might wish to digest in a work of fantasy (though it should be noted that Edward Bellamy did the same—and added a layer of economics lectures for good measure). But the intended effect is no doubt to underline the sentiments of the old great-aunt who, on her death, left Opal a letter that encapsulated her philosophy of life. Though no more imbued with Christianity than most other modern Britons, she retained enough common sense to be able to pinpoint the fatuity in mankind's worship of change and progress:

> I think it is the result of man being born immortal, and thinking (like an ass) that he has only this world to satisfy his immortal instinct with. Despairing of immortality in this world, and forgetting it in the next, he makes the human race the immortal unit, and so endows it with life. And, because he has been told that life means growth, he cannot be happy until he believes that the world in which he lives is growing, from something to something else. That is humanity's favorite dogma, and there is no atom of proof for it. Everything we know about history and natural history shows that there is a kind of progress in the world which is a progress from the less to the more complicated, from the less to the more organized: nothing suggests, except to our vanity, that there is a progress from the worse to the better—and what other kind of progress would any sensible person give a tinker's curse for?[9]

Opal was the beneficiary of that advice in early adulthood, when she was rather hoping for a more tangible bequest. Consequently, it fails to inform her outlook on life until she too has aged. In the meantime, political office looms as an outlet for her desire to be engaged in the world. She enters the lists of the Democratic Party in 1953 after paying a hefty fee to gain that right. Whether it is a successor to Labour or Liberal is unclear and indeed immaterial, since all the parties evolve

[9] Ibid., pp. 70–71.

into indistinguishable clubs. The prediction, perhaps slightly extravagant to Knox, that £7,500 would have to be donated to a political party to procure the right to stand for election, would of course pale beside the cash-driven electioneering of the modern world. By Opal's time, progressive thought has forced the enactment of legislation reforming the political process by disallowing any pledges by candidates to support particular measures as part of their appeal for votes. The old system whereby a candidate was held to account for preelection promises had too often straitjacketed public servants, and in the words of a great statesman had "hampered the operation of salutary afterthoughts, and left the Government free indeed to interpret, but not free to direct, the will of a civilized nation".

The major legislative action the government enacts during Opal's six years in Parliament is a reform placing coinage on the decimal system (which of course did take place about twenty years after Knox places it) but going further to decimalize distances as well. Had Knox been a less insular Briton, he might have foreseen the metric system's overthrow of traditional weights and measures. However, Opal decides to champion the duodecimal system, which one of her Oxford dons had convinced her was more useful. But since it requires the invention of two new digits (the new 10 equaling the old 12) and it upsets some familiar numbers ("the Battle of Waterloo had been fought in A.D. 1513"), her cause languishes without the support of the party leadership. The chancellor of the exchequer, who fears having to return to school to relearn the multiplication tables, charges her with the unpardonable sin of undermining the party system by adopting an independent line. And the leader of the party in the House of Lords is induced to send her a stern telegram without being in the slightest aware of what the disagreement is about:

> Deeply appreciate sincerity of motives which have contributed difficult situation. Impossible expect agreement great fundamental principles ensure seeing eye to eye matters of detailed application. But higher considerations than those mere party surely bid sink private differences co-operate generously in great cause. Implore you take no steps likely to jeopardize harmony Ministerial camp during crisis fraught grave national peril. No one more ready than Prime Minister or self to give full weight any criticisms administration when business Empire permits return. Know can depend strong personal

> loyalty already evinced hundred unforgettable instances during past years. Spirit of Gladstone not dead yet.[10]

Lady Porstock is gratified by the attention accorded her by the party leaders but is not deterred from promoting her plan. The decimal vs. duodecimal controversy is then remanded to committee, where the relative merits of the two systems occupy the members' attention for another twenty (or eighteen, by duodecimalists' reckoning) years.

Purely secular affairs continue to consume her time for another decade or so, but after the untimely death of Lord Porstock in a helicopter accident in 1963, she withdraws from public life to spend more time with her sons. Later in the decade, sensing the advance of years and the unsatisfactory nature of her interests, she takes another look at the consolations of religion. It is her ill fortune, however, to turn again to Canon (now Bishop) Dives, who writes to her in response to a letter seeking spiritual counsel: "From century to century, it seems to me we learn to get on with less and less of belief in supernatural things to encourage or to justify us, and I see no limit to that development. I go further, and say that I do not wish to see any limit to that development. The less we believe, clearly, the more creditable it is in us to call ourselves Christians still."[11]

Somehow this non-credo fails to satisfy Lady Porstock's desire for a firm anchor. The merry-go-round bores with its monotony, and the whiff of intoxicating instability Bishop Dives offers is apt only to engender spiritual vertigo in her. Meanwhile, the unobtrusive and uncolorful Cardinal Smith has been an occasional visitor at the Porstock mansion, never proselytizing but just biding his time as Lady Porstock continues her search. Just as undramatically, she enters the Catholic Church. No apologia accompanies her recital of the events leading up to her conversion, just a brief indication of the peace she senses in attending Mass at the Oratory.

And that is pretty much the whole story, except for the briefest of recollections of the war of 1972 to 1975, in which Britain, France, the United States, and Brazil fight an unspecified foe and achieve victory. She quotes the patriotic bombast on the conclusion of hostilities: "We have fought for honour, for civilization, for high aims and pure

[10] Ibid., p. 168.
[11] Ibid., p. 220.

enthusiasms: we have met the powers of evil, and forced upon them the conditions of a not dishonourable peace. And the power generated by these years of relentless friction of humanity, will if we but canalize it aright, galvanize through centuries to come the failing dynamos of humanity."[12]

But it impresses her no more. She concludes (in 1988) by wondering whether the memoirist of 2050 would be guilty of the same unconscious bias that she herself has shown, i.e., of idealizing the virtues of bygone days while viewing past cultural efflorescences as merely quaint. She has gone through enough of the mutable fashions of mankind over her seventy-three years to regard the slightly pejorative term "old-fashioned" with some skepticism, and she has also learned that human nature itself does not progress, despite each generation's declarations to the contrary. People always face the choice of clinging to the ephemeral or of accepting the supernatural heritage that gives life its meaning.

Thus the memoirs. Lady Porstock begs her readers' indulgence "for an old woman's gossip", which she hopes "will be lightly judged". The modern critic will abide by that request. Futuristic novels date rapidly, becoming anachronistic to readers whose vantage point lies beyond the temporal reaches of the author's imagination. Psychoanalysis, for instance, an up-and-coming preoccupation of the 1920s, assumes a disproportionately larger role in Lady Porstock's milieu than it has actually held in recent decades. And the tidbits of poetry and philosophy she passes on from the literary giants of those years, while no more fatuous than the actual oracles to which the media have often turned, are cumulatively palling. Yet Robert Speaight somewhat misses the point when he says, apropos of this novel: "Ronald Knox was still a comparatively young man when he looked into the future, and there was nothing in the prospect that pleased him. He realised already that he was out of tune with the modern world."[13] Whatever his quirks, Knox was not of a misanthropic cast, sulking in his sitting room because the nineteenth century had given way to the twentieth. What he was trying to bring to the cognizance of his readers, however good-naturedly, was that being in tune with the modern world is a trap, whatever age one has been placed in. Past, present, and future will

[12] Ibid., p. 238.

[13] Robert Speaight, *Ronald Knox the Writer* (New York: Sheed and Ward, 1965), p. 151.

always contain byways and blind alleys down which all too many people are content to wander. The straight path that leads to communion with God necessitates letting go of these transitory enthusiasms, however alluring they may be. *Memories* is a record of how one person might come to that epiphany. In any case, the book was not reprinted after 1923. It is a little too diffuse, and the central character too skittish a memoirist. A light piece, it has receded, along with much of Opal Porstock's fund of reminiscences, into the hazy past.

SANCTIONS

If *Memories* occasionally taxes a reader's patience with its flights of fancy, the same cannot be said of Knox's second novel, *Sanctions*.[14] Written in 1924, when he was beginning to enjoy the hospitality of Lord and Lady Lovat during summer holidays at Beaufort Castle in Scotland, it takes place entirely on the grounds of a fictitious castle that, whether or not it be a composite, must owe much of its captivating scenery to his hosts' estate.

Kingussie Castle is owned by a Catholic couple, but they let out rooms each summer to exiles from city life. Lord and Lady Denham, he a successful barrister and she a diligent cultivator of amusing party conversationalists, eagerly plan their summer according to their separate lights. Lord Denham, to whom the intricacies of the legal code present sufficient grist upon which to exercise his intellectual faculties, can readily justify a little mental atrophication during his leisure hours, so he fishes for salmon all summer. Lady Denham, however, foreseeing a gloomy passage of weeks spent listening to her husband recount the details of his daily catches, decides to invite a number of acquaintances to spend a week batting back and forth the conversational shuttlecock as they take in the other amenities of the locale.

About a dozen or so take her up on the invitation, conveniently representing a wide enough spectrum of philosophical stances to ensure that a vigorous debate, once engendered, will not peter out by week's end. Some are married couples, but even husband and wife never mirror each other's views. There are two clerics, both Anglican, but

[14] Ronald Knox, *Sanctions: A Frivolity* (London: Sheed and Ward, 1934; reprint, London: Sheed and Ward, 1932).

one is a suave Modernist while the other is an optimistic but unquestioning supporter of the Established Church. The rest are bachelors, except for a Hungarian emigré philosopher, who is divorced. Most of the guests are unknown to each other, so a jovial but somewhat bovine friend of the family, Mrs. Juliet Chulmleigh, is invited for her finely cultivated talent at jump-starting serious discourse between the just acquainted.

But it is not just Mrs. Chulmleigh's social graces that catalyze philosophical discourse. The allure of their surroundings gently nudges the guests to reflect on the wonders of life and the position of mankind within the universe. On the first full day at the castle, all are invited to bask in the beauties of the vast cultivated grounds. Knox describes the horseshoe-shaped garden bordered by a stone wall:

> From the door, one long sweep of grass stretches up to a giant box hedge.... [O]n either side of you a riotous border feasts the eye with clusters of alternating colour.... [W]ave upon wave, poppies and dahlias and gladioli and stocks and bergamot challenge you to halt. Aeroplane high, the effect of it would still greet you as that of a dazzling mosaic.... When you reach the end of the flower avenue, you find that after all it is only a turning point you have reached: a left-about turn discloses a fresh giant border, till now hedged from view, that runs parallel to the whole length of the other and then breaks away, L-shaped, into the far distance. This great L is a fresh grass strip, besieged with flower-armies as before: but down the middle of it a little mountain burn, caught and domesticated and put into Sunday clothes as it enters the garden, ripples decorously between its trim banks. All this is only to describe the two main arteries of the garden: you would still have to be told about the sweet-peas and the lavender, and the delicate hot-house blooms that tap their fingers against the nursery windows to their sturdier brothers outside.[15]

Later in the week, the action (if so it can be called) takes place at a picnic held

> on a little plateau, from which the riverbank fell suddenly in a deep ravine; Heather and bracken fringed its precipitous boulders, a few shrubs hung over, and seemed to shrink away startled from the abyss. Below, if you craned your neck to see it, the river swirled dark over

[15] Ibid., pp. 42–43.

> smooth ledges of rock that now made channels for it, now broke it into little waterfalls, and caught it again in fathomless pools. The sun, even so early in the afternoon, could not climb far enough down the hill-side to give any play of light to those depths; they lay abruptly exiled from the shimmering, insect-humming world.[16]

These extracts are cited not simply to summon into view the bucolic background against which the colloquies take place. They, along with similar passages dispersed throughout his detective fiction, show that, controversialist and logician and apologist as he was, Ronald Knox was firmly rooted in the created world. He had a very attentive eye for nature, and he celebrated the beauty of his physical environment in prose indicative of someone whose senses reveled in its offered gifts. He was in fact very much like his frequent fellow guest at Beaufort Castle, Maurice Baring, a poet before whose eyes no scene was a matter of indifference. The very sensuality of the surroundings also serves to keep the fictional conversationalists from straying too far from reality, however much they may enjoy exploring intellectual byways.

But at the same time, the enforced idleness of a vacation in a remote paradise somewhat levels the outward differences among the guests. With a daily diet of desultory tennis, billiards, walks, and short drives, no individual stands out from the rest for anything he accomplishes. The contrast in their outlooks on life is to be revealed solely through their words. The old adage about discerning the virtuous is consequently reversed: watch what they say, not what they do.

Canon Oxenhope, the Modernist clergyman, is not quite the travesty of liberal theologians that Canon Dives was. He fancies himself the defender of human initiative in the Church, a kindred soul to the mystical school of thinkers—Saint Catherine, Thomas à Kempis, and Johannes Tauler, who represented a reaction against a medievalist impulse to subsume the individual under "the claims of the Moloch-church". He preaches to a more rarefied sort of audience, finding uncongenial the common type of congregation that reeks a bit too much of superstition and crass self-interest. Yet he is also suspicious of a too great reliance on rationality as a road to God. "What the soul craves is illumination," he observes during a discussion on the nature of religious belief, "not by any barren formulas of reasoning,

[16] Ibid., p. 140.

but by a kind of direct access to the Source of all light." He cannot conceal his disdain for Catholicism, which is crawling with corruption and superstition. Its defenders align themselves "with the horrors of medieval monasticism and medieval Church diplomacy, with the tortures of the Inquisition, and the massacre of Saint Bartholomew". In spite of his harboring such a visceral dislike of the beliefs of his fellow guests, he comports himself impeccably, the very model of a Modernist vicar general.

John Lydiard is a widely read literary man—he reviews books for the press—whose private and professional sampling of the world's literature, combined with his de rigueur undergraduate taste for antinomianism, have left him a fragile agnostic, yearning for a secure foundation from which to view the world. Brought up to believe that God couldn't be proven to exist but was nevertheless a presence "just hiding so as to catch me out doing something wrong", he had naturally discarded the juvenile notion of the Schoolmaster Deity, leaving a void in its place. The appetite for logical thought fortunately has not deserted him, and he pursues with the greatest animation the search for truth during the vacation discussions. Frequently, the thread of conversation left dangling when the drawing room fire dies out late at night is carried over into the next day solely because Lydiard refuses to deny any discussion its ultimate resolution.

Gerald Chase is a rather self-assured Catholic layman whose choice in an evening parlor game of Thomas Aquinas as a historical figure whose identity must be guessed by the other players is entirely apt. (When Canon Oxenhope somewhat disapprovingly gives the correct solution, Lady Denham asks, "Sir Thomas Who?" appropriately reflecting the amnesia of the Protestantized English people respecting things medieval.) Chase is a thorn in the canon's side, forever trying to sap his illuminationist stronghold. He is the first person to introduce the word *sanction* when the conversation turns around the question of what we can know about right and wrong in moral actions, and true and false in religious beliefs. When the education of a boy is at issue, he asks, "How can I inflict my principles upon his mind, unless I have behind my principles some sanction, some authority which tells me they are right?" [17]

[17] Ibid., p. 61.

Sanction is a word that the puzzle solver in Knox delighted in employing: it has two almost opposed definitions, sometimes meaning "a penalty" but more often meaning "an authoritative approval for a given course of action". It is the second sense that is intended by the protagonists of the supernatural in this story. And credit for emphasizing its critical importance in a debate on ultimate truths belongs to Count André Kaloczy, the perspicacious Hungarian emigré. As a realist, he cuts through the shibboleths about a progressively more virtuous mankind. The late-nineteenth-century doctrinaire liberals, he avers, wanted to appear virtuous so that they could convince others that jettisoning religion would bring no harm in its wake. That generation of parents "used to read little green books about Evolution and Progress, which told them to be good because the human race was developing into something more splendid than before. But those little green books are put away now on the shelf with the family Bible, and the parents say only to the children, Be like us. And the school-teachers say to the children, Be like us. And they go away presently to the Pictures."[18]

When a bright young M.P. named Riseley and an atheist mathematician named Escrick argue that progress is palpable in the greater possibilities available for doing good today through medicine and other technological wonders, the count responds that "we are not better, but we are good in more complicated ways: our apparatus for virtue has developed. The good Samaritan does not pour oil and wine in the wounds, but only iodine; and he puts the wounded man in a motor-ambulance, and takes him to a hospital. It is better that all that should be so, but it is not a better Samaritan—it is the same kind of Samaritan."[19] Chase, who is of course in agreement with the older Kaloczy, though more upbeat than the lapsed Catholic philosopher, chimes in with an observation that could have been passed on to Opal Porstock by her great aunt:

> But the trouble about people like you, Escrick, is that you will insist on regarding it as a sort of inevitable scientific law that the world gets better and better. There is no such law; why on earth should there be? And, believing in this iron law of progress, you turn the process around (most illogically) and argue that simply

[18] Ibid., p. 107.
[19] Ibid., p. 115.

> because things are modern, simply because a certain phase of thought has developed out of an earlier phase of thought, we are all bound to sit by and applaud such developments.[20]

The foregoing comments are made in midweek. The next morning a sort of interlude occurs. The castle, as was noted earlier, was owned by Catholics, and every Thursday morning a priest arrives to say morning Mass in the chapel for those of the household who are of his faith. Afterward he joins the guests at breakfast. Under curious questioning from various quarters, Father Grant comes across as a man of no particular ambition but rather as a pastor placed in this out-of-the-way spot to minister to the young and old in his care. As with Opal's Cardinal Smith, it is in the ordinariness of the priest, a vessel in whom sacramental powers are present, rather than a great personage rising through the ministry by dint of personal attributes, that Knox sees authenticity. "Doesn't he ever think about the future of the race?" asks one of the party after the priest leaves on a sick visit. The same individual, a down-in-his-luck author, persists: "I should have thought a man like that would want to put his shoulder to the wheel more."

Again Kaloczy leads the discussion back to the realm of the concrete. Mr. Sanquhar, the author, has waxed from the particular (the priest's provincialism) to the universal by proclaiming that "surely the dignity of man lies, not in the history of the individual man, with his loves and hates, his prospects, his gout, his yearly visit to the seaside. It lies, rather, in the collective trend of human history, in the perfecting of our type, in the elevating of our human nature from its low, almost beastly origins, to the measure of its full perfection, which we look forward to one day."[21] This trust in conglomerate mankind is variously voiced through Oxenhope, Escrick, Sanquhar, and other characters. But Kaloczy will have none of it. Who, he asks rhetorically, has ever experienced this collective mind? "[Y]ou cannot collect all men's Minds together, and say these together form a single connected whole. There will always be one Mind missing from the collection. And which is that? Why, it is the Mind of you, who are thinking of that collection; you, whose experience alone unites all the rest of existence." Chase is at hand again to

[20] Ibid., p. 119.
[21] Ibid., p. 131.

drive home the staggering importance of the mundane, of those apparently routine and certainly unnewsworthy activities that constitute the unprepossessing priest's sphere of activity: "Every time Father Grant goes into the Confessional, each time the door of it clicks, Father Grant is confronted with a human soul, and that soul is half of existence—humanly speaking, of course."[22]

The arguments begin to exert a cumulative effect on Lydiard, the skeptic who has the initiative to question his skepticism. His ardor for answers is hardly extinguished by Mrs. Chulmleigh's admonition that if you wonder too deeply, life will be drained of zest, that object being the summum bonum to which she apparently aspires.

There is, however, one other perspective to be accounted for before all of Lydiard's doubts are to be dispelled. Doctor Donovan, a psychoanalyst, frequently intersperses an alternative explanation for many of the evidences put forward for any given outlook. For instance, when Canon Oxenhope outlines his theory of illumination by the divine, Donovan suggests that "the exact relation of the religious emotion to sex-consciousness" needs more investigation and draws out the parallel between mysticism and compensation for the absence of sexual gratification. He further puts a damper on free will, holding instead that all actions are conditioned and therefore unfree. Lydiard finds the latter argument unconvincing: "However little or however much this or that action is determined by the influence of your previous habits, there's always a tiny contribution made by the will, which will make it a tiny bit easier or a tiny bit more difficult to repeat the action next time the chance comes along."[23]

But the psychoanalyst can always checkmate a subjective proposition, one that relies on the all-too-frail prop of emotion. The second Anglican cleric in attendance at these discussions, the timid Canon Barton, offers man's yearnings for God as proof that he must be present and must indeed have planted those yearnings, which could not exist unless an object capable of satisfying them existed. Doctor Donovan asks: "How are we to assure ourselves that some urge in our nature, probably an erotic one, has not found a false direction here, and conjured up its own object in doing so? Believe me, that would not be

[22] Ibid., p. 133.
[23] Ibid., pp. 77–78.

stranger than many of the inversions our modern psychologists have come across." [24]

These counterarguments hasten Lydiard to Chase's room late on Thursday night to ascertain why the Catholic can remain so unruffled by the ebb and flow going on around him. Having been indoctrinated himself into believing that Catholics hold to their faith only by blind obedience to the dictates of Roman authority, Lydiard is pleasantly surprised to hear of the appeal to reason as an undergirding of faith.

But there is still more ground to be covered. Friday's lakeside discussion revolves around the type of moral character religion ought to produce. When Chase challenges Canon Oxenhope to come down on the side of either Christian or heathen ethics, the latter opts for the Christian but allows himself some wriggling room. "Your friends, Mr. Chase, would probably insist more on obedience as a quality than I should; and perhaps I should be disposed to insist more on openness of dealing." But the canon is not allowed to maneuver:

> "And which would be right?" asked Chase.
>
> "Oh, admirable!" cried Lydiard, getting up in his excitement and balancing himself on a rock, trembling with excitement. "Yes, hang it all, which is right? The heathen character, or the Buddhist character, or the Mahommedan character, or which of the three hundred odd types of Christian character? Sanctions! I thank thee, Chase, for teaching me that word." [25]

The canon attempts to deflect the thrust by implying that Chase would leave the heathens incapable of choosing a higher ethical code simply because they have not had the advantage of access to a supernatural revelation. But that is not at all Chase's point. A sermon on the Epiphany published by Knox around the same time as this novel can afford to get to the point more succinctly than can the congeries of houseguests:

> Right and wrong, sin and virtue, decency, modesty—do such names as these retain the old meaning and the old recognition? We still use them, and we still mean them, but somehow we're not quite sure what we mean *by* them. We have an uneasy feeling that we aren't quite sure

[24] Ibid., p. 171.
[25] Ibid., p. 200.

> whether there is money at the bank to back these symbols. . . . And it is because they find the ground thus treacherous under their feet that thoughtful people—for there are still people who think—are beginning to ask themselves where any fixed, permanent authority, and sure seal of values with a more than human sanction behind it, is to be found; they are beginning to wonder whether the answer to that question is not "only in the Catholic Church."[26]

But back to the protagonists of the novel: what Chase and Kaloczy are affirming is that there is an ultimate Arbiter of right and wrong who has implanted a law in the minds of each and every human person, heathen or civilized, and that this law is enforced by sanctions extrinsic to the person. These are the sanctions to which they are repeatedly calling attention as signals that men are not their own lawgivers. The relativist and the Modernist and the agnostic all shrink from this bald truth that must force on anyone who accepts it the fateful recognition that there is an ultimate Lawgiver who is, of course, God. Yet that conclusion is not paraded forward by Kaloczy, who is content merely to prove the unchanging nature of the sanctions governing man's activity.

In fact, it transpires that the count is writing a book on the subject. Lady Denham, who senses (without, however, in any way comprehending) the gravity of the week's intellectual passage through philosophy, goes so far as to suggest that he cast his book "in the form of a dialogue, and have all the problems in it discussed by a party of friends sitting around the fire—ourselves, for instance?" But Kaloczy rejects the format, indicating that such a book would appeal neither to readers of philosophy nor readers of fiction. Knox himself obviously did not share the count's reluctance to entrust philosophical investigations to a gathering of houseguests.

The arrival of the weekend offers a convenient premise for curtailing any further discussions, and all of them scurry to a train or a car to return to their own homes. But the succeeding days bring to Lady Denham by post a number of letters thanking her for providing an ambiance conducive to their holding forth so unreservedly. Acknowledging the limited power of purely intellectual arguments to dislodge

[26] Ronald Knox, "Epiphany", in *University and Anglican Sermons of Ronald A. Knox*, ed. Philip Caraman, S.J. (New York: Sheed and Ward, 1963), p. 308.

someone from well-worn ruts, Knox lets the reader know that not much has changed as a result of the colloquies. Canon Oxenhope, writing from the deanery at Barchester, is still a bit annoyed that he was ambushed so often by "the immature speculations of young men". It is a consolation for him to be attending as he writes a conference of like-minded theologians who are currently subjecting Saint Paul to some revisionist exegesis. The mathematician Escrick compliments Lady Denham for giving him an opportunity for doing nothing and enjoying it. Canon Barton expresses enthusiasm for the vitality of the young people and declares his optimism that the new generation he met during the week will solve the world's problems. Only Lydiard is sufficiently affected by what he has been through to want to pursue some loose ends. Not that there is anything overt in his letter alluding to that need. But he includes a sealed letter, which he asks her to pass along to Father Grant, whose address he does not have.

HOMAGE TO MALLOCK

Around the time Knox was composing this work, William Henry Mallock died. Mallock was very highly regarded in his time as a satirist and social critic, chiefly for a highly popular novel on which *Sanctions* is very consciously modeled. Indeed, when an annotated edition of *The New Republic* was brought out in 1950, the editor thanked Knox for having "spared time from his own more important research and translations to write a series of very helpful letters", the better to understand the book and its author.[27] Mallock was a well-bred Oxford graduate of Knox's father's generation, a nephew to Hurrell Froude, the Tractarian friend of Newman, and his two equally illustrious brothers, the historian James Froude and the scientist William Froude. Young Mallock found his Anglican faith shattered by the materialist and liberal philosophies he encountered at the university, philosophies then dominating Victorian thought. He wrote many works decrying

[27] A critical edition of *The New Republic* (Gainesville: University of Florida Press, 1950), edited and with notes and an introduction by J. Max Patrick, remains the most important scholarly study of Mallock's thought. The quote is taken from p. viii of that edition.

socialism, positivism, and atheism, but by far the most successful and penetrating portrayal of the shallowness of the underminers of Christian orthodoxy was *The New Republic*, first published in 1877.

In this novel, a young man assembles a group of friends for a weekend of intellectual discourse at the beautiful seaside villa he has inherited from his late uncle. The cast of characters includes virtually undisguised fictional counterparts to many of the influential literary voices of his day. Easily recognizable among them are Matthew Arnold, the promoter of desacralized Christianity; Walter Pater, the aesthete; Benjamin Jowett of Balliol College, the liberal churchman; Thomas Huxley, the materialist evolutionist; John Ruskin, the art critic and social reformer; and sundry other thinkers whose only common bond would seem to be their discomfiture with orthodoxy. The only Catholic among the guests is a demure young woman, patterned after Mallock's cousin Issy (the daughter of William Froude) who later became the sister-in-law of Baron von Hügel, a pivotal figure in the turn-of-the-century Catholic Modernist crisis.[28]

Whereas Knox was content to parody types, Mallock gave his readers every opportunity to recognize who his figures were, because he was endowed with an extraordinary facility for mimicking people's writing styles, even the cadence of their orations. His most youthful work, in fact, was an anthology of parodies of many of the nineteenth-century poets. Knox too, of course, had already demonstrated that same talent in his early swipes at theological Modernism (*Reunion All Round* and *Absolute and Abitofhell*) and was to do so again in *Let Dons Delight*. His sympathy with Mallock, with whom he grouped Samuel Butler and Hilaire Belloc as the finest of satirists, is very deep.

[28] For a sympathetic portrait of von Hügel (1852–1925) see Michael de la Bedoyere, *The Life of Baron von Hügel* (London: J.M. Dent and Sons, 1951). He figures prominently in a number of studies of the Modernist movement, the best introduction to which is Marvin O'Connell, *Critics on Trial* (Washington, D.C.: Catholic University of America Press, 1994). An Anglican clergyman and historian who was an admirer of the movement (and coincidentally also a good friend of Knox's Anglican clerical brother Wilfred) remarks that von Hügel "was the chief engineer of the modernist movement. He made it his business to seek out potential modernists, to stimulate and encourage them in their intellectual pursuits, and to introduce them to one another's work, especially to writings and ideas that would enlarge their understanding of what would be involved in a renewal of Catholicism." Alec Vidler, *A Variety of Catholic Modernists* (London: Cambridge University Press, 1970), p. 113.

Interestingly, Mallock showed a strong affinity toward Catholicism, which he saw as the only possible source of truth, if he could have recovered his faith. He was a good friend of Maurice Baring, and at the time of his death, he had just concluded a visit with the Benedictines at Downside. While at his Catholic convert sister's home, he fell into a coma and was apparently given conditional baptism by a priest.

But it is of course to the young Mallock of *The New Republic* that *Sanctions* is beholden. Dr. Jenkinson, the lofty divine who is patterned after the sonorous master of Balliol, conducts a Sunday morning service in the theater of the villa (there being no chapel) for the rest of the company. At length he expounds on his conceptions of belief in Christ and the Church, which must accommodate the latest scientific trends. The strong Christian is one who, with great alacrity, discards dogmas that are not in harmony with the physicalist's faith:

> Witness the discussions now engaging so much public attention on the subject of animal automatism, and the marvellous results which experiments on living subjects have of late days revealed to us; a frog with half a brain having destroyed more theology than all the doctors of the Church with their whole brains can ever build up again. Thus does God choose the "weak things of this world to confound the wise." Seeing, then, that this is the state of the case, we should surely learn henceforth not to identify Christianity with anything that science can assail, or even question.[29]

The peroration continues, the following extract no doubt inspiring the ecumenist gone to seed parodied in *Reunion All Round*. As the world ponders

> all the various opinions once so fiercely agitated about religion, it recognizes in all of them a common element of good, and it sees that all theologians and all sects have really agreed with one another, and been meaning the same thing, even when they least suspected or wished it. Nor is it, as modern study is showing us, varieties of Christianity only that this deeper unity underlies, but all other religions also. It has been well observed by a great Roman Catholic writer now living, that whenever any great saintliness of life is to be observed amongst infidels and heretics, it is always found to be due

[29] W. H. Mallock, *The New Republic*, rev. ed. (London: Chatto and Windus, 1878), p. 111.

> to the presence of certain beliefs and rules which belong to the Catholics. And in like manner, we may say too, that whenever any great saintliness of life is to be observed amongst Catholics, it is due to the presence of certain beliefs and rules that belong to the infidels and the heretics—and indeed to all good men, no matter what their religion is.[30]

Canon Dives could not have said it better.

Most of the novel is given to leisured dialogue, amid picturesque natural surroundings, of how the ideal society ought to be constructed. Dilettantism is the order of the day. The participants are almost uniformly animated by stunted world views, since they have deliberately shielded their eyes from the vista opened up by belief in God and in immortality. Mr. Rose (Walter Pater) counts himself among the fortunate few who "have thrown their whole souls and sympathies into the happier art-ages of the past" and finds the height of beauty and wisdom in fabrics or vases or other pretty artifacts. Yet his rhapsodizing over artistic treasures does not preclude him from offering his host £30 for a volume of pornographic essays that is tucked away in the villa's library.[31]

Mr. Luke (Matthew Arnold) is broad enough in his appreciation of tradition to ally Christianity with culture. However, that alliance is possible only because "culture sets aside the larger part of the New Testament as grotesque, barbarous, and immoral; but what remains, purged of its apparent meaning, it discerns to be a treasure beyond all price".[32]

[30] Ibid., pp. 112–13.

[31] The jab was hardly gratuitous. Walter Pater (1839–1894) shed his Anglican faith while an Oxford undergraduate and, as a fellow and tutor of Brasenose College, became obsessed with the search for physical beauty while his realization of its transience and his morbid fascination with decay and death induced only despair. His literary efforts, heavily tinged with homosexuality, were influenced by Algernon Swinburne and were in turn an important influence on Oscar Wilde, whom he first met when the latter was an undergraduate. See Michael Levey, *The Case for Walter Pater* (New York: Thames and Hudson, 1978), on his career and writings.

[32] Matthew Arnold (1822–1888) was, like many another Victorian liberal, a man of admirable moral qualities who endured personal tragedy heroically and who was sympathetic to the culture of Catholicism far more than to the Puritan culture of the Dissenters. He maintained a curious adherence to the Church of England as a civilizing force in society while reinterpreting dogmatic statements with a nonchalance that antagonized even his most devoted intellectual disciples. See, for example, G. W. E. Russell, *Matthew Arnold*

One of the more vituperative characters is based on the materialist mathematician W. K. Clifford, a disciple of the leading lights of materialism, Spencer and Huxley. When various speakers propose that the new republic they are fashioning should tolerate all shades of religious opinion and should be buttressed by a common morality, he erupts in a most illiberal manner: "[A]nd do I not really doubt that the degrading practice of prayer, the fetish-worship of celibacy, of mortification and so forth—do I not doubt that the foul faith in a future life, the grotesque conceptions of the theological virtues, and that preposterous idol of the market-place, the sanctity of marriage—do you think I do not really doubt that we must retain these? Do you think, on the contrary, I do not know they are already doomed?" [33] Whether that be an unfair parody of a scientific materialist can be gauged by the following quote from the real Clifford on the influence of Christianity:

> The old system which sapped the foundations of patriotism in the old world; which well-nigh eradicated the sense of intellectual honesty, and seriously weakened the habit of truth-speaking; which lowered man's reverence for the marriage-bond by placing its sanctions in a realm outside of nature instead of in the common life of man, and by the institution of monasticism and a celibate clergy; which stunted the moral sense of nations by putting a priest between every man and his conscience; this system, if it should ever return to power, must be expected to produce worse evils than those which it has worked in the past.[34]

With proponents of views like these well represented in the garden party, it is not to be supposed that a resolution of the outlines of a benign new republic should be achieved. Instead what awaits the guests is a ferocious tongue-lashing from the weary Mr. Herbert (John Ruskin), who reproves them for their forgetfulness of the needs of the lower social classes, for their studious avoidance of discussion of death and

---

(London: Hodder and Stoughton, 1904), especially the chapter on Arnold's theology. Park Honan, in his definitive *Matthew Arnold: A Life* (New York: McGraw-Hill, 1981), notes that Arnold was a communicant at Ritualist Anglican churches despite his disbelief in the Creed. It is also interesting to recall that his brother Thomas became a Catholic and taught at University College, Dublin, and that one of Thomas' daughters married Thomas Huxley's son Leonard and eventually counted Julian and Aldous Huxley among her children.

[33] Mallock, *New Republic* (1878 ed.), p. 158.

[34] Quoted in a footnote to *New Republic* (1950 ed.), p. 158.

the afterlife, and for their denial of God. The sentiments attributed to Ruskin are actually those of Mallock himself, who was a friend of the older social critic. The two shared a sense of wandering and aimlessness, having been cut off from the wellsprings of faith but, unlike so many of their contemporaries, feeling that loss for what it was rather than as a form of liberation. *The New Republic* is therefore, for all its incisive wit and erudition, a less self-assured, and certainly a darker, work of literary art than Knox would have written. As Knox wrote of him just after his death: "Mallock, born perhaps with something of a crooked temperament and even a crooked temper, found himself in a world where the Don still dominated, and Don-dogmas ruled English thought. He revolted, and was indeed a herald of revolt, against the tyranny of dogmatic skepticism. It was no good telling him that questions ought not to be asked in a hard, abrupt way. He *would* ask them; and the fact that he couldn't answer them did not make him in the least degree happier."[35] Nevertheless, *The New Republic* had a marked effect on Knox's own satirical writing, and he readily acknowledged his debt to this particular work of genius.

Another book, somewhat slighter in length and not as well known, may also have had some influence on *Sanctions*. It is likely that Knox would be familiar with *The Wish to Believe*, an 1885 philosophic dialogue written by Wilfrid Ward, who was the brother of Bishop Bernard Ward, the distinguished historian of pre-Emancipation English Catholicism and president of Saint Edmund's College when Knox arrived there in 1920.[36] Wilfrid Ward, best known as the biographer of Cardinal Newman and of his own father, Newman's sometime friend and sometime antagonist William George Ward, of course was himself the father of Maisie Ward, who teamed with her husband Frank Sheed to publish a vast array of Catholic books in the early to mid-twentieth century, including most of Knox's later writings.[37]

[35] Ronald Knox, "Mr. Mallock's New Republic", *Dublin Review* 173 (July/August 1923): 59.

[36] Wilfrid Ward, *The Wish to Believe: A Discussion concerning the Temper of Mind in Which a Reasonable Man Should Undertake Religious Inquiry* (London: Kegan, Paul, and Trench and Co., 1885).

[37] Wilfrid Ward (1856–1916) followed his father's footsteps as editor of the *Dublin Review*, a leading intellectual organ of English Catholicism. His life is recounted in Maisie Ward's two volumes *The Wilfrid Wards and the Transition*, vol. 1: *The 19th Century* (New York: Sheed and Ward, 1934), and vol. 2: *Insurrection versus Resurrection* (New York: Sheed and

The Wish to Believe, Wilfrid Ward's first book, follows Mallock's format by having earnest people engage in debate over fundamental truths. But unlike at Mallock's and Knox's gatherings, Ward's dialoguers include far more believers than unbelievers. In fact, there is only one skeptic, an Oxford-educated barrister who had dutifully absorbed an intellectual tradition beholden to Gibbon and Hume and who consequently assumed that a rational thinker could not be convinced by religious arguments. A chance encounter puts him in touch with an old university friend who has converted and become a Catholic priest. Through various venues, these two individuals, whose intellectual development has taken them to opposite conclusions, argue whether religious inquiry spurs a person to seek the truth or simply to catch at emotional palliatives. The fundamental argument of the priest is that since the stakes in religious truth—in other words, eternal life—are of such momentous account, the seeker demands far greater evidence before committing to religious truth than if the matter in question were a truth that had little consequence to life. This argument, obviously derived from Newman's *Grammar of Assent*, is carefully developed to dispel the common assumption that the more dispassionate the inquirer, the less likely will he be to accept a statement as true without sufficient proof. Ward does not have his skeptic embrace this line of reasoning by book's end, but his friend senses that the barrister's agnostic armor is cracking a bit, simply because of his tenacity in pursuing the issue and his conceding of some of the argumentative points. The barrister is consequently a possible source for the character of Lydiard in *Sanctions*.

More importantly, the plaintive wish to believe proclaimed by Mallock's mouthpiece, the host of the weekend party at the seaside villa, and by Mr. Herbert in his final discourse, signals that Mallock himself was in sight of his goal when he succumbed to death in 1923. *Sanctions* then is a homage to Mallock in more ways than one: certainly in its unmistakable adaptation of format but also in its affirmation that grace will exert an all-important pull on someone who cannot be satisfied by the dogmatism of a passing modern age.

Ward, 1937). A scholarly analysis of his mature philosophy as documented in his essays in the last decade of his life is found in Dom Paschal Scotti, *Out of Due Time: Wilfrid Ward and the Dublin Review* (Washington, D.C.: Catholic University of America Press, 2006).

OTHER EYES THAN OURS

Other Eyes Than Ours is the last of Knox's imaginative novels from the 1920s, appearing in print in 1926.[38] A satire on Spiritualism, it was topical at the time, given that a writer of the stature of Conan Doyle was crusading on behalf of the movement. It should be recalled that in the decade after World War I, the hopes of many a relative of a deceased soldier were raised by the prospect of communicating with the spirits of those who had "gone over". The intellectual atmosphere already prevalent among the upper classes in Edwardian times was conducive to the propagation of these ideas. For example, Lady Desborough, the mother of Knox's friends Julian and Billy Grenfell, who were killed in battle, was a sentimentalist who put stock in the occult. The chronicler of that socially prominent family notes how she and her friends "became interested in things like séances and ouija boards; they were searching for explanations, but not for change. Nothing, finally, seemed more absolute or interesting than death."[39]

To Knox, a light corrective to this trendy interest in the occult seemed in order. The hero of *Other Eyes Than Ours* is Arthur Shurmur, a retiring Oxford scholar whose reputation rests on his being one of two experts worldwide on the writings of an obscure Roman satirist named Persius. (The caricature of Knox's scholarly brother Dillwyn, whose claim to academic fame lay in his editing fragments of the obscure Alexandrian writer Herodas, is unmistakable.) The other expert is Otto Gaedke, a German who holds to different speculations about the definitive text and is therefore Shurmur's one mortal enemy. A palimpsest discovered in Viterbo promises to yield the victory to one of the polemicists: the previously hidden Persius fragment shows Shurmur to have conjectured correctly. But his glee is short-lived when he reads the obituary of his Leipzig counterpart, and he is robbed of the satisfaction of having his opponent concede defeat. Consumed with the desire to know whether Gaedke had acknowledged Shurmur's superior Persius scholarship before dying, the latter resorts to Spiritualist activities to find out. It is actually with a little reluctance that he allows

[38] Ronald Knox, *Other Eyes Than Ours* (London: Methuen and Co., 1926).

[39] Nicholas Mosley, *Julian Grenfell: His Life and the Times of His Death, 1888–1915* (New York: Holt, Rinehart and Winston, 1976), p. 75.

himself to be drawn into it by a formidable grand dame of Oxford salons named Mrs. Haltwhistle, who has attained heightened sensitivities to the spirit world. Her intellectual guide in these matters is a Mr. Scoop, who lectures widely and knowingly on the scientific basis of such contacts.

When an old school chum named Godfrey Minshull finds Shurmur being enveloped in this murky realm, Minshull invites the latter to his country home to show off a radio (back then, of course, still a commodity of some curiosity in a home) that he has altered so that it can pick up what appear to be spirit voices. Mrs. Haltwhistle and her blasé worldly niece Kitty Rostead, Mr. Scoop, Godfrey's sarcastic sister Mrs. Varley, a French abbé stationed at the local Catholic parish, and several other onlookers round out the weekend guest list.

The machine is put to the test and soon ethereal music and some hardly audible whispering are overheard. Different auditors interpret the sounds differently, some supposing them to have been spoken in English, Mr. Scoop holding out for Italian. Analysis ensues:

> "What I can't understand," said Shurmur, "is the language difficulty—difficulty of language. Did you say, Mrs. Haltwhistle, that you heard words spoken in English?"
>
> "Yes, oh, quite distinctly! But, you see, that's no new difficulty, because we've plenty of evidence from the séances of spirits talking in English; and sometimes even with English dialects."
>
> "Yes, but how? What I mean is, do the spirits all talk in their native languages, or do they all talk in English, or what?"
>
> "C'est sans doute le principe de la majorité [It's majority rule, no doubt]," murmured the Abbé to himself.
>
> "Well, you know, it was explained to me the other day" (Mrs. Haltwhistle always used this formula when she alluded to her automatic writing) "that the spirits don't really speak, don't use any medium of sound, but can just transfer their thoughts straight from one to another. So that perhaps their thoughts, when they become audible to us, clothe themselves in English because our minds are English."
>
> "Is Scoop partly Italian?" asked Minshull. "He doesn't look it."
>
> "No; I see what you mean. And of course Kitty heard a quite unknown language, which makes it more complicated still. It really seems as if the spirits must still *think* in their own native languages, just as we think in English, and that the impression which their

thoughts make on the ether around them clothes itself in language accordingly."

"You will pardon me, madame," suggested the Abbé, "but if the spirits play on musical instruments which make a real sound, why do they not also use real speech? Or will you say that the music also was not real music, it was the thoughts of these spirits expressing itself by vibrations just of that kind? Of course it might be that the voices express their thoughts, and the music only their dreams."

"Their nightmares, you mean, Abbé," shouted Mrs. Varley from her end of the table.

"Really I don't know," said Mrs. Haltwhistle.

"We might ask Planchette about it," added her niece.[40]

Further eavesdropping is rewarded when a spirit is overheard addressing an audience of its own kind. Evidently, all awareness of what transpired in their earthly lives has been obliterated, and they are reduced to speculating on whether the "tailless pithecoids" inhabiting the material world are worth making contact with (reminiscent of the preborn spirits of Erewhonian lore).

> If they have intelligences, these must be of a kind which do not ordinarily admit of intercommunication with our plane. But it has happened more than once of late, unless our investigations are at fault, that intelligible messages have been received from them.... The question, for example, "Are there any spirits present?" has repeatedly made itself felt, apparently in connexion with groups of these pithecoids, usually female. To such groupings our Physical Research Society gives the name of seances....[41]

A cautious note of optimism concludes the lecture, as efforts to proceed with attempts at contact are encouraged.

Mrs. Haltwhistle is crestfallen at the import of the intercepted talk. All the pious platitudes conveyed to anxious loved ones through mediums have lost their efficacy if the spirits don't even know we exist. But after some mental scrambling, Mr. Scoop asseverates that only the advanced spirits are privileged to lose memory of the past, while the contacts at séances must be made early on in the life beyond, before the dross of the old world has been sloughed off.

[40] Knox, *Other Eyes Than Ours*, pp. 79–80.

[41] Ibid., pp. 90–91.

Another bewildering communiqué causes a further shift in hypotheses, and finally a critical stage in psychic relations is reached. An urgent message, again confined to the spirits themselves, warns against any more attempts to contact earthly inhabitants. Too-easy converse will only cause men to fear death less. Hence they will take risks thoughtlessly, the suicide rate will rise, and soon enough the average age of death will drop to twenty-five. The concomitant population decline will finally put an end to the supply of new spirits. Also, the indulgence in psychic activity is accelerating the flight from human reason, a result not calculated to improve the quality of life among future denizens of the spirit world.

But Mr. Scoop rises to the challenge and composes a noble speech for transmission to the refractory spirits. Good will and openness on both sides is earnestly beseeched, and the alleged danger of human moral decline resulting from open commerce is dispelled in a grand peroration:

> We are coming to see, that just as the human race emerged from the reign of instinct into the reign of reason; so reason too, in its turn, must lay aside the sceptre, and make way for the higher claims of mystical intuition. The creeds and dogmas which rested their weight on the evidence of alleged facts have become old-fashioned; we have become familiarized with the idea that a historical statement may be false in the sense that the thing did not happen, yet true in the sense that it harmonizes with all that is highest in our spiritual nature. Mystical intuition steps in, and reprieves the statement, at the last moment, from being condemned as a falsehood. We are learning that man does not apprehend Truth—he *makes* Truth; that is Truth which satisfies his aspirations, the Light that never was on land or sea.
>
> This being so—and it is significantly so and increasingly so—it is doubtful whether the human intellect has much part to play in the momentous spiritual issues of the future. It will have its rightful place, of course, in assisting the scientist to unravel the mysteries of nature; it will be a hewer of wood and a drawer of water for the material progress of the race. But in that religion of the future towards which Spiritualism, in common with all that is best in all the religions, so confidently points us, the intellect will find itself inevitably superseded; it will be a landmark that we have left behind, a childish thing that we have outgrown. We are advancing, it has been

> recently and fearlessly said, towards a kind of Higher Cretinism. We embrace that destiny cheerfully, and shoulder it manfully; that star guiding us, we go forward we know not whither.[42]

The appeal finds a sympathetic minority on the opposite side, who are willing to ignore the warnings previously addressed to them by their compatriots. But they then ask to dematerialize one of the earthly communicators so as to convince the other spirits of the sincerity of the pithecoids. All those present in the Minshull house are requested to be alone in their bedrooms at 11:30 P.M., at which time one will be transported to the spirit world.

Shurmur, who participated in the experiments only to contact Otto Gaedke, has considerable misgivings but awaits his fate nervously. However, just before the appointed hour, he is called by Minshull to his room to observe from a window the hasty departure, one by one, of Mrs. Haltwhistle, Miss Rostead, and Mr. Scoop, all of whom had earlier evinced their interest in being selected. In the end, it is revealed that the weekend's unworldly phenomena were staged by Minshull and his butler, who used recordings to produce the spirit world voices in an elaborate hoax to disabuse Shurmur of his flirtation with Spiritualism. The final chapter is reminiscent of one of Knox's mystery novels, with the several clues dispersed throughout the narrative being illuminated to reveal what was really going on, unsuspected by earnest believers in the efficacy of séances. Yet in trading in fantasy for deduction, the novel is thereby deflated from the level of an amusing, if somewhat derivative, satire to the level of a detective story with a moral. Perhaps Knox simply felt compelled to pour cold water on a mushrooming movement fed by gullibility and greed. Possibly he was spurred on by reading a highly critical examination of paranormal phenomena published in 1922 by C.M. de Heredia, a Mexican Jesuit and former magician who earned some fame as a debunker of Spiritualist phenomena.[43] Interestingly, however, the English Jesuit

[42] Ibid., pp. 201–2.

[43] C.M. de Heredia, *Spiritism and Common Sense* (New York: P.J. Kenedy and Sons, 1922). Samuel Butler was once invited to attend a séance along with Alfred Russell Wallace, the evolutionary theorist, and according to his biographer, was totally unimpressed: "If ever a spirit-form took to coming near him, he told Wallace, he would not content himself with trying to grasp it: 'in the interests of science, *I will shoot it!*'" See Peter Raby, *Samuel Butler: A Biography* (Iowa City: University of Iowa Press, 1991), p. 107.

and prodigious scholar Herbert Thurston was also publishing articles, later collected in several books, which come to the conclusion that the description of some preternatural phenomena (including the infestation by ghosts of John Wesley's home) are historically reliable accounts.[44] In any case, an authorial tilt toward Thurston's angle would have strengthened *Other Eyes Than Ours* as a work of fiction. Evelyn Waugh accords it scant attention, except to comment that it could have had half the pages excised without any artistic loss. In Waugh's early satires, characters are immersed in a maelstrom of events through which they typically flail their way to their appointed ends without the opportunity for reflective conversation. Dialogue is clipped and the action frenetic. Knox on the other hand employs the drawing room as the backdrop for his satires, giving his characters the leisure to mouth fully developed philosophical viewpoints. Hence he could arguably need a greater word count to do justice to his theme. But the decline in the public's taste for purely intellectual exercises packaged as fiction guaranteed that *Other Eyes Than Ours* would never experience a reincarnation in a second edition.

[44] See for example Thurston's *Ghosts and Poltergeists* (Chicago: Henry Regnery, 1955 reprint). Herbert Thurston (1856–1939) lived in the Farm Street Jesuit residence in London and wrote regularly for the Jesuit publication the *Month*. Even though they were contemporaries, if a generation apart in age, it does not seem that Knox was in any way influenced by Thurston, the way he was by the Jesuits Martin D'Arcy and C. C. Martindale. On Thurston, who was a meticulous sifter of historical evidence, see Joseph Crehan, S.J., *Father Thurston* (London: Sheed and Ward, 1952).

CHAPTER FOUR

THE BODY IN THE TRUNK

THE SYMPOSIASTS

One of the distinctive marks of the modern world is the pervasiveness of communications media offering mass audiences ready access to information of all kinds. Ronald Knox did not live to see television reach its potential as a means of disseminating images and ideas, but he grew to maturity around the time Marconi and Fleming and Fessenden were perfecting radio. And he was in full bloom as a Catholic apologist at the Oxford chaplaincy when the government-owned BBC began broadcasting to the English public.

A new medium for talk soon attracts pundits, and religion especially invites punditry, being one topic on which all people believe themselves qualified by experience to have particular insight. The prudential question for Knox was to what degree one ought to pay attention to the profusion of talk on religion to which radio soon gave outlet. Is it to be ignored, to be parodied, or to be met head-on with a gravity befitting a struggle for the direction of minds and souls? There is, after all, a want of depth commonly inhering in theological speculation borne over the airwaves, a dreary superficiality much on a par with the scripted programming that cannot afford to be too subtle if it is to be popular and to make money for all involved in its production.

Given Knox's postconversion disinclination for engaging in polemics, a frontal assault on dispensers of popular religious thought was an unlikely option. Only persistent prodding by the indefatigable publisher and soapbox orator Frank Sheed would get him to focus on what was being fed to the English people as they read the daily papers and listened in to the BBC.[1] Both media would eventually supply him with sufficient stock of musings about God and the cosmos to require a book-length analysis of what was amiss in the suppositions and conclusions of the featured commentators, although the radio experts would be held accountable for their more durable published works rather than their evanescent on-air remarks. Knox began his task by lugging a huge cache of newspaper articles on religion to the Lovat estate in Scotland where he could sift through them, distilling from the heap of verbiage a fairly homogeneous statement of beliefs. These columns were the accumulated writings of what the newspapers called "symposiasts", a group of literary figures who would be invited by a mass-market daily to give their considered opinions on religious topics guaranteed to resonate with readers, topics such as whether there is an afterlife or what constitutes moral behavior.

Not surprisingly, barons of the British press such as Lord Beaverbrook and Lord Northcliffe were more interested in hiking circulation numbers than in plumbing the depths of scholarship in an effort to achieve certainty or even consensus on a controverted issue. Popular novelists were therefore an especially fruitful pool from which to select columnists who would not hesitate to speculate on the most profound religious issues. These individuals after all had already established a sympathetic relationship with the general reading public, and their thoughts could therefore be expected to command attention and engender admiration.

In the late 1920s that meant enlisting the talents of favorites like Arnold Bennett, Rebecca West, E. P. Oppenheim, and other writers of dramatic or mystery novels game enough to grapple with the meaning of religion in the modern world. By different routes these writers had arrived, not terribly surprisingly, at a fairly similar religious standpoint.

[1] Actually, as novelist Wilfrid Sheed observes in his lively and witty account of the lives of his publisher parents Frank Sheed (1897–1981) and Maisie Ward (1889–1975), his father was almost obsequiously deferential in his dealings with Knox, who by the 1940s was to become the company's "transatlantic meal ticket" and hence merited special consideration. Even more so, "Knox as an object represented something beyond the ungainly wooings of commerce, and the panting ones of hero worship. Ronnie was at the very nexus of those two great civilizations, Rome and Oxford University." Wilfrid Sheed, *Frank and Maisie: A Memoir with Parents* (New York: Simon and Schuster, 1985), p. 207.

Arnold Bennett, certainly among the most popular and highly compensated English novelists and playwrights of the decade, serves as an exemplar of the type of commentator with whom Knox had to contend. By all accounts Bennett was a fairly decent fellow. Unlike his friend H. G. Wells, he did not prey on young women and did not advocate the elimination of whole races of people. Granted, he had a predilection for yachts and fine dinners and could churn out stories about the well-to-do as nonchalantly as he could about those trapped in industrial towns. More importantly, he had a keen sense of what readers wanted to hear about, and he knew that their literary tastes did not extend to forays into traditional religion. After all, he himself had early on sloughed off the Methodism of the Potteries district and admitted later in life to "but a cautious disdain for the impassioned beliefs around me".[2]

Rebecca West, the authorial name adopted by Cicily Fairchild, was an equally promising font of acceptable opinion. She had emerged from dreary Scottish surroundings emotionally scarred from a childhood haunted by the dissolution of her parents' marriage under the strain of her father's infidelities. In reaction, she embraced Fabianism and feminism as a young writer. By the late 1920s, she was a successful critic and novelist and had extricated herself from a disastrous decade-long affair with the utterly self-engrossed H. G. Wells, an affair that issued in a son who in his mature years as a writer would add to her angst by lauding his largely absentee father at the expense of his mother. Her transformation into a foe of communism, wrought by her witness of the betrayal of Yugoslavia to Tito, still lay in the future, but her religious views by 1930 were already set. They were indistinguishable from those of other former Christians: humanitarian, sentimental, and far from focused.[3]

On the other hand, E. P. Oppenheim had led a rather charmed life as a prolific author of crime and mystery novels, many of them composed while he lived in a villa on the French Riviera, where he golfed and gambled and consorted with other rich and famous literary and

[2] The life of Arnold Bennett (1867–1931) is recounted in Margaret Drabble, *Arnold Bennett: A Biography* (Boston: G.K. Hall and Co., 1986). The quote is taken from p. 15.

[3] Her long life (1892–1983) is chronicled by Victoria Glendinning, *Rebecca West: A Life* (New York: Alfred A. Knopf, 1987).

sporting types. His memoirs, published in 1942 when he was seventy-six, reveal a man still thoroughly absorbed in the pursuit of physical comforts even as others suffered the privations of wartime. Conspicuously absent from his narrative is even the slightest hint of religious introspection.[4]

The tenor of these symposia was therefore already predetermined by picking suitable discussants, but it should be kept in mind that a press that knows what its public wants to hear nevertheless sees its relationship to its readers as a tutelary one: "Men, after all, are children, and the Press is a kind of governess that must first (for the sake of peace) find out what game the children want to play, and then (for the sake of discipline) appear to have been the originator of the suggestion."[5] So Knox describes the processes of professional journalism in his rejoinder to the symposiasts, *Caliban in Grub Street,* which appeared in 1930. The title, euphonious as it may be, perhaps needs as much explanation today as does the projected one—*Gigadibs upon Setebos*—which he wisely laid aside as too obscure. Caliban, the brutish slave in Shakespeare's *The Tempest,* is of course an archetype of the natural man with whom many of the symposiasts boast kinship, the modern for whom religious orthodoxy is a hindrance to full self-realization. Since Grub Street is the London locale once associated with literary hackwork, the title is a tip-off to Knox's estimation of the level of discourse upon which it was his duty to comment. The discarded title derives from two of Robert Browning's poems: the first is *Bishop Blougram's Apology,* in which a jaded Catholic bishop (a caricature of both Cardinal Wiseman and John Henry Newman) expatiates on his unbelief to a journalist named Gigadibs; the second is *Caliban upon Setebos,* in which Shakespeare's man-monster discourses on the anthropomorphized deity Setebos.[6] Knox deftly turns the tables on Browning by

[4] Oppenheim lived from 1866 to 1946. His autobiography, *The Pool of Memory* (Boston: Little, Brown and Co., 1942), is vivid but disappointingly shallow. For example, reminiscing about an old friend who enjoyed playing roulette at Monte Carlo, he can summon only bathos: "When I went to see him in his last illness, he pressed my hands, there was a gleam in his eyes and a faint smile. 'Don't forget that old quatorze, Opp,' he begged." See p. 107.

[5] Ronald Knox, *Caliban in Grub Street* (London: Sheed and Ward, 1930), p. 9.

[6] Browning's visceral hatred of the Catholic Church was roiled when Wiseman was named cardinal archbishop of Westminster in 1850 as part of the restoration of the Catholic hierarchy in England. Browning was a Unitarian by predisposition, and although he

letting the scoffers at traditional Christian beliefs display their incertitude in their own words, which merge imperceptibly into Bishop Blougram's. Like him, they value the emotions more than rigorous thought:

> All's doubt in me; where's break of faith in this?
> It is the idea, the feeling and the love,
> God means mankind should strive for and show forth
> Whatever be the process to that end,—
> And not historic knowledge, logic sound,
> And metaphysical acumen, sure![7]

In literary format as well as intellectual content, Knox's *Caliban* is, as Joseph Pearce has observed, also a lineal descendant of G.K. Chesterton's *Heretics* of a generation earlier but with the difference that whereas Chesterton rarely allows his antagonists to speak for themselves before he vanquishes them, Knox quotes extensively from their writings and merely assists the reader in seeing their inconsistency or want of logic.[8]

---

and Elizabeth Barrett Browning spent many years in Italy, they consorted almost exclusively with the English Protestant enclaves in Florence and other cities. For a discussion of his religious views and his frequent attacks on Catholicism, the biography by William Irvine and Park Honan, *The Book, the Ring, and the Poet* (New York: McGraw-Hill, 1974), is illuminating. Interestingly, G.K. Chesterton contributed the study of Browning to the English Men of Letters series, and despite a rollicking affirmation of Browning's poetry and philosophy, he studiously downplayed his antipathy to the Church. After discussing the poet's abhorrence of Spiritualists, Chesterton goes on to say: "Some traces again, though much fainter ones, may be found of something like a subconscious hostility to the Roman Church, or at least a less full comprehension of the grandeur of the Latin religious civilisation than might be expected of a man of Browning's great imaginative tolerance." G.K. Chesterton, *Robert Browning* (New York: Macmillan Company, 1905), p. 114. Chesterton's penchant for hearty exaggeration is curiously muffled in this statement.

[7] See, for example, *Bishop Blougram's Apology* in Adam Roberts, ed., *Robert Browning* (Oxford: Oxford University Press, 1997), pp. 212–37. The quoted lines are on pp. 227–28.

[8] Joseph Pearce, *Literary Converts: Spiritual Inspiration in an Age of Unbelief* (San Francisco: Ignatius Press, 1999), p. 179. Chesterton very neatly describes the malady at the heart of the writings of H.G. Wells, Rudyard Kipling, Joseph McCabe, and other "heretical" literary figures, anticipating Knox's task in dealing with a slightly newer generation of what Chesterton classifies as bigots: "Bigotry may be roughly defined as the anger of men who have no opinions. It is the resistance offered to definite ideas by that vague bulk of people whose ideas are indefinite to excess.... Bigotry in the main has always been the pervading omnipotence of those who do not care crushing out those who care in darkness and blood." G.K. Chesterton, *Heretics* (New York: John Lane Company, 1907), p. 296.

Despite minor divergences, the symposiasts speak with a common voice, one that assumes traditional religion to be outmoded, even as its rejection leaves them the burden of erecting an emotionally satisfying substitute. Oppenheim, for example, says he laments the passing of ages when people "accepted the priest-expounded explanations of the problems of the universe", an attitude that nevertheless has obviously "become impossible to dwellers in this bustling world of ours".[9] It is precisely because the reader is more intelligent than his forebears that the old orthodoxy will not do anymore. Independence of mind is an attribute few newspaper readers will deny having, and being credited with the ability to negotiate the perils of a bustling world can only reinforce the bond between columnist and reader. The astute symposiasts know that they are dealing primarily with readers who reckon themselves morally upstanding even though it rarely occurs to them to pause amid their duties to worship God, let alone cross the portal of a church. So to alleviate any lingering feelings of guilt about nonobservance, Rebecca West confides consolingly: "Certain forms which Christianity had to take to satisfy the needs of the man of that age are unsuited to the man of this age."[10]

The notion that one ought to accept any statement as true on the authority of a religious body, and particularly on the authority of the Catholic Church, is singularly abhorrent to her. Most of the literary commentators play on the inherent suspicion with which the average reader views authority, so that all dogmatic pronouncements take on an evil aspect. That they misrepresent the very meaning of the word *dogma* is a trivial point to them. As Knox reminds them, *dogma* "means, not something which one man tries to force down the throats of other men, but something on which a number of different people, coming to the question from different parts of the world and with different mental backgrounds, are all unanimously agreed".[11]

The dogmas of which they so freely divest themselves were held fairly unanimously for many centuries as traditions handed down from the age of the apostles. Many of them survived in England after the break with Rome, but only in the nineteenth and twentieth centuries

[9] Quoted in Knox, *Caliban*, p. 23.
[10] Ibid.
[11] Ibid., p. 15.

did they lose their palatability, and thereby they fall victim to a new set of dogmas, ones encouraged by the mass media.

Were their thoughts more coherent, the writers would speak with the voice of that noteworthy liberal essayist Matthew Arnold, whose critique of the Gospels in his *Literature and Dogma* assisted in the undermining of the faith of Mallock and others in the late Victorian era. Arnold had used the German term *Aberglaube*, or "extra-belief", to characterize all dogmatic statements as fanciful accretions on the Gospel message of morality and peace. The ancient Israelites were enraptured by the power that makes for righteousness, which they anthropomorphized into a personal God, and the evangelists mistakenly glossed Jesus' coruscating message of peace and light into a revelation about the Trinity. In actuality, God is no more than "the stream of tendency by which all things fulfil the law of their being". Reason as typified by the constructors of creeds is the enemy of religion, which can be experienced truly only as an "influence, which we feel we know not how, and which subdues us we know not when; which, like the wind, breathes where it lists, passes here, and does not pass there! Once more, then, we come to that root and ground of religion, that element of awe and gratitude which fills religion with emotion, and makes it other and greater than morality,—the *not ourselves*." [12]

To Arnold, the critical task is to salvage the strictures of the Bible on conduct while unloading the theology that he believed was causing the man in the street to dispense with the entire message. He believed morality could be underpinned by assurance that the nebulous "not ourselves" pervaded the universe. In that somewhat quaint hope, he was simply representative of the first stage in the inevitable progression of post-Christian British thought: the thinkers of the decades overshadowed by Darwin and by the German Biblical critics held onto the notion of a universal code of morality, but by the time of the symposiasts, the chafing under its strictures would in itself constitute the rationale for the dismissal of dogma.

Knox does not fault the symposiasts for reexamining traditional beliefs. Indeed, if only they would reexamine them, they might know better

[12] Mathew Arnold, *Literature and Dogma: An Essay towards a Better Apprehension of the Bible* (1873; reprint, New York: Macmillan Company, 1924), pp. 37, 208.

whether or not they are fulminating against tradition or against a caricature of tradition. He is puzzled, however, by

> an impression I get when I read all these essays in the reconstruction of belief. And the impression is this—that the authors, and countless others whom they represent, have grown out of the religion of their childhood without ever exactly discovering what it was; and that they are suggesting substitutes for it not because they have decided that there is nothing in it, but because they have assumed that there is nothing in it. They have thrown the creeds into the waste-paper basket, I fancy, not because they disbelieved in them, but because they were creeds. And when it becomes necessary to show why the creeds were unsatisfactory, they have a slight difficulty in remembering what it was all about.[13]

Perhaps not coincidentally, almost all of them had grown up in Protestant households, the one exception being Arthur Conan Doyle, who came from a well-known Irish Catholic family of artists and illustrators and who was educated by Jesuits at Stonyhurst before drifting first into agnosticism and ultimately into Spiritualism.

The standard debating tactic employed by these critics is to summon forth a doctrine couched in terms as it might have been first imparted to them as children. Then they proclaim, truly enough, that such teachings could no longer satisfy mature, thinking people. Hence their quest in search of a new religion. Henry De Vere Stacpoole is a case in point. He was the son of a Protestant doctor of divinity from Trinity College in Dublin, who (like Doyle) turned to writing after practicing as a physician and is best known as the author of the lushly descriptive romance *The Blue Lagoon*, which has been adapted to the screen a number of times since he wrote it in 1908. He is especially squeamish about hell. "I had the feeling", he maintains, "that the threat of eternal punishment for finite sins was a bogey put up to frighten me, not by God, but by my elders and betters."[14]

In a refashioned religion, consequently, the first dogma to be established is the nonexistence of hell. To be sure, it is the most

[13] Knox, *Caliban*, pp. 28–29.

[14] Quoted in ibid., p. 34. Stacpoole (1863–1951) wrote his picturesque and placid memoirs, *Men and Mice* (London: Hutchinson and Co., 1942), during World War II, and his religious views seem to have stabilized by then into the acknowledgment of a benign Providence tolerantly presiding over reincarnating souls.

uncomfortable legacy of the Catholic Church, and efforts to talk it out of existence have been at the root of many critiques of the Church's claims on men's consciences. Knox places their rationalizing in syllogistic form: "Eternal punishment does not exist; Christ was a true Prophet; therefore Christ did not believe in eternal punishment." The two alternative syllogisms positing either that (a) Christ believed in hell, or (b) Christ was not a true prophet, are not congenial to their preconceptions. The latter of the two amounts to a renunciation too radical to be accepted by a public loathe to part with all vestiges of Christianity. The symposiasts, one must remember, mirror their audiences' religious predispositions, and the sentimental humanist Christ is too appealing a construct to let go.

It is hell, therefore, that must go. And that calls for a God who wouldn't permit such a place to exist. "The Supreme Being enjoys, in their thoughts, a kind of constitutional Monarchy, limited by the will of those whose thinking lends him Existence; eternal punishment would be an abuse of his Prerogative—they would withdraw their intellectual support rather than admit it."[15]

Warwick Deeping, no doubt acquainted with the severely biased rendering of medieval thought popularized by writers such as the Cambridge historian G. G. Coulton, claims hell to be the invention of medieval "priestcraft", a tool to exercise power over nonconformers, "the crucible in which an established cult melted down contradiction". As such, its banishment into the dustbin of intellectual history must coincide with the progress of freedom, a process in which the English people, of course, have stood in the vanguard. Yet no concept, however distorted by the masters of the Dark Ages, is without some foundation in reality, usually explicable by modern psychology. Therefore, Deeping goes on, our "hells are personal. . . . What is hell for the wise man but the realization of his own failure?"[16]

The aphorism suggests that hell is a state of mind that can be avoided by the constitutionally upbeat, whereas the person who is by nature a

[15] Knox, *Caliban*, pp. 161–62.

[16] Quoted in ibid., pp. 164–65. Warwick Deeping (1877–1950) had already published many historical novels and romances before his service at Gallipoli and elsewhere in World War I caused him to probe the grim realities of war and of the disillusionment of the postwar era. Despite his authorship of over sixty novels, he has yet to be the subject of a biography.

pessimist is at serious risk of being plunged into its purely psychological fires. Should a believer in the traditional definition of hell reply that the occasional pangs of regret are a small price to pay for an accumulation of major transgressions throughout one's life, the symposiast responds that a religion based on fear of punishment is an ignoble one, and that the modern psyche does not need the threat of sanctions to lead a virtuous life. Rebecca West's criteria for happiness in the afterlife, in "a universe of greater beauty than this", are instructive. The blessed include "anyone who warmly loves anyone else; anyone who creates good art or sound thought, anyone who achieves courage or generosity, any one who does any work well". Meanwhile, the less fortunate—not indeed damned in her eschatology but gently obliterated—are typified by the superficial, "a man who spends his whole life in playing some game like tennis or chess" or a woman "who spends her whole life in trivial social activities".[17] One pauses to consider the quandary of the grandmasters of the chess world; not only might they suffer Warwick Deeping's hell for losing to a computer, but they are condemned to Rebecca West's hell for a life wasted on a frivolous pastime.

It is perhaps unfair to apply too remorseless a logic to such pronouncements. But when these hells are considered carefully, they threaten to include in their embrace a greater proportion of mankind than the hell recognized in Catholic theology. The orthodox theologian would point out that, after all, the Church proclaims some people saints, but she does not affirm the damnation of anyone. The critics also fail to realize that Catholic theology is far more reticent about what hell consists of than they are. No doubt the loss of God's presence, which the Catholic Church states is a consequence of an unrepentant will, does not impress them as a sufficiently horrifying torment, but then they do not concede that God is the source of *all* good and that therefore banishment from his sight would mean an interment in evil. Now, if God is only a benevolent force, the loss of that force may be a discomfort, but hardly a catastrophe. But once one accepts that God is

[17] Quoted in ibid., pp. 58–59. Rebecca West's heaven bears a strong resemblance to the Elysium pictured by Virgil, in which are found "those who bettered life, by finding out new truths and skills; or those who to some folk by benefactions made themselves remembered." *The Aeneid*, bk. 6, trans. Robert Fitzgerald (New York: Random House, 1983), p. 183.

indeed goodness itself, to forsake his friendship is to lose everything but existence, a far graver state than can be comprehended.[18]

Once hell is disposed of as the focal point of man's worries, the impulse to dismantle most of the other underpinnings of orthodox theology is hard to resist, beginning with its assertion that human reason can discern God's necessary existence and his plenitude of power. The concept of an almighty God is uncongenial to the symposiasts, so the process of rational thinking is laid aside as too tedious a vehicle to apply to transcendental issues. "I believe that to love is to be in God", proposes the poet and pacifist Max Plowman, and he follows this insight with the reflection: "Directly I love anything I cease from pure intellectual life, and by entering the world of sensuous and, finally, spiritual apprehension, acknowledge the insufficiency of intellect for the enjoyment of what I most desire."[19] Reason has been politely shown the door. In fact, many of life's thornier issues can dissolve within a murky sentimentalism when one posits that love for all people and all nature is all that matters. To be fair to him, Plowman, unlike many of the literary figures cited by Knox, was no hedonist. His letters show him to be repelled by egocentrism, commercialization, and the

[18] As a well-known Dominican moral theologian of the same era put it in a way that sounds superficially like what Deeping and West are trying to say but instead acknowledges the reality and horror of hell: "[S]in consists of setting up the ego in the centre of the personality instead of God; the immediate effect is isolation, loneliness, which is the essence of hell, so that hell is not so much a punishment *for* sin as the immediate and inevitable result *of* sin." Gerald Vann, O.P., *The Heart of Man* (New York: Longmans, Green and Co., 1945), p. 27.

Fr. Vann (1906–1963) was strongly influenced by his fellow Dominican Vincent McNabb (1868–1943), the friend of Chesterton and Belloc and proponent of social justice through distributism. It is also worth mentioning that Fr. Vann in the same book has a chapter on human sexuality (pp. 47–66) that anticipates the approach adopted years later by the future Pope John Paul II in his book *Love and Responsibility* (New York: Farrar, Straus, Giroux, 1981), therefore suggesting that the perfunctory dismissal by some popular moral theologians of the 1960s and 1970s of their pre–Vatican II predecessors as legalistic casuists is untenable.

[19] Quoted in Knox, *Caliban*, p. 49. Max Plowman (1883–1941) served in World War I in France but refused reassignment after recuperation in England from wounds. He became a leading promoter of pacifism in the interwar years, following Dick Sheppard as head of the Peace Pledge Union in the 1930s. After his death, Plowman's widow published his voluminous correspondence under the title *Bridge to the Future* (London: Daker, 1944). It displays a deep interest in the spiritual life. However, his youthful exposure to religion through the Plymouth Brethren left him closed to the possibility that Christ had founded a visible Church.

demeaning of human relations in the secularized world. But it is also the case that to this utterly sincere quasi Christian, the Catholic Church, in particular, with her rules and notion of sin, could serve only as a barrier to genuine religious experience. As Knox comments: "Religion, in the sense in which they are now using it, no longer consists in a system of sanctions which prevents them, in their own despite, from acting in accordance with their natural appetites; it is merely a sort of added grace, a bloom upon their otherwise blameless characters, which inspires them with great thoughts, makes them feel happy about the prospect of death, and consoles them for all the tragedies of life."[20]

An uncorkable glibness drives the symposiasts to describe their conception of God. Sir Francis Younghusband was a famous explorer of the Himalayas, whose contacts with adherents of Buddhism, Islam, and Confucianism, superimposed on his many experiences of the awesome in nature, engendered in him a growing interest in mysticism and induced him in the 1930s to found the World Congress of Faiths.[21] Knox's attention is arrested by Younghusband's notions about God: "Just as I, an Englishman, can feel England expecting me to do my duty, so also can I feel the Genius or Spirit of the Universe—what we call God—expecting both England and myself ... to strive with all our souls after what is best and noblest in life."[22] Is this mysticism or just imperialism? In any case, the analogy between something (England), that is an idea collectively shared by people, and its rhetorical counterpart, "what we call God", is jarring. The presumption of course is

[20] Knox, *Caliban*, pp. 40–41.

[21] Amusingly his biographer distinguishes between the muscular mysticism of Younghusband (1863–1942) and an inferior type associated with Catholicism: "There is a mysticism of the cloister, and there is a mysticism of what may be called the camp. The former is generally passive, quiescent, and life-denying; the latter active, ethical, and life-affirming. Younghusband's was of the latter type." George Seaver, *Francis Younghusband: Explorer and Mystic* (London: John Murray, 1952), p. 115.

[22] Quoted in Knox, *Caliban*, p. 75. Back in his days of adventure, during a confrontation with Hunza tribesmen in which Younghusband, the sole Englishman present (though backed by several Gurkha and Kirghiz guides), demanded that they desist their depredations, he had used strikingly similar language: "That I was able to do what I did was mainly due to the fact that I was an Englishman, that I stood for the British Empire.... I was to them the embodiment, the incarnation of the spirit which animates England.... And I could feel England expecting me to bear myself in a manner worthy of her." Seaver, *Younghusband*, p. 123.

that God is no more a being than England is and that our consciences are no more informed by God than our civic sense is enlightened by John Bull or Uncle Sam. Here indeed is an ethereal god, who can be conjured into apparent existence merely by capitalizing a phrase like "Life Force" and then can be as easily dissipated when the topic of personal accountability for actions is broached. Not that Sir Francis, a highly ethical man, would take advantage of his divinity's uncertain existence. But it might be a temptation to others drawn into his pantheist net.

Is there a God to worship? One author says that trying to be good "is the best form of worship of the spirit of good"; another rhapsodizes "on the mystery that irradiates every particle of matter". But surely Rebecca West tops the list with her counsel on behalf of tolerance, for "when we let people do what they like and say what they like we are giving the Divine a chance to express itself when it comes."[23]

With a divinity like that demurely hovering in the background, little good can be anticipated of the response to Christ's own query: "Whom do men say that I am?" J.D. Beresford, a novelist and critic with a penchant for suffusing his fiction with the latest in psychical research, faith healing, and inchoate mysticism, is adamant that there can be no connection between Jesus and a dogmatizing Church. When Jesus proclaimed that those who believed in him would not perish, he did not intend for his followers to submit to "an endless rigmarole of senseless ordinances and ritual originally imposed by priests for their own purposes". Instead, he was calling on them only to accept "the divine principle in himself and all mankind".[24]

[23] Quoted in Knox, *Caliban*, pp. 79–80. In 1950, West actually began instruction in the Catholic faith under the tutelage of the Dominican Gervase Mathew. However, she could not shake an essentially dualistic, Manichaean outlook on life and consequently gave up after eighteen months. See Glendinning, *Rebecca West*, pp. 221–25.

[24] Quoted in Knox, *Caliban*, p. 116. J.D. Beresford (1873–1947) led a penurious and unsettled life in England and France in the 1920s. He wrote almost fifty novels, along with many short stories and essays. A none-too-subtle predilection for burdening his fictional characters with his own unorthodox spiritual yearnings, and for supplying authorial commentary lest the reader miss the pitch for whatever key to life's mysteries Beresford was currently transfixed by, accounts for his limited popularity. He left his wife when he was in his sixties and teamed up with Esme Wynne Tyson to write tracts at a feverish pace until his death. For an appreciation of his life and literary career, see George Johnson, *J. D. Beresford* (New York: Twayne Publishers, 1998).

History is not the symposiasts' quarry of choice. The virtual eruption of Christianity after the crucifixion of its founder is hardly explicable without accepting the sober statements of the witnesses to Jesus' rising from the dead. The credo of the early Christian was built up on the fact of the Resurrection, and the specific truths about God that Jesus transmitted to his first disciples. Knox must remind the critics that Jesus was not merely the benign ethicist they envisage him to be. In their reading of history it would seem "that the world of Tiberius's time had been all agog to do its duty if only it could have found out where its duty lay; that the revelation it needed was given to it by the Sermon on the Mount, only, most unfortunately, this admirable programme was concealed from it by the machinations of the priests for nearly eighteen centuries".[25]

Again Rebecca West serves up a priceless specimen of sentimentalist prose when she interprets the life of Christ as a message "that poverty and suffering could be borne so sweetly that they exalted a man above the proudest and richest king; he struck back some of the world's swords by preaching the beauty of peace; he assured men that love was a power in the Universe by coming to render him these services, though he knew he must pay for it with his life". Her Christ is a tragic figure at best, a suitable hero for a novel or an opera, but hardly impressive enough to explain why so many Christians throughout the centuries would lay down their own lives for him. Peter laid down his life, and no one suffers martyrdom for Peter's sake; likewise Paul. But they do suffer martyrdom for Jesus' sake. Knox wonders whether her Christ would even have excited any anger among the rulers who plotted his execution:

> He must pay with his life—for what? For bearing poverty and suffering with sweetness? It is hard to see why Caiaphas should have minded that. For preaching the beauty of peace? But no such charge was made against him at his arraignment before Pilate. As a matter of fact, contentment with poverty and the beauty of peace were commonplaces of the period, and it would be much more exact to describe the poet Horace as concerned to preach them than our Lord.[26]

[25] Knox, *Caliban*, p. 128.
[26] Ibid., pp. 119–20.

If that were all that Christ supplied it, the world would have gone on as before, and a little sect of ethical Christians might have taken its place alongside the Stoics or the Plotinists.

In Knox's view, a supernatural motive cannot derive from an ordinary man, but it could from a Person who is both divine (in its literal sense) and human, someone who can tell the rest of mankind what God wants of the human race. If Jesus is to be viewed in light of his concrete historical impact, the stamp he left on his disciples, it would be seen that it is not open to individuals to define Christ in a way most coincident with their tastes. Instead, one must accept a particular Christ, the Christ set forth in the earliest documents, in which one will find "that there was *a* dogma of the Incarnation, *a* dogma of the Atonement, *a* dogma of the Resurrection, in the writings of St. Paul". Everyone accepts the fact that Saint Paul wrote his letters within twenty years or so of Jesus' time. Yet there is little evidence of Christ as ethical teacher, and an abundance of evidence of Christ understood to be God in those letters. Hence "the idea that Jesus was a great moral teacher, and that men afterwards came to think he had risen from the dead is simply unhistorical; you are putting the cart before the horse".[27]

The case against the symposiasts is best made by themselves, when they admit their (and by implication, their readers') inability to arrive at any real knowledge of God. Arthur Conan Doyle,[28] speaking of Christ, says it "is not for our mosquito brains to say what degree of divinity was in him"; E. P. Oppenheim claims to hold "the religion of the man in the street—an attitude of, I hope, reverent ignorance as regards the great unsolved problems of life and death"; and Arnold Bennett refuses to "agitate myself over a matter which exceeds my mental powers".[29] But their humble retreat from reason is inconsistently practiced. When a traditional teaching is hauled before their tribunal, it is condemned as irrational. Needless to say, it is rarely the

[27] Ibid., p. 113.

[28] The rational side of Arthur Conan Doyle (1859–1930) is heralded in the authorized biography by John Dickson Carr, *The Life of Sir Arthur Conan Doyle* (New York: Harper and Brothers, 1949), who quickly glided over the last decade of his life. Julian Symons, in *Conan Doyle: Portrait of an Artist* (New York: Mysterious Press, 1979), notes that he spent over £250,000 promoting Spiritualism in the 1920s and reproduces copies of doctored photographs that Conan Doyle gullibly accepted as genuine evidence of fairies haunting gardens.

[29] Quoted in Knox, *Caliban*, p. 191–93.

statements of Popes or Councils or Doctors of the Church that are thus treated, since it would be too tiresome a process to look them up. Instead, it is those hazily remembered catechism lessons from childhood, which are easily portrayed as repugnant to the intelligence of the modern thinker. Knox calls attention to the double standard, questioning "why they believe in their reason when it tells them a thing is untrue, but will not use it to find out whether a thing is true—to find out, for example, whether a God exists". He continues: "Miss West gives us to understand that the doctrine of the Virgin Birth is nonsense; she does not say 'My mosquito brain finds it nonsense.' Mr. Beresford writes 'The dogmas of the Churches seem to me to be utterly at variance with the Spirit of Christ;' he does not write 'The dogmas of the Churches seem to my paltry little reason to be utterly at variance with the Spirit of Christ.' "[30]

Even trained philosophers show their blind spots in reasoning when it is a matter of seeing the hand of God behind existence. Bertrand Russell, the aristocratic Cambridge philosopher and mathematician, makes a cameo appearance in the cast of symposiasts to put forward his alternative solution to the question whether chance alone can account for the presence of thinking beings. In all the galaxies making up the universe, he postulates, it should not surprise us that complex organized life should emerge haphazardly somewhere. The immense number of opportunities cancels out the immense improbability of each occurrence. His exact words are, "Even if it is enormously improbable that the laws of chance will produce an organism capable of intelligence out of a casual selection of atoms, it is nevertheless probable that there will be in the Universe that very small number of such organisms that we do in fact find." Suitably disentangled, this sentence is interpreted by Knox as follows: "Of course it is enormously improbable that there should be any intelligent organisms at all, but it is quite probable that there should be one or two." In other words, it leaves the basic question still unanswered. It does, however, afford Knox the opportunity of devising an apt analogy: "If the police were to discover a human body in Mr. Russell's Saratoga trunk, he would not be able to satisfy them with the explanation that, among all the innumerable articles of luggage in the world, it is only natural that there

[30] Ibid.

should be some few which are large enough to contain a body. They would want to know how it got there."[31]

Was it a worthwhile exercise to joust with these opponents? Even from an aesthetic point of view, this type of controversial writing did not appeal to him. He had to weave together a catena of quotes from more than a dozen writers and, after letting them make their often diffuse and sometimes even self-contradictory points, subject them to the searching light of logic in his rebuttals. And if anyone was sensitive to the fact that verbal combat rarely leads to conversion, it was he.

And yet it is uncanny how the arguments, almost the very phraseology, of the symposiasts are still aired generations after they themselves have faded from memory. The modern self-help manualists have nothing to add to the litany of propositions put forward in the 1920s. Psychology had already been mined expressly to banish moral norms and justify self-indulgence. And the classics of polemical "comparative religion"—the works of Frazer, Tylor, Durkheim, and others—were at hand as courts of appeal for any popular disparager of Christianity. Ronald Knox entered the fray against the tabloid columnists of his day, but his essays exposing their haphazard approach to logic are hardly just period pieces. Caliban remains a prominent character before the footlights, and Grub Street is always ready to hammer out in print his appeals to the baser susceptibilities of a mass audience.

THE OMNISCIENTISTS

It is therefore the less surprising that two years after finishing Caliban off, Knox had once again to face him in hydra-headed form. Only now the opponents he faced in literary combat were more sophisticated than their newspaper-column predecessors. Veteran philosophical foes of Christianity like Julian Huxley, Bertrand Russell, and H. L. Mencken had written treatises devoted to discrediting traditional beliefs. Huxley in particular would later become a fixture on radio as one of the "Brains Trust", a trio of savants upon whom the BBC could rely to express weighty opinions on a wide spectrum of issues. (Russell was also to make guest appearances on this program toward the end of World War II.) Their books at least afforded Knox a more substantial

[31] Ibid., p. 47.

target than newspaper clippings did. But it also tended to make the resulting counteroffensive, *Broadcast Minds*, a somewhat more discursive work than *Caliban*, and his readers are forewarned that the tactics of these writers, who attempt to elevate their own secularist constructs into a suitable replacement for a moribund Christianity, require that one "must tap every corner of the edifice to find out where it rings hollow", and that can be a formidable exercise.[32]

The title of the book is nonetheless appropriate, since however recondite the argumentation of some of the tracts Knox analyzes, each volume reflects a fairly uniform and highly ubiquitous stance toward religion, one that a tractable radio listener could fall in with quite comfortably. Like the symposiasts, the more professorial commentators are keenly aware of contemporary fashions in religious belief and unbelief, and they both mold and mirror such fashions. Much more than their journalistic counterparts, however, they are expected to impress their readership with a broad knowledge of scientific matters and in particular to broadcast the triumph of modern science over the beleaguered defenders of Christianity.

It is axiomatic among them that science and religion are always at loggerheads. But since history could afford embarrassingly few instances outside the Galileo case to demonstrate that state of conflict, an aggressive apologetic was required. That apologetic is what distinguishes these thinkers, whom Knox dubs omniscientists: it was their intent as prophets of a new age "to bewilder the reader with a series of confusing impressions; to impress him with an air of wide reading; to present the wildest hypotheses as if they were facts; to manipulate his evidence in the interests of a thesis; to treat the modern age as something sharply distinct in its whole outlook from every age that has gone before it, and to base that distinction entirely on modern science".[33]

Preeminent among these apostles is Julian Huxley, the noted botanist and ornithologist who was a grandson of Thomas Henry Huxley, Darwin's most ardent champion.[34] In 1927, he wrote a book entitled

[32] Ronald Knox, *Broadcast Minds* (London: Sheed and Ward, 1934), p. 38.

[33] Ibid., p. 156.

[34] On the life of Julian Huxley, and that of other famous members of his family, see Ronald W. Clark, *The Huxleys* (New York: McGraw-Hill, 1968). Julian Huxley was born in 1888 and was a contemporary of Knox at Balliol College, Oxford. Huxley occupied the chair of zoology at King's College, London, in the late 1920s and early 1930s, before

Religion without Revelation, in which he attempted to show how the former could be retained even after dispensing with the latter. Much of the book is a hymn to the religion of Darwinian evolution, which colors his outlook on every important topic. But within its covers, he exploits a philosophical movement associated with the Protestant theologian Rudolf Otto, who argued that the existence of God is demonstrated subjectively, by the otherwise unaccountable religious attitude common to virtually all men. If one finds the idea of the holy, the sense of awe, and the need to pray so widespread among all cultures, surely that is a forceful argument for the reality of the object of that focused reverence, God himself. Huxley accepts the universality of these emotions but argues that their object need not be God:

> [I]n origin religion has nothing whatever to do with belief in a God or gods, or with abstract good as against abstract evil, or with the salvation of souls, or with obedience to this or that revelation. These are all later growths, more elaborate dwellings for the religious spirit. But it is equally true that, inevitably and universally as man's accumulated experience grows and his logic comes into play, he will find certain things and ideas to which this quality of sacredness seems of necessity to adhere.[35]

Knox is not impressed with Otto's approach. The apologist observes that psychology can explain away feelings and states of mind sufficiently to undermine any proof of the supernatural resting on such foundations. But it suits Huxley's purpose to present this approach as the most compelling that Christians can offer in defense of their beliefs. For him, it is one of three ways used to argue the merits of theism, the other two being an appeal to revelation and (obviously his own method) "an insistence upon the study of facts, and upon inductive reasoning from the facts".[36]

It does not escape Knox that Huxley conveniently forgets to include the traditional five proofs from reason among the philosophical armaments of believers nor that he fails to acknowledge that the Catholic

---

becoming secretary of the Zoological Gardens in London and, in the late 1940s, the director-general of UNESCO. He died in 1975.

[35] Julian Huxley, *Religion without Revelation* (1927; rev. ed., New York: Mentor, 1958), pp. 106–7.

[36] Ibid., p. 89.

Church maintains unambiguously that it is through reason, not revelation, that each and every person ought to be able to arrive at the certitude that God exists. To Huxley, philosophical theology can mean discussion only of a nebulous Absolute, and he rather theatrically refuses to identify such a being with "the rich, vivid, and compelling experience of divinity which is enjoyed by many religious persons". Indeed, it is "one of the two besetting vices of religious systems, to over-exalt the purely rational and therefore communicable elements of religion at the expense of the non-rational but deeper intuitions and felt experiences which are unique and personal, difficult or impossible of easy communication to others, and yet the true material of religion".[37]

Huxley advances his own philosophical outlook as the most plausible on the arbitrary grounds that the best arguments for God's existence are irrational ones, which, not surprisingly, he can mine to his advantage. That approach allows him to acknowledge the emotions but to redirect the reverential feelings away from a personal Being and toward art and nature. Furthermore, he argues that, even if philosophy could prove God's existence, "there would still remain such a huge unbridged gap between the two aspects of the one truth that the problem can scarcely be regarded as much nearer solution than before." The Absolute of the philosopher is so far removed from the God supplicated by pious peasants that it is not worth the sustained effort to seek any reconciliation between the two.

But supposing, contra Huxley, reason *can* posit a personal Absolute, why should that philosophical conclusion be presumed to encompass the entire definition of God? Knox will readily concede "that the Absolute as defined by philosophers is no more like a mystic's understanding of God than the formula is like the reality it represents—than the formula of red on the spectroscope, let us say, is like the experience of red—why should it be? You might as well complain that Mars as defined by astronomers is not a bit like the Mars experienced by a man who has actually been there. What does it matter whether it is like, so long as it is the same?"

And, again accepting Huxley's condition that the philosopher's insight can reveal little about that Deity, Knox concludes that "the problem

[37] Ibid., p. 94.

of God's existence, in the case supposed, is not merely 'nearer solution'; it is solved. And if God exists at all, whatever questions as to his nature remain over for discussion, it is at least certain that he has the first claim on our capacities of worship, before we start lavishing them, as Professor Huxley wants us to lavish them, on sunsets and sonatas in B."[38]

Huxley, far from being a rationalist, is awash in nature mysticism. He sedulously cultivates an association with Wordsworth, who could turn into sublime poetry the raptures he felt during a stroll through the countryside. Since Huxley none too modestly owns to the same sensitivity to beauty in nature, he deems himself competent to analyze more elevated spiritual states revealed in the writings of religious mystics, for to him nature mysticism is the source and explanation of religious mysticism. He even attempts his own definition of grace: "a special inner illumination and peace which comes when conflicts are resolved on a high plane, when aesthetic or intellectual insight is vouchsafed, whenever, in fact, an unexpected or at least undeserved moment of spiritual achievement is thrust on the mind". The person who can attain to this state is someone who has "a reverent approach to reality".[39] But as Knox observes, this attempt to hold sacred all of nature, without recognizing a God who is the Creator of all of nature, must necessarily reduce the sense of awe to but a commonplace emotion. "The Hindu holds the cow sacred," he notes, "but if he held it no more sacred than anything else, then neither the cow nor anything else would be sacred at all."[40]

[38] Knox, *Broadcast Minds*, pp. 54–55. The whole issue has been succinctly treated in Jean Danielou, *God and the Ways of Knowing* (Cleveland: Meridian Books, 1960), especially in the first two chapters, on the God of the pagans and the God of the philosophers.

[39] Knox, *Broadcast Minds*, pp. 85–87.

[40] Ibid. Dom John Chapman proposed an analogy that seems useful to distinguish between natural and supernatural mystical experience: "The door to the unseen is connatural to *natura integra* (Adam), but filled up with lumber by original sin. But, in some souls, there is a little light shining through, and if they blow out or shade their terrene candles and lamps, they begin to perceive this light.... They do not look through the crack, nor get any communication with God, yet they get an impression of a higher light somewhere, a reality outside this 'cosy little universe' in which they are shut up. These are the Nature-mystics, like Tennyson and Wordsworth, or the children of whom Wordsworth wrote, who so often have impressions of eternity and that Imperial Palace whence they came." In *The Spiritual Letters of Dom John Chapman, O.S.B.*, ed. Dom Roger Hudleston (London: Sheed and Ward, 1944), pp. 71–72.

Huxley presses on, asserting that religious ritual would find a place in his new world. He solemnly proclaims acts of "obeisance, kneeling, or prostration" to be appropriate, not just in appreciation of nature, but directly *to* nature. Here Knox must remind him, "[O]ur human make-up includes not only a sense of reverence, but a sense of irreverence; not only an appreciation of the numinous, but an appreciation of the humorous. . . . And the churches of Huxleyism—well, I am afraid I shall never be able to pay them a visit for fear of disgracing myself." [41]

Smitten with the grand design he is constructing, Huxley proposes a new interpretation of the Trinity:

> God the Father is a personification of the forces of non-human Nature; God the Holy Ghost represents all ideals; and God the Son personifies human nature at its highest, as actually incarnate in bodies and organized in minds, bridging the gulf between the other two, and between each of them and everyday human life. And the unity of the three persons as "One God" represents the fact that all these aspects of reality are inextricably connected.[42]

This elicits the following commentary from an unmoved Knox: "In fact, his trinity consists of the real, the human mind and the ideal. That, doubtless, is what the early Fathers would have meant if they had had the advantage of a scientific education—three persons in no God." [43]

Yet in the long run, Huxley's religion does not seem a prime candidate to excite fervent interest, since it prescribes an ersatz ritual involving formal acts of worship to nature, and hence "the public, I gravely fear, will accuse him of having taken away its God without even saving it the bother of going to church." [44]

Implicit, of course, in the countertheologizing of the atheist natural philosopher is the desire to rid mankind of the consciousness of sin and the responsibility of submitting human will to God's will. After contemplating mankind's evolving perfectibility, the rate of which evolution can be accelerated by wholesale conversion to his new religion, Huxley identifies the roadblocks to progress, chief of which appears

[41] Knox, *Broadcast Minds*, p. 88.

[42] Huxley, *Religion without Revelation*, p. 37.

[43] Knox, *Broadcast Minds*, pp. 89.

[44] Ibid., p. 238.

to be "the refusal of the Roman Catholic and other churches to discuss such subjects as divorce or birth-control in any reasonable spirit".[45] Thus quickly does he descend from his Wordsworthian heights and take up the banner of sexual freedom.

Bertrand Russell was less coy about his atheism than Julian Huxley, openly admitting his rebellion against the moral code in *The Conquest of Happiness*, the next work to attract Knox's attention. Russell had expended much of his intellectual capital throughout the first decade of the twentieth century in writing (in collaboration with fellow Cambridge philosopher Alfred North Whitehead) his monumental *Principia Mathematica*, and by the 1920s he had turned to producing popular tracts on socialism, education, industrialism, and marriage. Despite his reputation as a logic machine, he was prone to contradictory impulses of asceticism and self-centeredness, icy rationalism and emotionalism, which when superposed on his resolute disbelief in God ensured that happiness was rarely within his grasp.[46] It is not surprising then that he was drawn to analyze the roots of unhappiness, which he ascribes to three aberrant personality types meriting reprobation: narcissists, megalomaniacs, and sinners. By sinners, he means people with consciences that acknowledge sins, not people who are so hardened by sin that they lose any consciousness of sinning. "Do not be afraid of irreverence towards the memory of those who controlled your childhood", he asserts. People have been too long victimized by an ethic

> not derived from any study of the individual's duty to the community; because it was made up of old scraps of irrational taboos; and because it contained within itself elements of morbidness derived from the spiritual sickness that troubled the dying Roman Empire. Our nominal morality has been formulated by priests and mentally enslaved women. It is time that men who have to take a normal

[45] Huxley, *Religion without Revelation*, p. 179.

[46] Bertrand Russell (1872–1970) was the grandson of Lord John Russell, the mid-Victorian-era prime minister of England. A modern biographer has drawn attention to the following quote from Russell's autobiography: "I have loved a ghost, and in loving a ghost my inmost self has itself become spectral. I have therefore buried it deeper and deeper beneath layers of cheerfulness, affection and joy of life. But my most profound feelings have remained always solitary and have found in human things no companionship.... I am conscious that human affection is to me at bottom an attempt to escape from the vain search for God." Caroline Moorehead, *Bertrand Russell: A Life* (New York: Viking, 1993), pp. 183–84.

> part in the normal life of the world learned to rebel against this sickly nonsense.[47]

Clearly he is not targeting the scrupulous soul here but instead all those people who examine their consciences in light of Judaeo-Christian morality. The spiritual sickness plaguing the later Roman Empire and all subsequent cultures is Christianity itself. Russell regards the moral code as nothing but childhood prohibitions transferred illogically to adult life and advocates "free affections and wide interests" as the true key to happiness in life. "Such a man feels himself a citizen of the universe, enjoying freely the spectacle that it offers and the joys that it affords, untroubled by the thought of death because he feels himself not really separate from those who will come after him. It is in such profound instinctive union with the stream of life that the greatest joy is to be found."[48]

These avowals pepper a book that also contains much unexceptionable practical advice on happiness, in fact, some advice that could have come from Thomas à Kempis. But what perplexes Knox is the claim that a lack of self-examination will yield a life filled with zest. Russell suggests that the more impulsive person will enjoy life more, an outlook that, it should be noted, the advertising industry has assiduously exploited. To his mind, the person distracted by work or hobbies from considering the four last things is well-rounded and happy. The emphasis on zest is also a recurrent theme in the writings of the mountaineering Younghusband and the formidable amateur pugilist and batsman Conan Doyle. While Russell was not an athlete comparable to either of them, he was a prodigious tramper and cyclist, like many another English writer of the period, Knox included. But much as he enjoyed cycling about the countryside, Knox demurs from apotheosizing the brisk adventurous life as the ultimate good:

> Unless we are to identify happiness with a fatuous kind of cheerfulness which commonly makes a man quite intolerable to his neighbours, it must have its light and shade, its chastening influences. And a life which contains no recollection of past failure to warn us against future misconduct or spur us on to greater moral effort may

[47] Bertrand Russell, *The Conquest of Happiness* (London: George Allen and Unwin, 1929), pp. 104–5.

[48] Ibid., p. 248.

induce a sort of bovine contentment, bred of thoughtlessness, but is not human enough to deserve the name of happy.[49]

And if, as Russell maintains, the sense of sin must be eradicated if happiness is to be realized, what meaning can adhere ultimately to any action in life? "Life, as it dwells in Lord Russell's ambitions, is no longer a Pilgrim's Progress; it is only a constitutional, undertaken by a nervous hypochondriac for the benefit of his health."[50] A sense of acedia brought on by resignation to evil may be presumed to be one among the causes of despair in hell, as it is when even temporarily experienced on earth. No amount of suppression or talking away of sin can disguise what it is, an absence of good that inexorably pulls the person enmeshed in it downward. In a world of Bertrand Russell's making, a pallid and banal rather than a zest-filled existence looms in front of a literally demoralized mankind.

Whether H. L. Mencken truly qualifies as an omniscientist, or whether his forays into religious subjects merely reveal him to be a dyspeptic crank, the popularity of his *Treatise on the Gods* forced Knox to accord him some notice. Mencken lived in an intellectual environment further removed from the wellsprings of debate over religious origins than did Huxley. He was a Baltimore newspaperman, a second-generation agnostic German-American, and despite his admirable autodidacticism, he read little in history and philosophy. But he knew where he stood, and he is certainly no less reticent than Huxley about confecting theories to suit his village atheist leanings. But, unlike Russell's book, which retains a certain charm in its outspoken hedonism, Mencken's treatise is bowed down by its leaden catalogue of disparate facts strung together to demonstrate the preposterous nature of religious belief.[51]

[49] Knox, *Broadcast Minds*, p. 102.

[50] Ibid., p. 117. Reality soon overtook theory. After advocating equanimity and a benign view of marital infidelity, Russell found himself in the early 1930s in the midst of a divorce case with his second wife Dora (who was also a voluble advocate of free love), embittered by the issue of the control of their two young children.

[51] H. L. Mencken, *Treatise on the Gods* (reprint, New York: Alfred A. Knopf, 1959). This is the second edition, originally published in 1946, fifteen years after the first edition, and is listed as "corrected and rewritten". The corrections were primarily in response to criticism of anti-Jewish sentiments expressed in the first edition. His animadversions on Christianity stayed put, including a typically raucous sentence describing immigrants as "an invading horde of moron Catholics, swarming in from Ireland and French Canada" (p. 252).

Whenever he finds others' speculations at odds with his own, Mencken simply brands those opponents sarcastically as "the learned" and proceeds unruffled with his castle-building. Like Huxley, he lectures the reader on the growth of religion from earliest times among primitive cultures, blissfully unaware (or culpably unconcerned) that his thesis is contradicted by the mass of evidence being published at that very time by the Viennese ethnological school under the direction of Wilhelm Schmidt. Their data, gathered in hefty volumes from painstaking field research among the vanishing true primitive tribes still extant in the early twentieth century, offered overwhelming proof that primitive religion is predicated on the existence of a spiritual High God.[52] Mencken prefers the aprioristic nineteenth-century theory that religion evolved from magic or superstition and runs roughshod over the facts exploding that myth. "The learned," he says, "in their speculations regarding the genesis of religious ideas in primitive man, would get further and fare better if they disregarded the dubious analogies presented by the thinking of relatively advanced savages, prehistoric or of today, and addressed themselves instead to an examination of the thinking of very young children."[53] In other words, anthropologists should cast their scientific methodology to the winds and instead pursue an arbitrary notion (i.e., that primitive adults think like small children). Knox notes the convenience of the hypothesis favored by Mencken, given that "very young children cannot speak, and therefore you can put on their behaviour any sort of construction which happens to suit your book, uncontradicted."[54] It is far less complicated than having to shoehorn recalcitrant data into a neatly contrived outline.

Mencken (1880–1956) intended this volume to be up-to-date and comprehensive, and a recent biographer cites his privately recorded observation that it was his "best book, by far". See Terry Teachout, *The Skeptic: A Life of H. L. Mencken* (New York: Harper Collins, 2003), p. 245. That it hardly ranks as a work of scholarship is evident from Mencken's sources for Catholic teachings, which are taken almost exclusively from recent Benziger catalogues, with Cardinal Gibbons' *Faith of Our Fathers* being his chief quarry.

[52] See for example Wilhelm Schmidt, *The Origin and Growth of Religion* (New York: Dial Press, 1935), which assesses theories and presents evidence based on the common religious beliefs of primitives; also his *High Gods of North America* (London: Oxford University Press, 1933). A useful discussion of his work can be found in Ernest Brandewie, *Wilhelm Schmidt and the Origin of the Idea of God* (Lanham, Md.: University Press, 1983).

[53] Mencken, *Treatise on the Gods*, p. 41.

[54] Knox, *Broadcast Minds*, p. 130.

When he moves on to Catholicism, Mencken adopts an already well-trammeled path of the hostile inquirer: show the similarities between Catholic ritual and belief and pagan ritual and belief to demonstrate that all religion is cut from the same cloth. "Who introduced such things as the dogmas of the Trinity, the Virgin Birth, and the Atonement we do not know with any certainty. Jesus Himself was unaware of any of them, and His disciples were apparently little the wiser. Most of them were not new, but had been heard of in other religions, in one form or another, for years." [55]

The predictable next stage in the argument is to excite democratic ire over priestcraft's accumulation of dominion over the common man. First, however, Mencken lays the groundwork with his hypothetical prehistoric magician claiming control over the elements. The same caste appears in Christianity as the clergy who perform the sacred rituals that keep the laity in check. The reader is expected to be impressed by similarities between pagan sacrificial meals and the Mass; with the fact that non-Christians pray with beads; that a cross appears as a symbol in some pre-Christian religions; and that incense is not a Christian monopoly. The list of course is selective and is not subjected to too-close scrutiny. For example, was the pre-Christian cross in any way associated with crucifixion, or was it just a symbol, in fact rather hard to avoid when one starts to play with two straight lines? But it is the second leg of his theory, the one about the conniving priesthood, that elicits a pointed question from Knox:

> What Mr. Mencken would like to prove, and ought to be proving if he wants to show us that his thesis is worth anything, is that the ceremonies and rites of Christianity, like those (he would say) of other religions, were invented by priests in order to make money out of them, and in order to enhance the dignity of their own position. But it is just here that his argument is so weak. For, whatever he may say of the sixteenth-century Church in England, or of the nineteenth-century Church in America, it is quite evident that our ceremonies come down to us from times when our priests, far from deriving either dignity or profit from their calling, found in ordination only a short cut to the lions.[56]

[55] Mencken, *Treatise on the Gods*, p. 226.
[56] Knox, *Broadcast Minds*, p. 140.

Mencken exploits his reputation as a canny cynic to underpin his arguments in *Treatise on the Gods*. The journalist who sniffed out hucksters could be relied on by his public not to fall prey to any claimant that would sweep him off his feet. But it turns out that there is one such claimant—science. Science would remove mystery from the world and dethrone the clergy once and for all. Its cures would obviate prayer, its discoveries relieve mankind of the need for God:

> [C]ivilized man has become his own god. When difficulties confront him he no longer blames them upon the inscrutable enmity of remote and ineffable powers; he blames them upon his own ignorance and incompetence. And when he sets out to remedy that ignorance and to remove that incompetence he does not look to any such powers for light and leading; he puts his whole trust in his own enterprise and ingenuity. Not infrequently he overestimates his capacities and comes to grief, but his failures, at worst, are much fewer than the failures of his fathers. Does pestilence, on occasion, still baffle his medicine? Then it is surely less often than the pestilences of old baffled sacrifice and prayer. Does war remain to shame him before the bees, and wasteful and witless government to make him blush when he contemplates the ants? Then war at its most furious is still less cruel than Hell, and the harshest statutes ever devised by man have more equity and benevolence in them than the irrational and appalling jurisprudence of the Christian God.[57]

In retrospect the faith evinced by the believers in science in the 1920s seems almost touching: the simple faith of the atheist, which confounds the discoverer of order in nature with the Creator of order in nature and which confidently foresees the imminent subjection of all forces, natural and societal, obstructing the perfection of mankind.

Since practitioners of science are occasionally too reticent to claim these powers, it devolves on popularizers and synthesizers of scientific information to become their mouthpieces. Gerald Heard was the son of an Irish Anglican clergyman and had lost his religious beliefs in the course of pursuing studies that would have led to his ordination. By 1930, on the recommendation of Julian Huxley, he was serving as editor of the short-lived journal the *Realist*, having attained some fame as the author of *The Emergence of Man*, an excruciatingly sententious

[57] Mencken, *Treatise on the Gods*, pp. 252–53.

survey of civilization viewed as a progressive unfolding of human consciousness. A consummate omniscientist, he would soon be tapped by the BBC to serve as its first science commentator.

In the aforementioned book, Heard indulges in reconstructing primeval society just as Mencken does, with the scantest concern that any physical evidence might upset his tableaux. To illustrate his contention that mankind once lived in a state below that of individual consciousness, he imagines the ancestors of modern humans residing in a tree and experiencing their first warding off of wild animals and even their first dispatching of an infirm elder with some satisfaction:

> Yes, life was good. The group was healthy. Three nights ago an old one had slipped and fallen out of the Tree. The next morning it was still at the foot dragging a broken leg and whimpering. As they looked down on it, suddenly they felt it had become something disgusting, hostile. Someone ran to the deep cleft where a store of stones was always heaped and, picking one, flung it at the monster. As the stone struck, it yelped. At once half a dozen more struck it. It broke away stumbling toward the bush. The rest howled their excommunication at it. The next day as they hunted they came on scraps of its carcase. A lion had eaten it. But looking at it they no longer felt disgust or even interest. Would the Tree feel love, interest or disgust as it looked down on the leaves it had shed?[58]

Knox suggests that this fantasy could be accepted at face value only by a generation of readers already desensitized to the boundary between the real and the fictional by the convincing fakery of cinema. He then summarizes Heard's further recounting of the march of evolution as follows:

[58] Gerald Heard, *The Emergence of Man* (London: Jonathan Cape, 1931), p. 33. Heard (1889–1971) wrote books on anthropology, theology, and psychology, and even on flying saucers. He also wrote several novels of fantasy and the weirdly supernatural. After settling in southern California in the late 1930s, he came under the influence of Swami Prabhavananda, a practitioner of the Hindu Vedantic philosophy. Together with Aldous Huxley, Heard opened a college to propagate these teachings, but it soon folded. Heard continued throughout the remainder of his life to adhere to its message of striving for the experience of Reality through successive reincarnations. A brief biography by his longtime personal secretary Jay Michael Barrie, titled "Who Is Gerald Heard?" and available on a website devoted to Heard's teachings, must suffice, in the absence of any printed critical study, to satisfy the curiosity of the interested reader. See http://www.geraldheard.com.

> Several millenniums elapse, during which the audience are requested to keep their seats; a fresh reel follows. It features the interior of an Aurignacian cave. Aurignacian man is playing about with chunks (called nodules) of flint, which for no apparent reason he appears to regard as living animals, which "look at you like a toad" and "bite." For a creature which has been heaving stones at lions these long centuries back, man does not seem to have progressed very fast. Now he manages to discover, rather late in the day, that flint cuts; later, that it produces a spark. That leads, of course, to a fire, produced by accident, which makes the acorns in the neighborhood taste better.... Then somebody sees a bison's head; he traces it out, to make it look more complete, and next day by good luck a bison is killed; so we enter upon the new phase of (i.) Art, and (ii.) Religion. The man who can draw is thought of as a wizard who can lure animals to their destruction. It is all quite possible, just as possible as a hundred other theories of how those inventions were made, or what those pictures represented.[59]

Heard's gallop through prehistory and on to modernity ultimately leads to the great crisis in intellectual history, the contest between religion and science. The Catholic Church, in particular, is cast as the foe of scientific progress. "For not only was the monastic knowledge limited—a third-hand recollection of Greek discoveries—but it was debarred by authority from the spirit of free inquiry.... To question, to ask for proof, to experiment, this was to be lost and excommunicated and damned. And the monastic spirit wished to have it so. The spirit that sought the monastery and found in it its highest expression, was a spirit which called for authority and dreaded exploration."[60] Among other signs of backwardness he cites is the Church's alleged opposition to dissection of human bodies, omitting to mention that pre-Christian Rome and the Arab world prohibited the practice, while late medieval European surgeons had no qualms about it. Knox supposes he burdens the Church with opposition to it because "Vesalius was made to do penance by a visit to Jerusalem; but this was for cutting up, not a dead body, but a live one."[61]

[59] Knox, *Broadcast Minds*, pp. 162–63.
[60] Heard, *Emergence of Man*, p. 239.
[61] Knox, *Broadcast Minds*, p. 182.

Oddly enough for a promoter of science, Heard sums up his disquisition on the ups and downs of man's mental evolution with the authoritative pronouncement that man can know very little about the universe because he is simply unable to think in a detached, rational way. The self-contradiction of this intellectual stance is patent. "If man is incapable of detached apprehension," Knox wonders, "how can he prove anything? . . . Pitiless in our scepticism, we others are not content to stop short at doubting our own mental processes. We go further, and doubt Mr. Heard's." The logorrheic polymath's intellectual edifice totters under the withering shafts of clear reasoning.[62]

Obfuscation is displayed in pure form in John Langdon-Davies' book *Science and Common Sense*. His purpose is to show that the two modes of thinking about the world are mutually antagonistic. Common sense, he claims, is useful only for evolutionary survival and, if pressed any further, deceives the human mind. Space and time are not what they seem to be: "Just as the eye has been evolved in such a way that it sees a three-dimensional space, simply because the perception of any other kind of space never had a survival value to the animal, so the mind may have evolved so that the one-directional past-present-future seems real to it because that sort of idea is valuable for the survival of the fittest to survive."[63]

But science is based on brute facts, mostly of a subatomic nature. What the ordinary person supposes to be a chair isn't truly a chair; it is merely a conglomeration of electrons whizzing about nuclei, with mostly space in between. The only reality is what the physicist formulates as a mathematical relation among these particles. Hence "what things are, whether they exist at all and why, are questions which have no importance whatever, and fortunately so, since they can never be answered or even profitably discussed by the human intellect or any

[62] Knox, *Broadcast Minds*, p. 184. Heard's proclivity for indulging in the most arbitrary generalizations about societies and epochs renders somewhat perplexing Martin D'Arcy's devoting a lengthy appendix, in *The Meaning and Matter of History* (New York: Noonday Press, 1967), pp. 284–301, to a searching analysis of his thought. While alert to Heard's "fantastic guesswork" and "arbitrary assumptions", D'Arcy credits him with an honorable effort to explain the Fall and the resultant lack of integration afflicting mankind.

[63] John Langdon-Davies, *Science and Common Sense* (London: Hamish Hamilton, 1931), p. 111. Langdon-Davies (1897–1971) was a British journalist who is best known as a Marxist partisan of the Republican side in the Spanish Civil War.

super-intellect either."[64] Granted that the physicist is not focusing on metaphysical questions when working out the mathematical model of the relations between physical entities, there remain serious problems with Langdon-Davies' blanket dismissal of those questions. If, Knox responds, he supposes it

> a question of no importance, and one which cannot even be profitably discussed, whether things exist or not, how is he going to persuade us that relations between things have any objective existence? For a relation to subsist without the substances which it related would be worse than the survival of the grin after the disappearance of the Cheshire Cat."[65]

Langdon-Davies and many other interpreters of the modern physicists have a tendency to translate a feeling of uncertainty about common sense into a like uncertainty about moral and theological concepts that are buttressed by common sense. He asserts condescendingly that medieval theology grew to maturity when the earth was assumed to be composed of four elements. In response, Knox admits

> that sometimes they built quaint superstructures of scientific belief upon these premisses; St. Hilary informs us, for example, that salt is made out of fire and water, I have no notion why. But, torture my brain as I will, I cannot see where our common notions of religion and ethics are based upon one form of physical speculation rather than another. If somebody discovered tomorrow that it was all a mistake about atoms and electrons, and that after all there was not and could not be anything smaller than a molecule, I should not find my faith in any way strengthened, or the work of Christian apologetic one tittle easier. I can see why people think that Galileo has made the world harder for Christianity, or why Darwin has made the world harder for Christianity; I cannot for the life of me see how my friend Henry Moseley or any of those scientists who have followed up his researches into the nature of the atom have made the world harder for Christianity.... It is all very well to tell me that the chair I am sitting on is in reality a mass of whirling electrons, but it is I who am based on the chair, not my faith. St. Thomas never told me that it was not a mass of whirling electrons; and

[64] Ibid., p. 51.

[65] Knox, *Broadcast Minds*, pp. 202–3.

> even if he had, and I was now forced to disbelieve him, I should not therefore conclude that his speculations about the nature of God were equally inaccurate.[66]

But the champion of science has one more arrow in his quiver for the theist. The smallness of man in the immensity of the universe suggests true insignificance:

> [T]he natural theologian seems to take comfort in the thought that protoplasm is so complicated and behaves so differently from the rest of matter that the chemist who first made it, in the stress of an earlier geological age of storms and unrest, must have been a god indeed. . . . [I]t is therefore as well to modify our common-sense feeling that the coming of life—that is, the formation of certain highly complicated chemical combinations containing carbon—was a watershed in the history of the universe. The universe, were it to write its memories, would certainly devote a chapter to this, just as it would to the first appearance of elements which had the quality of magnetism and the other special qualities we have mentioned; but it is doubtful whether it would deserve a whole new volume.[67]

The anthropomorphism is overwrought, especially when Langdon-Davies assures his readers that the "universe must be assumed to love all its children equally", but a thinker who finds common sense a hindrance to understanding can only with difficulty avoid such ways of expressing himself. And since his reduction of reality to the physicist's tools necessarily does away with "the psychological entities about which we talk in everyday life whenever we discuss ourselves as conscious beings—consciousness itself, mind, emotion, will, reason, conscience", he cannot be expected to marvel that men alone of all inhabitants of the physical universe can comprehend its manifestations on the immense as well as the minuscule ends of the size spectrum. His lucubrations about the universe are possible only because he disproves them by thinking, even if he is not a particularly compelling specimen of a thinker.[68]

All the authors surveyed resort to ad hominem arguments in their zeal to blunt the appeal of Christianity. Knox set out to show that

[66] Ibid., pp. 211–12.

[67] Langdon-Davies, *Science and Common Sense*, pp. 147–48.

[68] Knox, *Broadcast Minds*, pp. 214–15.

their desire to deflect the inquiring mind off the path that leads to God involves them in self-contradictions, non sequiturs, or misinterpretations of historical or scientific fact. And often enough he touches on the underlying current driving them on, that at bottom the symposiasts and the omniscientists are seeking freedom from God because it relieves them of the duty of following an externally imposed moral law. In stark contrast to the reputations for personal asceticism attaching to many of the great heresiarchs of past eras, austerity of life is not one of the charisms inexorably drawing people to the new gospels. The modern apostles of unbelief tend usually to be found offering incense at the altar of birth control, sexual freedom, or some other totem of self-gratification.[69] That ensures their popularity with the broadcast media, which well appreciate the advantage to commercial revenues of exciting unrestrained appetites. The defender of philosophical and theological sanity is therefore really fighting simultaneously on two fronts—the open one of ideas, and the less overtly touted one of morals.

Perhaps the most egregious example of a writer who promoted a philosophy of materialism to lend intellectual respectability to his unprincipled behavior was H. G. Wells, who exerted a strong influence on many of the writers cited above. The liaison with Rebecca West was but one of his connections to the omniscientific coterie: the first study of his literary work was written by J. D. Beresford in 1915; it has already been mentioned that he was a close friend of Arnold Bennett, whose

[69] Langdon-Davies devotes the better part of a chapter—innocuously enough titled "What May I Do?"—to arguing the psychological benefits of solitary sexual activity. Mencken's advocacy of birth control is passionate, as the following excerpt reveals: "To a clergyman lying under a vow of chastity any act of sex is immoral, but his abhorrence of it naturally increases in proportion as it looks safe and is correspondingly tempting. As a prudent man, he is not much disturbed by invitations which carry their obvious and certain penalties; what shakes him is the enticement bare of any probable secular retribution. Ergo, the worst and damndest indulgence is that which goes unwhipped. So he teaches that it is no sin for a woman to bear a child to a drunken and worthless husband, even though she may believe with sound reason that it will be diseased and miserable all its life, but if she resorts to any mechanical or chemical device, however harmless, to prevent its birth, she is doomed by his penology to roast in Hell forever, along with the assassin of orphans and the scoundrel who forgets his Easter duty." Mencken, *Treatise on the Gods*, pp. 97–98. These sentiments may have been inspired by his dalliance in the late 1920s with a movie starlet. At age fifty, he married a gifted but tubercular Southern writer who died after five years of devoted care on his part. Mencken's writings were in general more outrageous than his personal life.

rise to literary fame from an obscure background closely mirrored his; he was a supporter of Gerald Heard's *Realist*; but most ominously, his persistent advocacy of selective breeding to eliminate what he labeled inferior races is echoed in many 1920s putatively scientific works.[70]

Passivity and the pull of inclinations prohibit a large audience from responding enthusiastically to a spokesman for the Church. But in *Caliban* and *Broadcast Minds*, Ronald Knox utilized disarming wit along with unrelenting logic to expose the intellectual shoddiness of a variety of attacks on Catholic belief. The circumstances of their composition, and the necessity of having to break up a narrative with so many quotes *in extenso* of the writers he was examining, militates against these books surviving as exemplars of his prose. Neither has been reissued since the 1930s, while *Religion without Revelation* and *Treatise on the Gods* have gone through new editions (of course without their authors amending any assertions in light of Knox's critiques) and continue subliminally to inform new generations of newspaper and television consumers. The old canards have legs, and that renders these works of Knox—out of print and uncommon to find even in the age of instantaneous communication—still topical.

[70] See, for a balanced treatment of his life and philosophy, Michael Coren, *The Invisible Man: The Life and Liberties of H. G. Wells* (New York: Atheneum, 1993). Coren quotes the following selections from a book Wells wrote in 1901: "And for the rest—those swarms of black and brown and yellow people who do not come into the needs of efficiency? Well, the world is not a charitable institution, and I take it they will have to go. The whole tenor and meaning of the world, as I see it, is that they have to go." And lest the reader misunderstand his point, he remarks that undesirables will be tolerated "only on sufferance, out of pity and patience, and on the understanding that they do not propagate; and I do not foresee any reason to suppose that they [the New Republic's rulers] will hesitate to kill when that sufferance is abused" (pp. 66–67).

CHAPTER FIVE

PARODIES GAINED

THE WORLD OF BARSETSHIRE

Ronald Knox was not an inveterate novel reader. The literary fashions of his age, with the exception of the detective story, did not compel his attention. The past had furnished sufficient works of genius to satisfy his tastes in fiction. There were authors and books he had grown up with, and to these he was attached, and to Anthony Trollope most of all. More precisely, his allegiance was to a subset of Anthony Trollope's immense output, the five novels comprising his history of the mythical county of Barsetshire in western England: *The Warden*, *Barchester Towers*, *Dr. Thorne*, *Framley Parsonage*, and *The Last Chronicle of Barset*. Beginning with a relatively brief account of a clergyman's travails over retaining the wardenship of a hospital for twelve retired laborers, Trollope expanded his cast of characters in subsequent, far lengthier novels (the final installment in the series running to over nine hundred pages of close print in one popular edition) to include the entire clerical population and most of the leading gentry within a twenty-or-so-mile radius of the cathedral city of Barchester. The mild warden Septimus Harding; his son-in-law Archdeacon Grantly, who leads the high and dry clerical faction against the weak, Low Church bishop Proudie; and above all, the bishop's domineering helpmate, a truly classic comic figure—these and numerous other characters became as real as life to readers of the installments of these tales as they appeared in the 1850s and 1860s. That they should still be popular among the children of a clerical household after the turn of the century is hardly surprising. And yet, by the time Knox reached adulthood, Trollope's popularity among his countrymen had considerably waned.

But not with Knox. As with the epic journey of Aeneas and the escapades of Sherlock Holmes, the doings of the Barsetshire personages were worthy of constant revisiting and meticulous study. He wrote several essays attempting to explain their appeal and, not satisfied with those efforts, yielded to the challenge of emulation, one of his favorite literary pastimes, and wrote a sequel to the series in a style consciously patterned on that of Trollope. He was not the first writer to attempt such a feat. Thackeray had looked into the future of some of Sir Walter Scott's characters in *Ivanhoe*, penning a lengthy addendum to the tendentious potboiler of the Laird of Abbotsford, which, true to form, was a pasquinade rather than homage.[1] Knox would be far more respectful of his prototype. There was something fixed and reassuring about mid-Victorian Barsetshire:

> a world we were not born into, yet one that coloured for us the outlook of boyhood, when Archdeacons really preserved and drank port and quoted Horace, and country doctors dared to roll their own pills, and Lady Luftons brooded like a visible Providence over the country-side, and old Hiram's will, violated though it might be in the letter, was better kept in the spirit than our modern Quiverfuls keep it, and clerical controversies, however disedifying, did at least command the attention of the whole reading public.[2]

But it was more even than the aura of comfortableness it exuded. Trollope's was a voice, however seemingly flippant, for conservatism:

> For a moment, when he sketched out the plot of *The Warden*, Trollope half believed that he was on the side of the reformers. But when, in the first chapter of *Barchester Towers*, the Government went out just in time to secure the appointment of a Whig Bishop, the die was cast; from that point onwards the series is an epic of reaction; all Trollope's heroes are Conservatives, all his villains are Whigs. In the political novels, politics are only a game; in the "clerical" novels all is in deadly earnest—every contested election, every vacant

[1] Rowena, the fair maiden that Wilfrid of Ivanhoe marries at the end of the Scott novel, is a cold calculating shrew in the sequel, and King Richard a murderous tyrant, while Robin Hood is co-opted into the squirearchy, and Wilfrid slaughters French and Moorish combatants through ripe middle age. See "Rebecca and Rowena", in W. M. Thackeray, *Burlesques* (Boston: Estes and Lauriat, n.d.), pp. 267–321.

[2] Ronald Knox, "A Ramble in Barsetshire", in *Essays in Satire* (1928; reprint, New York: Sheed and Ward, 1955), p. 197.

> prebend, begins to matter. He could not save the old order of things, the world of privilege he so intimately loved, but his sympathies have embalmed the unavailing conflict.[3]

Ever ready to focus the techniques of the higher criticism on a body of writing—the better to show up the method's inevitable inbuilt presuppositions—Knox subjected the novels to searching inquiry to establish inconsistencies. Now, as Trollope himself boasted, and his biographers have amply documented, he was notoriously devoted to his craft for pecuniary gain and would no sooner be done with one manuscript than he would be starting on the next. Day in and day out, a hefty quota of words would be churned out, with no particular attention paid to ensuring strict conformity with previously penned segments.[4] For all that, the continuity in the Barsetshire series is quite remarkable, and the tying together of loose ends ingenious. The higher critic would have it otherwise, however. After using internal evidence to posit the dates for each novel's events, Knox details the indictment, beginning with Mrs. Proudie's age, which shows an unaccountable difference of at least six years in the two novels that feature her prominently. And it gets worse:

> Griselda Grantly is already seventeen in *Barchester Towers*: how comes it that in *Framley Parsonage*, when she ought to be twenty-three, she can be described as "little older" than Lucy Robarts, who is sixteen? Henry Grantly was her elder brother, and in the *Last Chronicle* he is under thirty; in *The Warden*, then, she should be less than nine, yet she has grown to be seventeen in the five years that have elapsed before *Barchester Towers*. Finally, Miss Dunstable is only thirty in *Dr. Thorne*, yet in *Framley Parsonage*, five years later, she is described as "well over forty." Homer, it seems, has nodded.[5]

There are problems too with geography, which Knox solves with a detailed map, which reconciles some very problematic trips taken over the years by characters. Interestingly, he seems unaware that Trollope

[3] Ronald Knox, "The Barsetshire Novels", in *Literary Distractions* (New York: Sheed and Ward, 1958), p. 143.

[4] See for example the excellent literary biography by James Pope Hennessy, *Anthony Trollope* (Boston: Little, Brown and Company, 1971).

[5] Knox, *Essays in Satire*, p. 195.

himself had sketched a map of Barsetshire, which bears only a passing resemblance to Knox's but is fraught with difficulties.

Needless to say, this cataloguing of minor errors is an exercise in shoring up Trollope's reputation rather than undermining it. Only the most devoted of admirers could expend the time to comb through some three thousand pages of chronicles and register discrepancies even the careful reader—not to mention the author—would miss. (By contrast, J. R. R. Tolkien spent much of his later decades reconciling minor linguistic and plot-related difficulties and lacunae brought to his attention by legions of devotees of *The Lord of the Rings*, a singular act of paternal care that Trollope would find incomprehensible.)[6]

But Knox's finest tribute was his exercise in imitation. As he noted of this mythical county in his prologue to *Barchester Pilgrimage* (1935), it "was a welcome escape from real life; like a fly in amber, it preserved for ever a moment of history".[7]

Trollope abandoned Barsetshire in 1867, turning his attention more to political novels and travelogues. But suppose instead Barchester to have lived on, the old standbys fading out while bequeathing their estates and their ecclesiastical pursuits to their heirs. How would the succeeding generations of residents fare in late Victorian and post-Victorian England? It would not be the first time Knox attempted a chronicle of this kind. Recall that in 1923 he had Opal Porstock reminisce about the decades leading up to 1988; now he would fill in the decades from the 1870s to the 1930s against a known backdrop but projecting how the descendants of the immortalized heroes of Barchester would act in that setting.

Knox begins with the career of young Johnny Bold, son of John and Eleanor Bold, stepson of the dean Arabin whom Eleanor (who is the daughter of Septimus Harding) marries after her first husband's early death. Johnny never figures in the Trollope novels past his early childhood, but he must be a young man by the 1870s, where the Knox narrative picks up his trail. He has become a medical practitioner and, much to the dismay of his High Anglican stepfather, has embraced agnosticism à la Thomas Huxley. In doing so, he frightens off his devout fiancée, only to fall under the spell of the infamous

[6] See Humphrey Carpenter, *Tolkien: A Biography* (New York: Ballantine Books, 1978).
[7] Ronald Knox, *Barchester Pilgrimage* (New York: Sheed and Ward, 1935), p. 2.

Signora Neroni on the rebound. This siren captivated many eligible bachelors in *Barchester Towers* despite her questionable past and her permanently injured feet, which required her to be sofa-bound during her interviews with her suitors. Now fiftyish, she has lost none of her facial beauty, but her cynicism about life and love still jars the doctor, whose cynicism extends only to religious truth. He proposes to her but flees when she tells him her former husband is still alive, a testimonial of course to the vestigial morality still clinging to the first generation of intellectuals who abandoned God.

The eponymous Dr. Thorne and Emily Dunstable had wed when he was in his fifties and she somewhere around forty and are not credited with children by Trollope in the later novels, but Knox grants them two sons, born (with some literary license) ten years apart. The younger, Marmaduke, seeks out the artistic crowd in Barchester:

> It was a set that belonged to the past; its great days had gone by, a dozen years before; but it was kept alive by *revenants* [ghosts] from that earlier period, who had the powers of fascination which thirty will always have over eighteen. Thus it was that Marmaduke Thorne learned to talk very slowly indeed, with a very clear pronunciation of consonants; and to talk languidly, as if it were really rather a nuisance to have to say anything at all, and a great casting of pearls before swine to make such clever remarks before his present company.[8]

Failing to impress Bishop Grantly (the archdeacon's younger son who has assumed the see after the death of Bishop Proudie's successor), Marmaduke flirts with the idea of becoming a Catholic priest before flirting with and then successfully wooing a rich American girl whose half sister is Mary Thorne Gresham, the doctor's niece. The reader is also introduced to the next generation of Greshams, who are still (as in *Dr. Thorne*) directed in social matters by their more aristocratic relatives, the De Courcys. But the more dignified demeanor of the mid-nineteenth-century forebears has given way to a rather frenetic search for thrills, so that the turn-of-the-century Lady De Courcy sounds very much like Margo Metroland, Evelyn Waugh's personification of 1920s vacuity.

[8] Ibid., pp. 61–62.

The early 1900s would not be complete without a Modernist theologian, and Knox puts forward Theophylact Crawley-Grantly in that role, grandson of the archdeacon and of the Reverend Josiah Crawley, the morbid Evangelical parson whose alleged theft of a check sets in motion all the events recorded in *The Last Chronicle of Barset*. Theophylact is as earnest as the *Foundations* theologians were, and no doubt the description of him owes something to one or more of those authors. He delivers a sermon at the cathedral, which opens by casting doubt on the historicity of Joshua and then proceeds to demythologize the entire Old Testament, thereby earning a reputation:

> He became, all at once, a familiar figure in Barchester; his shambling walk, his truculent look, his old-fashioned white tie (for by this time even the Low Church clergy of Barchester had adopted that collar which Dr. Catacomb, fifty years before, had derided as "Roman"); as well as the straw boater—white, none of your speckled compromises—which proclaimed his repudiation of clericalism. For it was an axiom with Mr. Crawley-Grantly, that the clergy should not seek to distinguish themselves from the laity by any peculiarities of appearance; although, as often happens in the case of such men, Providence had endowed him with so unmistakably clerical a face as had earned him the nick-name of "Sky-pilot" when he was still running about in cut-shorts and a woolen jersey at school.[9]

But then the Great War casts a pall over all other topics, and Mr. Crawley-Grantly regains his former notoriety only by preaching a sermon against forced conscription. The papers, which had rallied to his defense when his heresies were theological, now brand him a partisan of Germany, and he loses an appointment to a bishopric.

Meanwhile, the county is changing: Hogglestock, which in Trollope's chronicles was the site of Dr. Crawley's impoverished parish serving the local brickmakers, is now a manufacturing center. Demand for earthenware and wartime munitions work have combined to feed Hogglestock's growth so that it now outstrips the cathedral city in population. And there is now a Catholic see there, whose incumbent is the grandson of the erstwhile manager of the Gresham family estate. An opportunity to compare forces arises in 1925, when both the Catholic and Anglican communities hold separate pilgrimages in honor of

[9] Ibid., pp. 148–49.

the one-thousandth anniversary of the death of Saint Ewold. The Catholics, who number some ten thousand, come from as far away as London and congregate around the former site of the saint's miraculous well. The Established Church procession is far more resplendent, with the High Church faction guaranteeing the presence of copes and miters and thurifers but with the countervailing Low Church element requiring the absence of incense and litanies. And yet

> [t]here was a curious detachment about the citizens of Barchester when the procession went past, though naturally they stood there to watch it, and some few straggled on behind to listen to the sermon. They did not quite know whether to takes their pipes out of their mouths; nor did they register any interest, except in identifying some familiar figure in the *cortège* [procession]. On the whole, I am inclined to think that the citizens of Barchester did not feel it was any concern of theirs; it was no more a part of them than the Catholic procession which they witnessed, still gaping, a fortnight afterwards.[10]

The last vignette in this coda revolves around Hiram's Hospital and its warden, Septimus Arabin, grandson of Dean Arabin and great-grandson of Septimus Harding. The symmetry, for Hiram's was also Mr. Harding's charge, affords a neat closure to the cycle. But the hospital is no longer a home for valetudinarian workmen; it is now a flourishing public school, and Warden Arabin is being feted for his success in molding young manhood for the challenges of modern society five hundred years after Hiram's bequest in 1434. Mr. Arabin is undoubtedly highly appreciated: no one minds that he does not subscribe to the Thirty-nine Articles on the ground that he finds any theology emphasizing grace irrelevant. But he marries his secretary, Miss Stanhope (who happens to be the niece of the signora Neroni) despite the fact that she is a divorcée. The clergy attached to the cathedral are now in a quandary: on the one hand, the marriage seems to set a bad example to the boys; on the other, they don't expect the Established Church to hold the line on remarriage of divorced persons for long. They compromise by deputing the most liberal among them to ask Mr. Arabin to resign. But he has already decided to give up the wardenship, not from moral scruples about his own status, but

[10] Ibid., pp. 183–84.

simply because society has changed so completely that a public school education is obsolete. The economic hard times of the 1930s, superposed on the changes brought about by the Great War, have left enterprises based purely on secular affairs reeling. The slow slide since the 1870s, however, is most clearly brought home in the altered outlook on divorce: the rebellious agnostic of the Victorian era who nevertheless clung to certain dictates of the moral order has given way to the bland conformist who is equally indifferent to religion and to the moral law.

Barchester Pilgrimage was written in a style that is recognizably Trollopian in places, especially the asides to the reader in which a character's course of action comes in for criticism. Yet the relative brevity of the book with its whirlwind tour of seventy years of Barchester life is hardly characteristic of the loquacious Trollope, who could weave whole novels out of a few commonplace events. Trollope was out of favor in the more brisk-paced 1930s, so the whole enterprise was somewhat risky, as Maurice Baring (to whom the novel was dedicated) warned Knox. But Trollope has regained popularity in recent decades, and interestingly, Knox's act of homage, long out of print, was reissued by the Trollope Society in a 1990 edition.

ESSAYS IN SATIRE

One of Knox's short assessments of the Barsetshire novels was packaged with a number of similarly conceived writings in *Essays in Satire*, which was first published in 1928. Several of the other entries carry out for other literary works what Knox threatened to do for the Barsetshire series, i.e., a thorough examination of their authenticity as the product of a single genius. Here, for example, is found his classic "Studies in the Literature of Sherlock Holmes". This composition actually dates from 1911 and was taken seriously enough by Conan Doyle to merit a rejoinder. Knox subdivides the Holmes stories into eleven component parts, according each part a pedantic Greek label, just as the German critics of the Gospel would do:

> The first part is the Prooimion, a homely Baker Street scene, with invaluable personal touches, and sometimes a demonstration by the detective. Then follows the first explanation, or exegesis kata ton

> diakonta, that is, the client's statement of the case, followed by the Ichneusis, or personal investigation, often including the famous floor-walk on hands and knees. No. 1 is invariable, Nos. 2 and 3 almost always present. Nos. 4, 5 and 6 are less necessary: they include the Anaskeue, or refutation on its own merits of the official theory of Scotland Yard, the first Promenusis (exoterike) which gives a few stray hints to the police, which they never adopt, and the second Promenusis (esoterike), which adumbrates the true course of the investigation to Watson alone.[11]

And so forth, through a catalogue of parallelisms and inconsistencies that force the academic investigator to the conclusion that only certain of the Holmes narratives are historical, while the rest are fabrications by the Watson narrator. A peroration on the meaning of Watson's bowler hat could have come from the pen of Salomon Reinach or James Frazer:

> It is his apex of wool, his petasus of invisibility, his *mitra pretiosa* [precious miter], his Triple tiara, his halo. The bowler stands for all that is immutable and irrefragable, for law and justice, for the established order of things, for the rights of humanity, for the triumph of the man over the brute. It towers colossal over sordidness and misery and crime: it shames and heals and hallows. The curve of its brim is the curve of perfect symmetry, the rotundity of its crown is the rotundity of the world. "From the hats of Holmes's clients," writes Professor Sabaglione, "deduce themselves the traits, the habits, the idiosyncracies: from the hat of Guatson deduces itself his character." Watson is everything to Holmes—his medical adviser, his foil, his philosopher, his confidant, his sympathizer, his biographer, his domestic chaplain, but above all things else he stands exalted in history as the wearer of the unconquerable bowler hat.[12]

The satire becomes a bit wearisome when applied in later chapters to *Pilgrim's Progress* and to Boswell's *Life of Johnson*, but in fairness to

[11] Ronald Knox, "Studies in the Literature of Sherlock Holmes", in *Essays in Satire*, pp. 158–59.

[12] Ibid., pp. 164–65. Knox would henceforth be remembered as much for his contributions to Sherlockiana as for his Bible translation. In later years, in the midst of myriad other writing tasks, he contributed a chapter entitled "The Mystery of Mycroft" to a book edited by H. W. Bell, *Baker-Street Studies* (London: Constable and Co., 1934), pp. 131–58, in which he develops a coherent case for Sherlock Holmes' elder brother being in the pay of the evil Dr. Moriarty.

Knox all these pieces were written years apart and published separately in different journals before being placed in perhaps too-close proximity in this volume. In a somewhat different vein, however, is his cryptographic solution of the authorship of Tennyson's *In Memoriam*, which, by analogy with the Baconian hypothesis of who wrote Shakespeare, must have been composed by somebody other than Tennyson. By devising a wholly arbitrary mathematical series, Knox isolates eleven lines from 113 cantos to reveal the secret. But detailed anagrammatic work remains to be done:

> The letters of "I held it truth, with him who sings" yield, with a little arrangement, the following rather intriguing result: "Who is writing this? H. M. luteth hid." It was, no doubt, the word "harp" in the next line of the poem that suggested to the cryptographer the rather fanciful word "luteth." The implication is plain enough; the author of this poem is not its reputed author; somebody described as H. M. is really writing the poem, but prefers to remain hidden, that is anonymous. So far we have not much to go upon in the way of positive information; after all, there must have been plenty of people writing in 1850 who would answer to the required initials. We turn on, then, impatiently to canto 3, line 2, and are met with a startling announcement. "O priestess in the vaults of death" reads quite unmistakably "V.R.I. the poetess. Alf T. has no duties." Astounding—impossible! Yet there it is in black and white; there is no getting over the documentary evidence.[13]

More relentless reshuffling of the letters in the chosen lines lends credence to the suspicion that the reigning queen was the hidden creative hand:

> The tenth cryptogram raises the question—If Victoria was the authoress of the poem, how was it that Tennyson came to supply the cipher? There must, it seems, have been collaboration here, and there could be few more generous tributes than that which is paid in the words "Such splendid purpose in his eyes." For these, when read according to the cryptographer's intention, give you: "She lisp'd in sinuous ciphers deep"—the praise is the praise of Victoria, but the voice is the voice of Tennyson. And yet the man who could write such a line as that could take pride in signing himself at the

[13] Ibid., pp. 228–29.

conclusion of his cryptographic message: "A potent voice of Parliament," which, it need hardly be pointed out, stands for "Alf, poet-pen to Victoria. Amen."[14]

Absolute and Abitofhell, the first salvo at the *Foundations* authors, is reprinted in this collection, as is *Reunion All Round*, the 1914 satire on religious indifference masquerading as genuine ecumenism that infected official Anglican pronouncements. The particular incident that had occasioned this broadside in the manner of Jonathan Swift was a communion-sharing service between certain African Free Church Protestants and the local Anglican dioceses. Coupled with the loose doctrinal language of *Foundations*, it alarmed the "advanced" Anglicans, who of course at that time still included Knox among their number. The full title of the pamphlet is itself only slightly more wordy than the interminable title pages of seventeenth- and eighteenth-century tracts: *Reunion All Round, or Jael's hammer laid aside, and the milk of human kindness beaten up into butter and served in a Lordly dish. Being a plea for the inclusion within the Church of England of all Mahometans, Jews, Buddhists, Brahmins, Papists and Atheists, submitted to the consideration of the British Public.* Jael is the Kenite tribeswoman in the Book of Judges who drives a tent peg into the head of the recumbent Sisera, a Canaanite general who has just been routed by the Israelites. Interestingly, this minor incident in the fortunes of the Israelites looms large in a subplot in *The Last Chronicle of Barset*, when a painter executes a portrait of a rich young woman he is scheming to marry while she poses in the role of Jael about to strike the blow. So the reference to Jael is as much a sign of Knox's saturation in the Barsetshire novels as of his redoubtable knowledge of Old Testament minutiae.

The essay takes a benevolent attitude toward the distinctive notes of the several religions with which prospective unification with the Anglican Church is sought. All that is required is the allaying of a few scruples here and there and some tolerance for individual charisms. For example, the Muslim teaching on a plurality of wives need be amended only by allowing also a plurality of husbands to "meet a long-felt demand on the part of the lower classes in our country, as well as recognizing an existing practice in the case of their superiors

[14] Ibid., p. 234.

in social rank." Their habit of praying to the East for their devotions could be modified suitably to English inclinations by worshipping toward the West, the American centers of commerce. And their prohibition of bacon and alcohol (which would at first sight appear to be an insuperable obstacle to reunion) could be enshrined in the Book of Common Prayer alongside its equally ignored rubrics about Friday abstinence and fasting in Lent:

> This will surely be calculated to ease the consciences of our Eastern brethren, since it will show them clearly what the mind of our Church is upon this matter; whereas on the other hand, we shall have no scruple at all about the eating of the pig, but will continue to eat our pork chops on every day of the year, with the same assurance as we eat mutton on all Fridays: in short, no one will be at all affected in his manner of life, except a few scurvy High-churchmen, who impiously try to gain merit in the sight of heaven by observing these and other like ordinances imposed by the founders of our Church, instead of contenting themselves with a spiritual fast, which is far more acceptable to God, and far less prejudicial to the digestion.[15]

Even the Church of Rome might expect to enter the fold, once the pestiferous race of Irish is extirpated: "The Pope himself I would allow to take rank as a retired missionary bishop, thus leaving him the insignia without any sphere in which to exercise, or income with which to abuse it. The cardinals I would disperse among the common-rooms of Oxford and Cambridge, where they could exercise to the full their talent for intrigue without having any serious effect, for good or ill, upon the destinies of the nation."[16]

Having absorbed these previous groups, the broadened Anglican communion will have little trouble welcoming atheists into its bosom:

> [W]hereas the sectaries of one religion differ from those of another over a whole multitude of points, as niceties of ritual, quibbles of

[15] Ronald Knox, *Reunion All Round* (Rochester, Kent, U.K.: Faith, n.d.), p. 10. This pamphlet reprint from the early 1970s contains an introduction by David Knowles, the great medieval historian of the English monasteries, who feels compelled to warn its readers, that "satire always has in it an element of exaggeration and paradox. The true ecumenist, if he remembers this, will rise from reading Knox with his withers unwrung."

[16] Ibid., p. 16.

> doctrine, forms and postures in the recitation of prayer, etc.; in the case of the atheists we have only one single quarrel to patch up, namely as to whether any God exists, or not. If we could but ease their consciences on this matter, it is clear they would have no difficulty in accepting our forms and fashions of worship, having no inherited prejudice in favour of any other. There would be no straining at gnats, if they could but be brought to swallow the camel. I submit it, therefore, with all deference to our theologians, whether they could not find it possible to allow, that as God is immanent and yet transcendent, so we cannot see the whole truth, but only an aspect of the truth, until we have reconciled ourselves to the last final antinomy, that God is both existent and non-existent? We, who are conscious of the Supreme Being as existent, and those others who are conscious of Him as non-existent, are each of us looking at only one half of the truth, one side, as it were, of the shield; and we can surely hope that when we have studied each other's points of view, and come to understand them a little better, by common discussion and common worship, we shall all of us recognize the Divine Governor of the Universe as One who exists, yet does not exist, causes sin, yet hates it, hates it, yet does not punish it and promises us in heaven a happiness, which we shall not have any consciousness to enjoy.[17]

An introductory chapter in *Essays in Satire* offers a mock-serious explanation of the distinction between humor and satire, complete with an erudite survey of relevant literary milestones, reminiscent of the scholarly apparatus he employs in his preface to *A Book of Acrostics*. Humor, he concludes, is satire gone to seed. Satire is the normal outlet of human expression "born to scourge the persistent and ever-recurrent follies of the human creature as such". It would be difficult to imagine the younger Knox writing (or for that matter spending much time reading) anything like the novels of P. G. Wodehouse. And yet, among contemporaneous authors, he cites only three who are genuine satirists as opposed to humorists: W. H. Mallock, Samuel Butler, and Hilaire Belloc. Then there are those writers, George Meredith in *The Egoist*[18] for example, who employ irony rather than satire. "Irony

[17] Ibid., pp. 17–18.

[18] This celebrated novel offers a searing psychological portrait of an utterly self-absorbed bachelor, Sir Willoughby Patterne, who is consumed by the desire to marry the perfect young woman so that she can render him homage, and his acquaintances admire

is content to describe men exactly as they are, to accept them profoundly at their own valuation, and then to laugh up its sleeve." What of the modern predilection for the humorist, whose efforts he regards as ephemeral, fashions in humor changing so much from age to age (even though Wodehouse's continuing freshness belies that assertion)? He claims that it has been "debauching our sense of the ridiculous to such an extent as to leave no room for the disciplinary effect of satire".[19]

REFLECTIONS ON PROSE AND POETRY

No doubt satire provided some solace when the memory of a church yielding to every whim of modern society was still fresh in his mind. But it only irritated people like Arnold Lunn, who thought Knox was too hard on the Anglican clergy in his fiction. The ideas he lampooned, however, die hard, and their continuing reappearance in different circumstances breathes new life into pamphlets like *Reunion All Round*. In his later years, Knox did not resort to the chastening weapon. There is a world of difference between the mellow reflections on secular topics collected in the posthumous *Literary Distractions* (1958) and the barbed parodies contained in the volume of essays collected three decades earlier. In fact, self-deprecating humor pure and simple is sprinkled throughout many of these later essays. Consider the following specimen from a 1951 lecture on his difficulty in expressing himself in French, a language he could read with enough alacrity to digest Abbé Bremond's eleven-tome work *Histoire Littéraire du Sentiment Religieux en France* (Literary history of religious thought in France) and later to translate the writings of Saint Thérèse of Lisieux:

> If I were going out for a country walk with a Frenchman, I should find find myself immediately wanting to express more sudden and arresting thoughts. I should want to say, for example, "That cow

---

him the more for his effortless attractiveness. A representative sample of Meredith's style is afforded by the following description of his central character as he courts the young and beautiful Clara Middleton: "It was on the full river of love that Sir Willoughby supposed the whole floating bulk of his personality to be securely sustained; and therefore it was that, believing himself swimming at his ease, he discoursed of himself." George Meredith, *The Egoist: A Comedy in Narrative* (New York: Book League of America, n.d.), p. 80.

[19] Knox, *Essays in Satire*, p. 41.

> looks rather like a parson I know"—I am merely suggesting that by way of illustration. Well, it ought to be a simple sentence enough. But I am handicapped from the start by the consciousness that it is not what my French friend is expecting me to say; it will have to be done neatly and snappily if I am to get it across. "Cette vache-là," that part is all right; no difficulty about the gender of the beast; fortunately we are not talking German, in which a cow might quite possibly be neuter. "Cette vache-là"—or perhaps better "cette vache-ci" when you come to think of it, this one here, to distinguish it from the other cows which are *là*. "Looks like"—that is much more difficult. The word I want is *ressembler* or *rassembler*, I am not quite sure which; and the other verb, whichever is the wrong one, probably means to reassemble. Also, I cannot for the life of me remember whether it is an ordinary verb or a reflexive verb. It would be silly to find yourself saying, "That cow reassembles itself."[20]

Even topics that are ripe for satire—like the effort of the earnest Evangelical Canon Townsend to gain an audience with Pope Pius IX in 1850 to convert him to a religion suitable for an Englishman, or the retrospect on the hideously utilitarian poetry of the Scottish physician in the West Indies who wrote Miltonian blank verse on the sugar refining industry—are handled with the deft understatement of a mature chronicler of man's frailties. The latter essay is surely worth a glance. The perpetrator of "The Sugar-Cane: A Poem in Four Books", published in 1764, was James Grainger, and while it is only fair to note that his opus was panned by his contemporaries, it did make the cut in an anthology of British poets compiled in 1822. What caught Knox's eye was its achievement of bathos, which "demands a perfect craftsmanship in verse, no false rhymes, no missing caesuras, that bad taste, bad sentiment, bad imagination may find its just and inevitable expression. Bad verse you may find anywhere; bad poetry is of its essence a *faux ménage* (marriage of incompatibles)—verbal felicity married to mental imbecility."[21] That Grainger saw Virgil as his model only compounds the folly of his enterprise:

[20] Knox, "French with Tears", in *Literary Distractions*, pp. 225–26. *Là* means "there" and *ci* means "here".

[21] Knox, "A Neglected Poet (James Grainger)", in *Literary Distractions*, p. 98.

> ... that the subject of his choice is a process incurably pedestrian, the result of which can only be sugar or (at the best) rum: that while the Mantuan reaps corn Grainger hoes yams, while the Mantuan treads grapes Grainger must peel bananas; that local colour demands the superseding of the ash and the pine by the coconut; that machinery, which Grainger is far too conscientious to leave undescribed, does the greater part of the manufacture; that the human cries for labour involved is not that of jolly Apulian swains but that of negroes looted from the Gold Coast, whose presence has begun to need some explanation, even to the easy conscience of the eighteenth century. The situation cries for bathos, and gets it.[22]

But the great majority of the essay is given over to lengthy quotations from the epic poem, with little commentary provided or needed. The reader is left in Meredithian fashion to ponder the fatuity of ruminations about blights, machinery, discernment in buying slaves, and the variety of island insect life. Let one snatch suffice:

> Mosquitoes, sand-flies seek the sheltered roof,
> And with fell rage the stranger-guest assail
> Nor spare the sportive child; from their retreats
> Cockroaches crawl displeasingly abroad[23]

One can imagine Knox, who pleads elsewhere to catching his breath at lines of poetry that particularly move him—lines such as "Let them sleep, let them sleep on / Till this stormy night be gone" in Crashaw's poignant *An Epitaph upon Husband and Wife, Which Died, and Were Buried Together*—finding himself similarly speechless, but from what a different stimulus, as he scanned these leaden verses for the first time.

A good part, however, of *Literary Distractions* is devoted to essays on writers with whose works he had been intimate since childhood: Robert Louis Stevenson, for instance, who wrote prose as ringing as poetry; Samuel Johnson, the eminently quotable; and G. K. Chesterton, whose literary career was just sufficiently in advance of Knox's to provide him guidance from his early days at Eton. It is difficult now to imagine a romance like *The Napoleon of Notting Hill* serving to shake a

[22] Ibid., p. 100.
[23] Ibid., p. 102.

youth loose from preconceived notions of British hegemony, but it did, and it drew Knox into sympathy with the distributist economic and social philosophy.[24] Subsequent books such as *Heretics* and *Orthodoxy* resonated with him too:

> Chesterton was often accused of being a Socialist by people who heard him denouncing the great fortunes of the very rich, until they learned to recognize his devotion to the idea of ownership, as that is expressed in the lives of the moderately poor. Chesterton made us see the value of old institutions, the cogency of old truths, by dint of travelling around the world, as it were, to rediscover them—by re-interpreting truisms as the paradoxes they really were, things staled by familiarity as the exciting, adventurous things they really were.[25]

There is a very erudite appraisal of the work of the seventeenth-century poet and translator Richard Crashaw, a Cambridge scholar and Catholic convert whose brief life ended in Italy, where he was a canon of the Cathedral of Loreto.[26] Many of Crashaw's poems exist in Latin as well as English versions, and Knox, the trained classicist and inveterate puzzler, is intrigued by the exegetical task of guessing which version is anterior to the other. Not only that, but he recalls also trying his own hand at turning *A Letter to the Countess of Denbigh against Irresolution and Delay in Matters of Religion* into Latin back in 1917 when he was afflicted with the same irresolution. He quotes the lines:

> What magic bolts, what mystic bars
> Maintain the will in these strange wars?
> What fatal and yet fantastic bands
> Keep the free heart from his own hands?[27]

[24] At least one biographer of Chesterton has called it "possibly his finest book, certainly his most ambitious and successful of his early years". See Michael Coren, *Gilbert: The Man Who Was G.K. Chesterton* (New York: Paragon House, 1990), p. 152. But not all readers will be impressed by counterintuitive musings that are too frequently interspersed throughout the narrative. One wonders too whether Chesterton could have written the novel (first published in 1904) in the same vein after the carnage of World War I.

[25] Knox, "G.K. Chesterton", in *Literary Distractions*, pp. 165–66.

[26] For a brief biographical sketch, see the introduction by Michael Cayley to *Richard Crashaw* (Oxford: Fyfield Books, 1972), pp. 1–9.

[27] Knox, "Richard Crashaw", in *Literary Distractions*, p. 63.

Eventually the countess, who attended Charles I's wife Henrietta Maria, did convert, and the queen, whose company he knew during her exile in Paris, supplied character references for Crashaw to the Pope to facilitate his reception in Rome. His religious sensitivity long predated his own conversion to Catholicism. In his early twenties, he published his *Epigrammata Sacra*, reflections on the paradoxical truths of the faith:

> As he thumbs his Gospels, and meditates on them, Crashaw gets certain "lights" as we all do; he seizes, for the first time, some happy coincidence which links this occurrence, undesignedly, with that. The ordinary Christian's instinct is to make a note of the circumstance in some common-place book, some journal of retreat; the ordinary clergyman's instinct is to lay it up as the text for a sermon. Crashaw's instinct is somewhat different. He crystallizes his thought in the form of an English, or more probably of a Latin, epigram.[28]

What appeals to Knox is not only the sensuous religious mysticism of Crashaw's full-length religious poetry but also its clear stylistic affinity with the classical Roman poets. However, he is far from an uncritical admirer. To balance the ecstatic verses in his hymn to Saint Teresa of Avila, there are sycophantic paeans to his royal benefactress, as on the birth of a son:

> War, Blood, and Death (names all averse from joy)
> Hear this! We have another bright-eyed Boy!

which laborings unfortunately continue on a downward slope.[29]

Many of the essays gathered in this book can be dated by internal evidence, and some are reprinted from earlier works. Thus a lecture on detective stories derives in seed from a conversation in *Sanctions* (1924) and an introduction to an anthology of such stories in 1929. A talk entitled "The Greeks at Sea" was given during a 1930 cruise in the Mediterranean organized by Arnold Lunn. Reminiscences about *The Ingoldsby Legends* were elicited from Knox in 1945, the centenary of the death of their author, Reverend R. H. Barham.[30] It is not clear,

[28] Ibid., p. 64.

[29] Ibid., p. 69.

[30] Rev. Richard Barham (1788–1845) was from Canterbury in Kent and, after ordination, eventually became a canon of St. Paul's in London. Something of an antiquarian, he published the legends ostensibly collected by one Thomas Ingoldsby, consisting of several

however, from the context when he first wrote the piece on Crashaw, which remains a fine scholarly introduction to his place in English letters.

It is particularly easy to date one lecture in the volume, not only because it refers to a book published in 1957, but also because it was the last and most memorable lecture Knox gave, the Romanes Lecture of June 11, 1957, "On English Translation". The topic has bearing on one of Knox's major accomplishments, his translation of the Bible, and hence will be examined in another chapter as well. Suffice it to say here, however, that he worked on this talk while suffering from inoperable liver cancer and delivered it over the course of two hours, during which he never faltered. It is a rich feast of allusions to the Elizabethans, the classics, the Church Fathers, and assorted translators new and old and betrays his enormous lifelong study of, and love for, literature and language.

OXFORD THROUGH THE YEARS

In 1938, Knox turned fifty, an age that invites reflection, marking as it does a probable midpoint of adult achievements. He was about to resign the chaplaincy of Catholic students at Oxford to devote himself to his translation of the Bible, and that severance of ties no doubt

---

rather eerie short stories and a plethora of largely rollicking poems, which mined much of their humor at the expense of medieval Catholicism. The following extract is from a poem about the plight of a young girl who is being hidden from her overbearing suitor with the aid of St. Ermengarde, who addresses her pursuers:

> Come, make yourselves scarce!—it is useless to say,
> You will gain nothing here by a longer delay.
> "Quick! Presto! Begone!" as the conjurers say,
> For as the Lady, I've stowed her away
> In this hill, in a stratum of London blue clay;
> And I shan't, I assure you, restore her to-day,
> Till you faithfully promise no more to say "Nay,"
> But declare, "If she will be a nun, why she may."

For the rest of "The Lay of St. Odille", see *The Ingoldsby Legends or Mirth and Marvels* by Thomas Ingoldsby (London: Frederick Warne and Co., n.d.). The resemblance to the style of Theodore Geisel, that modern genius at versifying better known as Dr. Seuss, is unmistakable.

occasioned a retrospective look not only at the cultural changes coincident with his own lifespan but also over a period more appropriate to the venerable institution so much a part of him, in fact a period seven times fifty years, as seen through the eyes of the denizens of an Oxford senior common room. Mythical Simon Magus College serves as the locale, and the scholars' conversations, duly transcribed, serve as the text for *Let Dons Delight* (1939), a vehicle that allows full play of Knox's vaunted skill at confecting the idiomatic English of any century from the sixteenth onward.

The narrator is invited to dine with a friend, a fellow of the college, and is introduced to some of the lore surrounding some of the long-dead dons whose portraits peer down on him from the dark-paneled smoking room. As his host leaves to answer a telephone call, the effects of several glasses of port become pronounced, and he is soon dreaming. The dons around him, and their conversation, become merged with another set of men of a different era.

> You know how it is in dreams (mine, anyhow); you do not see people's faces, you just *know* that the man you are talking to (or throwing downstairs) is Such-a-one, belonging to your acquaintance. It may be that in the course of the proceedings, you look at his face, and find that it is the face of somebody quite different; this does not puzzle you in your dream, only afterwards; at the moment, you are content to let A act as a symbol (I think they call it) of B, and it is with an A-faced B that you round off the cycle of your adventures. So it was with me, that evening.[31]

Curiously too, the dream progresses through vignettes fifty years apart, the participants conveniently changing personalities but not seating order with each step forward in time. The stage is thereby set for conversations from the years 1588, 1638, 1688, 1738, 1788, 1838, 1888, and 1938 to be recorded. The underlying theme is the gradual drifting from the moorings of the old Oxford of the religious orders, beginning with the acceptance of the changes brought on by Henry VIII. The old provost in 1588 counters a young Protestant firebrand's call for a purging of all traditions with an affectionate but hazy defense of the advantages attaching to times gone by

[31] Ronald Knox, *Let Dons Delight: Being Variations on a Theme in an Oxford Common-Room* (1939; reprint, London: Sheed and Ward, 1973), pp. 9–10.

> when we sang the Mass lustily enough, yet the Pope's word never ran in Oxford, no, nor in the whole of England. And then King Harry died, and we were hard put to it to tell whether there was mass in the chapel or no; it was Kyrie eleison to-day and Lord have mercy on us to-morrow, with much expense to the College in continual procuring of new service-books.... As for her present Majesty, she hath blown hot and cold, but now we have all one mass again, and we must use that until she or some other send us a better. But you will find it is all one; the times go backwards and forwards, and no man can tell what will be the end of it. Honest men should put their coats about their ears for a little, and follow with the fashion of the time, not running off to Basel this day, and to Rheims the next, as if salvation should depend on an Ave Maria.[32]

The chief topic of conversation among the dons is the impending confrontation with Spain, a confrontation that causes acute embarrassment to one Mr. Lee, because he is committed to entering a seminary overseas but wants no part of Spanish dominion over England.[33]

After the dream segment fades out, Knox inserts extracts allegedly culled from actual historical works, which purport to detail several of the characters' subsequent careers. For example, he finds that Bishop Challoner's *Memoirs of the Missionary Priests* contains an account (under June 31, of course, "the feast of Saints Promiscuus and Miscellaneus") of the capture of Father Lee after the Gunpowder Plot and of his interrogation by a former colleague who back in 1588 had been an ardent champion of Catholicism but had since accommodated himself to the reigning religious opinions.

[32] Ibid., p. 22.

[33] Many Oxford fellows and scholars did quit the university to go abroad and be ordained as missionary priests in the 1570s and 1580s. Knox's own Balliol College was especially noted as a redoubt of Catholic sympathizers and produced Fr. Robert Persons, S.J., and St. Alexander Briant, who died alongside Edmund Campion. A government spy reported: "That Balliol College hathe not been free from the suspicion of papistrie this longe time it appeareth by the men that have been of the same house, namelye, Brian and Parsons. With Parsons and since his departure from the colledg hath Turner, Bagshaw, Staverton and one Pilcher been fellowes: all which were grevously suspect of religion. And certaune it is that this Pilcher is gone this year from thence to Rhemes, looking dailye for Bagshaw as he did report.... Staverton is in like manner departed the colledge, and it is thought that both Bagshaw and he be gone over the sea." Quoted in John Jones, *Balliol College: A History, 1263–1939* (Oxford: Oxford University Press, 1988), p. 80.

When the 1638 conversation opens, that interrogator is now the old provost, and religion is still being debated, but now Puritanism vies with the state religion for the sympathies of the academics. Mr. Kingsmill is scandalized that the government harries the practitioners of the pure religion and that Oxford tolerates depraved amusements:

> Already God is much offended by the profaning of his Sabbath, with the playing of football and at cudgels, with the holding of Whitsun ales and Maypoles, and the ringing of Church bells. If your boys here fall into such evil uses, from the daily consorting with low fellows in the ale-houses, how will you have acquitted yourself of your stewardship, who have received this pleasant inheritance to be a nursery of all godly piety?

This brings a retort from Mr. Fulwell, a High Anglican of the Laudian school:

> Mr. Kingsmill, I find in you what I have ever noted in my friend Dr. Berridge; that you will make a great to-do when any man would abridge your own liberty of conscience, as by bidding you set the communion table here and not there; yet, if a man will only shoot an arrow at the mark on the Lord's Day, you are instantly for having such a one clapped into gaol. Now, Sir, which way will you have it? Will you stand for the ordering of men's doings by public authority? . . . Or will you, *per contra*, have every man follow his own conscience, to do whatever he think well and right, as answerable to God and none other? Which if it be the case, why will you put restraint on Mr. Lilly here, that he should not go morris-dancing on the Lord's Day, ay, or play football, if he be in the humour for it?[34]

Mr. Fulwell is seconded by Mr. Lilly, whose later career in controversy is sketched out in some previously unpublished pages of Anthony Wood's history of notable Oxford men, published at the end of the seventeenth century. It seems Messrs. Lilly and Kingsmill went on to engage in heated polemics as the civil war between Cromwell and Charles I approached. The enumeration of the titles of their broadsides, so characteristically verbose, is high parody and excuses an extended quote. Anthony Wood's sympathies with the Royalists, it

[34] Knox, *Let Dons Delight*, pp. 61–62.

will be seen, are not muted. Mr. Lilly begins the pamphleteering, no doubt spurred on by the common room argument:

> *David dancing before the Ark, being a brief Apology for Whitsun Ales, Stage-plays, Bear-baiting, Morris-dancing, and all other Sports and Delectations which the sour-fac'd melancholy of these times holdeth abominable, in the form of a DIALOGUE between Hobbinol and Crop-pate.* By T. Y. Lond. 1638. To which a reply being put out in the same year, entitled, *A Reproof for taking the Ark of God into Battle, wherein Misochorus remonstrates with T. Y., who after the manner of Hophni and Phineas makes men to abhor the offering of the Lord* &ctr. &ctr., our author returned most courageously to the attack, publishing at some time in the next year,
>
> *The Hand of Uzzah stretch'd out to defend the Ark of God, in which a Warning is offer'd to Misochorus, and all other the pestilent sectaries by whose means the Ark of God is kept out from its true Place, and detain'd for this time at the house of Obed-Edom the Gittite,* by T. Y. Lond. 1640. Which work being now in the press, it seems the printer, or some other that contrived to come at them, did privately convey the sheets one by one to Mr. Kingsmill—by which dishonest practice he was able to put out his Reply more expeditiously. This was entitl'd, *The Ark carry'd by unserviceable Oxen, that turn to the right and to the left, and not upon the Narrow way to Bethshemesh, lowing as they go; which lamentable Lowings were lately Publish'd by one that calleth himself T. Y., under the title,* The Hand of Uzzah &ctr. This so incens'd our author, who (it seems) guessed well enough by what means it was that his adversary had gained this advantage upon him, that he determined he would continue the cannonade with heavier pieces. So that a full year and more before he published his last rejoinder in this controversy, which he called,
>
> *The Linen Ephod, wherein, namely in our Justification as Christian people, we do well to dance, yea and will dance, all canting and ranting of all melancholy Fanaticks notwithstanding; and that there shall be cakes and ale yet, as dancing David gave them to his people, when the Ark returned from its Captivity, to make both Misochorus and all humorous Conventicle-men roar with Envy.* Which as it was a work of more compass and import, and adorned with many weighty passages from the Fathers by way of proof, so it was not easy for Mr. Kingsmill, being but an empty and clownish person, to busy himself any further in this matter. Nevertheless that he did put out a reply, 'tis certain; whose merit is to be judged from the obscurity into which it has fallen;

> for I was never able to come by a copy of it, no, nor even to find out what title was given to it.[35]

No doubt Jael's hammer would have found its way into either of these combatant's arsenals had it not already done duty in a pseudo-Swiftian essay on the merits of religious reunion.

Each half-century stopping point conveniently coincides with major shifts in the political or religious order, and none of the dons appear to be reticent in predicting the course of future events, with almost unerring inaccuracy. In 1688, James II is pronounced secure in his fortune because he has Lord Churchill to command his army, Dryden is judged flexible enough in his creed to welcome the Protestant William and Mary, and even incidentals find a way to be confounded. After a discussion of the relative merits of several contemporary poets, one fellow extols the merits of *Hudibras* and exclaims, "So long as our tongue is read, I think there will be only one Samuel Butler", a statement the author of *Erewhon* would contest.

The academic world in 1788 is of course becoming far removed from religious questions, judging itself to have reached the pinnacle of modernity and scientific reasoning. But the religious establishment, to which all the dons at least nominally proffer their allegiance, remains and must somehow be reconciled with the pure air of rationalism. Mr. Watson sees a parallel in the mitigation of penalties for crimes that nevertheless remain capital offenses on the statute books. He maintains that "it is but following the order of nature, to allow what is unserviceable to fall into disuse; the withered limb has no need of an amputation". This, he says, holds true of the Thirty-nine Articles, and when asked to clarify whether he means only the penalties associated with not subscribing to them, he asserts that it is the theological content of the Articles themselves, which no longer binds consciences: "These are days of enlightenment, in which the most part of us are content to recognize that the Divine Author of our being exists, without making bold to quibble over *homoousion and homoiousion*, over grace efficacious and grace sufficient; we have seen the horrid contentions and wars bred by this sort of controversy, and we are minded to let it

[35] Ibid., pp. 75–77.

alone."[36] The temptation to outline the future is too great to pass up. Later in the conversation he waxes eloquent on the impossibility that bygone intellectual fashions could attract intelligent academics:

> Consider how the science of architecture improves, from one age to the next, our apprehension of beauty, so that the barbarous things which were formerly held in estimation no longer have power to delight the mind! In Oxford, we are slow to relinquish what is outworn; as witness how Hawksworth, not so very long since, disfigured All Souls' by retaining there the Gothic style of building; but who will be found to admire such a prospect now? So it is with these prepossessions I was speaking of; you will not persuade an Englishman to entertain in these days the notion of purgatory or the silly fable of the Mass.[37]

Pointed architecture would see a revival, no less than orthodoxy, in Oxford in exactly fifty years' time.

There are ingenious symmetries and asymmetries embedded everywhere in the text, which reinforce the inverted aphorism facing the title page, "*Plus c'est la même chose, plus ça Change*" (The more things stay the same, the more things change), and the easily misconstrued line "All This Waste of Time" placed under the dedication to Daphne Acton. Robert Speaight suggests that the latter phrase was written in a self-deprecating sense. Evelyn Waugh, writing with Knox's correspondence with Lady Acton available to him, rejects that interpretation but does not bother to supply one himself. It would certainly seem that the inference is to the time frittered away by the academics, raking over the same philosophical and theological ground, with progressively less to show for their efforts as the centuries pass. Reference is occasionally made (usually in a pejorative tone) to the religious houses that once infused the intellectual life of the university with the perennial philosophy.

In 1838, the Oxford Movement was creating ferment among the dons, and the provost, an atrophied Tory, likens the Romanizers' pestilential effect to that of the cholera epidemic of 1832:

[36] Ibid., p. 151. The words *homoousios* ("consubstantial") and *homoiousios* ("like") were used to describe Jesus in relation to the Father in the early Church controversy over whether Christ was fully divine.

[37] Ibid., p. 166.

> When the cholera broke out here, five or six years back—at least, they called it the cholera—and carried many off by death, it was thought by some this was because the sewers emptying into the river had contaminated the water. And in particular, this was said of the Trill Mill stream, which flows as you know next to Christ Church meadows. What did the students of Christ Church do? Did they let the matter alone? No, Sir, they built the wall which you will see on the Western side of the meadows, to keep the bad air away. And if this infection of Popery continues to flow in among us, it will be for the heads of Colleges to determine how they can build a wall against it and fend it away; you will see if that does not happen.[38]

He is reminded that the Franciscans and Dominicans used to inhabit that area, and the provost suggests that Christ Church should raze the dilapidated buildings.

What he would pull down is the Old Palace, the home in Knox's day of the Catholic chaplain. The last conferences Knox delivered to Oxford students were collected under the title *The Hidden Stream*, the reference being to "the Trill Mill stream, a true branch of Isis that has flowed modestly through the less frequented parts of Oxford, goes underground for a few hundred yards, to issue under an ornamental bridge in the Christ Church Memorial Garden". The preface to that work of apologetics pays homage to the Franciscan and Dominican houses that once stood astride that stream and invokes them as signposts pointing out the way of the intellectual morass into which the university is drawn: "[N]ot all the philosophies of Oxford are philosophies of negation and despair; she is fed by secret streams, not less influential to her life or less native to her genius."[39]

But the men of 1838 are too far removed from those times to have inherited their confidence in the Church as the font of truth. An adherent of the religious revival under Newman and Keble and Pusey bemoans Oxford's innate indifference to the quest for certitude, a moral supineness that will drive him and others out of the university's comfortable embrace.

> I don't know why, it is as if something in the very walls of this Common-room haunted me; all this evening the first eclogue has

[38] Ibid., p. 186.

[39] Ronald Knox, *The Hidden Stream* (New York: Sheed and Ward, 1953), p. vi.

> been coming back to my mind, and the shepherd who was dispossessed of his ancestral land; *sitientes ibimus Afros* [some of us will go to the thirsty Africans], he says,—we shall be off into the cruel desert, men such as I am; and we shall remember the greenery of Oxford only as better things, no, not better things, more companionable things, are remembered in dreams.[40]

He is indeed haunted: the same line ran through the mind of Mr. Lee when he was determining on going abroad in 1588 to study in a seminary, while in 1638 Mr. Fulwell invokes it to throw down the gauntlet to anyone dissatisfied with the established order. In 1938, a more materialist age, it is applied to the spoiled rich graduates who are to take overseas posts in the British Empire.

But the attractions of Oxford life are powerful, and timeless. One of the disputants of 1738 describes the view from a nearby hill when there

> was a little mist risen from the river, as I suppose, in the great heat; and the church spires and the towers of the Colleges rose out of it as if they had no more substantial foundation than air. You will think me a very foolish old man, Sirs, yet I could not help but think of the past, and how Oxford is its epitome. There were the walls, much overgrown with ivy, where the nunnery used to be at Godstow; and there was Binsey, with the well that men used to frequent for the cure of their eyes in the days of Popish superstition; there was the spire of St. Mary's and the tower of St. Martin's, there was Magdalen tower, and Merton, and the Cathedral Church; and with them some of these new-fangled edifices we have put up of late, which some admire more than I do, as Archbishop Sheldon's theatre and the Church of All Saints. And it was my humour to reflect, looking on them, whether we are indeed part of the past, and it of us; or whether that old Oxford of the monkish days is indeed something other, and we and our Church—I mean the established Church, although I am like to die myself outside its communion—a new foundation with but a century and a half of history, piled up on the ruins of the old.[41]

A like-minded descendant, a sincere Anglican holdout of 1888 who must contend with atheists and agnostics among his colleagues, takes

[40] Knox, *Let Dons Delight*, p. 198.

[41] Ibid., pp. 132–33.

the same walk and sees the same view, now however with the trees just blocking out the unseemly urban accretions, so that only an illusion of bucolic seclusion haloes the university spires and towers. He describes the same monuments of the past, with a far kinder eye even than the churchman of 1738:

> There was Godstow nunnery, with its grey stone basking in the sun-light; and Binsey with its miraculous well; the spire of St. Mary's and Carfax and Magdalen and Merton, and Tom Tower with the Cathedral shewing behind it, and the Sheldonian and the Camera and the City Church. I couldn't help reflecting, as I looked at all that, how inevitably we in Oxford are bound to our past; how the old Oxford of medieval days is still a part of ourselves, and we part of it,—the associations and the traditions of the place are so intertwined that you feel, like a living thing, the continuity of its history.[42]

Another don picks up the thread and muses over the question whether the dons of earlier ages would seem familiar to the moderns: "Should we find them exercised over the same problems, *mutatis mutandis* [with the necessary changes] of course, which exercise us, and giving the same answers that we give? Or should we have to admit that really we have nothing in common with them; that it is only the oak paneling which goes on and does not change, while the men who sit under it are changing, beyond hope of recovery, all the time?"[43] Not surprisingly, no consensus emerges, as several discussants try to pinpoint the source of the rupture: one dates it to the age of Hume, another to the fall of the Stuarts, another to the Civil War, yet another to the end of the Elizabethan age.[44]

The narrator then wakes up in 1938, to hear a conversation involving a research scientist, a Marxist economist, an ascetic philosopher of vague religious disposition, a doctrinaire psychologist, and a genial

[42] Ibid., p. 228.

[43] Ibid., p. 232.

[44] Of course, one major change that had occurred between 1838 and 1888 was the laicization of the Oxford colleges, abetted by government commissions in the 1850s and 1870s, which abolished the requirement of celibacy for most fellowships and elevated the nonprofessorial teaching staff (the tutorial fellows) into a profession. The consequences were predictable: most headships of colleges passed into lay hands, the number of clerical fellowships diminished, and the undergraduates no longer had to affirm the Thirty-nine Articles to take degrees other than in divinity. See A.J. Engel, *From Clergyman to Don: The Rise of the Academic Profession in Nineteenth-Century Oxford* (Oxford: Clarendon Press, 1983).

skeptic. To these is soon added the narrator's host, a classicist, finally returned from the summons to the telephone that precipitated the narrator's reverie. As might be imagined, the search for a common ground among such a disparate lot is futile. The scientist, whose appreciation of the search for truth is frankly limited, at least acknowledges the intellect of men as something superior to the workings of brute animals, but he is loath to countenance its other activities:

> [Y]ou've got to think of Science, ultimately, as a single body of knowledge; it's all building up an accurate world-picture, and you never know what'll come in handy, so to speak. But when you set people down to research into the causes of the Peloponnesian War, or something of that sort, that isn't going to help the human race survive, is it? It's side-tracking the primary purpose of the intellect, that's my point. Of course, I don't say there's any harm in it; only it's rather playing about, from our point of view.[45]

The economist would jettison the classics and all history prior to the French Revolution from the university curriculum because they perpetuate class consciousness. Science too would be stripped of its theorizing and set to work along purely utilitarian lines. When pregnant phrases like what the mind is "meant for" creep into the debate, the psychologist jumps into the fray with obnubilating explanations that would dampen any further inquiry:

> Well, you could say this, couldn't you—that the validity of our intellectual processes is guaranteed to us as long as we only make practical use of them? Because if you use them right, you survive; if you use them wrong, you disappear. The kind of people who thought climbing a tree was a good way of dodging a jaguar *may* have been right, of course, but they aren't alive to tell the tale. Whereas the question whether (say) Time has any absolute existence can't be decided by any such simple tests. You can answer Yes or No without any fatal results to yourself.[46]

When the economist, Dreschel by name, proceeds to heap scorn on truth as an impediment to the ruthless progress of the masses, the scientist is finally inspired to eloquence in its defense: "Whatever else

[45] Knox, *Let Dons Delight*, pp. 261–62.
[46] Ibid., pp. 267–68.

knowledge is or involves, surely it means that truth does exist, and is something to which we must bow, not something we can bow to our own ends." He continues with an analogy:

> I was going round Addison's Walk this afternoon, and I saw the fritillaries; they're early this year. You know the way they hit your eye suddenly, a kind of lake of purple and white where everything was green a week ago? Well, I'll tell you what it made me think of; it made me think of an Italian gardener I read of in some book or other, who said of a flower that was growing all over the place, "It flourishes like the thought of Man." That's a fine statement, Dreschel; and you'll find Man's thought will flourish in spite of you. It's not like the tulips in the garden there, that you can plant out in beds all at regular intervals, and they'll grow up as straight as ram-rods for you. It will take its own direction, not yours.[47]

Far earlier in time, back in 1688, another don had gazed upon the neat rows of tulips in a flower garden and then rode out of town to visit a friend; when he came upon the same field of fritillaries displaying their natural uncultivated beauty, he opined that Christian fellowship should be as natural as the field of flowers rather than a state-ordered affair like the formal garden. What a far cry from 1938, and yet the spirit animating the Royalist still breathes faintly on the rationalist who would defend the dignity of men. In 1688, the intellectual battleground was over whether the state could command all citizens to believe in one religion; by 1938 the controverted point is whether belief in anything is possible.

Mr. Mordaunt, the classicist, bemoans the cacophony in the common room and suggests a reason and a remedy: "Don't you think perhaps the background of classical education had something to do with it? I know this'll annoy you, J. D., but I do sometimes wonder whether we haven't lost something by not having a common classical tradition . . . being saturated with the classics, using ancient Greece and ancient Rome as two windows from which we can look out on life."[48]

As the last philosophical statement proffered before the conversation finally peters out, it would seem that this sentiment mirrors Knox's own views, classicist that he is. But that would be to forget the monks,

[47] Ibid., pp. 271–72.
[48] Ibid., p. 279.

and the Trill Mill Stream, and what that signified in his mind. Just as Eton owed its genius to the lingering spirit of the saintly king Henry VI, Oxford could deny its nurturing in the pre-Reformation Church only at the risk of denying all continuity with its past. The cacophony ringing through the common room throughout the past few centuries, then, is ultimately a legacy of the rupture engineered by Henry VIII.

CHAPTER SIX

A GUIDE FOR THE PERPLEXER

ACROSTICS

One of Waugh's underlying themes, as Knox's literary executor and biographer, is that Ronald Knox was not sufficiently appreciated by the Catholic Church after his conversion. The leading voice for orthodoxy in the Church of England prior to 1917 was relegated to teaching boys at Saint Edmund's—a step down from Shrewsbury, to which Knox had retired in his years of indecision—while still in the prime of his life, just when stalwarts like Hilaire Belloc were expecting great contributions from him on behalf of the English Catholic intellectual renascence. And if evidence were needed to reinforce the image of underutilized genius, the efflorescence of his prodigious talent for creating puzzles during those years can be cited to drive home the point. Idleness begat the weeds of frivolous wordplay; the talent that could have been exercised against the form critics was focused instead on fashioning brainteasers.

Knox was hardly concerned to deflect such whisperings about misplaced energy. The mental acrobatics that are required for solving all kinds of puzzles had been honed since childhood among the four brothers, and he could hardly erase the habits of a lifetime during the idle moments that continued to come his way. In fact, so proficient was he at puzzle making that he generated a sufficient number of one venerable type at odd moments on trains or while shaving to be able to publish *A Book of Acrostics* in 1924.

An acrostic is composed of a series of rows of words or lines placed one above the next, the first letter of which, when read vertically, forms another word or phrase. Knox noted that this form of entertainment was popular in the 1880s in England, and it seemed headed for a revival again in the 1920s. But being the sort of person who could not be satisfied with a superficial knowledge of a topic to which he was attracted, he wrote a disquisition on the origins of the acrostic (the word itself being derived from Greek words for "the end of a line"). He finds virtually no use of it in the classics, and he postulates an intriguing reason:

> All this habit of playing with words, of forming patterns out of their initial letters, of forcing them into the strange moulds of the anagram and the palindrome, is Christian rather than pagan. Rhyme itself, which is a form of playing with words, seems to be a purely Christian invention. There is a frivolity about the whole conception which never dawned on the pagan world, sad even in its pleasures. You must unlearn superstition before you jest with words and names; for to the superstitious mind all such things have still some faint aroma of magic and of religious mummery.[1]

Some early Christian hymns display the acrostic, but the first truly accomplished acrostician seems to be one Porphyrius Optatianus, a contemporary of Constantine, who composed a number of specimens of ingenious complexity. Modern English literature does not afford too many exemplars of the art, the poet Dryden and the critic Addison disparaging such wordplay as foolishness. But for some minds the appeal of a puzzle is irresistible, and its blossoming in mid-Victorian times and resurrection in the 1920s correspond, perhaps not coincidentally, with the fortunes of another art form soon to claim his attention, the detective novel. Knox waxes lyrical on the sublimity of the acrostic:

> And what an art it is! For here you have the marriage of two minds, the composer's and the solver's, after Heaven knows how many delays, false starts, misunderstandings. It is romance in miniature. Romance? Nay, a detective story, with clues to guide you and clues to mislead you, with the gradual realization of the plot, the sudden grasp of recognition. Or, if you will, it is a duel between two brains, the quickness of the solver's lunge developing in answer to the deftness of the composer's parry. Here is all the thrill, too, of scientific research: for what are the uprights of an acrostic but the working hypothesis

[1] Ronald A. Knox, *A Book of Acrostics* (London: Methuen and Co., 1924), pp. 4–5.

> on which the scientist bases his theory, and what are the lights but the series of observations and experiments by which he verifies it?[2]

Rather than continuing with excerpts from this paean, it might be beneficial to the reader to explain the terminology of the acrostic under discussion. For some obscure reason, the horizontal words are called "lights", while more obviously, the vertical words formed by the beginning (and end) letters of the lights are called "uprights".

Many of the definitions Knox employs are devilishly intricate puns and allude to persons, places, or items recognizable to people well versed in classical literature and Shakespeare. He advises that the puzzle solver have on hand the Bible, *Cruden's Concordance*, the complete works of Shakespeare, several handbooks of the *Bartlett's Familiar Quotations* variety, some encyclopedic works of science, and whatever other compendia can be thumbed through in a timely manner.

With that caution, perhaps a glance at a few of his definitions will provide an insight into Knox's artistry. When he announces that the two uprights, eight letters in length, are given by the cryptic definition: "Their difference in logic is obscure / This against that it's better to insure", the perceptive reader will quickly deduce the pair of words meant.[3] But who, upon reading, "A philosophy don and his pupil please name / Number Two on the banks of a river won fame / Which sounds like the Isis, but isn't the same", would think of Aristotle and Alexander, the river hinted at being the Issus? Or what about the pair of words suggested in, "Wherefore to alien countries fly / When there's a substitute close by?" Does the Cornish Riviera come to anyone's mind? Let us assume a peek at the back of the book to find that one; this shortcut is called "buying the uprights" and is a legitimate way out of an impasse. Now armed with the beginning and final letters of the horizontal clues, the puzzle solver can tackle the lights. The lights would be easier to solve if one knew in advance how many letters there were to each of them, as one knows in a standard crossword puzzle, but as the example below shows, there is no uniformity in length. The answer to clue 3, for example, begins with R (the third letter of "Cornish") and ends with V (the third letter of "Riviera"): "Return to scenes of childish memories—Is it superfluous? Of course it is." The answer to the first

[2] Ibid., p. 13.

[3] They are *property* and *accident*.

part of the clue is "Revisit", but the latter part of the clue suggests that the "isit" needs to be removed, leaving one with "Rev" as the final answer, with the requisite beginning and end letters. The clue for the fifth light is a clever one, but since we know it begins with I and ends with E, it is easier to solve: "To hint what's to someone's discredit—Adam to Eve might have said it." [4]

And so the process continues, through exactly one hundred complete puzzles composed of uprights and lights, many of them far more Delphic than the examples cited.

EARLY MYSTERY NOVELS

Knox first tried his hand at mystery novel writing at about the time he took on the Oxford chaplaincy. The move afforded him the opportunity to exercise his mind, creating puzzles more elaborate than the newspaper acrostics he could churn out at a moment's notice, and a concomitantly more substantial payment with which to supplement his meager priestly salary. His very first such novel was *The Viaduct Murder* (1926), which came complete with a map of the fictional environs around the murder scene and a cast of characters who could hardly raise enough three-dimensionality among them to obscure the physical evidence placed before the reader. Robert Speaight has observed that this novel can be read as "an amiable skit on the Higher Criticism".[5] But the careful deposition of clues throughout the narrative and the attention given to the retailing of the various theories proposed by the investigators stamps the book as a bona fide British detective story. It is a puzzler, but certainly not a thriller. The plot is simple enough, with the twists and turns being provided mainly by the competition among theorists to explain the facts. Four golfing partners find a dead body, with its face conveniently obliterated, at the base of a railroad viaduct running parallel to the fairway of the third hole. The course lies on the grounds of a former country estate, long owned by a recusant family that accepted the national religion only at the end of the seventeenth century, and the old owners' home has been converted into the clubhouse, with rooms let out to permanent residents. These include Marryatt, the parson for the village: "a man now

[4] *Insinuate*, or as Adam might have said, "In sin you ate."

[5] Robert Speaight, *Ronald Knox the Writer* (New York, Sheed and Ward, 1965), p. 131.

approaching middle age, a bachelor and unambitious. You would say that he had a clerical face—is that clerical face a mark of predestination, or does it develop by natural mimicry?—but the enthusiasm which it registered was, it is to be feared, principally directed towards one object, and that object a game."[6]

The reader familiar with *Sanctions* might suspect another vehicle for lampooning the complacent Anglican clergy, but this rural parson is no more sedentary than any of his fellow boarders, who are all about as faceless as the dead body literally is. They include Mordaunt Reeves, a former military intelligence officer, a visiting friend of his, and a college don who is a goldmine of ethnological trivialities. This foursome soon establishes that the victim was a Mr. Brotherhood, who lived in a nearby cottage during the week and took the train to London every weekend. He was an unsavory fellow who gained local notoriety by preaching atheist doctrines in the village square and who suffered a great financial reverse just prior to his disappearance. Curiously, a Mr. Davenant, an ex-serviceman Catholic gentleman known best for his low handicap in golf, has also disappeared. He used to live in the area on weekends and in the city during the week and so was never seen at the same time as Mr. Brotherhood. The most intriguing clues found on the body include a torn sheet of paper with a cipher message on one side and a partial list on the other, and a picture of a woman. She turns out to be the daughter of a former clergyman from the next village to the north, but she is unresponsive at an interview conducted by Reeves, who takes the lead in pursuing the case.

Their reconstruction of the murder (for they assume a murder despite an inquest verdict of suicide) revolves around train schedules and the time frozen on the victim's watch by his fall. Before anything is heard of Davenant's whereabouts, the college don concocts a theory that Davenant and Brotherhood must have been one and the same person, assuming alternate identities as blasphemer and practicing Catholic, as duffer and polished golfer, on weekday and weekend. Their known movements can be reconciled with such a hypothesis. But reality dispels such thoughts when Davenant is found lurking in between the walls of the clubhouse, which was used in earlier times

[6] Ronald A. Knox, *The Viaduct Murder* (New York: Simon and Schuster, 1926), pp. 4–5.

as a hiding place for hunted priests. It also transpires that the dead man was married to, but long separated from, the woman in the photo and that Davenant had once also sought her hand. The evidence seems to point to him as the murderer, who took flight to the hidden passageways of a house he alone knew well, for he is a descendant of the old landlords.

But Reeves is emboldened by his early successes in the case and refuses to acquiesce in such an obvious, almost pedestrian, resolution. For him, Davenant's innocence is established by an unverifiable intuition, fueled by his admiration for the woman in the portrait, who is herself convinced that her husband could not have perished at Davenant's hands. Timetables need to be reexamined, and some purloined bits of evidence, and even the idle chatter of the residents on the day of the murder, when they had been awaiting the passing of rain and fog that delayed their daily rounds on the links. The whole trail of information can indeed be woven into an incriminating case against one individual: the parson.

Unable to confront his old friend, Reeves resorts to a speaking tube connected to receivers between rooms to convey the damning indictment, but the parson is too frightened by his first words and bolts the scene. However, just as he finishes his masterful reconstruction of the murder with Marryatt as the evil genius orchestrating all the steps, word comes that Davenant has confessed.

The penultimate chapter, which Knox obligingly invites the impatient reader to skip in the interests of finding out exactly how Davenant accomplished his task, is largely given over to the philosophical musings of one of the four amateur sleuths. This character had not shared Reeves' enthusiasm for theories, and he compares their efforts to an exercise in literary criticism, in which someone "with a documentary hypothesis can defy the rudest assaults of common sense". He continues:

> You have to start out by saying, "This document consists of three parts. One part is genuine, one part is spurious, the third part is faked evidence put in to make the spurious stuff look as if it was genuine!" Then, you see, you are on velvet. You reject altogether the parts of the document which you don't like. Then you take the remaining part, and find that it still contains a certain sort of

> dross—Evidence which still conflicts with your theory. That dross you purge away by calling it a deliberate fake.[7]

The Viaduct Murder has many, though not all, the properties of Knox's mature detective fiction. Evelyn Waugh, in his biography, described Knox's concept of the mystery story as "a game between writer and reader in which a problem was precisely stated and elaborately disguised".[8] Notably absent from the stories is any violence: the body invariably appears only after the passions of the murderer have been spent. A meticulously precise trail of clues is then scattered about for detective and reader to uncover. One of Knox's brothers, Dillwyn, was a master cryptographer in the service of the British government—indeed, a key figure in the deciphering of German codes during both world wars. The same puzzle-solving genius animated Ronald as he diligently constructed his often tortuously complicated scenarios. Waugh even suggests that their very "austerity", their cool logic, might make them age far better than other works of detective fiction. Of course, the stories of Agatha Christie, Dorothy Sayers, and G. K. Chesterton have appealed to wider audiences for a longer period of time, but Knox's mysteries, being such cerebral exercises, have always attracted people who are challenged by the more recondite kinds of word puzzles.

With *The Three Taps*, Knox forswore all allegorical intent and produced his first bona fide whodunit. (The book even carries the subtitle *A Detective Story without a Moral*). Along the way he also introduces his detective hero, who would preside over the unraveling of all subsequent mysteries to issue from Knox's mind. His name is Miles Bredon, and he works for an octopus-like insurance company called the Indescribable, which maintains its headquarters in London in

> an enormously high building, with long, narrow windows that make it look like an Egyptian tomb. It is of white stone, of course, so time-defying in its appearance that it seems almost blasphemous to remember the days when it was simply a gigantic shell composed of iron girders. Over the front door there is a group of figures in relief, more than life-size; the subject is intended, I believe, to be Munificence wiping away the tears of Widowhood, though the profane have identified it before now as Uncle Sam picking Brittania's pocket.

[7] Ibid., p. 241.
[8] Evelyn Waugh, *Ronald Knox* (Boston: Little, Brown and Co., 1959), p. 188.

> This is continued all round the four sides by a frieze, ingeniously calculated to remind the spectator of the numerous risks which mortality has to run; here is a motor-accident, with an ambulance carrying off the injured parties; here an unmistakable shipwreck; there a big-game hunter is being gored by a determined-looking buffalo, while a lion prowls thoughtfully in the background.[9]

No wonder that, ensconced contentedly behind such an intimidating exterior, the Indescribable can make a fair claim to "insure every step you take on this side of the grave, but no one of them on such handsome terms as the step which takes you into the grave, and it is confidently believed that, if certain practical difficulties could be got over, the Indescribable would somehow contrive to frank your passage into the world beyond".[10]

Although Bredon's character is certainly never developed as is that of Poirot or Wimsey or Father Brown, the reader learns early on that he was in military intelligence in the Great War and obtained his present position as company investigator after demobilization. The only idiosyncrasy he displays is a passion for a form of solitaire (patience) involving four packs of cards, to which he retreats when all the clues of a case are in front of him, the puzzle is most baffling, and concentration of his energy on its solution is most fruitless. Like his creator, he also knows Bradshaw's Railway Guide inside out and is remarkably knowledgeable about the English landscape. He also differs in one important respect from most other supersleuths: "There was only one person who really knew how to manage him; and she, most fortunately, had married him. All he asked of Providence, beyond this happy arrangement, was to be left in his country cottage to play patience and solve an occasional cross-word. His wife saw to it that he was nevertheless uprootable when the Company wanted to uproot him."[11]

Angela Bredon in fact accompanies him on all his expeditions. In the first Bredon novel, one young son is mentioned and, in later novels, an ambiguous plurality of children, but they are always conveniently left in the care of nannies while the couple lights off to the

[9] Ronald A. Knox, *The Three Taps: A Detective Story without a Moral*, 7th ed. (1927; reprint, London: Methuen and Co., 1951), pp. 5–6.

[10] Ibid., p. 2.

[11] Ronald A. Knox, *Double Cross Purposes* (1937; reprint, New York: Dover Publications, 1986), p. 44.

scene of the crime. Consequently, Angela can immerse herself fully in the business at hand. The repartee engaged in by husband and wife is strongly reminiscent to the modern reader of that between Nick and Nora Charles, and it is intriguing to speculate that Dashiell Hammett, who began reviewing mystery novels in 1927, the year *The Three Taps* was published, may have modeled his sophisticated 1933 Thin Man couple on their British predecessors in criminal detection. Granted, Nick is boozier than Miles, but Nora resembles Angela far more than she does her reputed model, Lillian Hellman.[12]

The call for Bredon's assistance comes when an industrialist named Mottram is found dead in his room at the "Load of Mischief" inn while on a fishing vacation in the hamlet of Chilthorpe, asphyxiated by fumes from an acetylene gas lamp. The door of the room was locked from the inside, but the valves of the gas outlets (the three taps of the novel's title) were in a position that would allow no gas to escape. How could one person manage to arrange a possible crime scene so? When it is discovered that the victim had just altered his will to give over the benefits deriving from a euthanasia policy with the Indescribable to the local Catholic bishop should he die before his sixty-fifth birthday, the picture becomes murkier. The bishop, who was his neighbor, had befriended the old, nonbelieving bachelor and had in fact been invited to join him in Chilthorpe on the fateful day. An inquest is held and, as invariably occurs in English detective stories, duly returns a verdict of suicide. But did Mottram's secretary Brinkman (a man of pronounced anticlerical views) do him in and then alter the crime scene so that suicide would be suspected and the insurance policy thereby voided (the euthanasia clause)? Or perhaps Mottram's death was actually a carefully planned suicide occasioned by the discovery that he had a terminal illness and so would never benefit personally from his insurance policy, which converted to a generous pension upon his reaching sixty-five. Then there is Mottram's sole surviving heir, a taciturn nephew who may or may not be aware that he has been cut out of the will but who might have had access to his uncle's room with the assistance of his girlfriend, who works at the inn.

The solution, which of course is none of the above, is more complicated than the commonplace denouement of *The Viaduct Murder*. Once

[12] See the biography by Richard Layman, *Shadow Man: The Life of Dashiell Hammett* (New York: Harcourt Brace Jovanovich, 1981).

again other scenarios that sound equally plausible are put forward but always fail when one stubborn fact mars their airtightness. Chief among their proponents is the Scotland Yard inspector Leyland, the counterpart to Agatha Christie's Inspector Japp, the foil to Hercule Poirot. Leyland, however, at least gets the satisfaction of poking up some of the important clues, even if it is Bredon who ultimately unravels the puzzle.

In *The Footsteps at the Lock*, which appeared in 1928, Bredon returns to Oxford and its environs to solve another case of an apparent murder over an inheritance. Two dissolute cousins are in competition for their Victorian grandfather's estate. Should Derek Burtell, the elder of the two, not attain to his twenty-fifth birthday, his cousin Nigel would reap the windfall. And actually the survival of either one is problematic. The crapulous Derek had been sent down from Oxford after two years and is content to while away the time slowly sinking into inanition. And yet Nigel's reputation has easily eclipsed his, for he has flowered into an aesthete. Knox's description of Nigel is a masterful thumbnail sketch of the Oxford of Harold Acton, Cyril Connolly, and Evelyn Waugh, the Oxford it was now part of his duty to try to wean from sybaritic excess:

> Among all her immemorial traditions, Oxford cherishes none staler than that of aestheticism. A small group in each generation lights upon the same old recipe for setting the Isis on fire, and (since undergraduate memory only lives three years) is satisfied that it is a group of lonely pioneers. Nigel had read Wilde at school; he pillaged epigrams from Saki without appreciating that ironic reservation which is his charm. He offered absinthe to all his visitors, usually explaining that he did not really care for it, but kept it in his rooms in order to put temptation in the way of his scout. He painted his walls a light mauve, and hung them with a few squares of blank cartridge paper on which he was always threatening to do crayon drawings; the beauty of art, he said, lay in its promise—its fulfillment only brought disillusion. He talked in a very slow drawl, with a lisp and a slight stammer which he had cultivated to perfection. He never attended lectures; the dons did not understand, he complained, that undergraduates come up to Oxford in order to teach.[13]

[13] Ronald A. Knox, *The Footsteps at the Lock* (1928; reprint, New York: Dover Publications, 1983), pp. 5–6. For a good account of the Oxford literary set of the 1920s, see Humphrey Carpenter, *The Brideshead Generation* (Boston: Houghton Mifflin Co., 1990).

One of Knox's favorite recreations in Oxford, during both his student days and his chaplaincy, had been punting or canoeing on the Isis, and he brought to the fore in this novel all the descriptive power at his command to convey the natural beauty he had inhaled on those expeditions. Indeed, as he progressed further with his detective stories, he enriched them more and more frequently with his highly detailed evocations of scenery. The less-traveled reaches of the Thames bid him recall the panorama in midsummer:

> The woods that threw out their flanking battalions towards the stream were heavy with consummated leafage; the hay standing in the fields glistened and steamed with the evaporations of yesterday; the larks sang in the unconscious egotism of their perpetual encore; the hedges were still fresh with the year's last revelation, the dog-rose; white wreaths of cloud sailed lazily across the distance, as if assured that they had no speaking part today. The cows stood whisking their tails gently, reserving themselves for greater efforts in the coming heat; rabbits sunned themselves among the hillocks, and scuttled away, stricken with imaginary fears; school-children dotted the lanes, their heads together in earnest debate over nothing; the air was full of promise and expectation; a wind blew, steady but with no chill, from the south-west.... To meet haymakers in a field, to pass under one of the rare, purposeless iron bridges, makes you feel as if you had intersected an altogether different plane of life.[14]

But it is not so idyllic that murder cannot take place if a sufficiently feverish mind sets about the task. Derek had been advised by a doctor to take a canoe trip up the Thames to fortify his delicate health. He is accompanied by Nigel, who thoroughly detests him as a nonaesthete. The latter disembarks along the way to take a train to Oxford for an exam, allegedly intending to rejoin Derek at a downstream meeting place. But the canoe never arrives and is soon found overturned, with Derek missing. He is presumed murdered, with Nigel the obvious suspect.

Derek's body is nowhere to be found, however, and the abundance of clues that surface seems only to add to the confusion. Further complicating the case is the layout of Shipcote Lock's environs: a canal that divides into a lock stream and a weir stream around a

[14] Knox, *Footsteps*, p. 14.

small island and then weaves a twisting path to the inn at Eaton Bridge, where the Bredons and Leyland set up headquarters. There is also a second bequest, from a great-aunt, which is to fall Derek's way if the cousins prove their amity toward each other to her before she dies—which she does in the middle of the tumult. Nigel Burtell is also an adept at disguises, and Derek was clever with photography, and since one of the key pieces of evidence is a photograph of wet footprints on an iron bridge near where Derek's presumed murder took place, the correct interpretation of the photo is a key to reconstructing the scene of his disappearance.

It may well be that *Footsteps* contains Knox's most convoluted plot. Robert Speaight faults him for the profusion of clues "left lying about on the river banks" and suggests that the narrative's intricacy may make it pall, somewhat "like an impasse in a crossword puzzle".[15] But the accumulation of evidence is challenging, and the vignettes of scenes so familiar to Knox are often priceless. Take the following, for example, describing Bredon's visit to the Salisbury common room habituated by his own tedious uncle Robert:

> A Common-room dinner is an experience which strikes a chill into the heart of the bravest, when it comes to him for the first time. True, it has not all the horrors of High Table; he has not to endure the fancied scrutiny of an undergraduate perspective. But in Common-room the academic atmosphere is all the more pervasive for being concentrated at such close quarters. Who is this man next to you, to whom you have not been introduced? Is he a mere guest like yourself, or is he a Fellow? In the latter case, presumably, there is some subject on which he is a European authority, if only you could find out what it was. Are the frigid advances occasionally made to you an attempt at welcome? And if so, can you gauge from their frequency or heartiness the local popularity of your host? Uncle Robert was a supernumerary member of the Common-room, and a bore at that. His guests were usually men of his own kidney, and there was a general tendency to glare at them without speaking. Bredon felt, in an expressive modern phrase, like something the cat had brought in.[16]

[15] Speaight, *Ronald Knox the Writer*, p. 135.
[16] Knox, *Footsteps*, pp. 78–79.

THE DECALOGUE OF DETECTIVE FICTION

By now Knox was becoming a force to be reckoned with in the world of detective fiction. *The Three Taps* went through many editions, his reputation as a Holmes scholar was widely acknowledged (much to his embarrassment), and he was earning a highly creditable £400 a year on the royalties of his detective books alone.

Little wonder then that in 1929 Knox should be called upon to edit and write the introduction to a volume called *Best Detective Stories of the Year (1928)*, a collection of short stories by famous writers of the genre. More memorable, however, than the selections themselves (which included a Miss Marple story by Agatha Christie) is Knox's preface. It is the first printed version of a lecture he had previously given on the form and history of the detective story, and it contains his Decalogue for mystery writers. The true detective story, he claims, is a *hysteron proteron*, a tale told from back to front, with the body appearing early on and the detective trying to establish the facts leading up to the murder. Thrillers, which depend on shock value to keep their readers' interest, are not, properly speaking, detective stories. Since the detective story is so specific, it requires a set of rules to govern its structure, and he lists ten that come to his mind. They are all designed to ensure that the novel maintain a format and a consistency that will give the avid puzzle solver a sporting chance at cracking the case by using logic on a set of noncontradictory clues, even though spurious clues may well impede the process.

Commandment 1 requires that the "criminal must be someone mentioned in the early part of the story, but must not be anyone whose thoughts the reader has been allowed to follow". It would be grossly unfair to introduce a new character ex post facto and pin the crime on him; to give the reader insights into the train of thought of the yet-to-be-identified murderer would involve either tipping one's hand or creating an illusion of innocence. Commandment 2 lays down the line: "All supernatural or preternatural agencies are ruled out as a matter of course." There must be a logical explanation for every occurrence, and he convicts G.K. Chesterton of a minor infraction of this rule for even allowing suspicions of magic to color Father Brown's adventures. Commandment 3 specifies that "not more than one secret room or passage is allowable". Reference to his availing himself of that license (once) in *The Viaduct Murder* has already been made. Next, he prohibits the use of undiscovered poisons and then stipulates, "No Chinamen must figure in the story." His rationale for this exclusionary principle, perhaps necessary in an age less sensitive to racial stereotyping, is "our western habit of assuming that the Celestial is over-equipped in the matter of brains, and under-equipped in the matter of morals", and hence too likely to be the villain of a piece.

Knox also outlaws any "unaccountable intuition which proves to be right" on the part of the detective hero. That seems a bit stringent, so he qualifies it by saying that of course the detective may have inspirations about how to proceed on a case, but "he must not be allowed, for example, to look for the lost will in the works of the grandfather clock because an unaccountable instinct tells him that that is the right place to search. He must look there because he realizes that that is where he would have hidden it himself if he had been in the criminal's place."[17] While trying to reconstruct the crime committed on the Thames in *The Footsteps at the Lock*, Miles Bredon remonstrates with his wife when she accuses him of getting too fanciful in his speculations, "I have no instincts, no premonitions, no unaccountable intuitions. I just see the logic of the thing, nothing else."[18] Whether the reader's logical faculties can be trained on precisely the same clues as Bredon's, however, is another matter.

Commandment 7 contains what should be obvious: "The detective must not himself commit the crime", though Knox clarifies even that dogmatic statement as being applicable "only where the author personally vouches for the statement that the detective *is* a detective". Again in *Footsteps*, midway through the investigation, a new detective comes to Bredon's aid in establishing the meaning of various clues, but eventually he is unmasked as Nigel Burtell in disguise. However, a second read of the pages introducing the new character reveals that a few subtly placed details should have raised suspicions about his bona fides.

The following commandment is the only one that Knox himself can come under suspicion of breaking, especially in his final novel

[17] All the commandments are given in the introduction to Ronald A. Knox and H. Harrington, eds., *The Best Detective Stories of the Year (1928)* (1929; reprint, London: Faber and Faber Ltd., 1934), pp. xi–xiv.

[18] Knox, *Footsteps*, p. 38.

Double Cross Purposes. It states that no clues can be uncovered by the detective "which are not instantly produced for the inspection of the reader".[19] Commandment 9 dictates that the Watson character "must not conceal any thoughts which pass through his mind; his intelligence must be slightly, but very slightly, below that of the average reader". The Watson to Miles Bredon is his wife Angela. As often as not, her speculations would more than do justice to a clever reader, so perhaps Knox was paying a compliment to his audience with this commandment. Finally, Commandment 10 lays down a prohibition on identical twins or doubles "unless we have been duly prepared for them".

Knox reflected, in half-mock, half-serious tones consonant with the essay's overall cast, that "while the public demand for mystery stories remains unshaken, the faculty for writing a good mystery story is rare, and the means of writing one with any symptom of originality about it becomes rarer with each succeeding year. The game is getting played out; before long, it is to be feared, all the possible combinations will have been used up."[20] Already the bluff had been exhaustively mined, the technique whereby characters whose innocence would have been unchallengeable in Victorian-era detective fiction could now be assumed the likeliest of candidates for criminality. Perhaps the double bluff would follow, "when the author will make his heroes look like heroes and his villains look like villains in the certainty that the over-ingenious reader will get it the wrong way round".[21] But then he had already done that himself in *The Viaduct Murder*.

Different art forms boast their own exemplars, although to the only casually interested observer or participant, the claims to greatness may not be obvious. Why is the so-called Evergreen game, played between Anderssen and Dufresne in 1852, considered the greatest chess game of all time? Similarly, in detective fiction, there was but one answer according to Knox and others when it came to rating the greatest feat in that art form, and that was E. C. Bentley's *Trent's Last Case*. This is

[19] But it should be noted that one critic charitably points out, "The rules were written as instructive guidelines, not to be followed so much as inventively circumvented." See James Kingman, "In Defense of Ronald Knox", *Armchair Detective* 11, no. 3 (July 1978): 299.

[20] Knox, *Best Detective Stories*, p. xv.

[21] Ibid., p. xviii.

a finely crafted story of the murder of an American industrialist, which pits artist and amateur detective Philip Trent against an apparently irreconcilable array of clues, which can be resolved only by pointing the finger against the man's business assistant, who in the end turns out not to be the criminal. Knox's Decalogue reads as if it were conceived with Bentley's novel as template.

THE DETECTION CLUB

In 1929, Anthony Berkeley and Dorothy Sayers founded the Detection Club, and Knox, along with E. C. Bentley, Agatha Christie, G. K. Chesterton, and a number of other prominent detective writers became charter members. The popular creator of Father Brown was soon honored with the presidency of the club; Chesterton was later succeeded by Sayers, and after her death in 1957, Agatha Christie held the post for the duration of her life.[22] Although members swore themselves to secrecy, Chesterton eventually wrote an article revealing the text of the club's initiation ritual, in which each inductee was bidden to uphold certain literary standards, standards displaying a remarkable affinity to the Knoxian commandments. Among other demands made of neophytes, they were to "promise that your detectives shall well and truly detect the crimes presented to them using those wits which it may please you to bestow upon them and not placing reliance on nor making use of Divine Revelation, Feminine Intuition, Mumbo Jumbo, Jiggery–Pokery, Coincidence or Act of God". And if that were not enough to swear to, they must "promise to observe a seemly moderation in the use of Gangs, Conspiracies, Death-Rays, Ghosts, Hypnotism, Trap-Doors, Chinamen, Super-Criminals and Lunatics; and utterly and for ever to forswear Mysterious Poisons unknown to Science".[23]

[22] For the lives and literary accomplishments of Agatha Christie (1890–1976) and Dorothy Sayers (1893–1957), see Janet Morgan, *Agatha Christie: A Biography* (New York: Alfred A. Knopf, 1985), and James Brabazon, *Dorothy L. Sayers* (New York: Charles Scribner's Sons, 1981).

[23] Chesterton's further revelations on the initiation ritual, as well as basic information on the Detection Club, can be found in Maisie Ward, *Gilbert Keith Chesterton* (New York: Sheed and Ward, 1943), pp. 550–52.

Not content merely to dictate the lineaments of their art, the members of the club produced several composite novels, the most famous of which is *The Floating Admiral*. Twelve separate writers submitted one chapter each, beginning with Canon Victor Whitechurch, who set the table with the account of how a fisherman discovers the corpse of a retired admiral in a boat on the River Whyn. The boat belongs to a vicar who lives on the opposite bank of the river to the admiral's Rundel Croft estate. It is then up to later contributors, who were circulated the partial manuscript, to further the plot and eventually to account for the numerous clues each previous author carefully laid and finally bring the mystery to a satisfactory conclusion. Agatha Christie, Dorothy Sayers, Freeman Wills Crofts, Clemence Dane, and others, along with Knox, were architects of a plot that focused on Inspector Rudge's efforts to sort out the criminals among a cast including the admiral's niece and her fiancé, her brother, a retired ambassador, the vicar himself, and his estranged wife. Despite Knox's warning against Chinese intriguers, there is an Oriental connection, evocatively retailed in a G.K. Chesterton prologue written subsequent to the novel's completion. Knox, by the way, is responsible for a long middle chapter called "Thirty Nine Articles of Doubt", in which Rudge mulls over thirty-nine questions the evidence brings to mind but reaches no conclusions.

The Floating Admiral is saved from cumbersomeness only by the deft blending of writing styles and the conscious effort not to derail a previous author's trail of evidence while yet striking out on a new angle. One interesting feature of this book is that all the later contributors submitted their outline of a solution, and these are published as appendices. Interestingly, most converge on the same sinister figure as the culprit, only to be foiled by Anthony Berkeley's final chapter. As Dorothy Sayers observes in her introduction:

> Where one writer may have laid down a clue, thinking that it could point only in one obvious direction, succeeding writers have managed to make it point in a direction exactly opposite. And it is here, perhaps, that the game approximates most closely to real life. We judge one another by our outward actions, but in the motive underlying those actions our judgment may be widely at fault. Preoccupied by our own private interpretation of the matter, we can see only the one possible motive behind the action, so

> that our solution may be quite plausible, quite coherent, and quite wrong.[24]

And so, here again is the moral Knox tried to convey in *The Viaduct Murder.*

The Floating Admiral made money, with which, Knox reported, the club rented regular quarters to replace the restaurant-hopping in which they previously engaged for meetings at which plot lines and villainous enterprises could be hatched. Ironically, however, the place was burgled within a day of their obtaining their keys, and the perpetrator was never found, despite the formidable array of clever minds now hovering about the place.

Half a century later, when Julian Symons attempted to reconstruct the early history of the Detection Club, he found it curiously difficult to establish. "We have no papers of any kind relating to meetings before the fifties—their whereabouts, if they exist, is a mystery none of the present members has been able to solve, and all the original members are dead."[25] What did emerge from some investigating, however, were two more composite yarns, which had been broadcast in installments on the BBC in 1930 and published serially in the accompanying weekly the *Listener*; they were then lost to sight until the 1980s. The second story, titled *Behind the Screen*, includes a chapter by Knox. Far shorter than *The Floating Admiral*, it is an amalgam of contributions by Hugh Walpole, Agatha Christie, Dorothy Sayers, Anthony Berkeley, E. C. Bentley, and finally Knox. It concerns the death, by knife wounds to the neck, of a sinister middle-aged lodger in the quiet home of the Ellis family, whose daughter is engaged to the hero, a young medical student. When the hero visits the Ellises one evening, he is horrified to see a trickle of blood emerging from beneath a large Japanese screen in a corner of the drawing room while the family members are engaged in innocuous postdinner activities. Successive authors elaborate on the odd behavior of Mr. and Mrs. Ellis, their children Robert and Amy, the maid Mrs. Hulk, and various other suspicious characters lurking about the bushes. The only way Knox can tie up loose ends after five

[24] Agatha Christie et al., *The Floating Admiral* (1931; reprint, New York: Berkley Books, 1986), p. 4.

[25] Julian Symons, introduction, *The Scoop, and Behind the Screen* (New York: Harper and Row, 1983).

hands have contributed mounting evidence against multiple suspects is to allow two people with separate motives to have skewered the blackguard independently of one another after yet a third had drugged him. All in a day's work.

LATER MYSTERY STORIES

Every once in a while, Knox also produced a short story featuring Miles Bredon. For example, "Solved by Inspection" is a rather macabre little tale about a rich industrialist who pours his wealth into a faddish Eastern cult only to die of starvation in his bed in the middle of a converted gymnasium in his complex. Curiously, ample supplies of food are at hand, and no signs of struggle or restraint or any foul play are found. However, merely by observing the layout of the room, Bredon deduces that the other cult members, who stood to benefit by his death, drugged him and then availed themselves of four iron rings embedded in the ceiling, left over from the room's former use, to lower hooked ropes to grapple the bed railings, and hoist the bed, with its occupant, forty feet aloft. Earlier apprised of the victim's fear of heights, Bredon reconstructs the inevitable consequences when the victim awakened from his stupor, his cries for assistance repeatedly unheeded. But brief vignettes like this one showcase only Knox's ability to construct an unusual mode of committing a crime, a faculty by no means rare among detective writers, leaving no room for evocations of time and place, his literary strongpoint. Nevertheless, this story was included by the pseudonymous Ellery Queen in an anthology of the best one hundred detective short stories from 1841 to 1941.[26]

The Body in the Silo, published in the United States under the title *Settled out of Court*, is generally reputed to be Knox's best mystery. The reviewer in the *New York Herald Tribune* exulted that Knox "leads the mystery pack by an easy margin"; the *Philadelphia Enquirer* said his novels "are to be treasured—they are all too few"; and the *Chicago Daily Tribune* observed that "it moves so smoothly and convincingly

[26] Ellery Queen, ed., *101 Years' Entertainment: The Great Detective Stories, 1841–1941* (Garden City, N.Y.: Garden City Publishing Co., 1941).

to a horrid but inevitable conclusion that, though you have been completely mystified in its course, at the end you wonder why." [27]

The story takes place at Lastbury Hall, an incongruously Gothic farmhouse that fronts on the River Wye in Herefordshire. The grounds are distinguished by a forty-foot-high silo, which is used to store harvested grain. The estate is owned by a parvenu couple, the Hallifords, who invite the reluctant Bredons to a weekend party along with a number of other guests who have unusually little in common with one another. The hostess of the gathering arranges a "scavenging party", a typically 1920s amusement where people motor through the countryside in search of one vehicle, which is given a sporting head start, in an oversized version of hide and seek. One houseguest, Cecil Worsley, an important government figure, does not participate in the festivities because he must work on an important article that evening. The next morning Bredon, who was out with the others in the hunt until the early morning hours, is awakened to the news that Worsley has been found dead in the silo. Since everyone else had been preoccupied with the chase, it is assumed initially that he committed suicide, though he had shown no signs of depression (in fact, he was downright jovial) earlier in the evening. But why choose such a bizarre and cumbersome death? And if it was murder, none of the guests of the household had the slightest reason for doing him in, and he was financially backing Mr. and Mrs. Halliford. Inspector Leyland reappears and, as usual, makes out an almost convincing case against a young author who had been unpleasantly involved in a death in the United States, which he was trying to live down. But the Scotland Yard man has fingered the wrong suspect, whose suspicious moves are eventually revealed to have a matrimonial rather than a homicidal intent. The clues leading to a proper explanation of events are more subtle. The dead man had left a coded diary, which was missing from the effects returned to his executors and subsequently requested. A few torn extracts turn up in the library of the estate, and Bredon is encouraged by the Hallifords to decipher them. The full diary is then found, with its final entry altered. Bredon realizes that he has been

[27] Ronald A. Knox, *Settled out of Court* (New York: E.P. Dutton and Co., 1934). The quotes are taken from the frontispiece to his next detective novel, *Still Dead* (New York: E.P. Dutton and Co., 1934), first published in the United States the same year.

manipulated and turns his attention to several items found in a walled garden between the house and the silo. These too are ambivalent in their suggestion of who was in the garden the night of Worsley's demise, the victim or another guest. Eventually he discerns that a fateful confusion of two secret letters sent by the plotter—one to Worsley and one to the intended victim—had gotten mixed up through the cavortings of the family's pet monkey, so that a very carefully conceived murder went terribly awry. Just prior to the unraveling of the details, Knox and his publisher insert a caesura, a pause in the action, at which the reader is invited to solve the case, before proceeding in the company of Bredon. And perhaps sensitive to the criticism that his stories entwined the helpful clues in an excessive overlay of possibly misleading details, Knox also employs footnotes in this and his subsequent detective novels after the caesura to reassure the reader that the facts involved in the solution were dutifully aired earlier in the narrative.

Four of Knox's mysteries are set in estates of some kind, and he lavishes great care on their description. Although his concern was primarily with plot, the mood of a good detective story is incalculably enhanced by its physical setting, and his houses always evoked the appropriate ambiance. Of course, as Catholic chaplain at Oxford, he normally lived in the slightly shabby lodgings incongruously called the Old Palace, but summer vacations found him invariably the guest of Lord and Lady Lovat at Beaufort Castle in Scotland.[28] And although he rarely traveled beyond the English Channel, he knew his homeland thoroughly. Being a train aficionado, he saw the countryside in all its nooks and crannies while traversing the maze of lines connecting villages throughout the island. And like many reflective thinkers, he was

[28] The original Beaufort Castle had been destroyed during the uprising of 1745, and it was not until 1880 that the fifteenth Lord Lovat, Simon Fraser, began working on an imposing replacement overlooking the River Beauly while he lived in an adjacent, more modest, home. His son, who was the founder of the Lovat Scouts, which had a distinguished record in the Boer War and in the two world wars, was the husband of Laura Lister, and it was they who hosted Knox. Unfortunately, he died suddenly in 1933, and two years later the new castle was gutted in a fire. Consequently, his heir, the seventeenth Lord Lovat, later to become a World War II hero at Normandy, inherited a sized-down portion of the castle that Knox knew. The castle was finally sold by the family in 1994, and the seventeenth Lord Lovat died the following year. On the Lovats and other prominent British Catholic aristocrats, see Mark Bence-Jones, *The Catholic Families* (London: Constable, 1992).

also a prodigious walker, a pastime both he and his detective hero engaged in, more to clear their minds by contemplating nature's prodigality than to work out a solution to a vexing problem.

Given those summers at Beaufort Castle, then, it is not surprising that Knox's last two novels are set in Scotland, on the kinds of large estates that were already becoming by the 1930s decreasingly available in England as locales for mysterious occurrences. He explains this as an English predilection:

> We like to live in smaller houses, in which patent kitchenettes replace those long, chilly passages, as if we would draw our homes close about our ears against the wind.... [T]he gaunt mansions of the more fashionable suburbs advertise their emptiness with rotting boards that appeal for an imaginary purchaser, and their occupants live in dumpy maisonettes, a quarter of the size, compensating themselves for the loss with an undeniable garage and a few yards of crazy pavement. Meanwhile, those greater householders whose, once, were the dreaming parks and Georgian piles we have all coveted, have abandoned the expense of their upkeep and crowded into London flats, with a fine mews outlook and a postal address which looks respectable enough if you omit the 95B.[29]

Dorn House and its grounds in Scotland are anything but generous in relinquishing their secrets to an investigator, as Bredon finds out when called upon by his firm to look into the mysterious affair of Colin Reiver, heir to the estate. After Reiver notifies his family of his imminent return, his lifeless body shows up on the main road just outside the Dorn grounds. A peculiarly apathetic and dissolute fellow, he had been sent abroad after he accidentally ran over a child in a motoring accident but was exonerated of manslaughter charges. Strangely, his corpse is first discovered on a Monday morning, disappears before the household is brought to the scene, and then reappears two days later, *Still Dead*, as the title of the novel emphasizes. Bredon finds the mansion

> full of character, and its quaintness endears it to the habitué. But when you arrive just before dinner on a dark night, so that you have no external impression to go by, its odd corners and culs de

[29] Knox, *Still Dead*, p. 11.

> sac are enough to daunt even the resourcefulness of a detective. You open what was once the door of your bedroom, and find yourself in a cupboard; you come out of the bathroom, and find yourself suddenly surrounded by shut doors you have not the courage to try; staircases wander this way and that, passages run across one another without communicating, nothing seems to be on the same level as anything else. This, even if you are a legitimate visitor; the embarrassment of the experience is multiplied if you feel yourself to be a spy on the actions of your hosts, and nourish the suspicion that they regard you in that light.[30]

It is an appropriate backdrop for a case in which many layers of intrigue conspire to perplex Bredon. A rich assortment of relatives and acquaintances, many with plausible motives for murder, so crowd the canvas that both the detective and the reader are easily deflected from the true perpetrator, who is dutifully introduced early in the narrative and certainly harbors a sufficient grudge to do in Colin Reiver. There is the estate's old laird himself, admittedly bedridden throughout the proceedings but estranged from his sullen son so much that he alters his will so that all his money is to go to an Evangelical organization he has lately joined rather than to his family. The doctor who tends to him is equally suspect, as is Major Henry Reiver, an irascible cousin who may have designs on the estate as well. Both these characters notoriously plant evidence meant to deflect Bredon from reaching certain conclusions about the time and circumstances of the young man's death, but their motives remain unclear until the final exposition of the plot. Likewise, the deceased's sister and her husband have a vested interest in seeing the time of death fixed at the later date because a hefty insurance policy taken out on young Reiver's life had temporarily lapsed and, consequently, while in force by the Wednesday, was not in force on the critical Monday the body was first discovered by a tenant of the estate, before being spirited away by unknown parties.

A few years later, Knox came out with *Double Cross Purposes*, his final detective novel. It revolves around the quest of a rather louche young gentleman named Vernon Lethaby to find a treasure supposedly left on a secluded Scottish midriver island by Bonnie Prince Charlie during his abortive 1745 uprising against the Hanovers. The

[30] Ibid., p. 71.

atmosphere of the story is even darker than in *Still Dead*. Lethaby has a mysterious companion, Henderson, alleged to be a phenomenal man with a shovel, to assist him in his search, most of which occurs after nightfall. But even in daylight, Bredon finds the island disturbingly gloomy:

> It was an island fertile in decay. Overwooded, and visited by more than its share of Highland rain, its airs were continually dank, its soil spongy. By the fallen trees which lay there undisturbed, with their fantastic roots turned heavenwards as if in appeal against human neglect, grew toadstools, vividly coloured, mocking the forms of artificial things. Among the strange fungus growths you found, in springtime, that reputed delicacy the morel, an unshapely mass of edible corruption. The ferns which abounded in the rock crevices were, for the most part, of the simplest geometrical pattern, as if survivals from some undifferentiated, old days of nature's apprenticeship. This was in the woods; in the clearings, rare by comparison, heather and bracken and bogmyrtle delimited their own spheres, invaded continually by the vigorous burgeoning of rhododendrons and azaleas, man's importation. So rapid was their growth that every path, except the main drive, had to be cut afresh almost yearly lest it should relapse into jungle.[31]

Yet the Knoxian penchant for the light touch is irrepressible. The following gem is occasioned by Bredon's first approach to the island over the river Dounie:

> There is that about running water which makes us all want to stop and waste time. Why this should be so, it is for the psychologists to determine; you would have thought that a river, reminding us by its steady flow of the remorseless passage of time, might have spurred us to action, encouraged us to strike one blow before we too are carried away, like the people in the hymn. But whenever humanity has built a bridge over the river, there, unless you are traversing a wilderness, you will find people leaning over the bridge, absorbed in the spectacle of running water. Small boys, with all the opportunities of life opening before them, fritter them away the moment they come to a stream; a kind of ritual sense bids them halt, sail paper boats, throw stones at a bottle, or paddle. Bathing itself, the

[31] Knox, *Double Cross Purposes*, p. 62.

> adult's compensation for not being allowed to paddle, would lose half its seductive charm if it were not so evidently a pure waste of time. And there are those fearless enquirers into the nature of things who would maintain that the joys of the fisherman—most solid of all joys, and most incommunicable—are really determined by the prodigious waste of time which occurs between one rise and the next.... But I will not argue the matter.[32]

As for the story line, a fire breaks out in a shed on the island, a charred skeleton is recovered from the embers, and the digger has disappeared, but whether the skeleton is his, or whether he has absconded with the treasure, is open to surmise. Two secondary characters from earlier novels reappear in this tale, a pedantic elderly schoolmaster who previously showed up at the "Load of Mischief" during Mottram's fateful fishing vacation in *The Three Taps*, and Mrs. Wauchope, a grand dame who filled Angela Bredon in on the town gossip about the Reivers in *Still Dead* and who turns out to be Lethaby's aunt. The former provides a cover for the nonsmoking Bredons when they rent a cottage opposite the island where the excavating is going on, while the latter plays an unwitting role in upsetting her nephew's well-conceived plans. It transpires that Lethaby has never given much credence to the rumor of buried treasure. His aunt, however, holds a considerable trove of mid-eighteenth-century relics at a little-used estate, so he and his companion surreptitiously borrow some of them to create a bogus cache on the island. The plan is to uncover them in view of Bredon, the representative of the Indescribable, and then allow Henderson to escape with them before they can be evaluated, so that Lethaby can cash in on a sizeable policy he took out against the possibility that Henderson would do just that. But the plan starts to encounter difficulties when Mrs. Wauchope decides to pay an unexpected visit to that very home. Further confusing the issue is that Henderson may not be as dismissive of the legend of the buried treasure as Lethaby, and a photograph he takes of an old map figures as a multilayered clue, first to authenticate their finding of the bogus treasure but, then, more obscurely, to suggest a location where a real treasure might be found.

[32] Ibid., p. 59. Dounie was the name of the old castle (see footnote 28 above) burned after the battle of Culloden.

Earlier it was noted that in this novel, Knox took liberties with one of his commandments, the one in which the detective is bidden not to withhold evidence from his readers. Bredon oars over to the island earlier on the night of the fire, observes something concealed in the treasure hunters' moored boat, and then exchanges his vessel for theirs and returns to shore. What does he find there and take back with him? Knox does not let the reader in on the haul, which triggers Henderson's subsequent activities that night.[33]

DIVERSIONS FOR LEISURE HOURS

The last of Knox's six detective novels appeared in 1937. Within two years, Knox was to leave the chaplaincy at Oxford to take up residence at the Aldenham estate of Lord and Lady Acton, where he could begin work on the staggering task of translating the Bible anew, commissioned to do so by the hierarchy. It is idle to speculate what would have been the trajectory of his career as a mystery writer had he continued with the genre. The stories were merely exercises of ingenuity for him, opportunities as well to express himself in a style too lush for the more serious work of explaining doctrine or awakening spiritual faculties, and yet demanding outlet from an overflowing literary talent. The mystery novel allowed that talent to be channeled unpretentiously. He was a true connoisseur of the mind bender, whether it took the form of the *Times* crosswords he would solve by making use of only the horizontal clues because otherwise they were too transparent for him, or the novels he wrote in which important clues would be partially hidden behind inconsequential information lest the cleverest reader spy them without investing sufficient energy in the process. He wanted his contributions to the art of perplexing to be challenging enough to afford more than a fleeting pleasure to the leisure hours. Perhaps the complexity of plot may deter some readers from immersing themselves in these novels, although the numerous

[33] Because of this piece of obfuscation as well as other defects in the novel, a perceptive critic considers it inferior as detective fiction to *The Body in the Silo* or *Still Dead*. See William Reynolds, "The Detective Novels of Ronald A. Knox", *Armchair Detective* 14, no. 3 (1981): 275–83, for a thorough analysis of the strengths and weaknesses in all six novels.

editions they have run through, including paperback reprints, attest to the fact that an appreciative audience has consistently been at hand.

For sure, it would be inconceivable that any reader would have sought out his detective stories because of the magnetic appeal of Miles Bredon, who never assumed the celebrity status of a Hercule Poirot or a Jane Marple, let alone a Sherlock Holmes. But for stylistic beauty, and for an ability to evoke the English and Scottish countrysides and manors of the interwar years, Knox had few equals, and his detective fiction would remain enjoyable for that reason alone.

But the novels also testify to his rootedness in this world. Bredon may be colorless, but that is because Knox isn't the type of writer to place himself (Bredon's alter ego) front and center. The characters the detective comes in contact with, however, run the gamut of human types, usually with a preponderance of less desirable attributes. They are the creations of a keen observer and describer of people, and the lighthearted touch that graces his prose does not conceal his genuine fascination with the ordinary in life.

Anticipating Josef Pieper, he was comfortable with the concept of leisure, and he saw no incongruity in a priest writing merely to entertain. The golden age of the English detective story is the richer for his contributions to its body of literature, and as more of his novels find their way into print again, the intellectual rigor as well as the literary quality he brought to this form of writing will keep Knox's name alive among readers who may know little else about him than that he wrote six classic whodunits.

CHAPTER SEVEN

A.L. TO R.A.K.

For three years in the early 1920s, a skilled antagonist had been laboring over a book that would take aim at several major figures of English Catholicism, Ronald Knox among them. The book was called *Roman Converts*, and its author devoted a lengthy chapter to each of the figures he regarded as influential in a religion he believed to pose an alluring but ultimately debilitating threat to mankind's well-being. Among its trophies were Cardinals Manning and Newman, G.K. Chesterton, the ex-Jesuit George Tyrrell,[1] and Father Knox. Each was analyzed, some more sympathetically than others, with Tyrrell's peculiar blend of vague Modernist theology and earthy affection for the Catholic ethos drawing the highest marks, while Knox

[1] There are two modern studies of George Tyrrell (1861–1909), whose name has become synonymous with the Modernist movement in Catholicism. David Schultenover, *George Tyrrell: In Search of Catholicism* (Shepherdstown, W.Va.: Patmos Press, 1981), emphasizes his ambiguous ecclesiology and spirituality while downplaying his opposition to authority. But Nicholas Sagovsky, *On God's Side: A Life of George Tyrrell* (Oxford: Clarendon Press, 1990), goes out of his way to herald Tyrrell's bitter antagonism toward his Jesuit superiors (who often went out of their way to protect him), not to mention toward the hierarchy in England and the Roman officials to whom some of his works were predictably forwarded for censure. By the end of his tragic life he was reduced to espousing a view of Christ indistinguishable from Matthew Arnold's, as the following excerpt from a letter shows: "I do not mean that he is omnipotent but that He has the words of eternal life, that He makes Himself felt in me as a Power that makes for Righteousness—a redeeming strengthening power; that his words have a sacramental spiritual efficacy beyond their merely intellectual value; that I owe Him the same worship of obedience and self-sacrifice that I accord to my Conscience." Quoted in Sagovsky, *On God's Side*, p. 254. The best character study of Tyrrell is that given by Marvin O'Connell in his *Critics on Trial* (Washington, D.C.: Catholic University of America Press, 1994), while the most incisive analysis of his theology is the chapter devoted to him in Aidan Nichols, *From Newman to Congar: The Idea of Doctrinal Development from the Victorians to the Second Vatican Council* (Edinburgh: T and T Clark, 1989), pp. 114–35.

perhaps ranks below Newman as the least attractive convert in the author's eyes.

The asymmetry engendered by including a young priest in his mid-thirties among a cast of figures of historic proportions should itself be a clue to the author's contemporaneity with Knox, and indeed the two were exactly the same age. Arnold Lunn was born in 1888 in India, where his father was at the time a Methodist missionary. Unlike Knox, Lunn was educated at Harrow, but like Knox, he proceeded to Balliol College and was active as an editor of *Isis* and as an avid member of the Oxford Union Debating Society. He was actually one year behind Knox, having gone up in 1907, but whereas Knox completed his studies with great distinction in 1910, Lunn succumbed to the temptation to devour modern philosophy and Modernist theology rather than attend to the subjects bearing on his course of studies, and he consequently failed to obtain his B.A. Literary work and sports canalized his superabundant energy and innate competitiveness. An early intimacy with Swiss culture brought about by his father's departure from the ministry and entry into the travel business introduced him to the world of ski racing, about which he wrote prolifically. He is credited, in fact, with inventing the slalom race and was to become a prime mover in the development of the Winter Olympic Games. But mountain climbing perhaps even surpassed his passion for skiing, and whenever he was not completely felled by a broken leg, he would be in pursuit of the Matterhorn or another Alpine peak.

Never having appropriated the fervent Methodism of his father, Sir Henry Lunn, the young Arnold's religiosity suffered irreparably when he became an intellectual disciple of Leslie Stephen, the late-nineteenth-century literary critic best known as the editor of the massive sixty-three-volume *Dictionary of National Biography*, one of the monumental achievements of Victorian scholarship. Stephen too had been an accomplished mountaineer, a lean, tall athlete who thought a thirty-mile walk nothing out of the ordinary. He also shared with Lunn an Evangelical background. In fact, Stephen was ordained after studying mathematics at Cambridge, where he became a popular don and the coach of the rowing team. But what little faith he inherited from his civic-minded father wore down more rapidly than his boots did, and he soon renounced his clerical fellowship and set out to be a writer. He became a staunch agnostic, supported in his views by his second wife, Julia Duckworth, a widow whom he married a few years after the death of his first wife, one of Thackeray's two daughters. He and Julia had four children of their own, one of whom was to eclipse him in fame as a writer under her married name of Virginia Woolf.[2]

In addition to his biographical and literary studies, Stephen wrote philosophical essays championing the new unbelief being propagated by T. H. Huxley and others, a number of them collected in a small book under the heading *An Agnostic's Apology*. It was this book that found its way into Lunn's hands and converted him to its creed.

When one gets past the rhetoric, for example, the fanciful terming of Christians as Gnostics, Stephen's argument can be summarized under two main headings. The first is that if one grants that men do indeed exercise free will, then one has denied universal causation, which he associates with a rigorous determinism. "The anti-determinist asserts the existence of chance so positively that he doubts whether God Himself can foretell the future of humanity, or, at least, he is unable to reconcile Divine prescience with his favourite doctrine."[3] The second is the admixture of good and evil in the world, in many cases even the triumph of evil over good in the world, which does not instill confidence that a benevolent Creator oversees all events. The response given by the great Anglican theologians, that justice will be meted out in the next world, seems unconvincing:

> This is the Christian revelation according to Butler. Does it make the world better? Does it not, rather, add indefinitely to the terror produced by the sight of all its miseries, and justify James Mill for feeling that rather than such a God he would rather have no God? What escape can be suggested? The obvious one: it is all a mystery; and what is mystery but the theological phrase for Agnosticism? God has spoken, and endorsed all our most hideous doubts. He has said, let there be light, and there is no light—no light, but rather darkness visible, serving only to discover sights of woe.[4]

[2] A rigorous moralist in spite of his agnosticism, Stephen (1832–1904) was also a stern father who dominated his children and became excessively preoccupied with his own suffering after Julia's untimely death in 1895. Virginia had her revenge in subsequent, thinly veiled portrayals of him. An excellent modern study of his life and his thought is provided by Noel Annan, *Leslie Stephen: Godless Victorian* (New York: Random House, 1984).

[3] Leslie Stephen, *An Agnostic's Apology* (1893; reprint, London: Watts and Co., 1931), p. 13.

[4] Ibid., p. 22.

Marriage, mountains, and World War I all deflected Lunn from writing about ultimate issues until the European hostilities concluded. But in 1918, he published a novel called *Loose Ends* that was heavily indebted to Stephen's philosophy. Its hero is a young man whose faith begins to crumble while he is navigating his way through the usual horrors of a semiprestigious public school. Under the benign influence of a charismatic literature teacher, he rejects the heady but crude atheism of Ernst Haeckel, with which a fellow student plies him, and is guided to a gentle William Jamesian intellectual landing. Peace of mind is achieved only when he finds he can pray to and with a fallible deity rather than an omnipotent God. In the meantime, Rome and Jesuitism are so far removed from the ambiance of his school that they merit only the occasional derogatory remark while the hero wrestles with the tension building up between his budding agnosticism and the traditional exercises of the national religion as refracted through chapel services and a headmaster's talks.[5]

But then in 1921, Lunn began work on the book that he expected would explode the pretensions of the Romanists, by showing that conversion to the Catholic Church was tantamount to surrendering one's reason on the altar of blind obedience. Why the sudden interest if he, like his fictional projection, was now content with his newly adopted religious views?

Evelyn Waugh suggests that it was Chesterton's conversion that triggered Lunn's investigations, but Chesterton was received into the Church in 1922. On the contrary, it was clearly Knox's conversion, in particular his recounting of it in *A Spiritual Aeneid* (1918), that spurred Lunn into written reaction. Lunn accounted himself a good logician, and he clearly resented the imputation in Knox's writings and in the writings of Catholic theologians that logic was an integral ally to Catholic claims. A Jesuit author of a manual on natural theology especially irked him. When Father Bernard Boedder retailed rational arguments to delineate what one can know about God, Lunn charged him with "tactfully guiding his syllogisms towards the orthodox conclusions, even where those conclusions are contrary to logic and common sense".

[5] Arnold Lunn, *Loose Ends* (London: Hutchinson and Co., 1918). It is interesting to note that Evelyn Waugh's youthful slide into agnosticism was in part precipitated by reading this novel, so Stephen's skepticism had diffusive strength. See Martin Stannard, *Evelyn Waugh: The Early Years* (New York: W. W. Norton and Co., 1987), p. 62.

Chief among these inconsistencies in Lunn's estimation is the assertion of divine omniscience concomitant with the assertion that men have free will. So much was he beholden to Stephen's arguments that it is not clear whether he ever completely reconciled these concepts in his mind, but certainly in the early 1920s omniscience represented one of two major stumbling blocks keeping him from professing Christianity. He found it

> difficult to wax lyrical over the gift of free will, when the will, by hypothesis, is only free to travel along those paths which have been charted out in that plan of all history which has never varied since first conceived in the mind of God. Free will becomes a mere legal fiction, invented in order that God may send us to Hell with a clear conscience for committing those sins which he foresaw that we should commit, and for leaving undone those things which we could only have done if God had foreseen us doing them.[6]

As the trailing edge of the above quote shows, the other stumbling block was hell. Only the Enlightenment freed mankind from "an obscene conception of God" fostered by the Catholic Church and forced the Church to tone down her theology. Because "until the world revolted, the Church continued to teach that God by the fiat of his unchallenged will had called into being unnumbered millions with the foreknowledge, and, therefore, the intention that they should pass Eternity in excruciating agony".[7]

To drive the point home to readers with modern susceptibilities, Lunn cites the unfairness whereby a fellow who passes up Sunday Mass for a round of golf and is then killed in a car accident before repenting of his sin is eternally damned, while a profligate who outlives his capacity for satisfying his lustful urges and dutifully confesses his sins gets into Purgatory. "Conscience and common sense", he concludes, "are revolted by the lack of justice of the Roman Catholic scheme of posthumous punishments."[8] At the end of the decade, when Lunn wrote *The Flight from Reason*, a work that made a plea for a return to the respect for reason displayed by the scholastics, he still shuddered at Thomas Aquinas' treatment of the question whether the

[6] Arnold Lunn, *Roman Converts* (London: Chapman and Hall, 1924), p. 8.
[7] Ibid., p. 10.
[8] Ibid., p. 12.

saved rejoice in the justice of the punishment experienced by the damned. Aquinas calmly states that they will rejoice "for they will see in this the order of Divine justice and their own escape which will fill them with joy".[9] While it is evident that Aquinas did not exactly affirm any celestial delight in the contemplation of the torments of the reprobate, Lunn's mind was clearly still troubled enough to read into his discussion of the issue such an interpretation. By then, of course, he was reading Aquinas much more sympathetically on many theological points, but the concept of hell remained simply unacceptable to him.

Even in his 1929 biography of John Wesley, Lunn returns to the point. Wesley was forever expatiating on the love of God to the adherents of Methodism, but he had one very forceful sermon on the pains of hell, a sermon he did not shrink from preaching for fear of upsetting people's sensitivities. It was a device used by a sober realist to awaken people to the awful importance of conversion from a sinful way of life. But Lunn digresses at length once again on a theology that "postulates a Creator . . . who is not sufficiently civilized to reject torture as a means of punishment". And then he laments Protestantism's retention of hell and its rejection of Purgatory, which now seems to him a more humane, because temporary, vehicle for expiating sinful guilt.[10]

With a predisposition to regard Catholics as adherents of an intransigent world outlook—hostile to progress, bigoted in the extreme against outsiders, and unconscionably certain of the truth of the doctrines they hold—it is no surprise that Lunn should have been irritated by Knox's conversion story. When Lunn zeroes in on *A Spiritual Aeneid*, he wields an intemperate pen and a facility for distortion that does not do him especial credit as a rationalist or as a controversialist. There is too much of an ad hominem color to the essay on Knox, more so than in the other four essays in *Roman Converts*. Not too many years later, when he was writing the autobiographical portion of *Now I See*, Lunn admitted "that the essay was a travesty which I greatly regret", but he also says he "was not conscious of any unfairness" at the time

[9] Quoted in Arnold Lunn, *The Flight from Reason* (New York: Dial Press, 1931), p. 30.

[10] Arnold Lunn, *John Wesley* (New York: Dial Press, 1929), p. 319.

he wrote it.[11] That the essay was indeed the heart of the book was brought out in a book he wrote in 1958 shortly after Knox's death, which contained a lengthy panegyric recounting the events that brought about their meeting and subsequent friendship of over a quarter of a century. Reading Knox "exasperated me and I found relief in the catharsis of an essay on *A Spiritual Aeneid*. The next problem was to find a publisher. Nobody would publish the essay as it stood, but what about a book of essays on converts to Catholicism? Such was the genesis of *Roman Converts*."[12] And that recollection late in life effectively settles the priority of Knox over Chesterton as the burr in Lunn's hide.

Curiously, one of the things that particularly irritated Lunn was Knox's repudiation of his own father's religion: "The reasons he gave for his change of creed are so unconvincing, that you feel he might have spared himself the trouble of writing a big book to account for a conversion which he is said to have explained in a single sentence: 'I had to have some religion, and I couldn't stand Father's.'"[13]

Now, Bishop Edmund Knox's creed was not very different from Sir Henry Lunn's, and the reader who is familiar with the younger Lunn's writings during this period can see that despite his flirtations with Spiritualism and agnosticism, he was yearning for the kind of security his father found in Methodism. The Wesley biography, while poking some fun at the great revivalist's misfortunes in dealing with women, is withal suffused with profound admiration for the life of a most devout and learned Christian. Lunn detects impiety in Knox's refusal to be satisfied with his Evangelical upbringing, and his reticence in discussing the growing painful rift with Bishop Knox suggests instead flippancy. Evangelicalism had its muscular side, which eminently appealed to a mountaineer who viewed the Olympic Games in religious terms and envied the pagan religion of Rome its attraction to stouthearted men. Turning away from such an atmosphere could be accounted for only by a quirky affinity for precious posturing and for snide dismissal of other people's spiritual odysseys. Didn't the very title, choosing an "Aeneid"—a journey that implies a stable home at its end—offer a rebuke to searchers such as Lunn himself?

[11] Arnold Lunn, *Now I See* (London: Sheed and Ward, 1946), p. 42.
[12] Arnold Lunn, *And Yet So New* (New York: Sheed and Ward, 1958), p. 3.
[13] Lunn, *Roman Converts*, p. 168.

Knox is taken to task for recalling how he would attend Anglo-Catholic services in Pusey House Chapel all the while relishing the sense the visits gave him "of catacombs, oubliettes, Jesuitry, and all the atmosphere of mystery that had fascinated me so long".[14]

The reader catches the hint of self-mockery in the description, redolent of *Henry Esmond* more than of the Catholic milieu that Knox was already realizing to be far less romantic. But Lunn is not amused. It provides him an opportunity to caricature Anglo-Catholic clerics:

> Anglican Bishops exist to be baited; theologians to provide Knox with epigrams. It is all very jolly. It must be great fun to keep your friends waiting for lunch while you are occupied "in saying quint." You can imagine the pleasant evenings devoted to port, bananas and new schemes for an English Breviary, "a book of uncommon prayer". intended to replace the dreary compilation of Cranmer's prayers. One figures Knox lying on the hearthrug talking with brisk animation on the question of the hour. At what precise point should Ablutions be taken? It would really be great fun to transfer the Eucharistic Amen to the end of the Canon. How on earth can one manage to interpolate large chunks of the Latin Mass while saying aloud the rotten Anglican rite and yet contrive to complete Low Mass within thirty minutes *ab amictu ad amictum* [from putting on vestments to their removal]? It is all such fun.[15]

It was a clever idea to resort to parody against an accomplished parodist. But the grimace behind the quip is too evident, particularly since Lunn knew so little about the Anglo-Catholic movement. In his autobiography, he observes that while he was imbibing Modernist theology "I was ignorant not only of Catholic doctrine, but also of elementary facts about the Catholic liturgy. I did not, for instance, know that there was any connection between the Mass and the Anglican Communion Service. Until I had passed my thirtieth birthday, I had never been inside an Anglo-Catholic church, and never realised that Anglo-Catholics substituted Mass for Matins as the chief service on Sunday morning."[16] Since the years intervening between his thirtieth birthday and the writing of *Roman Converts* appear to have been devoted

[14] Ronald Knox, *A Spiritual Aeneid* (London: Longmans, Green and Co., 1918), p. 177.

[15] Lunn, *Roman Converts*, p. 178.

[16] Lunn, *Now I See*, p. 31.

primarily to research in Spiritualism, it would seem that he was caricaturing the opposition from a very uncertain base of knowledge.

Lunn also accuses Knox of being a party propagandist who is far more interested in advancing an institutional Church than of presenting Christ to the modern world.

> Jesus, according to Ronald Knox, is a mere lay figure. He fulfils his role by founding the Roman Church, and by bequeathing to Peter full powers of attorney.... Christ, as the second Adam, is a useful peg on which to hang a sermon, devoted to the disobedience of Eve and the consequent damnation of the great majority of Eve's children. But in all that Knox writes there is not one picture of Jesus the man.... Knox's Jesus never comes to life. His secret, his simplicity, the magic of his words, an alchemy which transformed all values and changed the world, finds no place in Knox's scheme.[17]

Blistering words, but is the indictment fair? For his background reading, Lunn relied primarily on Knox's autobiography; his critique of Modernist theology, *Some Loose Stones*; his two novels *Sanctions* and *Memories of the Future*; and his Anglican sermons collected under the title *The Church in Bondage*. Each of these works addressed issues of the day, some with gravity and others with some levity, but to belabor them with an alleged lack of Christocentricity is to misread them and their author. Had Lunn bothered to peruse Knox's reflections on prayer *Bread or Stone* from his Anglican years or his *Meditations on the Psalms* published two years after his conversion, he would probably have hesitated to dismiss him as a spiritual nonstarter. But what Lunn was about was trying to drive a wedge between formal religion, with which he was very uncomfortable at the time, and the humanist Jesus of Matthew Arnold and other liberal theologians, a Jesus whom one could admire without fearing as Lord and God.

So the polemics intensified. Lunn even questions the motivation behind Knox's vow of lifelong celibacy, a state of life that did not square with broad-shouldered Christianity but that instead allowed him leisure to indulge in superficial theologizing. "Had he joined an East End Church, the contact with reality might have had a salutary effect. A priest who has tested his creed experimentally by contact with sin,

[17] Lunn, *Roman Converts*, pp. 178–79.

suffering, poverty and crime soon ceases to feel an absorbing interest in the mere externals of his faith. But a clerical Don lives remote from these crude actualities, and has too much time for the mere politics of religion."[18] Presumably like Ernest Pontifex in *The Way of All Flesh*, whose experience of slum living disabuses him of his Ritualist leanings but also lands him in jail when he renounces his vow of celibacy in too sudden a manner, Knox would end up a reformed freethinker and journalist and thereby more of a credit to society. But on the other hand, Lunn's hero Leslie Stephen was not an East End curate but rather a Cambridge don when he decided for agnosticism. So the rhetoric is not that convincing.

At times, Lunn shifts away from the ad hominem to the realm of logic but frequently with less than marked success. One among a number of efforts to score off Knox's presumed slipshod reasoning will suffice for illustrative purposes. In *A Spiritual Aeneid*, Knox countered the notion that one must examine dogma to the fullest extent with the intellect with which one is endowed, if one is to be a good Christian. Knox suggests that it would be just as logical to state that the fullest development of one's physical fitness is a prerequisite to living the Christian life: "The same might, I suppose, be said of our biceps: yet I never think myself the worse Christian for not doing Sandow exercises." To which Lunn retorts: "Nor does [Jack] Dempsey think himself the worse boxer because he does not do the Spiritual Exercises of St. Ignatius. One could write this sort of thing with one's left hand, but it means precisely nothing."[19] Does it? Knox is merely reiterating classical Christian theology that it is faith, not intellect—or for that matter the development of any other God-given endowment either of a mental or physical nature—that leads to salvation. It is Lunn's inversion of the terms to accentuate a trivial skill that is a non sequitur.

There are, however, more serious problems with the essay, problems that touch on intellectual honesty. Examine the following paragraphs, which convey an image of a self-promoter:

> Knox enlivens his sermons during his Anglo-Catholic days with frequent references to dissent. No doubt he amused his congregations vastly by his quotation from an American paper describing a lecture

[18] Ibid., p. 188.
[19] Ibid., p. 196.

given in the Grace Methodist Church at New York. He implies, without giving any evidence, that this lecture took the place of a service, and that it was delivered on a Sunday. He appears rather shocked by the fact that the pulpit was surrounded by a block of ice, and that the audience were provided with fans in view of the heat wave which was then particularly severe. Catholic Cathedrals are heated in winter, and I do not see why it is more vulgar to cool a hot church than to heat a cold church. But let that pass. Catholic Churches in India, by the way, are always cooled by fans, and the fans are worked by perspiring Indians.

"Having thus fortified them against the elements he gave a lecture on sport in Norway, and the service concluded with a collection."

Knox then thoughtfully provides us with an effective contrast, a picture of himself at Benediction.

"All we saw was a curate in a rather shabby cope in front of something which looked like a circular piece of bread. All we heard was a few hymns in honour of a carpenter's wife who died nearly nineteen hundred years ago."[20]

The synopsis is based on an extract from a sermon preached at Saint James', Plymouth, in 1913. The obvious conclusion Lunn wishes to leave in the reader's mind is that Knox was describing himself officiating reverently at Benediction in an Anglo-Catholic service, by way of pious contrast with the vulgar American Protestant spectacle. But Lunn left out the following sentences after the quote about the lecture topic: "I rose from the perusal of this to attend the service of Benediction with the Blessed Sacrament in a small, and not very rich, Belgian parish church. It was a weekday, but I think the congregation was as large as you would find at weekday evensong in the greatest of our English cathedrals."[21] A quick reference to Knox's autobiography would have confirmed that earlier in 1913 he had been in Belgium, where of course he would have been a spectator, not an officiating priest, at Benediction. No doubt had the lecture that provided Knox with such a contrast between the mundane and the sublime taken place in any but a Methodist church and had the subject matter been other than the passion of Lunn's life, he might have been less offended

[20] Ibid., p. 200.

[21] Ronald Knox, "The Church in Bondage", in *University and Anglican Sermons*, ed. Philip Caraman, S.J. (New York: Sheed and Ward, 1963), p. 462.

by it. But editing it to add to an unfavorable portrait was hardly a forgivable ploy.

Another instance involves quoting Knox out of context. Lunn informs his readers that in his autobiography Knox "tells us that a First in Greats left him with 'a fierce love of sifting evidence,' a confession which does not prevent his remarking that he had 'no interest in discovering the truth, but believing myself to have found it, in making other people believe it.'"[22] But it is clear from the context in the autobiography that Knox was referring to his state of mind when he was trying to defend Anglicanism as a branch of the true Church when further investigation might have shown him the fallacy of that presumption. The quote begins with, "I had no interest", emphasizing that he had no interest at that particular time, a position he soon had to abandon. If Lunn had brought that fact out, he could not have left the desired impression, i.e., that Knox was arrogantly proclaiming a cavalier attitude toward ultimate truth.

Lunn concluded his essay with the observation that Knox would be "in no danger of reading this book, or of taking to heart the disinterested advice which is tendered in all humility by one of his many grateful readers". It is doubtful whether he believed anything of what he said in that sentence, nor should he have. He himself sent a copy of *Roman Converts* to Knox and awaited a reply. It came, and was surprisingly genial. Lunn reminisced later: "I remember thinking at the time that there must be unsuspected reserves in that strange religion of his, if he could reply with such humour to so hostile a study of himself and his book. Many years later, on the day before Father Knox received me into the Church, I remarked to him that if he had written the kind of letter I deserved, I should never have suggested collaborating in the book which had such an influence on my conversion."[23]

Not that a friendship ensued from this correspondence. Lunn was to spend the next six years gradually coming to the realization that secular liberalism held out no hope for mankind, a theme he explored quite fully in *The Flight from Reason*. Darwinism and agnosticism are tested and found wanting as philosophical systems, and his admiration

[22] Lunn, *Roman Converts*, p. 194.

[23] Lunn, *And Yet So New*, pp. 3–4.

for the medieval synthesis has grown by comparison. A sort of generic, Christian-tinted theism most closely describes his religious outlook by 1930. Knox was at that time doing public battle with some of the same thinkers Lunn now distrusted, and the appearance in print of *Caliban in Grub Street* encouraged Lunn to sound him out on the prospect of conducting a debate in letter form on the Catholic claim to be the true Church.

Knox agreed, and the book *Difficulties* was soon being pieced together by post. It comprises thirty-two letters, beginning with Lunn's laying the groundwork for the attack on July 22, 1930, and concluding with Knox's summation for the defense on October 5, 1931. The pace of the debate clearly picks up after a fairly desultory start: the first thirteen letters stretch out over a year, while the last nineteen are fired back and forth in the space of less than three months.

The reader looking for novelty in the line of attack or in the defense of Catholicism against that attack will be disappointed. Celsus in the third century had already marshaled the evidence against the Church, and Origen had countered him effectively, and since then the respective antagonists have largely built on their arguments. Of course, the accumulating historical record allows for more examples to be cited, especially by opponents of the Church, and Lunn certainly takes advantage of the labors of Henry Charles Lea and G. G. Coulton in unearthing scandals and hypocrisies that can be tied to Roman prelates and, by assumption, to the Church they serve.

Not surprisingly, many of the issues Lunn raised in *Roman Converts* reappear in the missives directed to Knox. The Inquisition, the bad Popes, and the eternity of hell vex him. He asserts that "the Catholic Church retained torture until she was forced to abandon it under the continued protests of men outside her fold" and that virtually all campaigns for reform and for the expansion of human rights were accomplished in the face of an intransigent Church. For a pronounced internationalist, he displays an unwonted level of John-Bullism by contrasting favorably English judicial mildness since the Reformation with Continental brutality. Reflections on the torture inflicted on Guy Fawkes, and the slow death of Margaret Clitherow when she refused to plead guilty to crimes suggest to Knox instead "that methods which give the police the advantage over the accused (and this is what we are really reprobating) come into vogue wherever you have a strong central executive and that executive has got rattled".[24] It is not, he avers, a distinguishing feature of either Catholic or Protestant countries but rather of fallen mankind.

The same holds true of the actions of the most venal of Renaissance Popes. It takes some explaining to disabuse Lunn of the notion that Catholics believe in the indefectibility and the oracular powers of the occupants of the Chair of Peter or that the Holy Spirit guarantees that the holiest candidate will always be selected in a conclave. Liberius and Honorius are instanced as the textbook cases of Popes who failed to live up to the supposed Catholic definition. But Lunn admittedly does not attach too much weight to that argument because the circumstances of the two unfortunate Popes have long been recognized as offering no exception to the formal definition of Papal infallibility. Indeed, their historical situations were hashed out at length by the assembled bishops at Vatican I before they composed the famous document.[25] Instead, adroitly shifting ground, he stresses the rarity with which infallibility is invoked and cites moral issues as being outside the purview of the definition:

> Moral questions may be divided into those on which all Christians are agreed, and those on which there is a great difference of opinion among Christians. No Christian is in any doubt as to the rights and wrongs of murder, theft, adultery or fornication. No Christian requires a ruling on these points. On the other hand, high-minded and conscientious Christians are divided on such questions as divorce and birth control. Is there any reason to suppose that the "ruling decisions" of the Roman Catholic Church on these disputed moral questions will not be reversed in the future, just as other "ruling decisions" on points of equal importance have been reversed in the past?[26]

The obvious parallel, Lunn urges, is with the Church's noninfallible statements on Biblical questions, statements that seem to be modified

[24] Ronald Knox and Arnold Lunn, *Difficulties* (1932; reprint, London: Eyre and Spottiswoode, 1952), p. 43.

[25] For a full exposition of the arguments leading to the definition, see Cuthbert Butler, *The Vatican Council, 1869–1870* (1930; reprint, Westminster: Newman Press, 1962), especially pp. 303–99.

[26] Knox and Lunn, *Difficulties*, p. 122.

under the pressure of scientific discoveries. Knox responds, however, that one would look in vain for an alteration in Church teaching on divorce or contraception, and the record of the decades since he wrote, with the Church remaining as a voice crying in the wilderness against the intense pressure of the media to reverse her teaching, would certainly fortify his argument. He denies the equating of moral teachings with Biblical interpretation, which he grants can be affected—though in detail rather than in broad outline—by new factual evidence.

Lunn scores his best debating points on those very pronouncements on Scripture. Particularly effective is his selection of a rhetorical flourish in an encyclical on Saint Jerome written by Pope Benedict XV, which refers to critics of a certain view of inerrancy: "Small wonder, then, that in their view a considerable number of things occur in the Bible touching physical science, history, and the like which cannot be reconciled with modern progress in science!" [27] The plain meaning of this sentence is that it throws down the gauntlet to scientists to show that Scriptural accounts of creation, say, are inaccurate. It likewise forces Catholic Scripture scholars into some contortions to attempt to reconcile the Genesis accounts with the scientific record.[28]

Lunn also quotes Benedict fulminating against writers who assert that Saint Jerome did not believe in the historical truth and sequence of events described in the books of the Bible but rather that events were sometimes related according to what people believed at the time. By contrast, Lunn favorably quotes Hilaire Belloc, who maintained that Catholics are not required to believe in such items as Balaam's ass or Jonah and the whale. He also cites an authoritative Catholic manual for Biblical study, which similarly discounts the possibility of a whale plying the eastern Mediterranean and urges restraint in taking the story literally. "Is there any reason why we should not read Jonas as a divinely inspired parable giving us through the medium of fanciful happenings a wonderful statement on the mercy of God, so that the whole becomes a commentary on the words addressed to God by Moses and here put into the mouth of Jonas: 'I know that Thou art a

[27] Quoted in ibid., p. 82.

[28] As Stanley Jaki has shown in *Genesis 1 through the Ages* (Chicago: Real View Books, 1998), such efforts are doomed to failure: the author of the creation account never intended to write a scientific treatise but rather intended to show the unlimited creative power of God through imagery that was well understood by the Hebrew mind.

gracious and merciful God, patient and of much compassion, and easy to forgive evil.' "[29]

Now, Lunn had already taken Knox to task in *Roman Converts* for his presumption in favor of the whale. Lunn had accused him of flippancy in *Some Loose Stones* when he had written in response to a critic: "What do we mean by not facing facts? Mr. Brook [one of the *Foundations* authors] does not believe that the whale could have swallowed Jonah, but Mr. Frank Bullen does, and Mr. Bullen has not only faced facts, he has faced whales."[30] No doubt the more mature Knox cringed when confronted with the bluff Chestertonian cadences of those lines written in 1913, which set him up for a devastating dismissal of the relevance of Frank Bullen's expertise on whale life: "It is not necessary to sally forth with harpoons to discover that normal whales do not act as couriers for minor prophets in distress, and it is clear that if we once posit a miraculous whale, there is nothing to choose between the opinions of a man who has never seen a whale, and the views of Mr. Bullen whose esoteric knowledge of whales is confined to those of the non-miraculous variety."[31]

In the correspondence of 1931, Knox is still hesitant to pronounce the whale episode a myth, because there is insufficient evidence to commit to any apodictic statement. If there are no whales in the Mediterranean now, it is still not certain that Jonah was in the Mediterranean or that there weren't whales there long ago. He does not concede the possibility that the story is not factual, that the author "was reciting a moral apologue which was not meant to be taken as history". What deters him from giving greater adhesion to this view is that Jesus refers to Jonah's three days inside the whale as an analogue of his impending burial in the earth for three days. Does Jesus mean the Jonah story to be taken as historical fact? Not necessarily, but Knox doesn't want to presume on something that hasn't been given an authoritative interpretation by the Church. He refers Lunn to an encyclical of Leo XIII, the wording of which is very moderate: "If you read *Providentissimus Deus* carefully, you will see that it is not strictly literalist. The expositor must not consider 'that it is forbidden, when just

[29] Knox and Lunn, *Difficulties*, pp. 106–7.
[30] Ronald Knox, *Some Loose Stones* (London: Longmans, Green and Co., 1913), p. 29.
[31] Lunn, *Roman Converts*, p. 196.

cause exists, to push inquiry and exposition beyond what the Fathers have done; provided he carefully observes the rule so wisely laid down by St. Augustine—not to depart from the literal and obvious sense, except only where reason makes it untenable or necessity so requires.' "[32]

Of course, what Lunn was doing with the encyclicals and the statements of the Biblical Commission was gliding by some of the nuances that protect them against the charge of strict literalism. When something "cannot safely be taught", the back door to its future acceptance is left open. Likewise, as Lunn himself observes in a postscript written in 1949, the phrase "offensive to pious ears" does not mean that an opinion is erroneous, but rather that it may be true but might shock unreflecting but pious people. During the correspondence, Lunn was still following the tactics of a no-holds-barred debater, collecting specific and often isolated texts as ammunition but not quite getting his finger on the bigger picture. Sometimes he is aware of that. In the letter in which he quotes Benedict XV, he attempts to show inconsistencies in the New Testament record of Jesus' sayings and of the events surrounding the Resurrection. Knox has no trouble explaining them, and in his next letter Lunn responds:

> I will admit that these discrepancies are not very serious. I am pretty well read in anti-Christian literature, and, as a result, I have taken it for granted that the discrepancies in the story of the risen Christ are great. This may be a good example of the way in which one's mind

[32] Knox and Lunn, *Difficulties*, p. 96. A good examination of the issues involved is presented by the noted scholar who founded the *Revue Biblique* and the Catholic Biblical School in Jerusalem. In particular, with reference to citations of Old Testament events, of which Jesus' use of the story of Jonah is certainly an example, he notes: "[I]f it be the case that St. Paul and our divine Saviour have argued from Holy Scripture according to the mental habits of the Jews, without seeking the exact text and without binding themselves down to its precise meaning, and that the Apostles set forth as the fulfillment of a prophecy what is merely an application based upon the similarity of the incidents, with how much more reason may they not have made use of current Jewish ideas in matters literary and scientific without seeking to rectify them? And if this course of action is not unworthy of the Author of our faith, why may we not presume that a similar course may have been adopted by other sacred writers in their exposition of divine teaching? The theological statement of the fact is not of recent origin; as is so frequently the case, the idea was stated by St. Augustine, St. Thomas moulded it, and, in his Encyclical, *Providentissimus Deus*, Leo XIII, has consecrated it anew." These words were written over a century ago by M.-J. Lagrange, *Historical Criticism and the Old Testament* (London: Catholic Truth Society, 1905), pp. 111–12.

> is affected by the "taking it for granted that Christianity is exploded" atmosphere in which we moderns live and move and have our being. And when, for the purpose of my letter to you, I sat down and reread all four accounts of the event, I was surprised to find that the discrepancies were much less than I had supposed.[33]

Yet ever the bulldog, Lunn still holds them sufficiently numerous to undermine Pope Leo's encyclical. It is worth noting, however, that nowhere in the letters does he put forward any arguments against the Resurrection itself. Far from being an agnostic any longer in the manner of Leslie Stephen, he has been led by his study to adopt a partially Christian perspective, but the obstacles standing between him and Catholicism are much more fundamental than alleged inconsistencies in the Bible. Instead, they have to do with his understanding of God himself and the meaning of Jesus' divinity.

The issue cannot but crop up in a discussion of the New Testament picture of Jesus. Lunn refuses to accept that Jesus was omnipotent and omniscient, and he quotes Mark 6:5 ("And he could not do any miracles there") and other passages in support of that view. The emptying, or kenosis, of God-become-man is to be taken literally: Jesus had the limitations of ordinary men. Knox's initial response strikes at the logic of the stance thus far taken by Lunn with respect to the books of the Bible:

> When you reach the kenosis it is evident that your Protestant upbringing is getting the better of you. To continue your argument, you clearly ought to be reasoning: "On this point the Church contradicts the Bible, and therefore the Bible must be wrong. The Agony, the Cry of Dereliction, etc., must be later insertions, not part of the true story." Instead of which it is evident that you are proceeding by force of habit to assume the inerrancy of the Bible and infer the fallibility of the Church.[34]

A good point. Consistency would demand skepticism of the accuracy of the verses; instead, he hangs his case for Jesus' limited powers on an interpretation of verses taken out of context. Lunn has a personal overriding view of the nature of God, of the battle between good and

[33] Knox and Lunn, *Difficulties*, p. 107.
[34] Ibid., p. 98.

evil, and of mankind's role in that battle, and the rest of the Scriptural and historical record needs to be accommodated to that perspective.

Highest on Lunn's list of certainties is the absence of omnipotence and of omniscience, not alone for Jesus as man but also for the God he posits as the Creator of the universe. "I contend", he says, "that just as we can argue from design to a designer, so we can argue from a process to a God limited at least in one respect, limited, that is, in so far as he is unable to achieve his ends instantaneously." And later: "God, I am prepared to admit, can forecast, perhaps, the vast majority of events. Free will can only properly be said to affect that small minority of events, if any, about which God himself is in doubt." Lunn won't concede God omniscience because to do so would rob life of its adventure: "If, at this particular moment, every detail, past, present, and future, of the struggle between good and evil has been foreseen, it is a little difficult to feel that the struggle matters. The result is certain and inevitable, and the events in history merely 'go through the formality of taking place.' The drama of this world is no more than a puppet show, every act of which has been written and rehearsed at the dawn of time."[35]

This point is the crux of his inability to accept the Catholic outlook. The God he hypothesizes operates within time. Never mind that time has meaning only in conjunction with space, and yet Lunn nowhere asserts that God is within the physical universe. But God in Lunn's view being bound by time, his foreknowledge of the future looks dangerously like a denial of our freedom to make choices, because if someone in the present already knows what the future holds, nothing we can do can alter that outcome. Knox attempts to help Lunn out of this conundrum by clarifying some terms: "It is true to say that I can only do the things which God has foreseen me doing; it is not true to say that I am constrained to do the things which God has foreseen me doing."[36]

Note that the issue between them is not the thorny problem of grace versus free will that caused so much bad blood between Dominicans and Jesuits in the seventeenth century. It is the more elementary one of predestination versus free will. Lunn stubbornly resists the

[35] Ibid., pp. 138, 140–41.
[36] Ibid., p. 150.

concept of God being outside time. He protests: "I know that, so far as time is concerned, the theologians are—for once—in agreement with the latest scientific fashion, but in spite of this formidable alliance I shall persist in believing in real objective time, and I shall refuse to believe that God is outside time until somebody brings that phrase home to me, either by analogy or otherwise."[37] This was a serious mental block, this inability to conceive of the source of the universe being unfettered by its limitations. Lunn's God could not be Knox's God, and Knox had to say so bluntly, describing a limited God as utterly unworthy of further notice. To Knox, the search for God is a search for the Almighty, for the one Being who necessarily exists and who out of his overflowing goodness created and sustains all lesser beings. The whole significance of the philosophical proofs of God's existence that Aquinas devised lay in their predication of an ultimate personal Being that all creation depends on for existence. If he is himself dependent on time, and is therefore unsure what the future holds, he has been relegated to a status too suspiciously like that of men for Lunn to avoid the charge of being "hopelessly anthropomorphic" in his theologizing. He was creating a god in the image of man: "He looks to me like a super-Lunn, enlarged to scale." Lunn may claim to find life more interesting with such a pale God watching the goings-on in our universe, but Knox demurs: "The great adventure of theology, to me, is that the Being who fulfills your conditions does more than that, escapes beyond the reach of our ambitions for him. Whether in natural theology or in revelation he is shown to be something more than a mere convenience for human thought: he dominates it and makes us reconsider all our values."[38]

An almost plaintive note appears in the second to last letter of Lunn to Knox, written on September 23, 1931. He quotes George Tyrrell to the effect that God should not make belief so difficult when such a weighty result—eternity with God or eternity totally cut off from him—depends on one's ability to find him. Lunn even suggests that if the credentials of the Church could be made clearer to him, the ensuing "struggle against sin would still be sufficiently interesting to keep us well employed".

[37] Ibid., p. 159.
[38] Ibid., p. 173.

Knox takes note of the crumbling of the edifice of skepticism and responds in a pastoral tone, befitting the turn the correspondence was taking. What must never be lost sight of is God's mercy; a fixation on eternal damnation is misplaced and misleading: "[W]e can only suppose that God judges with infinite tenderness the opportunities, the temptations, the natural disadvantages, the motives, the struggles of every soul that has ever lived.... All I know is that nobody goes to hell except through his own fault; and therefore, if and in so far as their unbelief is not their fault, I believe that God will make allowances for them."[39]

Knox had already admitted to Lunn that the doctrine of eternal punishment was not one he had accepted easily but had done so because the source for it was Jesus himself. And it was likewise with Lunn's father, committed follower of John Wesley though he was. (The founder of Methodism, as it was earlier noted, Lunn makes clear in his biography, had no doubts about the reality of hell.) During an examination prior to taking up the Methodist ministry, the elder Lunn skirted a direct question about his belief in eternal punishment by allowing that it was for the "finally impenitent" but refusing to acknowledge that such people have existed. Much the same evasiveness characterizes the younger Lunn's response to Knox. Two years after the conclusion of *Difficulties*, on the eve of Lunn's reception into the Church, Knox had been rereading their letters and asked him if his views on hell had changed since then. Lunn simply maintained that he believed what the Church teaches. When asked what the Church teaches, he replied that Knox should know better than he, and the issue was dropped.

As the final letters in the series were posted, a large gap still separated the two protagonists. In the meantime, however, they had met informally at Oxford at Lunn's request. Knox showed none of the signs Protestants associated with priests in pursuit of converts; being "gotten hold of" by a Roman priest was a fate the sturdiest of red-blooded Englishmen shuddered to hear of happening to a friend. Lunn was, on the contrary, almost miffed by Knox's diffidence. "Never did a priest make less apparent effort to win the confidence of a potential convert. Had I been easily snubbed we would not have met, but I

[39] Ibid., p. 208.

persisted and Father Knox allowed me to lunch with him at Oxford, and remarked as I left that if I wanted to come and see him again he would not mind much."[40]

Knox was not under the illusion that his responses to Lunn's attacks were drawing him closer to the Church. Lunn was still championing an experimental approach to religion in his final statement. He would take what he found convincingly argued (for instance, the Resurrection) and discard what he considered an encumbrance (for instance, the Immaculate Conception). Always with eternal damnation in mind, he objects to the absolutism of Catholic belief: "There are certain doctrines which are true for all time, and there are others which are the product of the mental climate of a particular age. The trouble with an infallible Church is that you saddle yourself with doctrines which went down very well in the thirteenth century, but which are a terrible incubus in the twentieth century." After reviewing some of the main sticking points in Biblical interpretation and other uncomfortable features he sees in Catholicism, he sums up: "I maintain, then, that the Church's doctrines on eternal torture, on indulgences, on inspiration of scripture, and on the first chapter of Genesis are the heritage of an uncritical age, and that the necessity to defend such doctrines in the support of an infallible authority is a greater handicap than the evils which are the result of a lack of authority."[41]

To Knox, the objections boil down to a desire to substitute experience and feelings for the whole truth:

> A man should not found some part of his faith upon an institution which, if it is true at all, is true altogether; it will give way under him. Oh, we are a convenience to the other Christianities, we Catholics; a lightning-conductor to draw the world's criticism away from them; a repository whose furniture they can reproduce without the worm-holes; a standard of theological currency, against which they can balance their rate of exchange. But, in the nature of things, we cannot accept the second-best positions you try to thrust upon us. Our whole witness is stultified if we are not to be the absolute thing we claim to be.[42]

[40] Lunn, *And Yet So New*, p. 9.
[41] Knox and Lunn, *Difficulties*, pp. 223, 226.
[42] Ibid., p. 237.

The admiration Lunn openly avows for much of the Catholic ethos, even for scholasticism and for the innumerable contributions of the Church to culture and art, is not enough, for it still falls short of acceptance of the principle of authority. "The wave of experience will always dash you up against the rock of authority, which dashes you back to seek refuge in experience again; 'he that wavereth is like a wave of the sea, driven with the wind and tossed.'" Finally he speaks directly to Lunn on a personal level: "There have been people—Mallock is the obvious instance—whose admiration for the Church seemed to kill in them all appreciation of other religious approaches, yet who never, at least till death was upon them, found their way in. I would not have you undergo that agony of the soul; this, I suppose, is to be a propagandist."[43]

Years later Lunn wrote that the reference to Mallock resonated within him and helped him off the theological fence he was straddling, into the Church. It took almost two years, however, with Knox receiving him on July 13, 1933. Other influences were important besides this correspondence: his friendship with Douglas Woodruff and with Father Martin D'Arcy, to whom Woodruff introduced him. And his favorable references in his letters to books by Karl Adam and C. C. Martindale, among others, suggest that the Catholic ambiance was already becoming more congenial to him. But he took the warning about Mallock seriously. "If I had waited until all my difficulties had been resolved," Lunn wrote in 1949, "I should be waiting still. I have, for instance, never read any attempt to reconcile free will and omniscience which gave me the slightest satisfaction. And there are other difficulties which are still unsolved. I became a Catholic not because the Catholic key unlocks every lock but because it unlocks ninety-nine locks out of a hundred and if I bungle the hundredth surely the fault may be in my wrist and not in the key."[44]

The remarkable feature of the correspondence in Knox's eyes, looking back at that later date, was that it captured on record the maturation of faith within Lunn's mind:

> You were clutching at straws, as we commonly do when we begin drowning in the well of truth; and all the time with less confidence,

[43] Ibid., p. 239.
[44] Ibid., p. 245.

> less hopefully. You were rationalizing your reluctance to admit that the Galilean had conquered, and as the book went on, more obviously. It was a good thing, I think, that you did not choose a more adroit opponent; it might have looked as if you were being battered, by sheer force of reasoning, into submission.... you were up against something you hadn't bargained for, and it wasn't me.[45]

This exercise did not by any means exhaust Lunn's capacity for controversy. Two of his subsequent books, coauthored with well-known advocates of positions he wished to challenge, followed exactly the same format. Virtually as the ink was drying on the last letter to Knox in October 1931, Lunn was initiating an epistolary debate with the Marxist biologist J. B. S. Haldane on the general topic of *Science and the Supernatural.* The tone of these exchanges is considerably more rancorous than was manifested in *Difficulties* because the common ground between the disputants is considerably smaller. Haldane is not only a skeptic about religion but also an outspoken atheist who pours ridicule on all serious efforts to interpret the supernatural. And Lunn, who has already entertained and subsequently discarded some of Haldane's antipathy toward Christian beliefs, is equally acid in his counterattacks.

It is interesting that well before Lunn's conversion, Haldane's arguments against the supernatural focus almost exclusively on Catholicism, about which he boasts: "I have made a certain study of the Catholic Church by discussion with Catholics, reading of Catholic literature, and observation of Catholic ceremonies and conduct, and have come to the conclusion that the Church is an evil. For this reason I consider it legitimate to use ridicule as a weapon against it." [46]

This self-acknowledged familiarity with Catholicism emboldens him to make a pronouncement on the doctrine of transubstantiation, which he sees as a vestige of a prescientific world view: "[T]he object which Catholics worship at mass is thought by them to be God. I think that it is a wafer. Not being addicted to masses, whether high or low, black or white, I admit that I may have been wrong in calling it a biscuit. But I am told that it is flat and round, and made of the same materials

[45] Ibid., p. 261.

[46] J. B. S. Haldane and Arnold Lunn, *Science and the Supernatural* (New York: Sheed and Ward, 1935), p. 59.

as certain biscuits, so I do not think that I am very far out." A reminder by Lunn of the philosophical concepts of substance and accidents employed in Catholic teaching to distinguish between unchanged appearances and a miraculous change into the Body and Blood of Christ fails to derail Haldane from pressing on with his crude materialism: "The fact that a consecrated wafer is said to have different effects according as the eater is or is not in a state of mortal sin reminds me of the different effects of eating an egg according as the eater is or is not sensitized to egg albumen—a matter of bio-chemistry." [47]

It is, of course, easy enough to be dismissive of doctrines of a religion that is antithetical to the Marxist materialist faith, but later in the argument, Lunn brings up the concept of beauty as evidence for the nonmaterial in human nature. The glorious mountain scenery, which drew the youthful Lunn away from dogmatic materialism, elicits the following utterly anfractuous piece of reasoning from Haldane:

> When you appreciate the Wetterhorn, the same universal, aesthetic beauty, is in you both, though of course in a different way. This implies a kinship between you and the Wetterhorn, which may be described in two manners. Your mind, I suggest, is a physical object which is often occupied with emotions such as hunger and other biological urges, to which it conforms as a result of natural selection, among other things. But in so far as your mind is not so occupied it may be expected to mirror the inner nature of matter in general, and to be impressed by objects which show that nature in a simple way. We may also say that just because our minds are not immaterial they are responsive to the universals embodied in other

[47] Ibid., p. 37. This kind of crude materialism is not the province of atheists alone. Knox refers in a sermon to the following incident: "I must apologize if I pause for a moment to consider a criticism recently made by a bishop of the Anglican Communion. He made, if you remember, the blasphemous suggestion that a consecrated Host should be subjected to chemical analysis, to see whether it would produce any reactions different from those produced by an unconsecrated wafer. It is, of course, a curious assumption that the forms of chemical analysis known to modern science are necessarily capable of penetrating the innermost secrets of physical reality. But I need hardly point out to you that however far Science may progress in the direction of reading that riddle, it is not possible that it should ever arrive at the point of separating accidents from their substance, since the distinction here, albeit real, is a metaphysical and not a physical distinction." Ronald Knox, *Heaven and Charing Cross: Sermons on the Holy Eucharist* (London: Burns, Oates and Washbourne, 1935), pp. 25–26.

> material systems. If you are really an immaterial being your feelings are much harder to explain.[48]

By far, however, the larger part of the debate revolves around issues related to evolutionary theory, with Lunn on the offensive. He declares himself a true agnostic on the concept of large-scale evolution, meaning by that the derivation of birds from reptiles, for example, and an outright disbeliever in the notion that major changes could have come about by chance or by Darwinian natural selection. He charges the generations of supporters of Darwin with clouding issues in an attempt to prop up a theory that has too many holes in it to stand the acid test of searching criticism. To Lunn, the debate boils down to a single sentence: "If Evolution be certain, then scientists are justified in interpreting awkward facts in accordance with the evolutionary theory, but if Evolution be the theory in dispute, it is a scientific crime to manipulate the evidence, geological or otherwise, in the interest of an unproven dogma."[49] Darwin's contemporary critic, Samuel Butler, effectively demolished the reliance on natural selection as the effective agent of evolution when he observed that the argument was analogous to assuming that mouse-traps or steam engines have arisen as

> the result of the accumulation of blind minute fortuitous variations in a creature called man, which creature has never wanted either mouse-traps or steam-engines, but has had a sort of promiscuous tendency to make them, and was benefited by making them, so that those of the race who had a tendency to make them survived and left issue, which issue would thus naturally tend to make more mouse-traps and more steam-engines.[50]

Darwin comes off as a rather hapless natural philosopher under the stern gaze of Butler. When Darwin wrote in *The Origin of Species* that "we must suppose that there is a power represented by natural selection always intently watching each slight accidental alteration", Butler was not impressed. Nor is Lunn, who quotes the Victorian critic: "[I]t is just as great nonsense as it would have been if 'the survival of the fittest' had been allowed to do the watching instead of 'the power

[48] Haldane and Lunn, *Science and the Supernatural*, pp. 369–70.
[49] Ibid., p. 221.
[50] Ibid., p. 110.

represented by' the survival of the fittest; but the nonsense is harder to dig up, and the reader is more likely to pass it over."[51]

When Lunn recalls the objection to Darwinism inherent in the complexity of the eye, the use of which depends on the coordination of so many components that would have had no function and therefore no pressure to evolve further until they combined to produce sight, Haldane's response is hardly to the point: "You say that its various parts cannot function unless they are accurately fitted into each other. But they do! My cornea and lens do not give a very accurate focus on my retina, so I wear spectacles.... This frequent incomplete adaptation is just what one would expect in an organ whose evolution is probably not yet finished."[52]

The gaps in the geological record are of course viewed differently by the two writers. To Lunn they show that the numerous missing links demanded by Darwinism have not turned up; to Haldane they are simply evidence that far more fossils need to be found to complete the picture of how life-forms developed. Lunn twits Darwin for having nothing to say about the *origins* of life in a book with the word "origin" in its title, instead considering only *adaptations* of species. Haldane will have nothing to do with creation of even the earliest living organisms:

[51] Ibid., p. 119. More modern critics of Darwin include several well-known cultural historians who have followed Butler's withering analysis, among them Gertrude Himmelfarb, *Darwin and the Darwinian Revolution* (New York: Norton, 1968), and Jacques Barzun, *Darwin, Marx and Wagner* (Garden City, N.Y.: Doubleday Anchor, 1958). Still underrated is the criticism by the contemporary of Darwin St. George Mivart. A highly accomplished osteologist and anatomist specializing in higher mammals, he saw too many differences in the creatures so easily placed on the same evolutionary tree by his mentor Thomas Huxley and others, that he had to break ranks with the rising tide of biological adherents to Darwin's theories at the risk of being ostracized by them. He cut through to the core of the problem with the Darwinians in his assertion that they simply ignored the mental chasm separating humans from other animals: "The failure to appreciate this distinction is not so much due to an exaggeration of our lower faculties, as to a want of apprehension of what is really implied in our higher mental powers. Perhaps the most remarkable circumstance connected with popular modern writers on this subject, is the conspicuous absence in them of any manifest comprehension of those very intellectual powers they continually exercise, and their apparent non-appreciation of that reason to which they so often appeal." Quoted in Jacob Gruber, *A Conscience in Conflict: The Life of St. George Jackson Mivart* (New York: Temple University Publications, 1960), pp. 137–38.

[52] Haldane and Lunn, *Science and the Supernatural*, p. 134.

> Some atheists have suggested that life is constantly being brought to the earth by spores driven by light pressure, and has had no beginning or end, to take one of the alternatives. However, I see nothing improbable in spontaneous generation. It was generally believed in until the eighteenth century by theists and atheists alike. Pasteur and others showed that the alleged generation of organisms large enough to be seen with a microscope did not occur when proper precautions were taken. But it would be very surprising if such relatively large organisms did start from scratch, so to say. If there is spontaneous generation it is almost certainly of much simpler living things, such as filter-passing viruses.[53]

Haldane remains extraordinarily plucky, and often vituperative throughout the correspondence. And well he might, given the great success he and his colleagues have had over the years propagating belief in doctrines that are a mixture of the unproven and the illogical. For example, when challenged to produce evidence for Darwinian natural selection in action, he refers Lunn to the progressive development of sea urchins in a limestone cliff, the persistence of dark moths over white moths on dark bark trees, and some experiments producing new species of certain plants. From these unimpressive facts showing a kind of evolution Lunn heartily accepts, he is asked to swallow whole the deduction that reptilian scales evolved into bird feathers, among other equally momentous changes in life-forms. Echoing Leslie Stephen confronted with the evidence for Christianity, however, Lunn can only acknowledge his agnosticism about the evidence, as well as the mechanism of evolution.

Lunn is unsparing in his charge that Haldane holds to a double standard of evidence: large-scale evolution must be accepted even when the evidence is not forthcoming, but miracles and other indicators of the reality of the nonmaterial world must be disbelieved despite overwhelming evidence supporting their occurrence. The Lourdes phenomena are a case in point. Instantaneous cures of the most intractable

[53] Ibid., p. 306. Of course with the tremendous advances biochemistry has wrought in scientists' understanding of living organisms, the arguments of evolutionary biologists based on visible similarities in form have become less compelling. The "irreducible complexity" of processes as commonplace as sight and blood clotting points, as Michael Behe showed in *Darwin's Black Box* (New York: Free Press, 1996), to a level of sophistication that leaves natural selection or random mutations wanting as explanatory mechanisms.

diseases, amply attested to by physicians of all and no creeds, leave Haldane speculating about possible future medical discoveries that will throw light on the now-inexplicable cases. But Lunn adduces the case of Émile Zola to show how blind to reality an unbeliever can become. The French journalist was witness to a terribly diseased woman's pilgrimage to Lourdes and then fictionalized the event in a novel. In actual life, she was cured, and the cure deemed miraculous by the doctors examining her; in the story, she has a relapse and dies. Why would Zola, regarded as a courageous freethinker, falsify an event, other than because he refused to acknowledge an inconvenient truth? It is a demanding creed that requires of its devotees that they avert their eyes when confronted by a miracle and at the same time exacts belief in blind evolution at the expense of disregarding the laws of probability. But, unshaken by the results of his wrangling with Lunn, Haldane proceeded years later to debate two professional scientists who viewed the evidence in favor of natural selection with as much skepticism as Lunn had. A philosophically neutral reader of the printed letters that appeared in a small, 1949 pamphlet titled *Is Evolution a Myth?* would likely give the edge to the anti-Darwinists. When pressed by Douglas Dewar, a well-known zoologist, for an explanation of the origin of hair, Haldane is reduced to pure hand waving: "Hair might have started as quills, and then fined down to fur. It is useless to speculate until we know more about the physiology and genetics of hair-growth; but the origin of hair appears to me to present no intellectual difficulty whatever." [54]

And with over a dozen more years of concerted effort on the part of a vast array of scientists to discover significant mutations, Haldane continues to fall back on minor variations within species to buttress his case. Directly challenged by the geologist L. Merson Davies to produce fossil evidence for an imperfect bat or insect or cephalopod, he cannot. The remarkable explosion of records of fully developed complex organisms in early geologic time defies a Darwinian explanation.

In the meantime, Lunn had come full circle in his disavowal of his early religious agnosticism. So much so, in fact, that he engaged G. G. Coulton in debate in 1944, twenty years after having sent him a

[54] Douglas Dewar, L. Merson Davies, and J. B. S. Haldane, *Is Evolution a Myth?* (London: Watts, 1949), p. 38.

complimentary copy of *Roman Converts*, which owed so much of its anti-Catholic ammunition to Coulton's prolific writings on the Middle Ages. Now they were on opposite sides of the question *Is the Catholic Church Anti-Social?*

Coulton was nearing the end of a long life devoted to controversial writing.[55] He was a Cambridge-educated clergyman who became a schoolmaster at various English public schools while indulging his antiquarian interests by collecting a formidable library of medieval manuscripts and books during his tramps through Europe on vacation. He sloughed off his chaplaincy duties, not dramatically à la Leslie Stephen, but gradually, almost imperceptibly, as the Thirty-nine Articles became too much for him to digest, until he finally declared himself a layman in his late thirties. (In view of later crossing of paths and swords with a member of the Lunn family, it is worth recording that he met his wife in 1902 on an Alpine vacation tour conducted by Sir Henry Lunn.)

Only in 1911, at age 53, did Coulton become a Cambridge lecturer and later research fellow. Despite his lifelong passion for abbey ruins and medieval monasticism, he was outraged by the success of Aidan (later Cardinal) Gasquet's books on the subject, which were based on some slipshod scholarship.[56] A meticulous collector of facts telling against the roseate depiction of monastic life Gasquet popularized, Coulton marred his reputation as a Cambridge historian by selectivity in his use of documentary materials, which were arranged to put the

[55] Coulton (1858–1947) wrote an engaging autobiography, which shows him to be possessed of a sense of humor absent from his polemical publications, as well as a keen appreciation of natural beauty. But with that stout Protestant disdain for authority that drove him to attack all things Catholic, he tellingly aligns himself with G. E. Lessing in opting for the freedom to choose error rather than contemplate truth in serenity, which, it would seem, would make heaven an irksome place for such people. Lessing's words, which Coulton quotes approvingly, are "If God held all truth in His right hand, and in His left nothing but the ever-restless instinct for truth, though with the condition of forever and ever erring, and should say to me 'Choose!', I should bow humbly to His left hand, and say 'Father, give! Pure truth is for Thee alone.' " Quoted in G. G. Coulton, *Fourscore Years* (Cambridge: Cambridge University Press, 1944), p. 229.

[56] For a favorable study of Gasquet's life, see the book by Knox's friend and collaborator on Henry VI, Shane Leslie, *Cardinal Gasquet: A Memoir* (New York: P. J. Kenedy and Sons, n.d.). The great twentieth-century historian of English monasticism David Knowles supplied a corrective to Leslie's encomia in an essay balancing the cardinal's merits and faults, "Cardinal Gasquet as an Historian", in *The Historian and Character* (Cambridge: Cambridge University Press, 1963), pp. 240–63.

Catholic Church in the worst of possible lights. He was also forever publishing tracts at his own expense—publishers had long since wearied of his crusades against this or that Catholic doctrine—and challenging Catholic historians to engage him in verbal combat. Like an insatiable pugilist, he was still smarting from the time he dared the Jesuit priest Herbert Thurston to back up his assertion that the American Protestant medievalist Henry Charles Lea was careless about his facts and averaged an error a page in his works. (Lea wrote books on the Inquisition, on clerical celibacy, and on auricular confession, three standbys of controversialist literature.) An impartial arbiter chose twelve pages at random from Lea's writings, and Thurston uncovered fifteen indefensible errors. Thenceforward, little volumes with titles like "Roman Catholic and Anglican Accuracy" and "Romanism and Truth" appeared with great regularity, and Thurston was the recipient of further challenges, which Coulton claimed he dishonorably ignored, up to the Jesuit's death in 1939. So the Cambridge historian was itching for a new antagonist, and Lunn eagerly accepted the challenge.

Coulton repeatedly likened the Church to the totalitarian regimes of the Second World War: "You are championing an elaborate and powerful institution which claims 120 adult millions of mankind as members, upon each of whom 'dogmatic facts' impose themselves. I stand for the 600 millions of outsiders whom, according to your theology, your Duce has the *right* (as apart from temporary or local *expediency*) of compelling into his fold, even by bodily punishment if necessary."[57]

Lunn notes, however, that the specifics Coulton marshals in favor of his thesis are largely culled

> from the writings of devout Catholics. It would not be possible to build up a case against Hitler from the writings of devout Nazis. The shortcomings of Nazism, Fascism and Communism have only been exposed by refugees from those countries or by disillusioned party members who have escaped into free countries, but the scandals of monasticism in the past and the defects of Church government and Church schools have been pointed out by men who

[57] G. G. Coulton and Arnold Lunn, *Is the Catholic Church Anti-Social?* (London: Burns, Oates and Washbourne, 1947), p. 235.

> continued to enjoy the confidence and the respect of the Hierarchy. All of which makes nonsense of your "totalitarian" thesis.[58]

Lunn quotes a review by a prominent non-Catholic medievalist, F. M. Powicke, who sensed the air of unreality in Coulton's treatment of religious history: "Why, just when one would fain be convinced, does one suddenly feel that the argument is like a discussion in a dream in which ordinary judgment is impossible?" Coulton had closed his mind to understanding Catholicism, pervasive as it was in the medieval world. Lunn proffers the word "museumist" to describe his encyclopedic knowledge of facts coupled with blatant ignorance of the actuating principles of Catholic life that characterize Coulton's work. The level of acrimony is fairly high in the pages of this book, and Lunn's task is made no easier by his opponent's hammering out a letter of over forty thousand words early in the correspondence. But most of the highlights of anti-Catholic historical research are duly presented and the Catholic counterattack ably carried through. Obviously no dramatic change of heart could be expected to ensue from the exchange, Coulton dying a few years later an unrepentant Catholic-baiter. But Lunn had by now effectively established himself as a leading Catholic controversialist, an occupation that Knox had shown little taste for holding on to after 1930. "I feel like an elderly cyclotron", he wrote to Lunn in the 1950 postscript to *Difficulties*, "that has played the midwife to an energy not its own."

That energy lasted until 1974, when the irrepressible mountaineer, with over sixty books—roughly equally divided between his passions of apologetics, travel, and skiing—to his credit, at last entered that realm where he could rest in contemplation of the truth he had grasped hold of many years earlier with an assist from Father Knox.

[58] Ibid., p. 180.

CHAPTER EIGHT

THE WATER OF CONVICTION

It is generally acknowledged that Ronald Knox was England's foremost expositor of the Catholic faith during the middle decades of the twentieth century, a time that was rich in noteworthy Catholic authors. What helped set him apart from some other equally brilliant writers and thinkers was that, although the immediate audiences he addressed might vary, he was especially gifted in composing his works of apologetics and of elucidation of all things Catholic with a widely disparate reading public in mind. Everyone from the schoolgirl under the watchful eye of the nuns to the skeptic disillusioned by the horrors of world wars and the fatuities of mass culture was being carefully considered as he wrote and spoke.

Knox could of course have been expected to write with the insight of a convert from the established religion of the land, who had cast his lot with a Church claiming only one adherent in twenty of the population. He could empathize with, and yet see through, the tangle of sentiment, patriotism, and cultural habit that gave Anglicanism an inertial hold over the souls of his countrymen. But the sympathy he evinces for minds alienated from all religion and the care with which he gently extends philosophical and theological lifelines to the genuine agnostic are what add a particular luster to his writings. He avoids the temptation to present apologetics as a matter of stockpiling argumentative armaments with which to bombard one's antagonists. Instead, he is forever the unobtrusive friend, letting the doubter put forward the most telling objections to this or that doctrine before patiently presenting the case for belief. To the believer, and (one must suppose) to the inquirer after truth, the most satisfying aspect of Knox's apologetics is its grounding in logic. One must not forget that he was not an academically trained theologian but rather an accomplished logician.

And logic, the apparatus of human reason, must be honored in any presentment of belief. It does not replace faith, but the very core of Knox's approach is that the act of faith ought not to be a blind leap but instead a conscious undertaking buttressed by all the natural powers at the mind's disposal.

Obviously, many of his writings are suffused with apologetic intent, but four book-length works and one fragment left incomplete at his death may be regarded as the most directed efforts on his part to convince people of the plausibility and ultimately the truth of the claims of the Catholic faith. First in order of publication is *The Belief of Catholics*, appearing in print in 1927 as a contribution to a series of books on the topic "What I Believe" by different authors. As such, it is the only apologetic work of his that was conceived in book form and for a general readership. The other works were originally delivered as conferences. *In Soft Garments* (1942) was a compilation of lectures delivered between 1926 and 1938 to the Catholic undergraduates of Oxford, whom he was then serving as chaplain. World War II found him in altered circumstances, working on his translation of the Bible at the home of Lord and Lady Acton in Aldenham. But the evacuation of London had necessitated the dispersal of schoolchildren throughout the countryside, and the girls being educated by the Convent of the Assumption were encamped with the Actons. His priestly ministrations during this period were therefore directed primarily to this audience, and *The Creed in Slow Motion* (1949) was one of the literary fruits of that interaction. Another batch of Oxford conferences, culled from talks given during his successor's tenure in the chaplaincy, resulted in *The Hidden Stream* (1953). Finally, with the retrospect of a more than four-decade immersion in apologetics, he began work on a project intended to supersede his previous efforts to reach out to the modern de-Christianized mind, by producing a work that would prove the ultimate truths "not merely with the effect of intellectual satisfaction, but with a glow of assent that springs from the whole being; 'did not our hearts burn within us when he talked to us by the way?'" This unfinished, indeed barely begun, work was published posthumously in 1959 in the English Jesuit journal the *Month* and then in pamphlet form as *Proving God*.

While Knox's return at the end of his life to overt apologetics indicated his unease with the comprehensiveness of his earlier efforts in that arena, it does not follow that his previous endeavors are consequently of diminished value today. He was a perfectionist who was forever dissatisfied with his past work, as can be seen in the introduction he wrote to the reissuing of *A Spiritual Aeneid* more than thirty years after its initial publication, in which he records how the passage of time elicits only a more jaundiced appraisal of its style: "Turns of phrase that passed muster at the time of writing jar upon the nerves of the senior self-critic as callow, or smug, or affected, or laboured, or cheap, or sanctimonious, or roguish, or pedantic, or fulsome, or mock-modest, or inflated, or provocative, or in a hundred less analyzable ways distressing to the educated reader."[1] That of a book which other well-informed critics regard as a modern masterpiece of spiritual autobiography. Evelyn Waugh notes that Knox was similarly diffident about *Let Dons Delight* and that, as he was putting the finishing touches on *Enthusiasm* in 1949, he wrote to Douglas Woodruff, complaining how poor his writing had become.

FAITH AND CERTITUDE

Specifically what he deprecated in his earlier apologetics was a somewhat impersonal approach, what could be perceived by the reader as a logical concatenation of evidences undergirding the rationality of the Catholic faith. The appeal to the nonbelieving person who yet is genuinely in search of the truth was not, to his mind, sufficiently strong to kindle the mysterious spark of faith. Yet he had never mistaken rational assent for faith. "To believe a thing, in any sense worth the name," he says in *The Creed in Slow Motion*, "means something much more than merely not denying it. It means focusing your mind on it, letting it haunt your imagination, caring, and caring desperately, whether it is true or not."[2] Reaching this stage, when faith is not a virtue that has already been nourished from childhood but is rather something on the horizon, requires an intellectual journey that leads first of all to moral certainty about theological truth. The apologist holds that faith is a gift from God, not a culmination of preparatory talks leading to baptism. He also knows that a moral certainty is not a mathematical

[1] Ronald Knox, *A Spiritual Aeneid* (London: Longmans, Green and Co., 1918), p. xiii.
[2] Ronald Knox, *The Creed in Slow Motion* (New York: Sheed and Ward, 1949), pp. 5–6.

certainty, that is, that the truths of religion will never be able to be demonstrated with the same kind of logical closure that attends a geometrical proof. Consequently

> the nature of moral certainty is that we can, if we like—we are queer creatures—neglect its claim on our intellectual honesty, and adopt the position of Nelson putting his blind eye to the telescope. That is where the will comes in. The decision we make is an intellectual judgment, but (as Aristotle reminds us) intellect by itself never gets a move on. We have reached our moral certainty, but we have got to face it, and take appropriate action about it, and that needs the use of our wills.[3]

Knox goes on to observe that the objective certainty of the evidences for Catholicism, many of which are based on historical arguments, *can* produce a response of certitude in the inquirer. That response is distinguishable from the kind of psychological certitude the Protestant "feels"—for by its nature Protestantism fosters a faith that is fueled by an emotional attachment to the Person of Jesus. Just as no priesthood is to interfere between man and God in the Protestant milieu, reason itself can be seen by the disciples of the Reformation as an enemy to pure faith. Instead, the seat of faith is in the emotions, "with frequent allusion to the misunderstood text, 'With the heart man believeth unto salvation'".[4] Catholicism, by contrast, has always accorded reason its due, and the apologist is only respecting the nature of human intellectual powers in appealing to that faculty. Yet the most sublime

[3] Ronald Knox, *The Hidden Stream* (New York: Sheed and Ward, 1953), pp. 169–70.

[4] Ronald Knox, *The Belief of Catholics* (New York: Doubleday and Co., 1958), p. 38. Compare for example the following discussion of the relations between faith and reason in an article on faith by the Anglican theologian Canon H. S. Holland: "It is well to recall briefly this character of the moral will, the affections, the love, of man. For these are faith's nearest and dearest allies. It is here, in these elemental motions, that faith finds its closest parallel. It is something very like an act of will, a movement of love, an heroic and chivalrous moral venture. And whenever we desire to understand its relations to reason, we must persistently recall the attitude towards reason taken by these fundamental forms of energy; only remembering that faith is yet more elemental, yet more completely the act of the central integral self, even than these. Where they leave reason behind, it will do so yet further. Where they call upon something deeper, and more primitive than reason, it will do the same, and yet more triumphantly." Taken from "Faith", in *Lux Mundi: A Series of Studies in the Religion of the Incarnation*, ed. Charles Gore (London: John Murray, 1891), p. 25.

apologetics cannot imbue anyone with faith and the certitude that that state of mind necessarily entails.

The task of the apologist is not to construct a watertight case for all the doctrines of the Church. It is to bring the person to the point where submission to the teaching authority of the Church is a compelling proposition. Then,

> [i]ntellectually speaking, the position of one who "submits to the Church" is that of one who has reached a satisfactory induction—namely, that the Church is infallibly guided into all truth—and can infer from it, by a simple process of deduction, the truth of the various doctrines which she teaches. He does not measure the veracity of the Church by the plausibility of her tenets; he measures the plausibility of her tenets by the conviction he has already formed of her veracity. Thus, and thus only can the human intellect reasonably accept statements which (although they cannot be disproved) cannot be proved by human reason alone.[5]

Obstacles that may have previously seemed overwhelming, for example, the opposition of family or the uprooting of congenial habits or the loss of career preferments, all of which Knox himself knew personally, loom less ominously when that state of conviction is achieved. An act of will overrules the timidity of irresolution. Knox is less than impressed with many of the metaphors used in Catholic manuals to relate rational conviction to the certitude of faith, but he proposes one himself, almost casually it seems, singularly felicitous. The supernatural grace of faith is finally poured out on the believer, and, in a manner symbolized by the miracle at Cana, "the water of conviction is changed into the wine of faith."[6]

Knox was a dispenser of the water of conviction. Ultimately, his efficacy can be judged not so much in the light of other apologetic or theological works as in his ability to draw people toward a mature acceptance of the teachings of the Catholic Church, and that is a

[5] Knox, *Belief of Catholics*, pp. 136–37.

[6] Ibid., p. 137. Earlier in the book he uses the same image: "The absolute certainty with which we believe the teaching of the Church comes to us from the supernatural grace of faith, which transforms our reasoned conviction into a higher quality—the water, as at Cana, is turned into wine. But *for apologetic purposes* a reasoned conviction is all we can offer to our neighbors; and it is this reasoned conviction which the present thesis attempts to maintain" (p. 43).

statistic not given a historian to know. But in the more mundane precincts of discourse on issues related to theology and philosophic truth, his writings can be examined and his perspicacity gauged in anticipating the questions of the intelligent inquirer, and his ability to engage in a perceptive manner the age-old stumbling blocks on the pathway to conversion can be appreciated.

Despite the advances recorded by science in each generation and the various trends prevailing as academic fashion in philosophy and psychology, the same fundamental questions recur in every age about the purpose of life. What can the human mind know with certainty? Even more fundamentally, is the human mind something above and beyond matter?

INADEQUACY OF MATERIALISM

Materialism had been flourishing in many scientifically attuned circles since the times of Huxley and Stephen in the second half of the nineteenth century (though interestingly enough, the three greatest English physicists of that era—Faraday, Maxwell, and Kelvin—were intellectually convinced Christians). Knox therefore thought it worthwhile to address its theses in his early addresses to Oxford students. He did so in part by focusing on the ordinary usage of the terms *mind* and *matter* as an indicator of deeper truths: "I think it will always be found that when we say, 'It doesn't matter,' we always mean, 'I shan't mind,' or 'somebody or other won't mind.' The latter formula is a more exact definition of our thought. If you say, 'It doesn't matter whether I get through Pass Mods at the end of this term,' you mean either 'I don't mind' or 'The dons won't mind' or 'My people won't mind.' " His point is that people mind about things, whereas things themselves may or may not matter. It is a happy feature of the English language to have these words used as verbs as well as nouns. Their everyday usage suggests a common presumption that persons who mind are more than matter. Which is the more important? Even though people will have a hard time conceiving how they could exist without matter, it is absurd to suggest that mind exists for the sake of matter: "The wagging of my tongue, and the twitching of your ears, do subserve an end . . . by making it possible for me to transfer my thoughts to your intelligence. But it would be ridiculous to imagine that my thoughts exist for the purpose of making my tongue waggle, or your ears twitch. That which exists for the sake of something else must have less value, in the ultimate nature of things, than that for the sake of which it exists."[7]

It is also evident that persons' minds reflect on what they do, that people are self-conscious:

> Man finds himself possessed of this apparently unique privilege, that he can become the object of his own thought. He can focus his attention, not merely on things outside himself, but upon himself the thinker, upon himself thinking.... The difference between this self-consciousness and mere consciousness is as real, as vital, as the difference between consciousness itself and mere life, or the difference between life and mere existence. This spiritual principle, this self-conscious life within man, is not accounted for (still less explained) by his needs as a mere citizen of the natural creation. It is something altogether outside the scheme of ordinary organic life; it exists for its own sake, and must therefore be regarded as a higher order of existence.[8]

Consequently, when people speak of minds they mean persons, not abstract forces or energies. And when they press on with minding about things that matter, they even approach an argument for the existence of God. Knox puts it succinctly: "Can anything matter, unless there is Somebody who minds?" He goes on to observe that the appeal to conscience cannot be ultimately satisfying, since conscience is only something inherent in individual people. Why, for example, is genocide wrong? Collective abstractions like world opinion are just that—abstractions: "I want to appeal to Somebody who minds, and has a right to mind, whenever the moral law is infringed; and he who minds must be a Person.... if there were no he, if there were only an it, to dictate commands to free moral beings like ourselves, could we reconcile ourselves to the indignity of it? I know I couldn't."[9]

But of all the arguments for the existence of God, surely that based on order is the most compelling, and the easiest to appreciate, even to

[7] Ronald Knox, *In Soft Garments* (1942; reprint, New York: Sheed and Ward, 1958), pp. 12–13, 15.

[8] Knox, *Belief of Catholics*, pp. 58–59.

[9] Knox, *In Soft Garments*, pp. 17–18.

the least philosophical of minds. To the schoolchildren at Aldenham, Knox sketches the standpoint of the fact-finding scientist who is impatient with the five classical proofs as enumerated by Thomas Aquinas:

> "All right" says the scientist, "we won't talk about causes and effects, if it has these uncomfortable consequences. We will content ourselves with observing the pattern of things as we find it in our experience; the wonderful order there is in nature, and so on." But, you see, that doesn't make them any better off. Order can only be the expression of a mind, and who has put that order in nature, which we discover with our scientific instruments? [10]

Elsewhere he is careful to distinguish this line of reasoning from the argument based on design, which had been a staple of Protestant theology since Paley but which is at root too subjective. It is essentially a counter-Darwinian approach, seeing in the world of nature the evidences of providential arrangement. Its weakness is that it "involves the assumption that you know what is best, and believe in God because you find him doing it". But the evolutionists will not buy that: they see the interaction of things as the outcome of a struggle for survival, not a delicately laid plan. Instead, he would pose to the convinced Darwinian the following, which is the actual Thomist line of reasoning: "The whole of creation leading up gradually to higher and higher stages of existence, with Mind as the last stage of all—and yet Mind must have been there from the first, or how, from the first, did cosmos emerge from chaos; how, from the first, could creation have contained the germs of Mind, unless Mind had put them there?" [11]

Or, as he drives the point home elsewhere:

> Surely, when a thing is unexpectedly found, we congratulate the person who has found it, but our next question is inevitably, "Who put it there?" . . . If the whole of our experience is not a phantasmagoria of unrelated facts, if water does not flow uphill, and gases do not double in volume when the pressure on them is doubled, who was it willed the thing should be so? Not we assuredly; not Boyle, not Newton. Not blind Chance, for there is a limit to coincidence. Not "Nature," for there is no such person, she is only an abstraction. What hypothesis is left to us except that of an ordering

[10] Knox, *Creed in Slow Motion*, p. 12.

[11] Knox, *In Soft Garments*, p. 6.

Mind? Instinctively we speak of a law when we find a natural principle; and have we no right to argue from a law to a Legislator?[12]

It is no good, too, falling back on the position of the Deist, for whom God is the primeval Watchmaker, content to leave his creation to run itself after he has brought it into existence. Philosophical reflection sees through the spuriousness of that notion, and frames another of Aquinas' arguments. The very contingency or dependency of the natural world demands a necessary Being to maintain it. The laws of nature are not themselves conscious arbiters; to follow through on the earlier analogy, the legislator still needs to enforce the laws.

EVIDENCE FROM SCRIPTURE

It was noted above that many of the evidences for the Catholic faith are historical, such being the evidences provided by the Old Testament about the uniqueness of the Jewish people and by the New Testament about Jesus Christ being the awaited Messiah and being God himself. One of Knox's strongest suits is his incomparable knowledge of not only the Biblical texts but also their nuances and their interrelationships. He was immersed in the thought of the writers of these texts and could explain their overarching themes with a sureness of touch available to few commentators. While a subsequent chapter will dwell in greater detail on this aspect of his work, suffice it for now to present a sampling of his utilization of the documents as they relate information concerning the divinity of Jesus and his founding of the Church.

[12] Knox, *Belief of Catholics*, p. 56. Fr. Martin D'Arcy, in a cogently argued philosophical treatise, observes similarly: "Now if man were the *chef d'oeuvre* of evolution, the final authority and measure, then truth and goodness would be relative to his personal wishes. But this is not so. In conscience he finds that he is subject to standards which he did not make, that duty and apparent self-interest do not always coincide; nevertheless, he is also aware that fidelity to this absolute serves also his own welfare. Again, in knowledge he does not make truth, invent it by consulting his own convenience. He is in the position of a disciple and pupil, and he can possess truth only on condition that his mind is candid and he himself disinterestedly in love with what is other and higher than himself. In this docility of the mind and asceticism of desire lies the secret of human perfection. It is because man, to use the phrase of Scripture, is made in the likeness of God that he cannot be himself until his desire is satiated with God and by the beholding of Him in an intellectual intuition." M.C. D'Arcy, S.J. *The Nature of Belief* (London: Sheed and Ward, 1931), p. 103.

That evidence comes down to the present time from the Gospels and from the traditions handed on by the early Christians. The response of that first generation of believers, transmuted from defeated adherents of a crucified leader into the most confident proselytizers of his message, is in itself a historical phenomenon explicable most easily on the ground that Jesus was who he claimed to be. Of course, there are many critics who would like to dismiss the Gospels as reliable accounts of Jesus' sayings, reducing them for example to Matthew Arnold's "sweetness and light" version of Christianity. But they are left in an untenable position:

> For, in the first place, you have to give some account of the following which our Lord had during his lifetime; you have already disallowed his miracles—if you censor his teaching too, what cause will you have left to explain his popularity? And in the second place you have to account for the origin of these alleged sayings—what source will you assign to them? It is true, the manner of our Lord's teaching is Rabbinical, and some of his utterances have their parallels in Rabbinical literature; but is it conceivable that the whole corpus of his doctrine is a mere anthology from earlier sources? Why, then, was it not challenged? For the records on which we depend were published within forty years of his death; and, if the modern critics are to be trusted, these records are themselves dependent on a much earlier document. Did no one, in those earlier times, question its authenticity? The utterances attributed to Socrates may be of doubtful genuineness, but that is because we know that his biographer was a Plato. What Plato had our Lord to report him? No one who values his reputation as a critic will dispute that, whoever Jesus of Nazareth was, he was the author of the words attributed to Jesus of Nazareth in the first three Gospels. Those Gospels are, on the face of it, the work of commonplace biographers, who can hardly be suspected of scientific editing.[13]

The God-Man

But who, precisely, does Jesus claim to be? The sentimentalists want him to be a man like the rest of mankind, except that he went about

[13] Ibid., p. 94.

doing good in a preeminent way. But do they get that idea from the Gospel records, the historical accounts?

> Do we ever read of his meeting an old woman carrying a heavy burden up a hill, and offering to carry it up for her? Did he ever jump into the water to save anybody's life? Do we even hear of his distributing money among starving people? Did he go around comforting the sick, and telling them to bear up? No, there is no trace of all that. He didn't jump into the water, he walked on the water. When people were hungry, he didn't distribute money, he distributed bread, miraculously multiplied. He didn't comfort the sick, he healed them.[14]

The critics who will adopt verbal contortions to explain away Jesus' miracles will also speak of his fulfillment of the role of Messiah as

> a notion which dawned on him gradually and strengthened as his Life proceeded. This is a pure speculation, which sins by going beyond the evidence. The evidence is not that the consciousness dawned gradually upon him, but that he allowed it to dawn gradually on the rest of the world. The fact that he forbade the "devils" to call him Christ early in his ministry, yet encouraged Peter to call him Christ later in his ministry, does not define the limit of what he knew, but of what he wished to be known.[15]

The Jewish people had associated the Messiah with a temporal rule, and many of them were even willing to ignore what the prophets foretold of his suffering, in order to convince themselves that their ultimate delivery from Roman hegemony was imminent. Weaning them from that image would take psychological subtlety, and it is far more credible to view Jesus' hesitation in identifying himself on those grounds than on some supposed uncertainty. There are simply no statements to back up the imputation of a hazy realization of a sense of mission. On the contrary, Jesus is always leaving hints about his identity. For example, there is his predilection for the phrase "Son of Man" when speaking of himself. Catholic commentators have frequently observed, of course, that "Son of Man" as used in Daniel is itself a title

[14] Knox, *Creed in Slow Motion*, p. 117.
[15] Knox, *Belief of Catholics*, p. 83.

connoting a more than human Being. But Knox suggests yet another significance:

> it emphasized his humanity; and what was the point of emphasizing his humanity unless he were something more than an ordinary human being? When Socrates assured his contemporaries that he really knew nothing, and was only asking questions because he wanted to learn from men wiser than himself, you can see at once he knew he was cleverer than they were. If you knew nothing about the Pope except that he called himself the slave of the slaves of God, you could infer quite easily that he regarded himself as the top man in Christendom, or he wouldn't have used such terms in describing himself. In the same way, you can give a good guess that our Lord wouldn't have been at such pains to call himself the Son of Man if he had not claimed to be something more than man when he did so.[16]

There is Jesus' consistent use of language, which distinguishes his station from that of his disciples. They do not bear the same relationship to God the Father as he does: "Constantly, he speaks to his disciples of 'my Father, who is in heaven,' constantly of 'your Father who is in heaven,' but never of 'our Father who is in heaven.' Could any clearer proof be needed that he thought of himself as the Son of God in a peculiar sense, in which that title could not be shared with any merely human creature, even with the apostles themselves?"[17]

[16] Knox, *In Soft Garments*, pp. 48–49. For a more complete investigation into the meaning of this title by a theologian who was a contemporary of Knox, see Karl Adam, *The Christ of Faith: The Christology of the Church* (New York: Mentor Omega, 1962), especially chap. 8, where he summarizes: "The phrase was a circumlocution for his messianic secret that he was on the one hand the coming king of divine dominion and the judge of the world, and on the other the servant of God, who gave his life as a ransom for many. This was both obscured and revealed in his circumlocution. The strange riddle was meant to draw the attention of those who had ears to hear to his manifestation and his calling. They were to experience in him that he was at the same time Lord of the future and Redeemer of the present, that the past and the present are one in him, and that his time and his generation will come with the turning of time" (pp. 138–39).

[17] Knox, *Belief of Catholics*, p. 87. A well-known Dominican who was no mean Biblical scholar offers this insight into what it must have been like when Jesus spoke of his Father: "No wonder, then, that the Sacred Humanity of Jesus Christ loved to have the word 'Father' in his speech. It was like a hidden brook, singing a quiet tune to still His heart in the rendings which were about Him. How good it is to sit in spirit beside some little quiet brook and just to hear it babbling. When in the hour of greatest anguish our Blessed Lord

And when Jesus performs miracles, he does so by his own authority, unlike the prophets or the apostles. In fact, the incongruity of the classic, misdirected, Western liberal modesty, which places Jesus as one among the world's great religious founders, is seen clearly when his sayings are placed on the lips of the other founders: "Did Confucius ever say 'all power is given to me in heaven and in earth'? Did Mahomet ever say, 'No one cometh to the Father but by me'? Did Buddha ever say, 'Whosoever confesseth me before men, the same will I confess before my Father who is in Heaven'?"[18]

So a sober examination of the Scriptures demonstrates that Jesus was human, but more than human. Knox even suggests that he knew that the first generations of Christians would have more difficulty remembering his humanity than they would his divinity and that that is why he wanted to make sure his disciples knew about the temptation in the desert (since only he could have been the source for that recounting of his dismissal of Satan's overtures) and about the agony in the garden of Gethsemane, to which he invited his disciples to be spectators. The rise of Docetism in the early Church, a heresy that taught that the humanity of Christ was not real but only an illusion created as a vehicle for God to communicate with mankind, showed how warranted was that concern.

Miracles of Jesus

But Docetism is hardly the refuge of the modern demurrer. Something more akin to Arianism, the view that Jesus was not truly divine, is the preferred standpoint of many critics of the doctrines of the Church. And they have to maintain a blanket refusal to countenance the miracles of Jesus as they assign him a place in their theological systems. In *Caliban in Grub Street*, Knox had reproduced an expurgated Gospel of Saint Matthew containing only those texts guaranteed not to shock the sensibilities of readers who are squeamish about miracles and about evidences of divine claims on the part of Jesus. The resulting text, reminiscent of the Jefferson Bible, required no more than four pages

had to find refreshment and strength for His soul, He found it in that one word, 'Father.' " Vincent McNabb, *The Craft of Prayer* (London: Burns, Oates and Washbourne, 1936), p. 5.

[18] Knox, *Hidden Stream*, p. 125.

of reasonably large type to display in full. A good 80 to 90 percent of Saint Matthew flew in the face of the hypothesis of Jesus as "sweetness and light". In the present set of apologetical works, Knox brings a number of salient points to light for assessing the Gospel miracles of Jesus. For one, they are recorded by contemporaries, and in a sober, matter-of-fact way that only heightens the contrast with the misty chronicles of the thaumaturges of the pagan world. They are also unique among first-century writings in emphasizing miraculous occurrences; far from that era being awash in credulous accounts of inexplicable wonders, it seems to have been singularly bereft of them:

> Belief in miracles (you might almost say) began, or at least began again, in the first century. The Jewish scriptures record hardly any miracles after the time of the Captivity; there is no atmosphere of the miraculous to be found in Josephus, and the occultist claims of a Simon Magus only testify to a local and a personal influence. Pagans connected their stories of the miraculous only with antiquity; the very oracles were dumb at the time when our Lord came. And then suddenly, in this extraordinary first century, a blaze of credulity flares up through the world. There is no question of "ignorant peasants" merely; rich men like Barnabas, educated men like Paul, medical men like Luke, are suddenly swept away on this odd stream of belief in miracle. When the moderns say that "ignorant people are always expecting miracles to happen," what they really mean is "ignorant *Christians* are always expecting miracles to happen." But there were no Christians till Christ came. When Christ came, people suddenly started believing in miracles—why?[19]

For sure the world at the time of Jesus' coming was saturated with superstition, and sorcerers and soothsayers abounded—no less than in more materially advanced but equally gullible ages. Such practitioners needed little concrete substantiating evidence to continue their lucrative careers. But when the truly miraculous did in fact occur, people took note and responded in a manner that highlighted its unexpectedness:

> When St. Paul healed the crippled man at Lystra, they all said, "The gods are come down to us in the likeness of man," and tried to do sacrifice to them. So, when St. Paul was uninjured by the bite of the snake, the people of Malta thought he was a god. They did not

[19] Knox, *Belief of Catholics*, p. 98.

> look upon a miracle as something ordinary or commonplace; it carried their minds straight back to their mythologies, to the stories of Philemon and Baucis, or the invulnerable Achilles.[20]

What is also curious is that the alleged wonders performed by pagan gods had been just that—wonders. They were astounding deeds serving no other purpose than to show off superior powers. Prior to Jesus, it is only among the Hebrew people, where of course God's miracles adumbrated those of the new dispensation, that they are performed to manifest God's goodness and mercy. Then, after the Gospels are written, other claimants appear on the horizon:

> I think there cannot really be much doubt that Philostratus' life of Apollonius of Tyana, written in the third century A.D., was a Pagan come-back deliberately designed to meet the overwhelming competition of Christian teaching. I understand it is true to say that the earliest lives of Buddha have no miraculous element in them, and that stories like that which represent him as born of a virgin date from a time when Christianity had already penetrated into India. And, as Paley pointed out, the miracles attributed to Mahomet are not recorded in the Koran—Mahomet himself seems to have made rather a point of the idea that miracles were unnecessary—but only came into circulation several centuries later, when Christendom and Islam were already matched in the struggle for world-domination. If all religions have their miracles, you see, that does not prove that there may not have been a certain infringement of copyright.[21]

The belatedly ascribed miracles raise an eyebrow; the preternatural powers of the Buddhist ascetic intrigue, but do not inspire. But with Jesus, the supernatural in a sense seems natural:

> The diseases, the leprosy, the deafness, the blindness, the disfigured and distorted limbs, the paralysis—they are all part of the world's darkness; and when the light shines, the darkness yields to it; this positive thing overawes our negations; the sick get well, the blind see, and so on. It is miracle, yes, in the natural order; and yet if you think what the supernatural is, the wonder would be if these strange

[20] Knox, *In Soft Garments*, pp. 67–68.
[21] Ibid.

> results didn't follow, when the supernatural breaks in upon us as it did at the Incarnation.[22]

The Resurrection

If it is impossible to obliterate the miraculous from the accounts of Jesus' life, then all the more so is it impossible to do so in the accounts of his death and Resurrection. The keystone doctrine of the Catholic faith is also an extraordinarily well-attested event in history. The greatest of Jesus' miracles, his rising from the dead, was common enough knowledge in Judea that, almost thirty years later, Saint Paul could summon the assistance of King Herod Agrippa (who was not a believer) to let a more recently arrived Roman official in on the facts, which, he says, did not happen in some remote corner but rather were the talk of the town. It is also clear from an obviously early speech of Saint Peter preserved in the Acts of the Apostles, in which he addresses Jews who had just come up to Jerusalem for an important feast shortly after Jesus' execution:

> He recalls to them a passage in the Psalms, where David says, "Thou, O God, wilt not leave my soul in hell, neither wilt thou suffer thy holy one to see corruption." Who, he asks, is this Holy One referred to? King David himself? No, King David *did* see corruption; we all know where his tomb is. Therefore it must refer to Jesus of Nazareth, who rose from the grave and did *not* see corruption. Now, St. Peter was talking exactly fifty days after the alleged event. The tomb of Jesus Christ was there, close to Jerusalem; about as far off, say, as Somerville is from here. And he challenges them to go and look for the Body of Jesus of Nazareth there. Or rather, he doesn't, because the mystery of its disappearance is on all men's lips. He does not prove the doctrine of the Empty Tomb; he refers to it as a fact and bases his whole argument on it. No; these things were not done in a corner.[23]

There is little that could be more concrete in evidentiary investigation than examining whether a body is or is not in the tomb in which it was placed, especially given the fact that a heavy boulder

[22] Knox, *Hidden Stream*, p. 115.
[23] Knox, *In Soft Garments*, p. 55.

covered its entrance and guards were placed in front of it to prevent the removal of the body. Of course, when Jesus' body was discovered to be missing, and the guards reported the extraordinary vision of a brilliant white figure sitting atop the rolled-away stone, the authorities fabricated a desperate story of the disciples coming and removing it while the guards slept. The one Gospel account that records this early effort at political spin doctoring was, Knox observes, likely composed in Judea, "and it may well have preserved the inner history, long-kept secret, of what the soldiers saw, and why, at dawn, the tomb was left unguarded." For by the time Mary Magdalen and the other women arrived, there were no guards there anymore, but they too saw a man—or men—in radiant garments by the tomb. "The evidence on these points of detail is not exactly clear. True evidence very seldom is. Bribe a handful of soldiers, and they will spread the same lie all over Jerusalem. Take three women to the tomb, none of them expecting to find anything unusual, and you will have to piece the story together for yourself." [24]

Knox's point is well taken. Many critics of the Gospels have belabored the authors over the small discrepancies in the accounts—was it one angel or two angels they saw? when did the women tell the disciples? why isn't Peter's vision of Jesus better documented? and so forth—as if these loose ends would cause the whole fabric of the narratives to unravel and the world would be relieved of the need to believe in the physical bodily Resurrection of Jesus. It is this type of argument that caused Samuel Butler to lose his faith and then portray Ernest Pontifex doing likewise, and it is this shattering of the edifice of literal inspiration that likewise abetted the slide into agnosticism of Leslie Stephen and of Arnold Lunn and of many others since Victorian times. But precisely the opposite is true: the differences in narratives are clear signs to the historical detective that no effort has been made to huddle the witnesses together and smooth out the apparent inconsistencies that arise when events are seen from the perspectives of different individuals. The anomalies are indeed as clear a signal as a seeker of facts could ask for that the accounts as they have come down through the ages are fresh and untainted, and they all blend together to prove the salient point that Jesus, to the

[24] Ibid., p. 57.

great surprise of both his disciples and his enemies, disappeared from his tomb.

Knox gives a masterful overview of the plausibility of assigning responsibility for the removal of Jesus' body to any of the participants in the unfolding drama. The Jewish authorities obviously had no motive:

> It was in their interest to keep the body, and to be able at any moment to produce it, should any claim be made that Jesus of Nazareth had risen from the dead. If they removed it from the grave, why did they not produce it afterwards? Nor had Pilate, the Roman governor, any reason for wishing to smuggle away the body of the man he had crucified; its presence might conceivably lead to rioting and disturbance, but its disappearance was far more likely to have that effect. The women cannot have stolen it, for they were not strong enough to move away the stone, let alone to overpower a military guard. Did the guard, then, desert their posts, and some other human agent remove the body before the women came? That was the only possibility which presented itself to Mary Magdalen. Could Joseph of Arimathea have carried it away, or Nicodemus? But, in any of these events, why did not the agent who had removed the body give any sign, afterwards, of what he had done? If he were friendly disposed towards the disciples, to the disciples; if he were ill disposed, to the Jews? And, whatever their motives, why did they leave the winding-sheet and the napkin lying there, instead of taking the body as it lay? The presence of the grave-clothes is also fatal to the theory, which has (I believe) been suggested, that the body was buried deeper in the ground as a result of the earthquake.[25]

And even supposing somehow, against all internal evidence of the Gospel records, which show the astonishment of the disciples when confronted with the empty tomb, that the original story put out by the authorities, that the disciples stole the body so they could proclaim Jesus' Resurrection and thereby perpetrate a massive and successful fraud, is held onto by the tenacious unbeliever, that unbeliever must explain away another very inconvenient historical fact: "What you have to decide is, whether such a notion is consistent with the behaviour of those same people two days before, at the Crucifixion, running away and leaving their Master to face his persecutors alone, and with

[25] Ibid., pp. 62–63.

the behaviour of those same people, in the years which followed, suffering imprisonment and dying in support of a story which they had made up to deceive the public."[26]

And then there are the post-Resurrection appearances of Jesus, appearances that, again by their almost haphazard recounting in the Gospels, bespeak an unretouched collection of incidents assembled and arranged to demonstrate that Jesus in flesh and blood conversed with and ate with his disciples for some forty days between his Resurrection and his Ascension. Here too the critics have looked for a nonmiraculous explanation and have offered the hypothesis of a "vision of Jesus". The more-straightforward unbelievers will speak of a collective hysteria, while the more-pious unbelievers (some in clerical attire) will suggest that the great faith of the disciples brought them such warm memories of Jesus that they could almost visualize him as they comforted each other with recollections of his sayings and deeds.

The attempt to dissolve the post-Resurrection body of Jesus into a vaporous warm glow, however, only multiplies the inconsistencies facing its proponents. As Knox points out:

> It is false to the evidence, for in Matthew xxviii. 9 the holy women take hold of our Lord's feet; in John xx. 17 he says to Mary Magdalen, "Stop clinging to me"; in John xx. 27 he invites the touch of an apostle; in Luke xxiv. 30 and 43, Acts i. 4, he breaks bread and eats. It is as easy to discredit the evidence for our Lord's reappearance as to discredit the evidence for his reappearance in a physical form. And such a view is equally false to the economy of criticism; for it explains the Resurrection appearances on a principle which does not explain the Empty Tomb; it insists that our witnesses have made two separate mistakes, not one. Further, although these appearances were not continuous, but were spread over intervals during forty days (Acts i. 3) it was clearly the impression of the first Christians that they depended upon the earthly presence of our Lord's natural Body, since they ceased after its (alleged) Ascension; the experience of Paul (1 Cor. xv. 8) being clearly exceptional, and quoted as such. No further report has come down to us of our Lord as seen walking on earth; why not, unless the first Christians were convinced that it was a physical Body which appeared to them, and then disappeared?[27]

[26] Ibid.

[27] Knox, *Belief of Catholics*, pp. 102–3.

Again, it is an argument of convergence, not one that demands assent from an otherwise cornered mind but one that the rational mind will find far more plausible than the spurious alternatives put forth by the deliberate doubter.

Jesus: Founder of the Church

The same can be said for the arguments proposing the founding of the Catholic Church by Jesus, and his bestowal on her of the commission to guard and promulgate his teachings. After all, what was the primary purpose of those forty days—spent very rarely in public, but instead closeted with his disciples—if not to indoctrinate them into the fullness of his teaching before he should ascend to heaven?

All the indications from the written sources point to a well-organized ecclesia, or Church, operating long before the Gospels were even penned:

> From the very outset of the Acts, you have the impression that the Church has sprung into being ready-made. Not that it has no lessons to learn from experience, needs no fresh revelations to guide it. But it knows already how to deal with each fresh situation that arises, and does so with a wonderful sureness of touch. The apostles, who owe their appointment to the command of a Divine Voice, have no hesitation in co-opting a fresh apostle on their own responsibility. They set aside, on their own responsibility, seven men to act in a newly created capacity as deacons. On both these occasions the multitude of the Church, being then a compact body, is directed to proceed to an election; but it is the apostles who lay their hands on the newly ordained deacons to invest them with their sacred character. This imposition of hands (nowhere prescribed by our Lord in any recorded utterance) appears, in early apostolic practice, as a normal supplement to the ceremony of baptism. About twenty years after the Ascension, an apostolic Council decides, once more on its own responsibility, what respect is to be shown, in areas where Judaism is strong, to the scruples of Jewish Christians. There is nothing amateurish, nothing haphazard in all this procedure; it reflects, surely, the administrative instincts of a self-contained and self-conscious institution.[28]

[28] Ibid., pp. 119–20.

It is an organic growth, like that to which Jesus alluded in the parable of the mustard seed and the leaven in the dough. In fact, as Knox reminds the reader, Jesus pays far more attention to the building up of his band of apostles into a Church than to healing the sick and preaching to the multitudes. His intent is very clear: it is not for him to go about trying to convert as many people as possible but rather to put into place a specific body of people who are to be his ambassadors to the rest of the world in the ages to come. In that sense, the Church as Jesus conceived her must be distinguished from merely a religion founded on, because found only in, a holy book.

> It was perfectly easy for our Lord Jesus Christ, if he had wanted to, to have dictated to his Apostles a book as long as the Old Testament or as the Koran, and to have left this book, after his Ascension, to guide all the world into his truth. But he didn't do that; and for a score of years, perhaps, after his Ascension, the Christian religion was preached everywhere by word of mouth; nobody studied the Gospels or preached about the Gospels, because there were no Gospels to study or to preach about.[29]

Here is stated concisely the fundamental weakness of the Biblical literalist. The Gospels are the outgrowth of an oral tradition of apostolic origin. The continuity of the tradition and its apostolicity (one of the marks of the Church), passed on from generation to generation of her leadership, are what ensured that the Gospels as they have come down through the ages, chosen out of a vast literature, are repositories of authentic knowledge of Jesus and his teaching. Thus they are perpetually to be venerated as inspired by God and free from error. There is need to be precise here, however:

> It is not true to say that the New Testament depends upon the Church for its authority. The Church teaches that the Scriptures, whether of the Old or the New Testament, were written under the inspiration of the Holy Ghost, and are consequently free from error; no other title is needed to claim for them the assent of Christians. Their authority springs from their own origin. But it is true to say that we should not be conscious of this authority if the Church did not assure us of its existence. In the order of our knowledge, belief

[29] Knox, *In Soft Garments*, p. 75.

> in the Church is antecedent to belief in the Scriptures, and is the condition of it. Historical criticism assures us, indeed, that the books of the New Testament are veracious in their main outline, but only Revelation could make us confident in the belief that they have God as their author. It is the Church which assures us, for example, that the Epistle of St. Jude has a higher authority than that of the Epistle attributed to St. Barnabas; it is the Church, further, which assures us that St. Jude wrote under the direct inspiration of the Holy Spirit.[30]

Selecting the Word of God as the sole source for truth while dispensing with the vehicle that defined what precisely constituted the Word of God is a logically untenable position to maintain. As the subsequent playing out of the history of those religious groups who have the Bible alone for their guide shows, schism looms inevitably when opposing interpretations of important texts find their champions, and no ultimate authority exists to adjudicate among them.

THE CHURCH AS HOLY

But even admitting the existence of a body of people whom Jesus had chosen to propagate his message, one must examine the position taken by those inheritors of the Protestant world view who hold that the true Church is the sum total of people who are ultimately saved. In other words, they do not equate the Church with any visible corporate body on earth but instead with the elect whom God alone can identify. Yet it is difficult to square the words of Jesus himself with this doctrine; rather, his parables and other preserved sayings indicate that when he spoke of the kingdom of heaven, he meant a visible Church composed of a mix of the saintly and the reprobate. Knox states, for example, that when Jesus warned, "Many are called, but few are chosen", he had in mind the ecclesia, the Church, not all of whose members will be saved. Knox notes parenthetically, with an eye on those who believe that the saved constitute only a small fraction of mankind (a notion entertained by some medieval theologians and preachers, and later by many Protestant sects), that the word "few" should more

[30] Ronald Knox, *The Church on Earth* (New York: Macmillan Company, 1929), pp. 33–34.

properly be translated as "less than a hundred percent", and therefore the phrase offers no clue about the relative populations of heaven and hell. But to return to Knox's main point:

> The kingdom of heaven, the Church, is like ten virgins, five wise and five foolish—only five of them are saved, but all ten of them are in the Church. The kingdom of heaven is like a great supper, to which a number of people are called, but one of them is found to be without a wedding garment, and is cast out into the exterior darkness. It is like a net thrown into the sea, which brings in some fish that are eatable, and some that are worthless; it is like a field, in which some of the crop is honest wheat, and the rest mere useless cockle. Now, when our Lord goes out of his way to talk like that, does he not make it clear that his Church is something different from that ideal assembly of the elect which the old-fashioned Protestants declared it to be? Does he not make it clear that it consists of a recognizable body of people, some of whom but not all of whom, will attain everlasting life?[31]

If the question suggests itself why God would allow imperfection in the kingdom founded by himself, Knox proposes the following consideration: "God does not want it to be known, in this life, which souls are his and which will meet with final rejection; it is better for our faith that we should belong to a Church which has imperfect as well as perfect members; better for our watchfulness over ourselves that we should realize the possibility of being a baptized Christian, and yet not bound for heaven."[32] And he goes even further, echoing Jesus' own words about the necessity of scandals arising: "It is part of our probation, he would have us understand, that we should be puzzled by all these anomalies of religious history, and distressed at them, and yet have enough strength of resolution to see behind them and beyond them, and recognize the Church as his own Bride, the inheritor of his promises and the completion of his life."[33]

Many years earlier, during the darkest hours of World War I, when he was still in Anglican orders, he gave a series of conferences on prayer. The daily mounting carnage had caused some people to lose

[31] Knox, *In Soft Garments*, p. 78.
[32] Ibid., p. 92.
[33] Ibid., p. 95.

faith in God's omnipotence, but Knox reminded his auditors that God foresees every consequence of every act, however contrary to his purposes it may seem: "He foresaw how each soldier would fall, what effect that loss would have, or ought to have, upon those who loved him, how every single human soul living in the world would be affected by the upheaval." Only in heaven shall it be appreciated "how the purposes of God ran, like a single straight line, fulfilling every need, allowing for every exigency; tested at every point, and at every point found true." [34] From the temporal side, the world may seem especially bleak, the Church far from pristine, but there must be room to exercise the virtue of faith in God, amid apparent disharmony, so that the believer can, by a meritorious act of the will, seek repose in God's will.

At the same time, Christians must constantly guard against the fashionable temptation to belabor an institution over alleged unjust structures, a posture too often assumed in order to facilitate the sidestepping of moral blame for wrongs committed by themselves. The larger the institution (and what is larger than the Catholic Church?), the more diffuse the guilt. The psychological need to assign a cause for evil is assuaged in a way that does not require personal penance and reform. That is the tempting thing about collective guilt: it affords the very mundane sinner the chance to don the mantle of the prophet by exposing the unholiness of the Church, and even to use that righteous indignation as justification for leaving the Church altogether. But Knox reminds his readers that it is in the Creed that the Church is called holy, so it is part of the ancient deposit of faith, not just a by-product of post-Tridentine triumphalism, to hold fast to the image of holiness inhering in and emanating from the Church.

> Judas betrays his Master—Judas, the Catholic; and we still say, "The Church is holy." Cardinals poison one another, in the history books we read, and we still say, "The Church is holy." We go to Mass in Farm Street, and there's such a pious-looking man saying his rosary just behind us, and when we come back from making our Communion the pious-looking man has disappeared, and our bag has disappeared, too, and we still say, "The Church is holy." What is it

[34] Ronald Knox, *Bread or Stone: Four Conferences on Impetrative Prayer* (London: Society of SS. Peter and Paul, 1915), pp. 23, 25.

> that leaves our faith quite undisturbed after all these uncomfortable incidents?[35]

There are, to be sure, the external marks of holiness that the unbiased observer can see: the succession of saints in every generation who draw sustenance from the Church, the organized religious orders that she produces, the works of mercy flowing naturally from her adherents, and the elevation of man's dignity throughout history that she has wrought. But all that enumeration of specifics, which is fairly telling in itself—and is compellingly brought out in, for example, the writings of the nineteenth-century Spanish theologian Jaime Balmes—underscores a unique feature of the Catholic Church, one that can easily be taken for granted:

> Other Christians think it is up to *them* to be holy in order to bring up the average of holiness, so to speak, in their particular denomination: but we Catholics have a quite different instinct—we think of the Church as a holy thing, whether we are holy or not. We expect it to make us holy; we don't imagine it to be our job to make it holy.... It is a reservoir, a power-house of holiness, this Church of ours; not a mere collection of holy people.[36]

The Church is composed of sinners, but she is the source of grace for the forgiveness of sins. She shows the way to holiness, but she does not exact holiness as the price of admission into her ranks. Or, as Knox puts it succinctly in a talk on the communion of saints: "The Church in heaven is All Saints. The Church in Purgatory is All Souls. The Church on earth is all sorts."[37]

[35] Knox, *Creed in Slow Motion*, p. 165.

[36] Ibid., p. 168. The book referred to is J. Balmes, *European Civilization: Protestantism and Catholicity Compared in Their Effects on the Civilization of Europe* (Baltimore: John Murphy and Co., 1850).

[37] Knox, *Creed in Slow Motion*, p. 197. One of the more influential critics of Catholicism as a religion of externals was Auguste Sabatier of the Sorbonne, who argued that the early Church crowded out a pure religion of the spirit with rituals and dogmas. His thesis was countered by Cuthbert Butler in an essay in the *Hibbert Journal* in 1906 bearing the title of Sabatier's book "Religions of Authority and the Religion of the Spirit". Butler observes: "Doubtless there are souls able at a certain stage of their spiritual growth to nourish their religious life on this immaterial food; those who have read Sabatier's books will not question that, at any rate in his later years, it was so with him.... But is it not an atmosphere so rarified that only the *Intellectuels*, and of them only those of a strongly mystic and pietistic temperament, can breathe in it with comfort? Can it ever be the living religion of the

SACRAMENTS

How do all sorts become All Saints? Primarily through continued recourse to the sacraments instituted by Christ precisely to aid fallen mankind along the way stations of life. Given that some Catholic theologians question whether Christ instituted *seven* sacraments and bring up as contradicting witnesses the medievals who tabulated a different number, Knox's introductory remarks on what a sacrament is are most germane today. After citing Saint Peter Damian, the eleventh-century theologian who held that there were twelve sacraments, among which he included the anointing of a new monarch, he notes that any fuss over discrepancies in lists arises because the word *sacrament* was for the longest time a loosely defined term translating the Greek word for *mystery*. "All the mysteries of the Christian faith, in primitive language," he observes, "are sacraments of the Christian Church."[38] It was not until the Council of Trent that a dogmatic statement first pinpointed the meaning of *sacrament* in the seven rites familiar to modern Christians and distinguished them from all other rites in use by the Church. But these seven rites are coterminous with the Church: there is no question of confession of sins or ordination or any other sacrament being a later accretion. They all have a foundation in the New Testament.

To the critic who disputes this, Knox submits the case of the Greek Orthodox as evidence in favor of the antiquity of the seven sacraments. Western theologians began to narrow the definition of the term to the seven later solemnly defined at Trent as early as the time of Peter Lombard in the thirteenth century. And yet the Greek Church, by then long estranged from the Latins, had held the same seven rites to be sacraments. Knox comments:

> Is it not clear that, although seven rites may only have acquired the exclusive label of "sacraments" in the twelfth century, the unique importance of those seven rites was recognized even before the ninth

crowds, of the poor, the overworked, the ignorant, the unspiritual, the dull of heart, the tempted, the sinners whom Christ came to save?" Cuthbert Butler, *Religions of Authority and the Religion of the Spirit with other Essays Apologetical and Critical* (New York: Benziger Brothers, 1930), p. 43.

[38] Knox, *Hidden Stream*, p. 196.

> century, in what Protestants call the "undivided Church"? The fact that they had as yet no common name to distinguish them from the other rites of the Church makes the circumstance of their recognition doubly important. Language may react upon thought to its confusion; but here thought had preceded language by at least three centuries.[39]

The squeamishness of the antagonists toward the sacraments has undergone some vicissitudes over the centuries, and Knox characterizes their opposition according to one of two arguments: sacraments are too materialistic (making use of matter, which the medieval Manicheans held to be evil), or they are too magical (resorting to ceremonies rather than a direct communication with God, in the view of the leaders of the Reformation). A third attitude, typified by the Jansenists, who were not disbelievers in sacramental efficacy, tends to isolate people from the sacraments because they claim the Church holds too lax an attitude about their usage, especially when it comes to frequency of reception of the Eucharist.

Of these objections, the imputation of magic is today favored most by critics. They couple it with a portrayal of Jesus as a great spiritual teacher who could hardly be held responsible for inaugurating a system so starkly based on material actions. But obviously the criterion by which they judge what is and what is not spiritually edifying is not at all based on the historical record of Jesus' doings. Else they are hard put to explain how a prophet could put spittle on a man's tongue and apply his hands to the man's ears to give him speech and hearing. In doing so, "he made a deliberate display of the sacramental principle, combining with that internal prayer—which surely might have been efficacious by itself—the use of form and matter. He went through the gestures of a physical cure, and made those gestures the vehicle of a miraculous cure."[40] Thwarted in their attempts to divorce Jesus from a supposed grosser later Christianity, the critics still cry magic at any sacramentalism. But are the two concepts at all parallel? Not when the means and the end of them both are examined:

[39] Knox, *Belief of Catholics*, p. 165.
[40] Ibid., p. 162.

> Magic, surely, means using supernatural means—or so they are regarded—to produce a natural effect; to cure an illness, to get the wireworm out of the mealie-crop, something of that kind. Whereas the sacramental process is using natural means to produce supernatural effects. The blow on the cheek and the smudge of oil on the forehead are expected to fortify the soul with a higher measure of the Holy Spirit's influence; surely we ought to call that ceremony by some name which is the exact opposite of magic?[41]

Knox echoes the historian Thorndike in suggesting that the medicine man, far from being the ancestor of the priest, is the ancestor of the scientist; and of course the ethnological and folklore studies of Andrew Lang and Wilhelm Schmidt had already debunked the notion that magic was the precursor of religions honoring an all-powerful God.

And yet the Catholic need not recoil at the suggestion that some similarity might exist between the ceremonies of the mystery religions and the ceremonies of the Church. Since God has situated men as "a kind of liaison officers between matter and spirit", he uses physical means to effect spiritual ends, and those means can have been anticipated in part by mankind's fumbling efforts prior to the full revelation in Christ.

If anything, the imputation of magic lies more heavily at the Protestant's door than the Catholic's. Just as magic is resorted to in the hope of producing a natural effect by invoking the supernatural, the Evangelical kind of Protestantism, as typified by the Wesleyans and other sects Knox examines in *Enthusiasm*, promises physically measurable consolations, a feeling that one has been touched by God. On the contrary, the Catholic concept of sacrament carries no such connotation. "We don't expect to *feel* much as the result of the grace which, we know, we are getting. We are accustomed to the idea of supernatural transactions going on; affecting quite really the state of our souls; and yet nothing in the way of external feelings to show for it. We are content to go on in faith, knowing that we have received spiritual benefits without having the itch to take our spiritual temperatures all the time."[42]

[41] Knox, *Hidden Stream*, pp. 202–3.
[42] Ibid., p. 204.

PRIESTHOOD

In his discussion of the priesthood, Knox recalls the oft-noted fact that the New Testament authors chose a different term to denote the Christian ministers (*presbyters*) from the term employed for the Hebrew or pagan ministers (the Greek *hierus* and the Latin *sacerdos*). The terms for the latter directly squared with the notion of the minister or priest as a sacrificial agent, while the Christian term means simply an elder, or a charter member. Protestant controversialists have seized on that verbal distinction to imply that Jesus never meant to institute a sacrificial priesthood, and indeed if nothing but the New Testament were available to decide the case (or as Knox puts it, if Christianity "died out about A.D. 70"), the conclusion would be impossible to gainsay. But of course the Church did live on, and there is a substantial amount of apostolic and early postapostolic tradition to guide the inquirer through troubled exegesis. If every record of the Church in action shows a functioning sacrificial priesthood with the Mass being celebrated much as Saint Paul describes a Eucharistic liturgy, then the onus of proof lies with the critic to show when the innovation took place. This is a very important point in apologetics. The Church claims continuity with Jesus' establishment of the original community of followers. If any change of direction occurred, or any accretions contradicted the primitive outline, clear signs of the schism would have reverberated down through history:

> [Y]ou've got to shew when it was that the development [of a hierarchy] took place, and what protest was made against it at the time, or alternatively why the protest wasn't made. The favourite supposition used to be that the Church went all catholic about the middle of the second century. But, most unfortunately, there was a schism in the middle of the second century which would quite certainly have made capital out of it if the Church, at that very moment, had been declining from the simplicity of her primitive ideals. I mean the Montanist schism, which is amply documented for us by the writings of a really brilliant heretic, Tertullian. And there is no suggestion to be found in the writings of Tertullian that there had been any funny business going on.[43]

[43] Ibid., pp. 209–10.

This principle of an appeal to early Church history is a distinguishing mark of the balanced exegetical approach flourishing at the time Knox wrote, particularly among French Biblical scholars like M.J. Lagrange and Pierre Batiffol.[44] The New Testament texts must be analyzed in relation to the Christianity that emerged in the first generations after Jesus. Otherwise an ultimately sterile building of hypotheses, which is characteristic of the rationalist school (and is mirrored as well in the fanciful treatment of primitive religions and folklore made famous by *The Golden Bough*), inevitably results because the documents are treated as if they exist *in vacuo*. Of course the ahistorical method induces not only a loss of depth in criticism but, whether deliberately or otherwise, also sows unnecessary seeds of doubt about the worth of the text under discussion.[45]

Why then didn't the early Christians make use of a word for priests that would suggest a sacrificial aspect to the role? Displaying his wonted psychological insight into the Biblical milieu, Knox posits an answer that makes eminent good sense.

> By a kind of unconscious instinct, human language shrinks from ambiguity. And the first Christians will have avoided the word hiereus, without asking themselves why they did it, simply because it was the ordinary word for a priest attached to the Temple at Jerusalem, and it would have been confusing to apply it, all of a sudden, to a quite different class of people. A curious verse early on in the Acts of the Apostles tells us that a large number of priests had given their allegiance to the faith. What became of them? Did they go on functioning as temple priests? We don't know. There is no evidence that they stopped. In any case, what we tend to forget about the very early Church is that it existed side by side with the synagogue, and,

[44] Examples of the fruit of such scholarship available even to English readers at the time include Pierre Batiffol, *Primitive Catholicism* (London: Longmans, Green and Co., 1911); Battifol, *The Credibility of the Gospel* (London: Longmans, Green and Co., 1912); M.J. Lagrange, *The Gospel of Jesus Christ*, 2 vols. (Westminster, Md.: Newman Bookshop, 1938); Ferdinand Prat, *Jesus Christ: His Life, His Teaching, and His Work*, 2 vols. (Milwaukee: Bruce Publishing Co., 1950); and Louis Duchesne, *Early History of the Christian Church*, 3 vols. (London: John Murray, 1909–1924). An excellent synthesis can be found in Henri Daniel-Rops, *Jesus and His Times* (New York: E.P. Dutton and Co., 1954).

[45] A classic example of this ahistorical approach occurs in a short book by an otherwise highly competent Catholic Biblical exegete: Raymond Brown, *The Virginal Conception and Bodily Resurrection of Jesus* (New York: Paulist Press, 1973), a work that would have elicited from Knox no less vigorous a rebuttal than did *Foundations*.

in Jerusalem at any rate, at very close quarters. And if a presbyter of that period had taken to calling himself a priest, it would have been just as confusing as if a Catholic priest in modern England took to describing himself as a parson.[46]

KNOX'S AUDIENCE

Extensive extracts from Knox's primary works of apologetics have been quoted to give a sense of his approach in explaining the Catholic faith. It may legitimately be asked whom he supposed his audience to be, preliminary to pronouncing judgment on the continued validity of his method. Obviously, the dependence on logic and the adherence to a traditional intellectual argumentation, from the natural evidence pointing to God's existence, through a sober appraisal of the evidentiary value of Scripture, to acceptance of the divinity of Jesus and his continued presence in the Catholic Church, is not in vogue today in many popular expositions. Too cerebral, too Counter-Reformation neo-scholastic, the critics would say. Who today, they say, would be convinced by *The Belief of Catholics*? Indeed, back in 1965, Robert Speaight suggested that a chasm of maturity separates the Ronald Knox of *Broadcast Minds* in 1932 from the Ronald Knox of *Proving God* in 1956. He regards Knox's assertion in the latter that the will as well as the intellect is involved in the apprehension of God as a marked advance on his earlier apologetics. Likewise Speaight cites Knox's criticism of the apologetics of the manuals as too mechanical to stimulate belief as a repudiation of his previous œuvre. Writing in his later years, Knox even says that what an old man looks for in religious disquisition "is not so much truth as reality".

Proving God, it should be recalled, is an unfinished fragment of a book. Having begun it on New Year's Day in 1956, Knox shelved it when asked to translate Saint Thérèse's autobiography, and ill health and death overtook him before he could return to the project. But even though the opening chapter presents thoughts meant to startle the possibly complacent reader out of the illusion that the Catholic faith is but a series of syllogisms to be assented to, the approach is completely congruent with his previous writings. There were some

[46] Knox, *Hidden Stream*, pp. 210–11.

Catholic thinkers of midcentury who drifted with prevailing intellectual currents as the conciliar years approached, caught up perhaps in eddies of Eastern mysticism or existentialism or pantheism. Knox was not of their number: his friend and confessor, Dom Hubert van Zeller, characterized him as "an arch-conservative" in an interview in 1983, a time far enough removed from the years of turmoil to assess fairly where someone like Knox stood with respect to ideas resonating in Catholic circles.[47]

What then would an archconservative mean when he speaks of the priority of reality over truth? Within a few pages, he answers his own rhetorical question: "Am I suggesting that we should haul down the flag of intellectualism? ... If such a gesture were possible, I should be the last to recommend it. 'An unintellectual salvation' (the phrase, I think, was Philip Waggett's) 'means an unsaved intellect'; and if muddle-headedness is a mood of our age, and a vice of our fellow-countrymen, we whose traditions are age-long and worldwide, are committed to an attitude of protest.' "[48] It would be a dishonor to the very reason with which men are endowed to dismiss it as unnecessary when attempting to think about God. Obviously then, his protest is being registered only against the divorcing of rational

[47] From an interview with Milton Walsh, the transcript of which appears in Walsh's dissertation, "Ronald Knox as Apologist" (dissertation, Pontifical Gregorian University, Rome, 1985).

[48] Ronald Knox, *Proving God* (London: Month, 1959), p. 15. The limits of reason in the eliciting of the act of faith have been well described by Martin D'Arcy in his work cited earlier in this chapter, *The Nature of Belief*: "There at the parting from the natural to the supernatural, where the natural looks most like its divine neighbour, the soul has to make a sacrifice which to the eyes of human prudence appears uncalled for; it has to surrender its glory, to change its shield and throw away the very weapon which has won for it its safe journeying so far. For the natural man reason and private judgment are inalienable rights, and now, as a lover does to his beloved, but with how much greater wisdom, he has to give up his most cherished possessions and have no word but 'Speak, Lord, for thy servant heareth'" (p. 322).

Fr. D'Arcy (1888–1976), whom Knox admired as a philosopher and theologian, extolled the power of human reason and in fact devotes much of the book cited to a critique of Newman's theory of the rational grounds for faith developed in his *Grammar of Assent*, which posited an illative sense, a sort of intuition based on probabilities, to account for certitude. D'Arcy instead ascribes certainty about truths to rational interpretation, when the mind is confronted with a unity of indirect reference. Hence his description of the act of faith is all the more powerful in contradistinction from certitude in the natural realm. An excellent biography of this thinker is that by H. J. A. Sire, *Father Martin D'Arcy: Philosopher of Christian Love* (Leominster: Gracewing, 1997).

argumentation from an exposition that touches the moral and spiritual faculties. He then envisions some future writer who could tap all a reader's faculties when proving God's existence, so as to evoke the same response as that of the disciples on the road to Emmaus: "[D]id not our hearts burn within us when he talked to us by the way?" He goes on to outline other features of an effective apologetics, one that could "reconstruct the picture of Our Lord Himself" and that would portray the New Testament "as the breathless confidences of living men" and the Church "as a patient pioneer washing out the gold from the turbid stream of her own memories".[49]

Milton Walsh, surveying the vast corpus of Knox's sermons, conferences, and overtly apologetical writings in light of the above-enumerated goals, comes to the conclusion that Knox had himself already met the criteria of the sought-after apologist. "In many of his sermons," Walsh writes, "Knox touches the hearts of his listeners as profoundly as any of the great preachers of the twentieth century; these 'pictures of Our Lord Himself' are among Knox's most effective apologetical writings."[50] Sermons such as "The Window in the Wall" on the Eucharist, and even somewhat fanciful short stories like "The Rich Young Man", are extraordinarily compelling and evoke respectively a perception of Jesus hidden and Jesus walking among his fellow Jews that no formal theological treatise could manage to equal.

There does, however, remain the question Knox himself puts in the mouth of the doubter of the worth of apologetics: "Can you point to a single instance, in history or among your own acquaintance, where a man has been led on, unwillingly by sheer force of argument, to a position in which mere intellectual candour forced him to make the surrender of his soul?"[51] The question of course cannot be answered with any certainty because it is impossible to

[49] Knox, *Proving God*, pp. 16–17.

[50] Walsh, *Ronald Knox as Apologist*, pp. 128–29. And yet when Walsh argues, "The Christ of *The Belief of Catholics* emerges as the sum of an equation, the computer printout of Gospel data" (p. 163), in contradistinction to the "more appealing and apologetically more convincing" Christ of Knox's sermons, he is surely exaggerating in the interests of a thesis. As the references above to *The Belief of Catholics* aim to convey, Knox's mellifluousness and persuasiveness were in full bloom when he wrote that short 1927 work, and its potential for stimulating belief in readers can hardly be slighted.

[51] Knox, *Proving God*, p. 36.

plumb the depths of anyone else's mind to proportion all the factors weighing in to induce conversion. And yet there are many people in all walks of life who have been nudged to the brink of conversion by the written word. Newman's reading the article by Nicholas Wiseman in the *Dublin Review* on Saint Augustine's strictures against the Donatists can be said to be one such occasion, one that pulverized (to use Newman's own word) his elegant theory of Anglicanism as a middle way between extremes in religion. And there is the "*Tolle, lege*" ("Take, read") of Augustine himself. Among the less famous too, the phrase "He read his way into the Church" is common enough not to startle the hearer into incredulity.

But it is important to remember that the value of apologetics lies less in its power to convince the obdurate (because it is true that an unwilling mind may yield to the notion of a truth merely to disengage from an annoying argument but will not give it a real assent) than in its power to amplify the faith, and thereby strengthen the witness, of those who already believe. The act of conversion is typically fostered by a combination of intellectual reflection and personal influence. The personal influence comes from believers who are confirmed in their belief, people who have overcome the doubts that Knox associates with the sleepless worries of four in the morning. Those doubts, like many predawn worries, are not always quantifiable as specific points of unbelief. They may take the form of a general unease, a sense that there is no firm intellectual ground underfoot. In an age not committed to clarity of thought, one that equates metaphysics with Eastern religions and reflexively distances itself from anything redolent of the Catholic tradition, many believers can be expected to be assailed by such doubts.

Once he found his way into the Church of Rome, Ronald Knox was never in doubt about his own faith. He was, however, sensitive to the doubts of others, and he strove to achieve a level of apologetical writing that would meet doubters on their own ground and gently lead them to the threshold of belief. At the same time, his primary audience consisted of people within the fold—Catholic schoolgirls, Oxford Catholic undergraduates, and the faithful who heard his sermons in parish churches. One can rather confidently suppose that many of these people found their faith strengthened by his words, and in a way imperceptible to the historian but foreordained by

Providence, they in turn helped nourish a spark of faith in other people, people formally called unbelievers, with whom they would come in contact. What Knox was supplying, to outwardly radiating circles of his contemporaries and future generations of readers who would come to know of him only through the printed word, was a generous ladleful of the water of conviction. Unseen grace, the prerogative of God himself, could then be left to transform it into the wine of certitude.

CHAPTER NINE

ODDS AND ENDS AND ARMAGEDDON

During Knox's stint on the faculty at Saint Edmund's College and the early years of his chaplaincy at Oxford, encompassing the decade of the 1920s, he contributed columns to several newspapers, the bulk of them to the *Evening Standard*. These occasional pieces supplemented a modest clerical stipend and introduced his name to the nontheologically minded public.

And yet to categorize him at this stage of his literary career as a journalist, in the sense that Chesterton was a journalist, would be to miss the mark. Chesterton at a comparable age was propagating his views far and wide in the press, and when sufficient quantities of columns had accumulated, he was steadily sandwiching them between hard covers (*Tremendous Trifles* and *All Things Considered* come to mind) for posterity. For him, of course, metaphysics loomed large in almost every installment for the papers: he was out to convert his readers to the buoyant orthodoxy that had taken hold of him. For Knox, on the other hand, newspaper articles seem rather to have been a diversion, an opportunity for spinning out reflections and reminiscences that might engage the attention of weary readers commuting to and from work on the railway system he so idolized. Unlike Chesterton, whom he greatly admired and had read extensively as a young Anglican cleric, Knox rarely availed himself of the opportunity to reach for the reader's conscience via the coat lapels. Perhaps his known status as a Catholic priest provided sufficient apologetical weight to essays that display his humanist far more than his theological interests, and in any case the general English public still needed some assurance that Romanists were not consumed by the desire to hoard gunpowder underneath Parliament buildings. Adopting a lighthearted vein while treating of topics like punting on the Thames, the taxation of wireless sets, and the preservation of the country churchyard that occasioned Gray's elegy, sounded just the right note.

Then of course there were the trains. And not only the trains themselves, but even their guidebook, the immortal Bradshaw, which educes several panegyrics from a man who from early childhood was an adept at extracting from its tables of departure and arrival times the most efficient route for traveling between any two termini in England, Scotland, and Wales. A visit to a house that contained in its library one of the earliest of these timetables, dating from 1840, evoked in Knox reflections on passenger comfort in that rugged era when second-class fares afforded exposure to the elements in open-sided carriages, and the slower pace of railroad transport necessitated setting aside a full day for a trip from London to Manchester. Slow perhaps, but at least it meant that parsons would have been prevailed on less frequently to accept out-of-town preaching engagements. Modernity of course required a greatly expanded version, so the former thirty-page, duodecimo booklet was transformed

> into the ox-Bradshaw of to-day, that noble volume which all of us, if we thought the matter over with proper deliberation, would pack next to the Bible in our desert-island bookshelf. Nowhere else, assuredly, can Fancy roam so free; nothing else affords the same opportunity for solitary pastime.
>
> The game of putting an imaginary traveler down at Cheltenham and finding his quickest route to Cambridge; the game of reading through the hotel advertisements and finding out what is really wrong with each; the game (better than either) of choosing a page at random, covering the top with your hands, and guessing from the names of the stations which county you have strayed into.[1]

Given its inherent capacity for allowing the shipwrecked sailor to while away the hours more fruitfully than in scanning the horizon for a rescue ship, Bradshaw is obviously worth consulting for far more than the merely utilitarian purpose of finding the next train northward, a property of little advantage on the island.

A few years later, Knox returned to the same theme, a reader having supplied him with some historical lore in the form of several pre-Bradshaw guides of the late 1830s.

[1] Ronald Knox, "The Traveller's Bible", in *An Open-Air Pulpit* (London: Constable and Co., 1926), p. 39.

> In those more spacious days, it seems, travelers were not greatly exercised over such material details as times of arrival and departure. What they wanted was a sort of Baedeker, which would tell them the exact population, history, etc., of all the towns they visited *en route*; which Seat they passed belonged to which Gentleman (in the surrounding landscape, I mean, not in the train); which were the principal ruined abbeys, gasworks, rivulets, coal-mines, and grottos in the vicinity—it was all one to them. Note you, in those days they had not learned to be ashamed of machinery; the grandiloquent periods and the formal tastes of the early nineteenth century are combined with a frank, Cockney admiration of the march of science, unknown to Ruskin. Thus Freeling (in the neighborhood of Bilston): "There is nothing worthy of note until we have cleared this cutting. At the 86th post to the right we then have a view of the coal-pits, for which this part of the country is celebrious. The steam-engine may be seen." "Celebrious"—I like that word. And the steam-engine may be seen—what a privilege![2]

Indeed, train travel was one feature of modernity that Knox embraced wholeheartedly. He was less sanguine about automobile travel; not about the vehicles themselves, but about their intrusion into the byways that the fixed rail lines left as the domain of the pedestrian. The prospect of fifty thousand new vehicles being churned out each year to congest the English road system did not please him. In 1926, of course, the automobile was still sufficiently a novelty that one of its primary uses was for joy riding, which only compounded a pedestrian's distrust. On the other hand, in 1928 he had to endure a ride in a horse-drawn "conveyance" in a country town, and his jaundiced view of motorized vehicles was henceforth considerably softened.

> I had ever fancied myself a resolute enemy of internal combustion, sighing for the day when all the world's petrol should be exhausted, and every possible substitute for petrol exhausted in its turn. I had even supported such views, only the other day, at the Oxford Union. And indeed a motor-drive of over twenty miles seems Purgatory to me. But for these short distances—how did anybody ever live in the country, I mean, deep in the country, when every journey had to be prefaced and concluded with a taste of this dog-cart business for

[2] Ronald Knox, "Bradshaw's Early Rivals", in *On Getting There* (London: Methuen, 1929), pp. 69–70.

> its *hors d'oeuvre* and its savoury? One didn't read in a dog-cart; conversation about the crops cannot really have been very stimulating. What on earth did one do all the time? How did one occupy the immortal mind during those long hours of bumping? Yet there were days, once, when such locomotion was regarded as a sport of the rich; Lucretius has satirized for us the attitude of the *blasé* plutocrat, who "flies to his villa in desperate haste, driving his ponies," to cheat the cares which beset his mind. What an anodyne!
>
> It does not do, really, to go back into the past. We are so much the creatures of circumstance that the conveniences of our bustling age breed in us a new time-sense, a new capacity for boredom. Let us respect the good old coaching days, but be glad we were not there to share them.[3]

Knox frequently went on walking tours, routinely covering fourteen or fifteen miles on winding roads and pathways along which hardly anyone else would be met. At the end of the day, the country inn beckoned, where, despite the lack of interesting reading matter found in the rooms and the poor substitute for fresh coffee they served, "there is hospitality, and a fire lit in late spring, old prints, and Niersteiner at five shillings a bottle, and that atmosphere of crooked passages, alternating levels, projecting beams, which tells you that the house is old without self-conscious antiquarianism."[4]

Like Chesterton, but less assiduously, he was not averse to collecting a year or so's worth of articles into book form, and the above quotes come from two such volumes, *An Open-Air Pulpit* (1926) and *On Getting There* (1929), neither being anywhere near as popular as Chesterton's compilations. The latter of the two takes its title from yet another essay on locomotion, specifically on the value of pilgrimages to religious shrines, with Knox's point being that the essence of the ritual is in the mode of arrival (like the pilgrims who go to Lough Derg in Ireland walking barefoot over stones) rather than in what is seen at the end (which is the tourist's goal and earns a snapshot). Here too modernity intrudes an ambiguous note:

> On their spiritual side there can be no doubt that the pilgrimages of to-day make up in tedium and in expense (as expense is reckoned

[3] Knox, "Memories", in *On Getting There*, pp. 13–14.
[4] Knox, "The Contented Vagrant", in *Open-Air Pulpit*, p. 175.

> among the poor), for the want of personal effort involved. But there is a loss of picturesqueness; there is a loss also, I think, of the sense of achievement. Either you must be trundled along in railway carriages to Lourdes, or Lisieux, or Rome, seeing nothing of the country you pass through and (incidentally) getting no exercise; or you must take an afternoon train to Canterbury or Lancaster or St. Albans, and there walk through the streets in a merely ecclesiastical procession: the love of the road is a thing altogether divorced from pilgrimage.
>
> It is characteristic of our modern specialization. You cannot enjoy, nowadays, the combined sensation of pedestrianism and penance. You must sort out your emotions, and decide to spend your holiday either in tramping the roads without a devotional object, or reaching your devotional objective without tramping the roads.[5]

Certainly his essays brought out a mildly anarchic streak in Knox. He was especially irked by the interference of government with human liberties. The wireless tax is a case in point. Knox held no aversion to radio as a means of communication; in fact, in January 1926, he broadcast a satire over the BBC, which in format and in consequences prefigured Orson Welles' *War of the Worlds* sensation over a decade later. In Knox's script, a live performance of music is interrupted by news reports of an uprising in Piccadilly Square that turns into a full-scale rampage against London's treasured buildings. A sufficient number of listeners failed to recognize the lampooning of the way news was (and still often is) reported over the airwaves that the ensuing commotion made headlines in the newspapers the next day. But the notion that a government could require people to pay a regular fee for the right to receive the radio waves being propagated through the air over their homes struck him as inherently preposterous. The British authorities even wanted to search homes for illegal receivers, and it was only at that incursion on privacy that a public outcry emerged:

> But this is to begin at the wrong end. It is too late to protest against the right of search, with our doors scarred all over by the school inspector, the sanitary inspector, the gas, the rent, and the rest of their tribe. What we ought to be asking is whether, in the nature of the case, a private wireless set can be regarded as a contraband thing—

[5] Knox, "On Getting There", in *On Getting There*, pp. 206–7.

> whether, in fact, the broadcast licence has any right to exist. Why should a man need a licence to make use of his own property in a way that cannot possibly cause any annoyance to his neighbours? Granted the right of private property in ether, it is surely obvious that the B.B.C. is putting itself in a very questionable position by sending sound-waves through it. Why should we not recall the precedent of the railways, and demand heavy compensation? Or, at least, if we are content to forgo our claims here, a man must be allowed the right to bring down a sound-wave that is traveling over his own garden, just as if it were a pheasant.[6]

The income tax assessor was a scourge too. Knox does not begrudge paying an income tax: he thinks the amount he owes an embarrassingly small sum. It is the tedium of filling in details on a form and the imperious demand that it be returned by April under threat of severe penalties that are offensive to his sense of justice and propriety. By way of amelioration, he suggests that the twenty-one-day grace period allowed to British citizens who have questions about specifics on the form be informally stretched out to three months' duration before the commencement of threats.

A proposal to tax profits from gambling attracted his attention because of the vociferous opposition raised by the Puritan constituency of the population, who argued that a government sullied its hands by partaking of the gains of an inherently sinful enterprise. Knox empathizes with but does not countenance their position: to be consistent they ought on the same grounds to advocate repeal of the liquor tax. And by their logic, which seems to presume that only virtuous activities should yield revenue, Bibles should carry the steepest tax. Affected by his own Puritan-tinged upbringing, he feels betting to be a vice but notes that his fellow Roman clergy, most of whom are Irish, entertain no such scruples. Catholic theology, he reminds his readers, does not condemn games of chance as intrinsically wrong; what is sinful is an imprudent indulgence in them.

Every once in a while Knox lets his clerical collar show in these essays. Even mundane topics will lead a thoughtful person back to some facet of the Christian philosophy of life. Take, for example, the tradition of April Fools' Day. After the stern remonstrances from the

[6] Knox, "Eavesdropping-In", in *Open-Air Pulpit*, p. 16.

Proverbs of Solomon against foolishness, Knox finds comfort in the fact that Saint Paul uses that very word in conjunction with the embrace of Christianity in the letter to the Corinthians. And in comparison with the pagan world, the toleration of foolishness in the Christian world is startlingly rampant:

> The truth about the pagans, surely, is that we cannot really like them or really feel at home with them because they were so abominably dignified. I suppose I have been brought up on the classical tradition as much as most people, but there was ever this barrier between me and the heroes my authors held up to me. You could not read Cicero without feeling that he habitually admired people for having no sense of humour; and this dull suspicion about Cicero becomes a nightmare when you get on to the younger Pliny. . . . It is a tiresome habit to claim too much for the Middle Ages, but one thing is surely evident—the medievals may at times have been pompous and dignified, like the heathens, but at least they reminded themselves that they were fools; at least, they paid homage to folly. . . . Buffoonery became an honoured thing, often in perilous proximity to religious observance; our Lady had her Tumblers as well as her Troubadours; Fra Juniper won an honourable title as the Jester of the Lord.[7]

And then there is an essay on bells. The classical world never used bells the way medieval towns did; the Latin language offered no equivalent for the term until a Carmelite monk used the word *campana*: "It was Christendom that developed the bell, and with the bell the bell-tower, from the slim campaniles of Italy to those giant musical boxes that brood over the hills of Somerset. The church chime was the conscience of the medieval village, whether it called men to prayer, or warned them of bedtime, or sent them hurrying out into the street at an alarm of fire." The best that the de-Christianized world of the Industrial Revolution can offer as an alternative is the shriek of the whistle, which harries the workers in manufacturing towns to their stations in the service of mechanized production. And yet

> Christendom dies hard in a half-paganised country, and it is characteristic of us that we still connect bells with two pious institutions that precariously survive—marriage and Christmas. We have not

[7] Knox, "The First of April", in *On Getting There*, pp. 85–87.

> yet arrived at the stage when it will be necessary to write, "Shriek out, wild sirens, across the snow," or "No wedding-hooters for him!" Bells are still a thing of joy to men. That is why they must ring all through the Gloria in the Mass of Maundy Thursday and in the Mass of Holy Saturday, but between these every bell in the house must be silenced, and meal-times only announced with a wooden rattle. All which is fresh proof that bells are a Christian product; for it is the instinct of the Church, when she goes into mourning, to return to primitive conditions—new-fangled inventions like the bell and the organ must for the moment be put aside. It is a wonderful thing to have a long memory.[8]

But these columns are the exception to the rule. The morning commuter could not be expected to ingest a too-substantial portion of serious fare, rumbling along in a passenger train. Which, by the way, brings to mind just one more essay on modes of travel. Knox decided to take a stand in the controversy over whether a tramway system, a subway system, or a bus system would be more efficient for a metropolis to support. After noting the advantages of the former two, he eventually opts for the bus on the "*quod semper, quod ubique, quod ab omnibus*" (what is always, and everywhere, and by everyone) principle: service continues if one unit fails, they are not as dependent on tracks, and they appeal to a wider clientele. But perhaps of more interest than his solving the mass transportation problem of mid-1920s London is his citation of a limerick that would stubbornly cling to him as its author, despite his futile efforts to notify newspapers that it was already going around when he was born:

> Damn!
> At last I've found out what I am,
> a creature that moves
> in determinate grooves,
> in fact not a bus, but a tram.[9]

Human foibles remain a staple of his musings: for example, busybodies just waiting to pounce on him with help, who are as much an irritant as government obtrusiveness posing as concern for citizens'

[8] Knox, "Concerning Bells", in *Open-Air Pulpit*, p. 153–54.
[9] Knox, "Tubes, Trams and Tyranny", in *Open-Air Pulpit*, p. 161.

welfare. A cheery waiter offering him more toast when he was already munching on a roll in the dining car of a train sets him off on a disquisition on philanthropists, whom he suspects must not be kind at home. The irreclaimably shy, like himself, cannot hope to compete with the self-assured interferers in people's lives who earn accolades for their timely dispensing of invaluable assistance. Reflection on his own skills in this line produces only a modest list of accomplishments:

> (1) Digging out obstructions from a pipe when no scientific apparatus for the purpose is available;
> (2) Writing Latin inscriptions;
> (3) Helping small children to break the furniture;
> (4) Taking unused stamps off envelopes.
>
> When I have done any of these things I would, if I had an ounce of honesty in me, say, "Thank you," to the person who gave me the opportunity of doing them. Even as I write there is a cow outside scratching itself with great difficulty against a post. If I were really altruistic, I should go down with a stick and help it. But, then, cow-scratching is not one of my fortes.[10]

Then there are the letter writers who assert that dogs have an intellectual life comparable to that of men. Chesterton's distinctions between human laughter and what passes for animal laughter, and between human drawing and a chimpanzee's doodling, come to Knox's mind as able retorts to such correspondents' vapid conjectures. It is the ability to reflect that accounts for the development of humor and of art in people but not in animals. There too lies the appeal in books like *The Wind in the Willows*, in which animals are given human attributes, which they manifestly do not have, to the delight and amusement of the reader. He continues, warming to the subject:

> What is so baffling is that people will go on telling you stories about their dogs and cats which conclusively prove that their dogs and cats possess intelligence without seeming to see that in that case the whole of our views of life must be entirely revised. If a dog has intelligence presumably it has a soul, and, if it has a soul, are we not committing murder when we shoot it in its old age? If a dog really "understands every word you say," are you always careful to turn it out of the room before one of these smoking-room stories is told?

[10] Knox, "Helpfulness", in *Open-Air Pulpit*, pp. 129–130.

> If a dog is really "the best friend you have," why don't you let it kill the chickens? Until the philosophers have succeeded in providing us with a cheap substitute for intelligence, may we not as well use our intelligence when we talk about animals, and get rid of all this metaphorical nonsense?[11]

Not that he had it in for animals. Writing a column on the centennial of the birth of Reverend J. G. Wood, whose *Illustrated Natural History* was given to Knox on his fifth or sixth birthday, he recalls the magical effect the book had on him. For one, it was his and his alone. His stepmother, Ethel, recalled in a 1930 article the first view of the family she was to inherit with her marriage to Bishop Knox, and the image of Ronald was of a child in front of the fireplace absorbed in the study of Wood's pages. The recollection of this gift elicited from him some advice to parents, that they not bestow on a child too many presents of books.

> See to it that he gets one large book, on an informative subject, but preferably about animals. If he is the possessor of one large book, it will be a point of honour with him to possess himself of its contents. If one of his brothers or sisters takes it up for a moment, he will rush forward with cries of, "No, that's MY book!" Especially if he is the youngest of a family he will carry it with him everywhere, curl himself up with it prominently on the sofa, to let his brothers and sisters know that he too has a book, a five-shilling book, all his very own.[12]

And what did the Reverend Mr. Wood impart to him? Much, it seems, that he retained throughout adulthood, although he never became a naturalist, or a visitor to the zoo:

> How vividly its text, and still more its plates, stand out in memory! The ocelot, useful to me in later life, when cross-words came along; the toco-toucan, which I always imagined to be the size of an ostrich; the eland and the oryx, the honey-ratel and the duck-billed platypus, the coloured page of humming-birds; the John Dory, and the narwhal, and the rock-python, and the tapir! Who more skilled than I to distinguish between the camel proper and the Bactrian or

[11] Knox, "The Stupidity of Animals", in *Open-Air Pulpit*, p. 104.
[12] Knox, "Every Boy's Friend", in *On Getting There*, p. 16–17.

> dromedary, between the ear formations of the Indian and the African elephant, between the stripes on the zebra and on the quagga?[13]

He concludes that despite his turning aside from taxonomy in maturer years, and the realization that the volume contributed to his frittering away his youth in idle fancy, nevertheless Wood's history may have taught him something valuable—"some grammar, perhaps, and some rudiments of logical arrangement. Only do not let them talk to me about the formative years of one's life. I wish I had the book still, to turn up some of my old favorites."[14]

Years later, in 1946, when his stepmother died and the family sorted through her belongings, he did indeed recover the revered volume and "sat reading the anecdotes, all of which he professed to believe, aloud: 'When cut grass is given to giraffes, they eat off the upper part of it, and leave the coarse stems, just as we eat asparagus.' He was lost in rediscovery."[15] Language is another topic that attracted his attention. An article is devoted to the merits of Fowler's *Modern English Usage.*[16] Fowler's was a daunting task even in 1925. His goal was to cleanse the language of sloppy word usage and syntax, and he had patiently sorted through specimens of writing culled from literature, newspapers, and various sorts of ephemera to hunt down instances of deplorable English:

> For this is not a mere manual of orthography, to help us choose between "criticise" and "criticize," "practise" and "practice"—difficulties which the printer's reader is always ready to solve. It probes, remorselessly, the very stuff of our composition. (Would Mr. Fowler mind that adverb in front of the object? I believe he would, but I cannot humour him there.) Here is a whole section on Wardour-Street English, which proscribes "anent" and "belike"; and I am glad to see that the word "galore," the most nauseating, I think, of

[13] Ibid., p. 17.

[14] Ibid., p. 20.

[15] Penelope Fitzgerald, *The Knox Brothers* (New York: Coward, McCann and Geoghegan, 1977), p. 261.

[16] This mononymous arbiter of acceptable written English was actually Henry Fowler (1858–1938), a former schoolteacher turned lexicographer, who coincidentally was the closest friend of G. G. Coulton, Arnold Lunn's nemesis in debates over the Church. See Jenny McMorris, *The Warden of English: The Life of H. W. Fowler* (Oxford: Oxford University Press, 2001).

> all words in the language, is condemned in a separate article all to itself.[17]

Fowler makes even a natural grammarian like Knox a little self-conscious about substituting "as to" for "about", invites his skepticism on using a hard *g* before *i* in words derived from Greek, and disappoints him in allowing the split infinitive.

Since he was often a guest in people's homes, Knox had ample opportunity to browse in libraries, and he had an eye for the curious. Among such items was an eighteenth-century book of English proverbs, quotations from which serve to show how quickly phrases can become thoroughly obscure. Proverbs, he notes, were the ammunition used by elders to counter a child's desires: "They seemed to have been invented by long generations of aunts and nurses, so pat did they come, so nimbly did they head us off when we wanted to do anything a child ever does want to do." He recommends Mr. Ray's 1737 anthology of contemporary sayings as a potential gold mine of child control, but many of them, he admits, have sadly lost their trenchancy:

> An Alphabet of Joculatory, Nugatory, and Rustic Proverbs is attractive, but strangely mystifying. "He capers like a fly in a tar-box"; what imaginations these proverb-makers have! "The way to be gone is not to stay here"; this, I take it, must have been a polite hint in rustic circles. I should know what to do if I were accosted like that; but what exact sense would apply to the phrase "Great doings at

[17] Knox, "Is It Twilight?" in *On Getting There*, p. 51. One must not assume that Henry Fowler was devoid of a sense of humor merely because he was a grammarian. The following entry, on pedantic humor, should disabuse anyone thumbing through his reference work of that notion: "A warning is necessary, because we have all of us, except the abnormally stupid, been pedantic humourists in our time. We spend much of our childhood picking up a vocabulary; we like to air our latest finds; we discover that our elders are tickled when we come out with a new name that they thought beyond us; we devote some pains to tickling them further; & there we are, pedants and polysyllabists all. The impulse is healthy for children, & nearly universal—which is just why warning is necessary; for among so many there will always be some who fail to realize that the clever habit applauded at home will make them insufferable abroad. Most of those who are capable of writing well enough to find readers do learn with more or less of delay that playful use of long or learned words is a one-sided game boring the reader more than it pleases the writer, that the impulse to do it is a danger-signal—for there must be something wrong with what they are saying if it needs recommending by such puerilities—& that yielding to the impulse is a confession of failure." H. W. Fowler, *A Dictionary of Modern English Usage* (Oxford: Oxford University Press, n.d.), p. 426.

> Gregory's, heat the oven twice for a custard"? Or "Toasted cheese hath no master"? Or "This is the world and the other is in the country"? Most of us have laughed at jokes we could not see, but it must have been heavy work spending an evening with Mr. Ray's tenants when they were joculatory.[18]

Another stay at a well-stocked home turned up grist for another article, when he found a book styled *Knowledge for the People, or the Plain Why and Because, Familiarising Subjects of Useful Curiosity and Amusing Research*, the literary effort of a pedant named John Timbs.

> Mr. Timbs's formula is of the simplest; there are various pieces of information which he is determined to inflict on the public; and he tempers the crudeness of his design by throwing the whole book into the form of a catechism. I conceive that he found his model in Plutarch's *Roman Questions*. Thus, for example, "*Why is 13 December Called Raminudia, or Barebough-day?* Because the leaves by this time are all fallen, and the branches bare." Does the man think us fools, that he supplies us with so obvious an explanation? Not at all, but we did not know that 13 December *was* called Raminudia, and Mr. Timbs knew that we did not know. It was the question, not the answer, that he was wanting to get off his chest.[19]

A VOICE IN THE WILDERNESS

The descent of Europe into World War II would require a different voice for the general public. Knox spent the war years at Aldenham working on his translation of the Bible, but he continued his preaching engagements, and his sermons from the period often attempt to situate the suffering experienced by so many families within the framework of God's unsearchable providence. Politics did not consume him, and the remembrance of the loss of friends' lives in World War I hardly inclined him toward bellicosity, but he did contribute a chapter to a symposium on the menace facing civilization from Nazi Germany. The title, *Nazi and Nazarene*, strikes the only Knoxian chord in an otherwise derivative enumeration of the steps by which the Nazi Party encroached on the prerogatives of the Catholic Church in Germany

[18] Knox, "Proverbs of the Past", in *Open-Air Pulpit*, p. 84.

[19] Knox, "General Knowledge", in *Open-Air Pulpit*, p. 63.

in the 1930s.[20] The denial of a political voice, the closing of schools and youth organizations, and the discrediting of religious orders are the classic tools of a totalitarian regime tightening its grip on a people. Knox's conclusion, that Nazism is inherently antagonistic not only to Catholicism but to all Christian beliefs, should seem patently obvious. But at the time, there were two distorted views coming from opposite sides of the spectrum that held some currency in England, namely, the view that Nazism represented a sort of muscular Christianity that found its only religious enemy in Judaism, and the view that the 1933 concordat with the Vatican signaled a Church blessing of the regime. The latter view was of course promoted by people who were unsympathetic toward the Church and were eager to associate her in the public mind with a hostile military power. Hence the emphasis in his essay on facts that are irreconcilable with a purported Vatican-Berlin axis.[21]

But it was the end to the war that provoked one of his more noteworthy literary endeavors. From the vantage point of the twenty-first century, decades of living with the vicissitudes of nuclear power has dimmed, if not yet wholly eradicated, the luster attaching to the label "the atomic age", but when it was first coined in 1945, the images it evoked sent shudders up Knox's spine. Its sudden entry on the world scene drew from him a lengthy essay in which he attempted to restore a sense of equilibrium and perspective in a climate giddy with total war and unconditional surrender. *God and the Atom* was written in short order and initially serialized in the *Tablet* within weeks of the dropping of the atomic bombs on Hiroshima and Nagasaki. These devastating displays of military and technological power had the intended effect of drawing the Pacific war to a rapid conclusion, but they also cried out for moral analysis and reflection. They represented the final crescendo in the cacophony of the Second World War, and the temptation on the part of people living in the victorious countries was to

[20] Ronald Knox, *Nazi and Nazarene* (London: Macmillan, 1940).

[21] A thorough modern study of the background of the concordat, Stewart Stehlin's *Weimar and the Vatican, 1919–1933* (Princeton: Princeton University Press, 1983), presents convincing evidence that the agreement was actually the culmination of negotiations with the previous regime and its constituent states and was signed with the Nazis only to guarantee a framework of church-state coexistence agreed to in Weimar days. Of course the Nazis soon blatantly ignored its provisions.

celebrate and move on, in a world desensitized another notch or two to the mass carnage both endured and still unfolding in the postwar reconfiguration of spheres of influence.[22]

The use of nuclear weaponry alarmed Knox on several counts. First of all, it was clear to him that the cessation of war would bring no relief to millions of people. Mass starvation, deportations of whole populations, the settling of old scores: this was the human backdrop across Central and Eastern Europe as victory celebrations played out in more comfortable quarters. And now, with all the infernal machinery of war already at hand to wreak havoc on people's lives, another had just been added:

> Weapons whose blast comes around the corner to kill you; weapons that are not content to kill with blast, but leave people with incurable burns on them, impregnate the earth where they fall with the properties of fire.... There is, of course, no reason whatever why a man should not entrust those he loves to God's safe-keeping when these are the dangers they are threatened with, any less confidently than in the old, primitive days of rocket-bomb; for the intellect, the principle is the same. But the imagination will make pictures for us, and there are some which hardly bear thinking of. Even if we were only concerned with the safety of our immediate friends, we would give much to be able to banish this kind of nightmare from our dreams.[23]

Intellectually, the person of faith would still have recourse to the reassuring conviction of God's omnipotence, but a calculable erosion of confidence was manifest in the human psyche. Life seemed much more tenuous, as the possibility of instant incineration could not but seep into the thoughts of even the stoutest of optimists. Knox could see little comfort in the fact that the weapons of mass destruction remained the possession of the United States, noting the likelihood (soon realized) that "the latest and most effective use of atomic power

[22] The melancholy history of the early postwar years has not been given due recognition, largely because the victors dictated how the history of the times would be written. Over two million German-speaking people died during forced repatriation schemes. The acquiescence of American and English governments in these largely Russian-enforced mass deportations has been chronicled in Alfred de Zayas, *Nemesis at Potsdam: The Anglo-Americans and the Expulsion of the Germans* (London: Routledge and Kegan Paul, 1979).

[23] Ronald Knox, *God and the Atom* (New York: Sheed and Ward, 1945), pp. 61–62.

should fall into the hands of some enemy of civilization, as ambitious, as unscrupulous, as ever Nazi Germany was; that the whole world may be enslaved to some evil philosophy, unless it will accept the alternative of annihilation."[24] The world of Stalin and his successors lay ahead, decades when those stark alternatives were vividly before the world's eyes, and a third of its population had to accept the yoke, while the remainder debated which of the grisly choices was the lesser of two evils. Already, however, as Knox noted elsewhere, the war's aftermath meant a resignation "to mere co-existence in a world from which perfect fear had cast out love".[25]

But geopolitics was not the focus of his reflections. Rather, it was the effect on the individual person's way of thinking in the light of this new source of power. The splitting of the atom seemed to portend an encroachment on a forbidden frontier of science. The whole subatomic realm, which depended on statistical mechanics for its elucidation, seemed an affront to the traditional understanding of the common sense law of cause and effect.

> To say that no such law *exists* would be to dogmatize; and it is the boast of science not to dogmatize. We are assured, however, that there is proof. Whoever has the skill and the patience to follow an intricate mathematical argument will find that the hypothesis of such a law existing leads to an absurdity. This, like all our modern arguments, ends up in an appeal to the expert. And since I am writing, not for experts, but for the profane, I have no option but to believe what I am told; or at least to argue on the assumption that what I am told is true. And, after all, even if the physicists were content to report that they could not trace the influence of any law in this one department of nature, it would be sufficiently strange. Wherever else we have questioned Nature closely, she has been more communicative. She does not always allow us to find out the reason for the things, but she lets us trace a rhythm in them.[26]

Knox does find some consolation in the constancies that are displayed everywhere in nature. This unit of matter, puzzling in its properties, is nevertheless a building block in a universe that is ordered, so

[24] Ibid., p. 63.
[25] Ronald Knox, *Lightning Meditations* (New York: Sheed and Ward, 1955), p. 116.
[26] Knox, *God and the Atom*, p. 108.

it too must give evidence of the Creator at work. But he senses his own inadequacy in attempting to incorporate atomic physics into the proofs of God's existence.

> Our age is in need of a great philosopher; one who can thread his way, step by step, through the intricate labyrinth of reasoning into which scientists have been led, eyes riveted to earth, by the desire to improve our human lot, the desire to destroy life, or mere common curiosity; one who can keep his mind, at the same time, open to the metaphysical implications of all he learns, and at last put the whole corpus of our knowledge together in one grand synthesis. He must be able to gaze through the telescope, to peer through the microscope, with a mind unaverted from that great Source of all being who is our Beginning and our last End. He must be at once Thomist and Atomist; until that reconciliation is attempted, the pulpit and the laboratory will be forever at cross-purposes.[27]

Arguably, the required synthesizer, scientist and theologian, historian of science and philosopher of science, would enter the literary scene a generation later in the person of the polymath Benedictine priest Stanley Jaki.[28] In his seminal work *The Road of Science and the Ways to God*, he would point out that the basis for the unease felt by Knox and others about the atom's presumed disregard for cause and effect is attributable to the Copenhagen theory of quantum mechanics (not to quantum mechanics itself) as espoused by Niels Bohr and Werner Heisenberg but vigorously opposed by Max Planck and Albert Einstein. Bohr's rhapsodies on the modern physicist's way of looking at the subatomic world included the assertions that "even words like 'to be' and 'to know' lose their unambiguous meaning", and he

[27] Ibid., pp. 110–11. Robert Speaight quotes this passage and asserts that Teilhard de Chardin (of whom Speaight was a biographer) answered to the description, though he admits he "was neither a philosopher nor a theologian, but he was a poet and a priest, a scientist and a seer". But in truth Teilhard could offer nothing to satisfy the doubts to which Knox gave voice. Speaight cites with admiration Teilhard's response "*il faut croire*", seemingly oblivious to the fact that irrational belief was antithetical to Knox's epistemology. Robert Speaight, *Ronald Knox: The Writer* (New York: Sheed and Ward, 1965) p. 250.

[28] Anyone interested in the major themes of the history of science should become familiar with at least three of Jaki's many books dealing with science, philosophy, and religion. In addition to the title cited in the text, the two others are *The Relevance of Physics* (Chicago: University of Chicago Press, 1966) and *Science and Creation: From Cosmic Cycles to an Oscillating Universe* (Edinburgh: Scottish Academic Press, 1974).

proclaimed that the new approach to modeling the behavior of particles involved "a radical departure from the causal description of Nature".[29] And yet the observation of orderly tracks in cloud chambers presupposed either order—and hence cause and effect—in nature, or else, as Paul Dirac felt compelled to believe, the "assigning to nature the ability to choose from among an infinite number of possibilities, all equally probable, the one that appeared to produce a coherent set of events".[30] So the qualms Knox felt in the 1940s about an apparent instability in some of the underpinnings of the proofs of God's existence were a false alarm, which an eventual clearing of the philosophical fog surrounding quantum mechanics would resolve.

More immediate consequences from the dropping of the bombs also worried him. While on the one hand the execution of war involves enforced sacrifice of individual goals for the common good, whether on the battlefield or among those at home, it also inures people to violence. He reminds his readers that Thucydides charted a decline in public morals after the Peloponnesian War and that the countries of Europe might expect the same. Brigandage, vendettas, and assassination are habits learned that may not easily be unlearned in peacetime. Add to this an outlook conditioned by newspaper headlines into believing that a new age has dawned, and the moral restraints imposed even as a residue of the Christian heritage in the recent past will be removed. The image of slow but inevitable progress in mankind idealized by the Whig interpretation of history will give way to one of immediate and unrestrained force personified by the splitting atom. And yet self-restraint must be the order of the day, even abstracting from moral considerations. The postwar Europe he was surveying looked bleak:

> The whole economic machinery of Europe has suffered a breakdown; the business of repairing it will be slow, and it will have to be run in gently. There will be controls everywhere, and all the prizes of life will have to be queued up for, unless we want a free fight. There will, please God, be enough to go round, but only just enough. And comfort means, not having all you need, but having a

[29] Stanley Jaki, *The Road of Science and the Ways to God* (Chicago: University of Chicago Press, 1978), p. 202.

[30] Ibid., p. 207. Dirac also took issue with and felt hemmed in by the philosophical inhibitions imposed by the Copenhagen school.

> little more than you need, so as to leave a margin. To be always counting the biscuits and measuring the remains of the pressed beef, to work and sleep in the same room, to pinch yourself when you are going to entertain a visitor, save up for a fortnight so as to make a spread for some festive occasion—all these are not hardships, but they interfere with the smooth running of life; it is like a hard chair without a cushion, a tap without a washer. There must be a certain largeness in our surroundings, if we are to be effortlessly happy. To make your career, to marry a wife, to have a family, in a world where everything is a tight fit, robs youth of its pleasant carelessness, makes it more apt to brood, more selfish, more ready to revolt against its chains, where revolt seems possible.[31]

In the end, the economic hardship was endured, no doubt with personal tragedy in many cases, but in the aggregate with resiliency by the recovering nations of Western Europe. But other psychological aftereffects were harder to expunge. Knox recalls the postwar sense of guilt that infiltrated English society after the 1918 armistice: "We tacitly acknowledged in ourselves a kind of moral second-rateness which served as an excuse for low standards; we were poor creatures, and morality must not expect too much of us." He continues:

> I may be wrong, but I anticipate a similar reaction not many years from now, which will threaten to plunge us still lower into the depths of self-abasement, and of consequent self-despair. In what precise way we shall rationalize this mood of ours, I do not pretend to predict. But I think what will chiefly help to fasten it on us is the memory of having called in a sinister weapon to win the fight for us, a weapon which may recoil on humanity, and possibly on ourselves. We shall feel like men that have sold themselves to the devil; we have conjured up the Atom, and the Atom henceforth is to be our master.[32]

The civil turmoil that enveloped Europe and the United States in the late 1960s was in part attributable to a sense of despair, the sense that the two world powers would eventually engage in a catastrophically destructive third world war. The specter of that conflagration had been seared into the minds of rising generations of adults by film

[31] Knox, *God and the Atom*, p. 89.
[32] Ibid., p. 92.

footage of multimegatonnage nuclear bomb tests, by the Cuban missile crisis, by an escalating war in Vietnam, and by tanks rumbling through Budapest and later Prague. The atomic world had produced the threat of instantaneous annihilation, and the response of many was to find an outlet for despair in rage. For others, the response was a dull acceptance of the possibility of nuclear warfare with a concomitant lowering of expectations from life. In either case, the result verified Knox's perception

> that emerging from childhood into your later teens is no longer an emancipation, the entry into a larger world, as it was a generation ago. On the contrary, it is the adolescent that begins to feel himself or herself unwanted; school days, instead of being a thralldom, are a sunshiny world with a dark tunnel at the end of it.... [I]t does seem obvious that in these next years the rising generation will be called upon to exercise a self-restraint uncongenial at once to its time of life, and to the instinct of its period.[33]

Knox's one venture into direct political commentary is to observe that, had the decision been made to drop the atomic bomb on an unpopulated site, a note of magnanimity would have been infused into World War II that might well have forestalled the feeling of thralldom imposed on mankind by the weapon's use, and the sense of shame and guilt for participating as a nation in a morally dubious if not outright indefensible exercise of destruction of life.

But the action could not be revoked, and it was certainly not Knox's intent to fix blame for it on any individual. The reality of nuclear weaponry, however, demanded a Christian response, and the only response possible in a potentially unstable world was to practice the Christian virtue of hope.

> Hope is something that is demanded of us; it is not, then, a mere reasoned calculation of our chances. Nor is it merely the bubbling up of a sanguine temperament; if it is demanded of us, it lies not in the temperament but in the will. Indeed, we can hardly doubt that the Christian is at his best when he is, as we say, "hoping against hope." Hoping for what? For deliverance from persecution, for immunity from plague, pestilence, and famine, from worldly discomforts

[33] Ibid., p. 90.

> in general? No, for the grace of persevering in his Christian profession, and for the consequent achievement of a happy immortality.[34]

Knox sees an analogy with that sense of desolation often encountered by saints in their journey toward God, who seems to hide his face to test their perseverance. And it is Knox's presumption that such a test is being administered to mankind as a whole in the postwar era. During such trials, the exercise of the virtue of hope is acutely needed, even though it may seem beyond one's ability to summon up in a world rife with a contagious despair. He finds the right note in the *Imitation of Christ*, in a parable about a man suffering the agonies of fear who receives a message from God to act as if he were saved, and then his doubts would dissipate. Knox concludes, "*To go on behaving as if we hoped* may be, for some of us, at bad times, the nearest approach we can make to hoping. But if we do not make at least that effort, there is grave danger that we shall really lose our souls, by taking leave to treat them as if they were lost." [35]

Carrying further the analogy between mankind and the favored soul, Knox entertains a proposition entirely at odds with the gnawing sense of gloom that has been gathering about his soul:

> God means the human race, or some large part of it, to grow towards himself, to become more perfect. Not necessarily in the sense that, as this movement goes forward, a larger number of souls will attain Heaven in one century than in the century which went before it. He makes, we must believe, infinite allowance for our opportunities; and, for all we know, there may be thousands of souls dying at peace with him in some environment which seems utterly hostile to the reception of his graces. No, but, viewed in the bulk, humanity will become more what he would have it become. Nations will be more at peace with one another, governments more just, public opinion more humane and more enlightened—all the rosy dream of the Victorians will tend to come true, and at the same time, a thing they wasted little time over, religion will progressively come into its own. It will be a reign of Christ the King; not a millennium, but a progress towards the millennium. All this may be—I do not say is,

[34] Ibid., p. 119.
[35] Ibid., p. 121.

> but may be—God's effective will for the human race, destined to reveal itself more fully in the centuries that lie before us.[36]

If that is the case, then it is not the Christian's duty to belittle the stumbling efforts at progress in human affairs made by people and nations possessing only a dim remembrance of the true priorities in life.

> It is not necessary to conclude that the world is hurrying to its dissolution, and raise, in a theological sense, the cry of "Sauve qui peut." It may be that mankind is being called upon to exercise the virtue of hope; and, if so, Christian people must think twice before they abandon themselves to the luxury of world-despair; before they wash their hands of our communal guilt, and betake themselves, singing "O Paradise, O Paradise!," to the hilltops. We shall do better, I think, to help man the pumps of the labouring ship, and let the world see that hoping is one of our specialties.[37]

There is a sustained tension throughout the narrative between the call to hope and the chronicles of dissolution. The temptation of an older man is to counsel withdrawal from the world's anxieties, but a disciplined striving to exercise the virtue of hope counters it.

One of the keys, perhaps, to understanding the interior mental struggle to which Knox gives uncharacteristic voice in the essay is supplied at the very beginning of the text, when he dedicates it to Hubert van Zeller, the Benedictine monk and spiritual writer who was his confessor and friend. They had first met in 1927 when Knox visited Downside Abbey while van Zeller was serving as guestmaster. In his autobiography, written in 1965, van Zeller recalls that the friendship was built on opposite personalities. One marked difference was manifested by their views on death. Knox, like most people, did not look forward to a separation from this world, with all the beauty with which God had suffused it and all the activities and relationships marking a life's progress through time. But van Zeller, since his youth, had felt otherwise:

> I saw in death the means to a more important emancipation. Nobody has been able to talk me out of it, or to persuade me that so to think and so to hope can be in any way wrong. Idle for people to

[36] Ibid., p. 124.
[37] Ibid., p. 128.

> tell me that life is something good: I know. Idle to tell me that life is God's gift and must be lived fully, positively: I know. I am not, I think, a sombre person. I doubt if my friends think of me as a melancholic. It is just that I do not much like living. Certainly at no time in my adult life have I so enjoyed being alive as not infinitely to prefer the prospect of being dead.[38]

Not that van Zeller in any way distanced himself from the created world. The reminiscences of this noted artist and spiritual writer demonstrate that even fifty years after the fact, he could recall in the minutest detail every article of clothing worn by people he had met on various occasions, and all the sights and smells of the cities he had passed through. He was as much in this world as anyone; he just had a gift for experiencing it without being attracted to it.

When Knox was hurriedly composing *God and the Atom*, van Zeller was a guest of the Actons at Aldenham, and the emerging text was read aloud to him and to Lady Acton every evening for critical comment. The audience for whom Knox was writing was composed primarily of people like himself: "Of people who are not sanguine by temperament, yet would fain see justice done, truth apprehended, humanity grow more human and more humane, in this world, without having to wait for the next." But wouldn't it be far easier to live in the shadow of atomic war if one were differently disposed? "There are some temperaments so eager for the supernatural adventure that all their hopes are set on heaven; like Noe's dove, they find no rest for the soles of their feet in a world that is transitory." [39] The personification of that mood was well known to him, indeed sat across the room from him as he read those words aloud before committing them to the public. Surely he would have liked to have experienced the same sense of detachment and perfect equilibrium that was ingrained in van Zeller's personality while contemplating an unstable world:

> In every event, trust in God is the key-attitude these people recommend to us. Let the framework of our lives be as comfortable or as uncomfortable as you will, it will all be according to schedule. That consideration breeds in them the same debonair attitude towards

[38] Hubert van Zeller, *One Foot in the Cradle: An Autobiography* (New York: Holt, Rinehart and Winston, 1966), p. 71.

[39] Knox, *God and the Atom*, pp. 154–55.

> the future which you find, also, in the shallow, selfish character who tells you, "It's all a gamble, anyhow." The struggle is more difficult for us, who have enough decency to care, but not enough self-abandonment to trust.[40]

As it still is. The ultimate point of *God and the Atom* is less tied to a specific technological development that threatens human society than it is about the temptation to despair of God's continuing governance of all creation. The philosophical arguments, based on the indeterminacy principle, that would attempt to dethrone the Creator lack all logical foundation, as even an agnostic like Einstein could see. There remains, however, the potpourri of popular beliefs—mind as computer, body as randomly evolved, universe as infinite—all equally without any scientific merit but that collectively corrode religious faith. And to the extent that these superstitions and others continue to garner widespread credence, the likelihood of large-scale damage being done to societies remains far greater than in a world in which God was universally recognized as the Creator, Redeemer, and Final End of mankind.

[40] Ibid., pp. 162–63.

CHAPTER TEN

HEART-RELIGION

The very title of Knox's most famous book taxes the determination of the curious reader seeking in it an introduction to the author's writings. Here is the book Ronald Knox admits to laboring over during the hoarded free moments secreted out of three decades of varied literary and spiritual duties, and therefore the most illustrative of his interests as well as being his intellectual testament to posterity, and he calls the lengthy tome *Enthusiasm*. How tempting to bypass it unexamined, supposing it to be a disquisition on a lesser-known theological virtue. Even the subtitle, *A Chapter in the History of Religion with Special Reference to the XVII and XVIII Centuries*, fails to completely disabuse the browser of that presumption.

But in actuality it is a chronicle of waywardness: one learns that the label *enthusiasm* in religion signifies a disequilibrium resulting from allowing the emotions too great a role as a spiritual thermometer, whether individually or more commonly as a community of believers. Steeped as he was in the idioms of eighteenth-century English, Knox may be pardoned for supposing that the connotations of that word *enthusiasm* would still be transparent to the educated mid-twentieth-century reader. However, for a good part of the half century and more that has elapsed since the book's appearance, two factors have successively conspired to render the title obscure or at least archaically quaint. For roughly the first twenty-five years, up through the mid-1970s, there was so little evidence of contemporary enthusiastic movements within the Catholic Church that the encyclopedic information he provided on the subject could maintain the full-fledged attention of only a limited audience, one with antiquarian interests. By contrast, since the mid-1970s, trends that owe their origins to religious movements profiled by Knox have become rife within and outside the Catholic Church. Their practitioners' assurance that they have found the key to a spiritual renewal that has lain dormant since the age of the apostles inhibits their capacity to see an affinity between their own movements and past ebullitions of like-minded sects that would have steered the institutional Church differently than along the path she has followed. The word *enthusiasm* has now lost its remonstrative power.

It is ironic that a major book on a festering temptation of man's spirit should recede into the less accessible corners of library bookshelves, its six hundred pages of close text kept mute, at a time when its penetrating analysis would be most salutary. It is unlikely, given Knox's oft-repeated reminders of the solidity of the Catholic edifice, that he could have anticipated that within two decades of its issuing, his magnum opus would have direct relevance to the internal affairs of his own Church. But the unforeseen prophetic aspect of *Enthusiasm* may provide sufficient impetus for the modern reader to follow the many strands Knox pulls together from the annals of Church history to show the dangers of emotionalism in religion and of a reliance on perceived new revelations over the unchanging teachings of a two-thousand-year-old institution.

EARLY CHURCH

There is indeed much pulling-together to do, because although the book's subtitle indicates that he focuses primarily on sects of the seventeenth and eighteenth centuries, he scans all twenty centuries of Christian history to find the origins and the continuous undercurrents of the ultrasupernaturalist urge. In fact, given the wealth of information contained on the nascent Church in Saint Paul's letters, it is not altogether surprising to find the first evidences of an eruption of the emotional impulse there, namely, in Corinth, within the first decade of the Gospel being preached to its inhabitants.

Corinth

One hallmark of many of the later rebellions against the authorities of the Church is the casting off of laws that seem to oppress man's liberty. Not uncommonly, those laws governing sexual relations are a primary target. Corinth, of course, had a history of libertinism already, but it is new converts, not jaded unbelievers, who cause Paul anguish by claiming liberties with respect to the flesh on the grounds that the Mosaic Law no longer bound them. He would anchor them in the natural law; they are impatient with such thinking and dismiss the notion that marriage is an integral part of the law ingrained on man's behavior for all time. Knox observes that their attitude can, and subsequently does, lead to two opposite extreme tendencies in dissentient groups:

> The same ultrasupernaturalist point of view which looks upon bodily impurity as a mere imperfection among the elect, because it is only something carnal, will, in other moods, condemn the whole institution of marriage as a carnal institution. Some of the Corinthians may have held the doctrine attributed to Molinos, that sins committed in the body could not defile those who were living in the Spirit; others, with Ann Lee, may have tried to make celibacy a condition of Church membership.[1]

There are other clues too in this letter, which, like an overture, presents themes that will be developed in their fullness in later centuries of enthusiastic movements. The Corinthians are mindless of scandal to their weaker brethren when they nonchalantly eat meat sacrificed to idols. Here they presage the seventeenth-century sectarians who will engage in bizarre antics under allegedly divine influence with utter disregard for the sensibilities of bemused outsiders. There is also the prophesying of women in church, to which Saint Paul takes exception. The first full-fledged enthusiastic movement, Montanism, will be fueled by prophetesses' utterances, and history will multiply the phenomenon. Too, there is a subordination of the sacramental life to the charismatic that requires the Apostle to the Gentiles to reassert the meaning of the Eucharist. Finally, there is his exhortation on charity as a unifying force among the new Christians. "What Saint Paul evidently fears", Knox writes, "is that an unwholesome preoccupation with the *charismata* in their more startling forms is creating an atmosphere uncongenial to the exercise of

[1] Ronald Knox, *Enthusiasm: A Chapter in the History of Religion with Special Reference to the XVII and XVIII Centuries* (Oxford: Oxford University Press, 1950), p. 16.

charity; it fosters pride, jealousy, backbiting, and other uncharitable emotions."[2] Once again history is to provide ample instances of the latter coming to the fore when members of an elite sect such as the Jansenists find themselves at odds with ordinary Catholics. Saint Paul has put his finger on all the symptoms of willfulness that emerge whenever a coterie becomes impatient with the institutional Church and sets out to create a more perfect movement. And as the apostolic age gives way to a more established order in the Church, this tendency will only be aggravated.

Montanism

Of the vices deprecated by Saint Paul at Corinth, it is pride that served as the catalyst for the first formal heresy of an enthusiastic cast, that of Montanus, which flourished in Phrygia. Little is known about this late-second-century personage, except that he declared that a new revelation had been transmitted to him: the age of the Paraclete had dawned. Two prophetesses named Maximilla and Priscilla accompanied him; the women spoke in ecstasy, a departure from the mode of prophesying characteristic of the apostolic age. Montanus himself would claim identity with the Father, the Word, and the Paraclete. Very much a localized sect, they might not have made much of a mark on ecclesiastical history except for the conversion of the great legalist and apologist Tertullian. "It was", Knox muses, "as if Newman had joined the Salvation Army." But once convinced of their message, he became the most tenacious of publicists, rather as Pascal was to become for the Jansenist cause many centuries later. And the lawyer and journalist in Tertullian inclined him to unfair rhetoric:

> He is often cheap; to accuse the *psychici* (that is, the members of the Church universal) of "marrying oftener than they fast," because they only keep one Lent, and allow widows to remarry, is obviously cheap. Sometimes he comes refreshingly near the border-line of blasphemy, as when he says "Let us leave the Holy Spirit out of the discussion, because after all he is a witness on our side." He is never

[2] Ibid., p. 23.

> profound, never opens a new window on some aspect of theology; he will stick to his brief.[3]

Knox even suggests that the rigorism Tertullian upholds on behalf of the sect is not so much appealing to him on its merits but instead attracts him simply because it provides an opportunity to argue a cause.

Of course the Catholic Church has always recognized the weakness of human nature and does not close her doors to sinners. A sect, by contrast, can be as restrictive as it likes and can measure its superiority to the run-of-the-mill (what the Montanists called *psychici* or "earthy", as opposed to *pneumatici* or "spiritual") by the degree to which its own membership is shorn of moral laggards. Tertullian and the Montanists would not allow widows to remarry; nor would they grant absolution to anyone who committed adultery or even fornication. And they cited the Holy Spirit as their authority for this new rigorism, because it had been revealed to Montanus that remitting such sins would only encourage people to sin again.

> To justify itself, the new prophecy must find something to forbid which the Church tolerates. That is the impression, I think, which Tertullian's propaganda leaves on you; there is no genuine moral enthusiasm about it, only a perpetual manœuvring for position.... The history of Montanism is not to be read as that of a great spiritual revival, maligned by its enemies. It is that of a naked fanaticism, which tried to stampede the Church into greater severity, when she had not forgotten how to be severe. And its chief importance for our present subject is that it helped her to make up her mind,

[3] Ibid., pp. 45–46. Timothy Barnes, in his *Tertullian: A Historical and Literary Study* (Oxford: Clarendon Press, 1971), presents convincing arguments to show that the traditional assumption that Tertullian was a lawyer is incorrect; rather, he was a classically trained rhetorician. Interestingly, he also notes that neither Tertullian nor any other Latin Christian writer ever said "*Credo quia absurdum*" (I believe because it is absurd), a phrase that critics have attributed to theologians of the early Church. Yet despite his erudition and lengthy analysis of his subject's surviving works, Barnes is disappointingly weak on the ambiance of Montanism. The relevant chapter in Louis Duchesne, *Early History of the Christian Church from Its Foundation to the End of the Third Century* (London: John Murray, 1909), pp. 196–206, is more informative. On Tertullian's theology, see Jules Lebreton and Jacques Zeiller, *The History of the Primitive Church*, vol. 2 (New York: Macmillan Company, 1947), pp. 811–42. Also useful is Pierre de Labriolle, *The History and Literature of Christianity from Tertullian to Boethius* (New York: Alfred A. Knopf, 1925), pp. 55–105.

thus early in her experience, about the recurrent problem of human weakness and her own commission to forgive.[4]

Donatism

The desire to set oneself on a plane higher than one's co-religionists can be assuaged in other ways than by prophesying, as the North African Donatists showed with their exhortations to martyrdom. This movement took its start from charges of laxity against clerics who responded to pagan demands to burn copies of the Scriptures by yielding up other texts to the illiterate pursuivants. The rigorists objected to the subterfuge and went so far as to deny the consecrating power of bishops who countenanced this adroit avoidance of sacrilege or martyrdom. A counterhierarchy of hundreds of bishops led by Donatus of Carthage formed the rigorist camp, which peaked in strength around A.D. 400. But to maintain its hold on the populace, the sect had constantly to reaffirm its distinctiveness, and it did so through a most extreme band of enthusiasts known as the Circumcellions: "Roving fanatics, with wooden clubs which they called Israels . . . who swooped down on cultivated neighbourhoods and terrified all, Catholics especially, with their war-cry of *Laus Deo*; pillagers of churches, murdering their theological opponents or blinding them with a mixture of lime and vinegar; lunatics who would stop the traveler and demand martyrdom at his hands, under pain of death for himself." [5] Admittedly these thugs constituted the fringe of the Donatist church, but even the proper members evinced a smugness that precluded them from offering even the most innocuous of civilities toward a nonconverted neighbor. Knox is reminded of the Puritans who affected a similar mode of speaking: their reference to the Evangelical faith and to "the people that shares our warfare in the truth of the gospel". Even the Donatists' taunting of Catholics to "turn Christian" and save their souls suggests comparison with "the kind ladies who used to ask us, 'Are you saved?' in omnibuses".

There have, of course, been innumerable heretical movements occasioned by doctrinal disputes and schisms that have national roots, and Knox is conscious that a knowledgeable critic might question his judgment in arraying Donatism among the ranks of enthusiastic

[4] Knox, *Enthusiasm*, p. 49.

[5] Ibid., pp. 61–62.

movements while leaving out the myriad of other fourth- and fifth-century dissenters from the Catholic Church. But he does so because it represents "a protest of the rigorist against a supposed betrayal of the Christian conscience", and given that the protest emerged over such a flimsy issue, and at a time when the primitive faith still burned brightly, the rending of the North African Church boded ill for the future "when men of real spirituality should rise in protest against real abuses and relaxations; when there should be a real case for rigorism, and when a world more removed from the fervour of apostolic times should greet it with impatient rebuke".[6]

MEDIEVAL TIMES

The medieval world, far from stamping out all traces of heresy, saw so many upwellings that it takes half a page for Knox simply to enumerate them. Their relationship to each other is often difficult to ascertain, but for the purposes of tracing the genealogy of ideas that loom large in the seventeenth century, he concentrates on two rather disparate strands that grew side by side in and after the twelfth century. They are the Waldensians and the Albigensians. The former are of interest chiefly because they harbored a deep distrust of the sacerdotal nature of the Church. They were doctrinally more or less Catholic, but anticlericalism and a skewed understanding of the priesthood of the laity kept them at arm's length from ordinary Catholics. The Albigensians had a much richer, if more bizarre, theology. They were dualists, sprung from Asiatic Gnosticism, and therefore thoroughly at odds with the tenets of Catholicism. Seeing spirit and matter in opposition,

[6] Ibid., p. 70. W. H. C. Frend, the modern historian of the movement, does not dispute Knox's aligning of Donatists with subsequent outbreaks of enthusiasm, although he observes that much of their righteous indignation was stirred by what they saw as the alliance of Catholics with wealthy Romanized landowners in the coastal regions of North Africa while Donatism caught on with the poorer inland farmers who suffered economic oppression. He also notes that Donatism, with its uncompromising hatred of secular society and its castigation of Catholicism for absorbing classical culture, paved the way for the ultimate victory of Islam: "With primitive people who considered government in terms of theocracy, the Koran merely replaced the Bible, the Kadi and Emir the dissenting clergy, and martyrdom could equally be attained in holy war against the infidel Franks as against infidel pagans and Catholics." W. H. C. Frend, *The Donatist Church: A Movement of Protest in Roman North Africa* (Oxford: Clarendon Press, 1985), p. 335.

they denied that Christ took flesh of the Virgin Mary or suffered crucifixion. They also denied the efficacy of the sacraments, especially infant baptism. And since marriage presumes the goodness of materiality, it too was reprobated, with consequences no different from those Saint Paul found festering in Corinth.[7]

A nineteenth-century admirer of one late medieval group that owed some of its ideas to the Albigensians claimed of them: "In the overflowing fullness of their joy, the sting of human passion found no place; for they lived on earth as the angels live in heaven."[8] And after them, many post-Reformation sects will think themselves as well capable of carrying off this platonic relation of the sexes while denigrating the value of Christian marriage. But to Knox, the presumption that the member of the elect society has transcended human frailties weighing down the less illuminated of mankind is a sign par excellence of the enthusiast. Time and again, the results—hollow-eyed debauchers and listless colonies of dubiously related "families"—are predictable. Not surprisingly, the medieval heretics also bequeathed to later generations the belief that the institutional Church cannot be the true Church because she accepts too many unfit people into her communion. "That there could be tares in the wheat, that worthless fish as well as eatable ones could be found in the net, was a doctrine incomprehensible to Wycliffe and Huss, for all their insistence on the Gospel. For the enthusiast, there is only one Church, a Church 'invisible.' Its membership consists of the names which are written in the book of life, whatever their sectarian affiliations."[9]

[7] In his classic study of the dualist tradition in the Eastern and Western Christian world, Steven Runciman notes that since the Albigensians deprecated the flesh as evil, adherents who had not yet risen to the highest level of membership could afford to indulge in sexual excess without compunction. He also convincingly traces the lineage of the sect to the Bogomils of Bulgaria and points out that a derivative of the latter word as *Bougre* entered the lexicon of Western languages as a synonym for unnatural practices. See *The Medieval Manichee* (New York: Viking Press, 1961), pp. 175–78.

[8] Knox, *Enthusiasm*, pp. 103–4. The allusion is to Mk 12:25 and is but one instance of the danger of freewheeling interpretations of Scriptural texts taken out of context.

[9] Ibid., p. 112. Knox bypasses several of the more egregious manifestations of perfectionist millennial enthusiastic sects that erupted within the turbulent medieval social landscape. However, Norman Cohn focuses on these in his seminal study, first printed in the year Knox died, titled *The Pursuit of the Millennium: Revolutionary Millenarians and Mystical Anarchists of the Middle Ages*, rev. ed. (New York: Oxford University Press, 1970). The flagellants, armies of nomadic anticlerical penitents who flourished at the time of the Black

ANABAPTISTS

The various streams of antinomianism, perfectionism, and even dualism met head on in the Anabaptist sect that was to cause Luther so many headaches in Reformation Germany. The defining mark of these radicals, indeed what gave them their name, was their opposition to infant baptism, which they held to be irreconcilable with a salvation that had to be consciously sought by any true believer. State-supported Protestantism, as epitomized by Luther, who relied on the secular arm to cement his territorial gains at the expense of the Catholic Church, was insufficiently godly to the Anabaptists. They could be satisfied with nothing less than theocratic rule. Leave the machinery of the state to legislate for the reprobate; the elect could not bow to servants of the natural order. Some of their tenets were to be adopted by John Knox in Scotland and the Puritans on both sides of the Atlantic Ocean in the seventeenth and eighteenth centuries. "Under such discipline sin became a crime, to be punished by the elect with an intolerable self-righteousness. And the Presbytery, grim in its dealing with its own subjects, could cultivate an attitude of bloodthirsty ferocity when it went to battle, and had the enemies of the Lord at its mercy." [10] Likewise Luther would not let private interpretation of Scripture outpace Lutheran orthodoxy, a stricture under which the enthusiast chafed: "Anabaptism had enough logic in its Protestantism to claim that the Bible might and should be interpreted by the individual Christian according to the light given him, while official Protestantism, recoiling from such a vista of confusion, reposed its confidence in

---

Death, were notorious opponents of the Catholic sacramental system, claiming instead to be infused directly with the Holy Spirit. Likewise, the Brethren of the Free Spirit, who originated in the Low Countries, were an antinomian sect whose elite members claimed to have attained divine status, thus being henceforward incapable of committing a sin. Sister Catherine, one of their ecstatic writers, proclaimed what that meant: "You shall order all created beings to serve you according to your will, for the glory of God.... You shall bear all things up to God. If you want to use all created beings, you have the right to do so, for every creature that you use, you drive up into its Origin." Quoted in Cohn, *Pursuit of the Millennium*, p. 179. These strictures, needless to say, countenanced all manner of licentiousness, theft, and other anarchic behavior in whatever lands into which the Free Spirit doctrines were imported.

[10] Knox, *Enthusiasm*, p. 133.

the comparative certitude of scholarship."[11] Luther had divined his theory of grace by his exegesis of Saint Paul. What would prevent someone else coming along with a different explanation of sin and redemption if the Bible were truly open to all to interpret? The Anabaptists, faithful to the enthusiast tradition, mistrusted any kind of Biblical scholarship. Instead, they would rely on the Spirit to suffuse the prophet with an understanding of God's Word. Knox stresses the dichotomy between charismatic, anti-intellectual Protestantism and the established reformed creeds:

> To the enthusiast, the Bible is infallible when interpreted by an inspired person. To the Reformers, it possessed an inherent infallibility, and needed only clarification, which was a matter for the learned.... Thenceforward, simple folk might read the Bible for themselves if they could derive any spiritual profit from the exercise; but their rule of faith was not, in fact, to be any private inspiration of their own. They were to be guided by the Scripture as interpreted by Luther, and Calvin, and Zwingli, and Beza, and Knox, by the pundits.[12]

Antinomianism rarely fails to surface when free interpretation of the Bible is encouraged. One Protestant Reformer asserted that the Anabaptists deliberately left out the phrase "forgive us our trespasses" from the Our Father and that they looked benignly on promiscuity among the elect. The following contemporary extract also parallels the bizarre antics to be found in many later ultrasupernaturalist outcroppings in various cultures: "On February the 11th ... some Anabaptists having met at a house in Amsterdam, at the call of one named Richard they stripped themselves of their clothes and ran through the streets crying, 'Woe, woe, woe, the wrath of God, the wrath of God!' Brought before the magistrates, they refused to dress. 'We,' they said, 'are the naked truth.' "[13]

[11] Ibid., p. 129.

[12] Ibid., p. 134–35.

[13] Ibid., p. 136. The Anabaptists were far from a merely eccentric sect. Under the megalomaniac John of Leyden's theocratic rule, the residents of Münster were subjected to months of terror, executions, debauchery, and finally starvation before his capture in 1535. For the grisly details, see Cohn, *Pursuit of the Millennium*, pp. 252–80.

QUAKERS

If Anabaptism evokes images of fanaticism, the Quakers certainly do not. Quiet contemplativeness and passivity would appear to be of the essence of their system. But their resolute founder, George Fox, hinted at a more steely side to the sect when, in response to a probing question on religious toleration by Roger Williams, he proclaimed that if a ruler "is in the light and power of Christ, he is to subject all under the power of Christ into his light". Pacifism was not an original mark of a Quaker; only after the Puritan victory of Cromwell against the Stuart monarchy proved not to usher in the millennium but rather only furthered the persecution of Fox's band did they opt for nonconfrontation with the worldly.

Instead it is the "inner light" that is their distinguishing tenet. This inner light was the prompting of the Spirit, who guided all of life's choices. With direct communication between the Spirit and the soul, any need to consult the Bible or tradition evaporated. Prayers and supplications were equally useless. Fox himself said he received an illumination that "there was a mystical, but Divine, light in the hearts of men, a light which would, if followed honestly and steadily, infallibly lead to God: and that without the aid of either the Bible or any ordinances." Given that this light could indwell in anyone, a certain anarchy was bound to accompany the group's expansion. Whose inspired utterances at a Quaker meeting would be normative, and whose should be disregarded? Even more troubling, when the inspiration wells up within an individual, and that person proceeds to utter thoughts apparently steeped in mystical meaning, where is the line to be drawn between the *exalté* and the Spirit presumably speaking through the person? When one of Fox's admirers refers to him as "O thou bread of life" and "O thou father of eternal felicity" and when Fox himself says, "He that hath the same Spirit that raised up Jesus is equal with God", trouble is sure to arise.

And it did in 1656 in the person of James Nayler, a convert to Quakerism whose facial resemblance to portraits of Christ only heightened his confusion about whence arose the light within him. He was credited by his followers with raising a dead girl to life, and he reenacted the entry of Christ into Jerusalem with a horse ride to

Bristol, replete with cries of "Hosanna!" Even before this ultimate charade, members of his little schismatic Quaker group hailed him "as the 'dear and precious Son of Zion, whose mother is a virgin and whose birth is immortal,' as 'the fairest of ten thousand and only-begotten Son of God,' telling him that his name should no more be called James Nayler but Jesus".[14] But this public display of adulation caused Nayler to fall into the hands of the Puritan Parliament, who flogged and maimed him for his blasphemy. Interestingly, Fox himself regarded Nayler not as a heresiarch but as a usurper of his primacy, so much had the belief in the Person of Jesus receded in Quaker theology before the doctrine of the inner light. To give Nayler the benefit of the doubt, he most likely did not believe that he alone was the Christ, but he was so befuddled by the notion that Christ dwelt in him that he could not make the distinction that even an elementary grounding in Catholic theology clarifies. The language of the enthusiast had produced its logical conclusion, to the embarrassment of official Protestantism:

> In the last analysis, Puritan England was concerned not so much to exact punishment, as to make a gesture; the world must be assured that English religion had not gone into the melting pot. Catholics were twitting Anglicans with the existence of Puritanism; Anglicans were twitting Puritans with the existence of Quakerism; Puritans were twitting Quakers with the existence of

[14] Ibid., p. 162. This type of hyperbolic language was not reserved for only the more outlandish figures in early Quakerism. Margaret Fell, the foundress along with George Fox of the movement, is addressed by an adherent in the following terms: "Oh my dear heart my love and life is with thee ... blessed art thou amongst all women ... for with thee there is a fresh spring which flows freely to the lambs and plants of god.... My tongue cannot utter the joy that I have concerning thee ... my dear and near and eternal mother, by thee I am nourished." Quoted in Phyllis Mack, *Visionary Women: Ecstatic Prophecy in Seventeenth Century England* (Berkeley: University of California Press, 1992), p. 174. The author is clearly on the side of the ecstatics, lamenting the transformation of the early, uninhibited Quakers into a more structured, socially responsible community valuing rational discourse under the influence of William Penn in the later 1600s, although she sees the development of formal women's meetings having control of the social side of Quaker life as partially redeeming: "Tracking the movement's evolution from sect to church, one watched prophetic women, once the bearers of considerable charismatic authority, slowly disappear behind the rising edifice of the new structure, their voices muffled by the clearer discourse of the proponents of new rules and values" (pp. 274–75).

Naylerism. And Nayler must be the scapegoat. He suffered as the *reductio ad absurdam* of the Reformation experiment.[15]

JANSENISM

There is more than a touch of priggishness as well as fanaticism in the strands of enthusiasm Knox forges into a catena. And with seventeenth-century Protestantism falling a prey, it would have been astonishing if Catholicism had avoided having to deal with these efflorescences, human nature seeking as it does an outlet for one-upmanship. So when a Dutch bishop named Cornelius Jansen wrote a theological tract on Saint Augustine that purported to explicate the saint's rigorist doctrine on grace and fallen mankind while managing to inject a twist that held out salvation only to an elite, a ready audience was at hand to gravitate to the new teaching. Enlisting the services of the numerous talented members of the Arnauld family and coopting the genius of Blaise Pascal, Jansenism soon hardened into a sect. Its spokesmen engaged their theological archenemies, the Jesuits, in rancorous debate over the ability of people to cooperate in the attainment of their salvation. The Jesuits were taxed with latitudinarianism. They advocated frequent reception of Holy Communion for individuals whom the Jansenists viewed as hopelessly reprobate; they had the temerity to suggest that sins could be forgiven without the severest penance; and they believed that heaven was accessible to more than the most accomplished of spiritual athletes.

At this point in the narrative, a comment too relevant to be relegated to a footnote needs to be inserted. No foray into the maze of seventeenth-century French ecclesiastical history can be undertaken without invoking Henri Bremond, whose monumental series of studies supplied Knox with much information about the religious milieu in which arose authentic mysticism and its Quietist counterfeit, as well as what Bremond calls the "devout humanism" of Saint Francis de Sales and his followers, a view of the relations between God and mankind that served as a counterpoise to Jansenism and its severities. Abbé Bremond was a generation older than Knox and had left the Jesuits—but not the priesthood—in 1904. But for his association with the excommunicated Tyrrell culminating in his officiating at a prayer service for

[15] Knox, *Enthusiasm*, p. 164.

him at his Anglican gravesite in 1909, he was impeccably orthodox in his theology and an astute judge of where and how others sometimes flirted with unsound notions.[16]

Bremond was not concerned, as Knox was, primarily to catalogue errant spiritualities. With the whole history of French religious thought as his subject, Bremond had the more arduous, if also more fulfilling, task of sifting through literally thousands of biographies, histories of religious orders and communities, works of devotion and of spiritual direction, indeed any manuscripts casting light on trends within French Catholicism from the days of Henri III to those of Louis XIV, the better to understand the growth of orthodox spirituality. He reminds his readers that France in the early seventeenth century produced Madame Acarie, Cardinal Berulle, Madame de Chantal, Charles de Condren, Jean-Jacques Olier, Vincent de Paul, and many other saints and mystics alongside the contentious souls that Knox's argument requires highlighting.

With the apposite phrase, he could frame distinctions a less felicitous writer would take pages to delineate. Witness for example his contrast between devout humanism and Jansenism at the end of his first volume of investigations. The former

> is as yet neither perfect saintliness nor the higher life of mysticism, but it favoured the ripening of these rare fruits. Strictly speaking, one can say as much of all sincere and fervent devotion, no matter in what direction it be found, for instance, that of Port-Royal; the goodness of Mère Angélique, Mère Agnes, M. Hamon, and many others may not be questioned. We merely affirm that Devout Humanism is a leaven of holiness and of mysticism far more active and far surer.... Strong in its invincible optimism, Devout Humanism makes short work of the paralyzing scruples engendered by and encumbering the opposite doctrine; it frees and dilates the soul, teaching it that, although fallen by original sin, human nature still remains

[16] Bremond (1865–1933) was ordained in 1892 and wrote for the Jesuit periodical *Études* until his separation from the Society of Jesus in 1904. Much of his subsequent life was devoted to his encyclopedic history, though he managed to write close to forty other books, about half before and half after commencing with his magnum opus. He was elected to one of the forty seats occupied by "*les immortels*" of the Académie française in 1923, succeeding Louis Duchesne, who had died the previous year. A somewhat inadequate biography in English is Henry Hogarth, *Henri Bremond: The Life and Work of a Devout Humanist* (London: SPCK, 1950).

> the marvel of creation; that the wound of the Old Adam has not gangrened all our being; that redemptive grace is always and fully offered to all.[17]

Likewise, Knox draws attention to the stifling spiritual atmosphere encumbering the Jansenist elite, which he notes was always threatening a schism with Rome and which finally erupted in a bizarre display of ecstatic phenomena half a century after the principals had gone to their rest. Mère Angélique Arnauld, he observes, "was incurably self-conscious". Although she stoutly proclaimed her desire to subject her will entirely to God, she and her colleagues never "got rid of that self-consciousness which makes you see yourself out of the corner of your eye at every turn in life". She had a flair for the dramatic spiritual gesture. The world had to know how much anguish she suffered on account of petty ecclesiastics. At one point, she made a point of her preference for her Jansenist spiritual director over the Pope: "[S]he would rather be canonized by M. Singlin than by the Pope; unconsciously, you see, she takes the canonization for granted."[18] Her band of nuns at Port-Royal relished persecution by the authorities, because the siege mentality it created confirmed their sense of superiority. Yes, of course, Port-Royal would grieve at the pervasiveness of sin, but "the more its inmates find themselves cut off, by the peculiarity of their views, from the rest of Christendom, the more freely their tears flow that the rest of Christendom should be so wrong."[19]

And yet the Jansenists' immiscibility with commonplace Catholics did not engender passivity, as the pamphlet wars with the Jesuits amply demonstrate. With Antoine Arnauld and Pierre Nicole, the most combative of lawyerly features come to the fore. Endless disputes about what was and was not meant by Jansen in his book, about what was and what was not condemned by various Roman documents, and about what authority those documents carried cloud the literature of that period. Its dismal record is more drawn out in Ludwig von Pastor's relevant volumes on the seventeenth-century Popes, but Knox gives

[17] Henri Bremond, *A Literary History of Religious Thought in France from the Wars of Religion down to Our Own Times*, vol. 1: *Devout Humanism* (New York: Macmillan Company, 1928), p. 404.

[18] Knox, *Enthusiasm*, pp. 189–90.

[19] Ibid., p. 195.

sufficient instances of the argumentative and hairsplitting strategy employed by the Jansenists as they sought to exonerate their side of all culpability in a war of wits with Rome. While most Jansenists in France flaunted their disobedience, remarkably they managed to remain just on the right side of formal schism; only a Dutch contingent went far enough to precipitate a permanent split from the Church.

Yet for all their cleverness and evasiveness, when it came to pinning them down to doctrinal formularies that would establish once and for all whether they were inside or outside the Catholic fold, they exhibited a blunt outspokenness about everyone else's odds of perdition. "Of all the Jansenist tricks," Knox avers, "none is more clearly un-Catholic than the readiness with which they assume their neighbour's damnation." Their elitism showed even in their punctilious maintenance of a necrology that "included only the names of those who were thought, somehow or other, to have supported their own side of the quarrel".[20] How well the Jansenist world view was summarized by François Bonal, a Franciscan contemporary of Arnauld, as

> that sombre religion ever living in fear, restless and feverish, which in efforts after virtue at once austere and arrogant, vaunts melancholy as perfection and sadness as a celestial grace; which claims the dreamer as one inspired, the scrupulous as a saint, the dismal as a prophet; which canonises its fears, vapours, dreams, convulsions, ecstasies, illnesses, as visions, oracles, revelations, and the pains of love. Nothing of all this is Christianity, since, for the inner man, the end of the precept is the charity that arises from the depths of a purified heart and good conscience, far removed from all tremblings of a sombre and sickly superstition fearing God as a tyrant instead of loving him as a father.[21]

One of the recurring motifs of Knox's survey of two thousand years of enthusiastic movements is the danger of assuming that persecution is necessarily a sign that its victims are God's elect. The beatitudes certainly indicate that those who are persecuted in Christ's name are blessed, but it is ever the temptation of the members of the downtrodden sect to see themselves in the role of the Remnant who will be saved. On the other side is the institutional Church, large and admitting many lax and

[20] Ibid., pp. 203, 206.
[21] Bremond, *Devout Humanism*, p. 321.

many evident sinners through her portals. She scandalizes the little community of the perfect by doing so, and consequently they challenge her credentials as the Church founded by Christ. All too often then, the mainstream Catholic authorities will team up with, or passively comply with, the secular arm to bring the dissenting company to heel. With their rigorous teaching, the Jansenists certainly saw themselves in that role of the true followers of Christ. And it would become clear to the world that they, and not the "corrupted" Church headquartered in Rome, were the repository of the true teaching as exemplified by the witness they would give through penitence and austerity: "Just as Donatism had to produce synthetic martyrs, Port-Royal had to produce synthetic penitents; the world must be shown what being contrite for your sins really meant; and how you must set about it.... The visitor was meant to go away, not so much reflecting on the high place these people would take in heaven, as wondering whether he himself would find any place in heaven at all."[22]

There was always that fillip. The sect that basks in its righteousness likes to elevate the walls a bit so outsiders feel more keenly the divide between themselves and a hope of salvation. The quarrel over frequent Communion is really the touchstone issue with the Jansenists. Reception of the Eucharist must be made prohibitively difficult; otherwise Jesus will be accessible to too many people who just haven't earned his company. Antoine Arnauld was the most prolific propagandist on the point, and Knox's commentary on his reasoning is worth reproducing in its entirety because it so aptly encapsulates the Jansenist mindset:

> The trouble about Arnauld is the old trouble which Saint Francis [de Sales] had pointed out to his sister; he was content to catch only a few fish in the net of salvation—a Le Maitre here, a Pascal there, and the small fry did not matter. The *avertissement* of the book tells us that the bishops who have approved it regard it as "un excellent moyen pour imprimer aux pécheurs l'horreur de leurs fautes." If it was really intended to do that, it is to be feared that the book has not often fallen into the right hands; not many obdurate sinners are prepared to read through a stout quarto of patristic quotations, out of curiosity to know why they have been refused absolution. No, the book was meant to be read on the other side of the grille. Priests were to be encouraged to think with the mind of the early

[22] Knox, *Enthusiasm*, p. 211.

> Church, and defer the absolution of every penitent until he should attest, by repeated applications for pardon, the genuineness of his sorrow. The French Oratory was all wrong about this; St. Philip Neri had not understood the doctrine of penance. And it is no use to object that St. Philip understood something better than the doctrine; he understood sinners, whom Arnauld had not met. Isolated in his study from the world of common living, Arnauld saw sinners only as a class; and as a class they were unsaveable. Our rigorist does not understand the maxim *sacramenta propter homines*; he will let the generality of men perish in a dry wilderness, while an *elite* of souls, "pure as angels, proud as Lucifer," forms the bodyguard of the Holy Eucharist.[23]

There is one other aspect of Jansenism that perhaps deserves highlighting, because in the long run it partially explains the odd sequel to the movement in the eighteenth century. Blaise Pascal, the leading intellectual of Port-Royal, not only left a brilliant volume of propaganda on their behalf with his *Provincial Letters*. He also was a philosopher, and the excerpts that constitute his most famous work, the *Pensées*, are thoroughly imbued with the Jansenist outlook on life. These writings, which offer arguments for an apologetic, show a distinct downgrading of human reason as a road to knowledge of God. The traditional proofs of God's existence are acknowledged but not given the primacy of place that Thomas Aquinas would accord them. One would think that Pascal, as a scientist and mathematician, would make of them a cornerstone of a rational philosophical edifice, but he was obsessed with the misery of human existence, and his portrayal of the

[23] Ibid., p. 216. And yet the Jansenists are not without their modern sympathizers. Marc Escholier, in *Port-Royal: The Drama of the Jansenists* (New York: Hawthorn, 1968), portrays them in a uniformly positive light as high-minded saintly victims of persecution by the worldly Jesuits. Of Arnauld's book, for example, the author summarizes it with the comment that it "proclaimed what many believed: namely, that to commune with the Crucified we must know and love him, putting aside everything that separates us from him" (p. 63). He neglects to mention that it was condemned by the saintly Vincent de Paul at the time of its publication for its contention that reception of Communion be restricted to the heroically virtuous. A distinguished French church historian records Monsieur Vincent's observation "whether there could be any man on earth who held such a high opinion of his own virtue as to believe himself worthy to receive Holy Communion" and his contention that if it drew a hundred people closer to the Eucharist, it alienated ten thousand from the sacraments. See Henri Daniel-Rops, *The Church in the Seventeenth Century* (London: J.M. Dent and Sons, 1963), p. 348.

utter degradation of human nature required that it be incapable of any insight into the divine governance of the universe. Human reason is to be distrusted, and only the infusion of a rush of grace, such as he experienced during his famous epiphany of November 23, 1654, can reveal anything of God's nature to mortals.[24]

The Jansenists were nothing if not stubborn. Their tedious badgering of Rome left them secure in the knowledge that they were in the right about matters theological and legal, but they also appealed to the charism of the miraculous to buttress their case. A spiritual elite could hardly avoid being showered by God with otherwise inexplicable cures of maladies. In the 1730s, following the death of a Jansenist deacon reputed to be saintly, extraordinary manifestations of the power of God were reported to be taking place at his tomb in the cemetery of Saint-Médard. The Abbé Gregoire, a Jansenist politician and historian of a later era, describes the altered states experienced by those congregating at the gravesite as follows: "violent convulsions or contortions of the whole body, rolling on the ground, leaping about on the pavement, rigours, tumultuous shakings of the arms, the legs, the head, and all the limbs, resulting in a difficulty of breathing, a quickening and an irregularity of the pulse".[25]

The aberrations did not stop there. Some individuals inflicted the most excruciating tortures on themselves to show their imperviousness to injury and pain. What had begun as manifestations of miraculous cures had degenerated into the grossest exhibitionism, where swords, clubs, and heavy weights all proved incapable of harming the convulsionaries.

EXTREME MANIFESTATIONS

Interestingly enough, the same kind of activity had been noted a few years earlier, across the English Channel, among a group of violently Protestant Huguenots called the Camisards. They too shook uncontrollably at their meetings and fell to the floor, swelling at the neck and

[24] For an excellent treatment of Pascal, placing his contentious *Provincial Letters* in context, see Marvin O'Connell, *Blaise Pascal: Reasons of the Heart* (Grand Rapids, Mich.: William B. Eerdmans, 1997). Although he was an extreme defender of Port-Royal, which housed his sister Jacqueline as well as two nieces, he died at age 39 completely submissive to the ministrations of a parish priest who had no ties to Jansenism.

[25] Quoted in Knox, *Enthusiasm*, pp. 377–78.

stomach, and then they would rise to prophesy. "Sometimes the prophets would fall from rocks 12 feet high without injury. Some drove knives into themselves leaving no mark, or gave proof that fire could not burn them. Without any education they preached an exalted piety and quoted Scripture texts aptly enough. They talked sometimes in languages they could not have known; made prophecies or told of things which were happening at a distance and were proved right by the event."[26] Unlike the Jansenists, these shock troops of the Huguenot party, whom Knox likens to the Circumcellion fringe of the Donatist church, engaged in political and military activity, as well as polemics. They massacred their religious opponents with a ferocity that only fanatics who believed God authorized them to punish all infidels could summon, and they shed their own blood with equal abandon. It would consequently appear difficult to draw a connecting line between them and the Quakers and Moravians, who adhered to a pacifist tradition. But too many similarities mark all these groups to discountenance a common patrimony. The Quakers, before they calmed down to await the promptings of the inner spirit, "did use to fall into violent tremblings and sometimes vomiting in their meetings, and pretended to be violently acted by the Spirit" according to a mid-seventeenth-century observer.[27]

The Moravians were descended from the Hussites and the Anabaptists; they had coalesced under Amos Comenius and after him Count Zinzendorf in the eighteenth century. These leaders showed a marked flair as organizers, setting up highly regimented communities throughout central and western Europe, with headquarters in Germany. They were pietistic and childishly sentimental in their devotions, adherents of the Lutheran doctrine of justification, and consequently called upon to glory in their conviction of themselves as saved sinners. Count Zinzendorf apparently pushed a dangerous inclination beyond the bounds of even a semblance of propriety in the 1740s when he informed the brethren that since they were utterly in God's hands they "were not to use their own brains; they were to wish they had no brains; they were to be like children in arms; and thus they would overcome all their doubts and banish all their cares".[28] Exhortations continued for four

[26] Ibid., p. 360.
[27] Quoted in ibid., p. 150.
[28] Quoted in ibid., p. 414.

years to cast aside all inhibitions, and witnesses attest to the holy buffoonery unleashed. Good works, even Bible reading, were disparaged in favor of clowning, and anyone who stood aloof from the antinomian sporting was accused of being an agent of the Devil. Those years were afterward referred to under the vaguely sinister appellation of "the Sifting Time". Its excesses were clearly a cause of embarrassment to later generations of Moravians who had to sanitize the hymns that emanated from the era and place a judicious veil over what had all the hallmarks of a drunken orgy. But that, once again, was the price paid for giving free rein to emotionalism in religion.

QUIETISM

At first sight, the lengthy treatment Knox accords to Quietism, a movement associated with the Spanish priest and spiritual director Miguel de Molinos, seems to herald too great a contrast with the foregoing to warrant inclusion within the same dragnet. It did not spawn quaking and shaking enthusiasts whose uninhibited antics show all too visibly the deleterious consequences of seeking a short circuit to God outside the Church and her sacramental system. Quietism is the antithesis of holy-rollerism. But it merits attention in his pages (indeed, he devotes 125 pages to its history and doctrinal singularities) because it pushed the concept of passive mystical communion with God so far that its doctrine of the "prayer of simple regard" became virtually indistinguishable from the Quaker notion of the inner light. And just as the Jansenists argued with the Jesuits over grace and the degree of man's dereliction, the Quietists argued with the Jesuits over the value of meditative versus contemplative prayer.

Far less than Jansenism does Quietism qualify as an organized movement—it would be against its initiate's nature to do anything so concrete. It is instead a tendency, and it caught on in salons and even among churchmen, but its chief promoter after Molinos was the celebrated Madame Guyon, who in her turn influenced the archbishop of Cambrai, François de Fénelon. Molinos had been stationed in Rome, where he acquired a reputation as a director of souls with his advice to penitents to allow a passive devotion to God to be their rule of life. They were not to think of prayer as a means to achieving virtue. The Spiritual Exercises as taught by Jesuit directors were deficient in that sense, in that they used imagery and required discipline and concentration to lead the soul to deeper communion with God. Knox aptly observes why the exercises seemed unsuitable for a significant portion of seventeenth-century society and why Quietism found fertile ground:

> St. Ignatius's object had been a simple one—to make the thoughtless, whose attention was all directed to outward things, turn back upon themselves and see their own souls in the light of eternity; he would turn extroverts into introverts. But the age which immediately followed the counter-Reformation was, on the whole, an age of introverts.... it demanded, hardly less than our own, a method of devotion which should turn introverts into extroverts. It must have its gaze, somehow, directed outwards upon God, not concentrated eternally upon itself. These affections, these acts of the will, how was the mind to make them successfully when it was watching all the time to see whether it was making them successfully or not?[29]

It is difficult to pin down the Quietist apologists with overt theological errors.[30] When the famous Bishop Bossuet charged that Fénelon's book on the mystical state as evidenced in the lives of the saints was riddled with heresy, leading to a lengthy investigation by a panel of theologians in Rome, the decision arrived at in 1699 was far less

[29] Ibid., p. 246. Here too Bremond has some interesting comments, suggesting that St. Ignatius himself meant his Exercises to accentuate worship of God rather than self-examination, hence to be theocentric rather than anthropocentric, but subsequent generations of Jesuit directors shifted the emphasis. See Henri Bremond, *A Literary History of Religious Thought in France from the Wars of Religion down to Our Own Times*, vol. 3: *The Triumph of Mysticism* (New York: Macmillan Company, 1936), pp. 21–25. This last volume of his to be translated into English is immensely valuable as an introduction to the great French Oratorians and Jesuits. Incidentally, all three volumes were translated by "K. L. Montgomery", the name used by two Irish-born Protestants, Kathleen and Letitia Montgomery, one of whom died in 1930, while the other died at the age of 97 in 1960. One can presume that with Bremond's death in 1933 shortly after the death of Letitia, the project of continued translation of the remaining volumes already in print in French languished. It would be a worthy enterprise for a gifted translator of French—who is also conversant with mystical theology—to continue where the Montgomery sisters left off three-quarters of a century ago, much as several hands had to combine to translate the staggering forty volumes of Ludwig von Pastor's *History of the Popes* into English.

[30] For a detailed discussion both of writers such as Francis Malaval and John de Bernières who paved the way for Quietism with their overemphasis on spiritual passivity, and of the Quietists themselves, see Pierre Pourrat, *Christian Spirituality*, vol. 4: *From Jansenism to Modern Times* (Westminster, Md.: Newman Press, 1955), especially pp. 67–260.

conclusive than that for which he had hoped. Pope Innocent XII was known to be favorable to Fénelon, and historians have subsequently looked askance at the unscrupulous politicking employed by Bossuet to engineer a condemnation of his fellow prelate. To complicate matters further, Bossuet was highly tinged with Gallicanism, while Fénelon was an ultramontane and had the support of the Jesuits.

More instructive is the fate of Molinos, and even his published writings were not condemned on their own account. At the height of his popularity as a guide to thousands of Spaniards seeking a heightened spiritual life in Rome, Molinos was arrested in 1685 on unspecified charges obviously bearing on moral turpitude. The implication is that his teaching on passivity extended to nonresistance to temptation. He abjured a number of errors and died eleven years later, never again free to expound his method. Previous to that abrupt termination of his ministry, he was voluble enough in his writings. His impassive acquiescence in his condemnation could allow for either of two constructions, either an acknowledgment of guilt or a following through of his own preaching on noninterference with God's permissive will. Enough evidence, including evidence given by Molinos, is on record to show that he counseled penitents to remain unperturbed when temptation overwhelmed them, he devalued confession of sins, he advocated resignation to the thought of eternal damnation, and he held that prayer ought never to be used to ask anything of God, even assistance for souls in Purgatory. How then to characterize the proponent of this new spirituality? Some critics thought him a charlatan; Knox sees in him traits of the enthusiast:

> Molinos believed himself to be a prophet, and as is the way of such men (where the belief is ill-founded) thought himself superior to considerations of ordinary moral prudence. His temptations were those of the exhibitionist, and he readily induced himself to believe that the laws of decency were made for the common run of mankind, not for the spiritually perfect.... Penitents had told him about grave sins, committed while they seemed to be in a state of uninterrupted prayer. Pedantically true to his own principles, he had assumed the manner of an oracle, and told them there was no known harm in it; it was only the Devil making use of their exterior faculties to humiliate them; a Divine light assured him of it. Now he began to take advantage of his own lax principles; encouraged dangerous

> intimacies, perhaps partly with the idea of experimenting, of making sure that it was all right. He did not quite take himself in; he still indignantly repudiated the doctrine of the Alumbrados, who claimed that a man should yield to his temptations rather than abandon the state of repose. But all the time he was falling into lower depths of abasement, while self-conceit assured him that he, Doctor Molinos, could not really be sinning.[31]

Then there is Madame Guyon, the famous widow who adopted Quietism as her mode of spirituality contemporaneously with, but certainly independently of, Molinos. She overshadowed all the clerics in France who advocated its methods of freeing the advanced souls from all the snares of formal prayer and dependence on good works. Ostensibly under the care of the unfortunate Père Lacombe, she badgered her poor director until he became wholly her adjunct. He was later imprisoned for his role in her spiritual adventures, and eventually he went mad. She, however, was formidable enough to enlist the support of various dukes and duchesses and, of course, Fénelon, who consistently vouched for her mystical insights but blanched at the prospect of reading her spiritual autobiography. No wonder, since Père Lacombe had instructed her to record all her thoughts on paper, a suggestion upon which she followed up with the most immodest alacrity. Of this effort, one among an eventual output totaling over twenty volumes, Knox simply remarks that "the mind which produced it seems to labour under the want of any proportion".[32] In one of her volumes appropriately titled *Spiritual Torrents*, she

[31] Knox, *Enthusiasm*, pp. 317–18. Bremond gives a concise definition of Quietism that belies Knox's occasional insinuation that Bremond was insufficiently clear presenting the difference between it and true mysticism: "Quietism despises and neglects the ordinary practices of the Christian life, such as vocal prayer and meditations, frequent use of the Sacraments, and the practice of Christian virtues, substituting for these an indolent abandonment to the mystic work of grace in certain elect souls. According to the Quietists, the perfect will be raised into a state of bliss in which mystic contemplation will be easy and constant, if not altogether uninterrupted—a crying absurdity." Henri Bremond, *A Literary History of Religious Thought in France from the Wars of Religion down to Our Own Times*, vol. 2: *The Coming of Mysticism* (New York: Macmillan Company, 1930), p. 442. And in volume 1 he refers to Madame Guyon as "sinister" on p. 194.

[32] Knox, *Enthusiasm*, p. 328. Michael de la Bedoyere, an English Catholic writer who was the founding editor in the 1930s of the *Catholic Herald*, takes issue with Knox's characterization in de la Bedoyere, *The Archbishop and the Lady: The Story of Fenelon and Madame Guyon* (New York: Pantheon, 1956). But unlike Knox, he seems not to have delved deeply into her many writings or at least is reticent to expose the full array of her spiritual effusions

lays claim to powers of discernment of spirits, the ability to transmit messages mentally to people at great distance, and to concourse with the saints. Bossuet compared her to the prophetesses accompanying the heretic Montanus (incidentally drawing the ire of Fénelon, who did not like the implication that he was the counterpart of the heresiarch). Similarly, Knox suggests a filiation to other female enthusiasts such as Ann Lee, the Shaker foundress, and the Countess of Huntingdon, who was an influential backer of the early Methodists.[33] Of course the latter represented sects much further removed from Catholicism than Madame Guyon—who always avowed her absolute fealty to Rome—could ever imagine, but she shared with them an excessive confidence in the fevered lucubrations manufactured in her overwrought imagination.

Similarities abound too with other pious women who fall outside Knox's purview simply because they were not associated with major movements inside the Church, but whose writings are hardly less unsettling than Madame Guyon's. Herbert Thurston, a historian a generation older than Knox, chronicled the eccentricities of a number of these figures in a series of articles in the English Jesuit journal the *Month* and later collected in book form as *Surprising Mystics*. Mary of Agreda, who authored voluminous treatises purporting to give details of the lives of Jesus and his Mother, falls into the same category as Madame Guyon. She claimed that the Virgin Mary told her that any doubters of her narrative "will incur the indignation of Almighty God as well as mine, and that he will be punished, in this life and in the next, with all the rigour of the divine justice". Doubters enough

---

to his readers lest they not accept his contention that she was purely a victim of Bossuet's spite (as Fénelon more arguably was). Surely the historian is far more reliable who says that "her neurotic temperament was better adapted to Quietism with a pantheistic basis than to Teresian mysticism and its encouragement of moral energy." Pourrat, *From Jansenism to Modern Times*, p. 196. It should be noted that Madame Guyon had early been elevated to heroic status by English Protestants through a decidedly oleaginous 1847 biography by Thomas Upham, which, as Knox notes, transforms her into an estimable nineteenth-century Evangelical.

[33] Knox quotes one French priest in this regard: "Les hommes font les heresies, les femmes leur donnent cours et les rendent immortelles" (p. 319). On Mother Ann Lee and the Shaker theology, see Diane Sasson, *The Shaker Spiritual Narrative* (Knoxville: University of Tennessee Press, 1983). Lee's religious outlook, which branded the act of procreation sinful, was dualistic not only with regard to nature but also in that after her death in 1784 her followers elevated her to divine status alongside Christ as his Second Appearing, "required in order to reveal clearly the sexual root of all evil" (p. 198).

there were, which explains the checkered history of *The Mystical City of God* with the Index of Forbidden Books, and the hopeless task involved in squaring her visions with those of other mystics or with known historical facts. Father Thurston is inclined to ascribe to this woman the highest degree of sincerity, even of devotion, but he cautions that her "mental health has to be considered, and hysteria, while it is itself no bar to sanctity and may not involve any form of self-seeking, is singularly apt to lend itself to exaggerations and pervert the sober judgment".[34]

Madame Guyon certainly attached the same gravity to her experiences. But she goes a step further and "crosses the line between mysticism and pantheism, between theocentricity and deiformity", frequently conflating her state with that of Jesus himself. She appropriated to herself Gospel statements of his, going so far as to recommend her disciples to God the Father, with the wish that he watch over them. Knox quotes her statement that she, after all, is no longer "capable of giving any reason for my conduct, for I no longer have a conduct; yet I act infallibly, so long as I have no other principle than the infallible One".[35] The orthodox student of mystical theology could handle the idea of being suffused with love of God while yet remaining distinct from him. Madame Guyon could not, and Knox's comment that she fell into the same trap as James Nayler, who let people shout Hosanna to him, is incontestable. It is ironic that a movement that sought to minimize the human contribution to the quest for sanctification, indeed to minimize the quest itself, should end up blurring the distinction between God and man. But then, precision in language is never the strong suit of enthusiasts, and a few ill-conceived catch phrases invariably leave them mired in inconsistencies.

JOHN WESLEY

No doubt many stout Evangelicals would be offended by the primacy of place given John Wesley in Knox's gallery. The indefatigable founder of Methodism seems such a practical reformer, preaching up and down England and even in America a simple Gospel message, not letting

[34] Quoted in Herbert Thurston, *Surprising Mystics*, ed. Joseph Crehan (Chicago: Henry Regnery Company, 1955), p. 132.

[35] Knox, *Enthusiasm*, pp. 333–34.

fatigue sap his apostolic zeal until death caught up with him at the age of eighty-eight. He personally visited all the seventy thousand or so souls in the British Isles who accepted his message and were thus directed "Godward". And he was such an authoritative figure that he could expel any backsliding adherents—which he did with great frequency—without endangering his leadership role. An ordained Anglican minister, he was not averse to drawing inspiration from Catholic sources, even Jesuit sources. In the fervor of the revivalist meetings he held, he could stand aloof from the emotional upwellings of his congregations and analyze them coolly in his journals.

The opportunity to be dragged into the full flowering of enthusiastic sects lay all about him when he was attempting to discern his mission. Despite the fashionable overlay of Deism, England in the early eighteenth century still contained a welter of groups from Anabaptists to Quakers and Moravians that could capture an earnest seeker's spirit. But despite an attraction to Count Zinzendorf's circle, he could not accept their approach to spirituality, which smacked of antinomianism and even licentiousness. In his subsequent dispute with them, he even reminds Knox of Bossuet battling the Quietists.

Even within his own circle, he was the more measured theologically. George Whitefield, cofounder with Wesley of Methodism, unrivaled orator and originator of the lay preaching that was a hallmark of the movement, was a rigid believer in the Calvinist doctrine of predestination. Wesley saw Calvinism as opening the door to antinomianism: if man's free will played no role in determining whether or not one was to be saved, why exert any effort to live a moral life? For thirty years, the two pillars of Methodism labored side by side holding these diametrically opposed visions of what conversion (the essence of their missionary work) entailed. "The inevitable separation was only staved off by the immense respect which the rival controversialists had for one another; against their own better judgment they persisted in trying to convince themselves that their differences were of minor importance. Never were theologians so resolved to make a molehill out of a mountain."[36] But the issue came to a head at a conference in 1770 when Wesley and his allies engineered a condemnation of the predestinarians, only to find themselves outvoted the

[36] Ibid., p. 496.

next year at a similar meeting called at the behest of the Calvinist Lady Huntingdon, financier of the movement and ally of George Whitefield. The schism was so deep that the composer of the Evangelical hymn "Rock of Ages" castigated Wesley as "a venal profligate" and "a grey-headed enemy of all righteousness" among other less flattering epithets.[37]

That schism would invade his own movement could not have been utterly surprising to Wesley. What he did not anticipate was that his own followers would break with the Anglican communion to which he was wedded, however jaundiced a view toward his ministry was adopted by its bishops. He sought no separation, just a wider latitude. But the centrifugal forces tearing at the church were actually more jurisdictional than doctrinal. Anglicanism tolerated a spectrum of believers and sinecure seekers among its leadership, so Wesley could have maintained a toehold in its establishment. But the lay preachers upon which he relied developed an appetite to do as the ordained Church of England ministers did. And when the Revolutionary War in America discredited the Anglican clergy there, he was left with a fertile field for growth and no means at hand to get ordained ministers sent over to the new republic. So he commissioned five men himself to act as ministers, laying his hands on them ordination-style. One of them then ordained others in America, one of whom (Francis Asbury) then assumed the title of bishop. Wesley was furious at this turn of events but eventually adopted a dual approach to orders: in England, Anglican orders had to be obtained; in America and elsewhere, the Presbyterian mode was sufficient. Bishops in these lands were to be elected from among the presbyters and then perpetuate the ministry more democratically.

But even that slippery slide away from sacramentalism does not qualify for Wesley's inclusion among the enthusiasts. It is in what happened at Methodist gatherings that one sees the overpowering emotionalism that bears such a striking resemblance to the spectacles occurring during the Sifting Time of the Moravians or at the cemetery where the Jansenist convulsionaries displayed their preternatural powers. Wesley himself could raise a congregation to a fever pitch so that a predictable response would ensue:

[37] Quoted in ibid., p. 502.

> There is a cry, or a roar; usually (not always) the afflicted person drops to the ground; you can see that he or she is something in the position of the demoniac healed after the Transfiguration; Satan is letting his prey go, with the utmost reluctance. The bystanders fall to prayer; if there is no immediate deliverance the interrupter is carried out, and prayer goes on, often till late at night. We do not hear, commonly at least, of people foaming at the mouth; but in these as in other cases of religious convulsions we are often told that it took so many strong men to hold the energumen down.[38]

These are the symptoms of a congregation undergoing "convincement" during an outpouring of God's grace after a Methodist sermon. It is sometimes claimed on Wesley's behalf that they were the normal accompaniments of the birth of a new movement, that they disappeared early in his ministry, and that he himself did not put much stock in them. But the entries in his journal belie that explanation. While his early preaching in some communities called forth emotional excesses not to be repeated later at that locale, the phenomena reappeared throughout his fifty-year ministry whenever he brought his revivalist message to a new community. He recorded the reaction meticulously and saw in it a visible proof that the Holy Spirit was at work among the people.

At the same time, Wesley was well aware that others were eliciting even more remarkable responses from their adherents, including a sect known as the Jumpers, of whom he records the following description: "Some of them leaped up many times, men and women, several feet from the ground; they clapped their hands with the utmost violence; they shook their heads, they distorted all their features, they threw their arms to and fro, in all variety of postures; they sung, roared, shouted, screamed with all their might. . . . The person of the house was delighted above measure, and said, 'Now is the power of God come indeed.' "[39] Wesley has no qualms about ascribing these displays to satanic influence. However, an account he penned in 1772 of one of his own revivalist meetings seems to record hardly more edifying behavior:

[38] Ibid., pp. 521–22.

[39] Quoted in ibid., p. 533.

> On Saturday evening God was present through the whole service, but especially toward the conclusion. Then one and another dropped down, till six lay on the ground together roaring. . . . Four young men . . . came out of mere curiosity. That evening six were wounded. . . . One of them, hearing the cry, rushed through the crowd to see what was the matter. He was no sooner got to the place, than he dropped down himself, and cried as loud as any. The other three, pressing on, one after another, were struck in just the same manner. And indeed all of them were in such agonies, that many feared they were struck with death.[40]

The disinterested observer might be forgiven for not being able to discern which scene was of God's doing, which of Satan's. But John Wesley knew.

What is especially important to recognize is that the concept of hysteria, of overwrought emotionalism, does not suggest itself to him as a plausible alternative to supernatural agencies. That is because he took it for granted that the emotions must be engaged to the fullest in the unfolding of God's commerce with mankind, and hence there are no extremes to be met with when an outpouring of God's mercy is being experienced. The very notion of a calm intellectual acceptance of the Gospel was alien to Wesley and his fellow preachers. A turnaround in one's behavior could take place only in consequence of a searing experience of God's presence, one that in most instances is so vivid and so irrevocable that the date of its occurrence can henceforward be memorialized as a birthday. Against a Mennonite minister who had stigmatized Wesleyanism as a fanatical sect, he countered that his movement "is no other than heart-religion, in other words, righteousness, peace and joy in the Holy Ghost. These must be *felt*, or they have no being. All therefore who condemn inward feelings in the gross, leave no place either for joy or peace or love in religion, and consequently reduce it to a dry, dead carcase."[41] One should palpably feel a love of God, and sense too that one is loved by him. The emotionally charged atmosphere at the revival meetings was to be expected as the Holy Spirit poured forth grace on the newly regenerated.

[40] Quoted in ibid., p. 530.

[41] Quoted in ibid., p. 537.

Yet as Wesley matured, his private journal entries recorded occasional doubts that God always granted sensible consolations to favored souls. The common teaching of the Catholic mystics that the emotions are a most unsure guide to the state of one's soul came again into view, thereby redeeming Wesley partially in Knox's view from thralldom to what he calls a "terrible doctrine".

But the damage was already inflicted on the English psyche. Centered around an emotional response to the preaching of John Wesley and his heirs, the religion of many English Protestants was bound to become a subjective affair.[42] After being slain in the Spirit or convicted of God's Word, the beneficiaries of that grace could proclaim that God had transformed their lives but would have difficulty imparting to an outsider anything more enlightening than an account of the emotional thrill undergone in the experience. Rational argumentation of the kind that Catholic apologetics employs to fan the spark of incipient faith in the seeker would hold no place in the new converts' arsenal of proselytizing weapons. But the insufficiency of such a religion does not lie only in its incommunicability. While the enthusiast is impervious to rationalist detractors of faith (remember that Wesleyanism took root against a backdrop of Deism, in an eighteenth century where cynicism was de rigueur among the fashionable), reliance on the consolations of faith runs high and needs continual reaffirmation: "[H]e expects much (perhaps too much) of his religion in the way of verified results; he is easily disappointed if it does not run according to schedule. It must chime in with his moods, rise superior to his temptations; a decent average of special providences must convince him that it works. Otherwise, though without rancour, he abandons the practice of it."[43] From the standpoint of modernity, the evanescence of the Wesleyan spirit could

[42] An exhaustive account of the same phenomenon as it manifested itself in one particularly fertile domain in the United States a generation or two later is the classic study by Whitney Cross, *The Burned-Over District: The Social and Intellectual History of Enthusiastic Religion in Western New York, 1800–1850* (New York: Harper Torchbooks, 1965). An emotional brew of Evangelical revivalism, teetotalism (some of the proponents of which wanted to ban coffee and tea as well as all alcoholic beverages!), abolitionism, and other causes resulted in a strange assortment of religious ventures. Most famous of these are Joseph Smith's Mormonism, William Miller's Adventist millennial campaign announcing the Second Coming in 1843, the Oneida Community's sexual communism, and the spread of Spiritualism in the 1850s.

[43] Knox, *Enthusiasm*, pp. 547–48.

hardly be more evident. Methodism has retreated to a place among the more subdued Protestant creeds. But more importantly, the English people's distrust of philosophical precision, already undermined by heart-religion, poisons the well for a Catholic apologetic undergirded by appeals to reason and common sense. Knox characterizes the altered religious landscape thus: "You needed neither a theology nor a liturgy; you did not take the strain of intellectual inquiry, nor associate yourself whole-heartedly with any historic tradition of worship. You floated, safely enough, on the little raft of your own faith, eagerly throwing out the lifeline to such drowning neighbours as were ready to catch it; meanwhile the ship was foundering." [44]

SPEAKING IN TONGUES

While the experiential religion of Wesley is the last movement of the eighteenth century to occupy front and center in Knox's history, the

[44] Ibid., p. 589. For a vigorous denunciation of Wesleyanism from an Anglican viewpoint, see Sabine Baring-Gould, *The Evangelical Revival* (London: Methuen and Co., 1920). Baring-Gould (1834–1924) was a colorful Devonshire parson, antiquarian, folklorist, and travel writer who is best known as the author of the hymn "Onward Christian Soldiers". He deplores the Evangelical movement in the Church of England as the source of lapses into dissent, skepticism, and conversions to Rome, because it became a vehicle for pernicious doctrines such as Calvinist predestination and Methodist instantaneous conversion. The following extract suffices to convey his opinions of its Calvinist strain: "[S]uch Christians as had not been sent to an Evangelical Sunday school, had not been fed up on, and relished, the Religious Tract Society leaflets, had not been roused to conviction by Mr. Jabez Jaques, or Mr. Ezechiel Hornblower, all these, and every Papist, the humble priest living with and ministering to the lepers, every little Sister of the Poor, every child that dances 'round about the mulberry bush,' every reader of Scott's novels, every play-goer, every Sabbath-breaker who, having toiled all the week in a close office, mounts his bicycle to fill his jaded lungs with fresh country air, the ragged slum-girl, who toils all day dragging about in her arms a fretful baby-brother, soothing it with kind words and loving kisses, sharing with it her slice of bread with a smear of treacle on it, the rough unscripturally instructed sailor, who helps the women into the only boat from a wreck, and himself, with folded arms, waits on deck to go down into the deep; the soldier unacquainted with the Evangelical shibboleth, who is blinded with liquid fire, fighting for his King and Country; the nurse who succumbs to cancer contracted through ministration to a peevish patient, because she is a Catholic; aye, and the babe that dies in convulsions in its mother's arms, rained on from her eyes, before it has intelligence to acquire a Saving Faith—all these, failing to produce their coupons, meet with the same sentence from the inexorable would-be Judges in white chokers: 'Be damned, all the sort of you!' Veritably the Jacobin committees in the Reign of Terror, the Bolsheviks of Moscow, were mercy and justice compared with these men" (p. 247).

nineteenth century supplied too many new emotionally charged religions to ignore completely, though many of their features can be traced back to spiritual ancestors whom he has already subjected to close scrutiny. There is, however, one curious phenomenon, which appears with the Scottish preacher Edward Irving around 1830 and which is far less common than has often been supposed.

That is the practice of glossolalia, or speaking in tongues. Irving was a gifted revivalist of Presbyterian stock who actively sought a renewal of the Pentecostal experience of the apostles. He and his own disciples believed that the utterances elicited at their meetings were precisely what Saint Paul had in mind when he spoke of the tongues of men and angels. Some of the verbalizings were taken to be specimens of foreign languages, usually sufficiently obscure that the procurement of a natural speaker as an interpreter might take so long that the afflatus would have long since ended before it could be put to the test. Or else they were reported to be of a heavenly dialect, though why pure spirits needed to utilize acoustic vibrations to communicate (as Knox had one of his characters wonder in his novel *Other Eyes Than Ours*) is not clear. It should be recalled by way of contrast that the historical occasion documented in Acts when the Apostles preached under the inspiration of the Holy Spirit describes them as speaking in perfectly intelligible local languages to multitudes of people of different nationalities gathered in Jerusalem.

Knox sees a different process at work in the modern phenomenon:

> It must be confessed, however, that the characteristic specimens of Irvingite glossolaly which have been preserved to us are beyond the reach of any lexicon. Such utterances as "Hippo gerosto niparos boorastin farini O fastor sungor boorinos epoongos menati" or "Hey amei hassan alla do hoc alors lore has heo massan amor ho ti prov his aso mi," hardly bear out the claim that "the languages are distinct, well-inflected, well-compacted languages." The philology of another world does not abide our question, but if we are to judge these results by merely human standards, we must admit that a child prattles no less convincingly.[45]

Two points Knox brings out are especially instructive on this phenomenon, which has reappeared with some gusto in modern times.

[45] Knox, *Enthusiasm*, p. 553.

The first is that Irving himself looked askance at certain noninitiates' efforts to fathom these tongues. Even a sympathetic observer who possessed some facility in various languages was rebuked when he suggested some benign translations of what he heard spoken in Irving's London church. Far from wishing to impress on people the rationality of what his preaching wrought, Irving gloried in the suspension of that faculty and the yielding to pure emotional release entailed in glossolalia. Only the willingness "to abate thy trust in thine own understanding" provided fertile ground for faith.

More curious still is that there does not appear to have been much of a lineage for the phenomenon, despite the appeal to Pentecost. Of all enthusiastic sects from Montanists to Wesleyan revivalists, only a small Jansenist sect and an extremist Huguenot offshoot, both extant in the late seventeenth century, laid claim to the gift of tongues, and then only for a short time. Loose assertions to the contrary in encyclopedia entries under *glossolalia* are too quick to identify prophecy (such as the Montanists practiced) with the gift of tongues. But the Montanists, and other sects, were never belabored by their antagonists for speaking in unintelligible sounds, and surely if they had thus spoken, the charge would have been laid against them.

But once the Irvingites discovered its efficacy, glossolalia caught on with the early Mormons and then spread around the globe with various smaller cults. Knox was not alive to see its full flowering in the charismatic movement, which crossed denominational boundaries. There is no doubt, however, that he would have recoiled at the sight of people engaging in this emotion-laden activity in Catholic services and would have regarded as wholly misguided the emphasis placed on being slain in the Spirit by otherwise orthodox Catholic believers.

It can be seen from this brief survey of the most far-reaching and ambitious literary endeavor of his near half-century as an apologist that Ronald Knox was thoroughly convinced that the emotions are a faulty guide to one's spiritual state. The great mystics in the Catholic tradition could all be lined up as witnesses to that very point. The practice of virtue and the experiencing of the presence of God in this life are achieved in very unspectacular ways. A close reading of most saints' lives reveals little, and sometimes nothing, on record of an experience of ecstasy, while their work in the vineyard is seemingly mundane, consisting of the spiritual and corporal works of mercy.

There will always be people seeking a shortcut to spiritual fulfillment. Recent decades have, perhaps more than ever before, witnessed to people's urge to fulfill themselves rather than accept life as a journey marked with signposts to heaven. Psychology, political ideology, consumerism, and nontraditional spirituality all conspire to turn people inward to examine their wants and needs. The age is impatient with duty and with submission to time-tested authority. Enthusiasm has even found its way into the Catholic Church and seduced many who several generations ago would have been immune to its charms. It is therefore a time when Knox's great admonitory historical work can serve as a check on imprudence and downright folly.

CHAPTER ELEVEN

THE TIMELESS WORD

No book is written without a stimulus. To understand what motivated Ronald Knox to undertake a translation of the Bible, a brief excursus on the status of what was available in English in the mid-twentieth century is necessary.

BIBLE TRANSLATIONS

Protestant Bible Translations

Among very many English-speaking Protestants on both sides of the Atlantic, there remained (as there still remains today) a sturdy belief that the team of forty-seven scholars convened by King James I of England brought forth in 1611 the Scriptures as God himself would have dictated them in our tongue. All later Bible translations were measured—and usually found wanting—in the popular mind against that touchstone, judged worthy or not in proportion to their fidelity to its sonorous phrases and cadences. No matter that those seventeenth-century translators based their work on Greek manuscripts that later scholarship revealed to be more corrupted by copyists' errors than other texts were. The King James Bible was the Authorized Version, and although no record remains of how it became authorized to displace the Great Bible of 1539, the Geneva Bible of 1560, or the Bishops' Bible of 1568 (the records having perished in a 1619 fire), the popular presumption has been that God authorized it and that attempted alterations represent tampering with his Word.[1] Of course as profoundly

[1] Indeed, the records of the whole process of the King James translation are sparse, including how many scholars actually worked on it. A lively account of its production is

as spoken and written English were subsequently influenced by the monumental work put before the public with the King James translation, the language inevitably continued to evolve as all living languages do, and many hallowed verses found in the Authorized Version appeared progressively more stylized and less limpid.

The Anglican hierarchy took note of this fact, as well as of the advances made in evaluating Greek texts and in understanding Hebrew nuances, and brought out a Revised Version in the 1880s, while their American counterparts completed a separate revision, appropriately called the American Standard Version, in 1901. The reception accorded each of these texts was what might be expected: satisfaction on the part of some scholars who sensed greater precision and clarity, dissatisfaction on the part of other scholars who sensed obfuscation and desacralization, and indifference on the part of many who were committed to passing on the Authorized Version from generation to generation as an inviolable heritage. The American translation was then updated again by a team of experts who began work in the 1930s, with the Revised Standard Version appearing under the auspices of American Protestant churches in 1952. Finally, after World War II ended, the Church of Scotland and the Church of England began collaborating on a new translation into modern English, which finally appeared in the 1960s as the New English Bible.

While these revisions carried the weight of some church body behind them, it should not be supposed that they represented the only non-Catholic efforts at Bible translation into English undertaken in the nineteenth and twentieth centuries. On the contrary, bookshelf space in the pious Protestant's library could be filled with competing texts, several of them the work of individual translators. For example, an

---

given in Adam Nicolson, *God's Secretaries: The Making of the King James Bible* (New York: Harper Perennial, 2005). He points out that it did not overtake the Geneva Bible in popularity in England until the 1660s, while across the Atlantic the exigencies of life produced a different response: "Seventeenth-century America was a country of strictly enforced state religion and as such needed a Bible much more attuned to the necessities of nation-building than anything the Separatists' Geneva Bible could offer. It is one of the strangest of historical paradoxes that the King James Bible, whose whole purpose had been nation-building in the service of a ceremonial and Episcopal state church, should become the guiding text of Puritan America. But the translation's lifeblood had been inclusiveness, it was drenched with the splendour of a divinely sanctioned authority, and by the end of the seventeenth century it had come to be treasured by Americans as much as by the British as one of their national texts" (p. 230).

amateur linguist named Ferrar Fenton completed a loose translation in 1903 that proved fairly popular. James Moffatt, a professor of church history in Glasgow and later at Union Theological Seminary in New York, published his own translation in the 1920s, and Edgar Goodspeed, with some collaborators, brought out a version intended for American readers in the 1930s.[2]

Nevertheless, the Authorized Version remained the wellspring of the Word of God for countless preachers, devotional readers, and even for those whose Scriptural knowledge extended no further than catch phrases picked up through popular culture.

Martin's Douay-Rheims Bible

Among British Catholics in Ronald Knox's time, the picture was considerably less complicated. Thirty years before King James' scholars completed their work, and ten years before Rome adopted a revised official Latin version of the Bible, known as the Clementine Vulgate, an English translation of the New Testament was published by Gregory Martin, a scholar of the English College then at Rheims. This college, founded by Cardinal William Allen in 1568 at Douay, was the intellectual center of the Catholics living in exile during the reign of Queen Elizabeth I. The disorder attendant on religious warfare in the Low Countries necessitated the college's temporary removal to Rheims, but by the time Martin's translation of the Old Testament was printed in 1609, the college had returned to Douay. His Old Testament translation was actually completed in 1582, the year of his death, but its publication was delayed because in the meantime the Vulgate was being revised in response to the wishes of the Council of Trent. An edition appeared under the name of Pope Sixtus V, and then the Clementine version reached its final form in a 1598 edition. Martin's successors at Douay made minor adjustments in his translation accordingly. Hence the name Douay-Rheims Bible. The translation was based on the then-current version of the Latin Vulgate, but Martin kept a close eye on the Greek and Hebrew texts as well, and it is of interest to note that

[2] A detailed account of these and other translations is given in F. F. Bruce, *The English Bible: A History of Translation from the Earliest English Bible to the New English Bible* (Oxford: Oxford University Press, 1970).

the Anglican architects of the Authorized Version made copious use of his New Testament in arriving at their translation.[3]

Challoner Bible

However, the erosion in the allegiance of English-speaking people to Catholicism throughout the seventeenth and early eighteenth centuries is amply illustrated by the fact that the Old Testament, after being reissued in 1635, saw no later printing for almost one hundred years. By the mid-eighteenth century, when Bishop Richard Challoner oversaw a small and dispersed Catholic community, he recognized the need to update language already a century and a half removed from contemporary written English. But while Martin was an accomplished Hebraist and classical scholar and had colleagues at Douay in Cardinal Allen and Richard Bristow who could advise him, Bishop Challoner had to proceed without the aid of critical reviewers, trusting to his own sense of the apposite phrase or word to replace an obscure Tudor turn of speech. So whereas the Douay-Rheims was a translation, albeit one heavily laden with Latinisms because of Martin's desire to render Vulgate terms faithfully, Challoner's contribution was simply an updating of the English of that translation. And yet John Henry Newman, who himself had been considered by the English hierarchy in 1855 to oversee a new translation of which nothing came, claimed in an 1859 essay in the English Catholic periodical the *Rambler* that Challoner's work was more than a revision:

> Looking at Dr. Challoner's labours on the Old Testament as a whole, we may pronounce that they issue in little short of a new translation. They can as little be said to be made on the basis of the Douay as on the basis of the Protestant version. Of course there must be a certain resemblance between any two Catholic versions whatever, because they are both translations of the same vulgate; but this connection between the Douay and Challoner being allowed for, Challoner's version is even nearer to the Protestant, than it is to the Douay; nearer, that is, not in grammatical structure, but in phraseology and diction.[4]

[3] See Hugh Pope, *English Versions of the Bible* (St. Louis, Mo.: Herder, 1952), pp. 263–65.

[4] Quoted in Edwin H. Burton, *The Life and Times of Bishop Challoner (1691–1781)*, vol. 1 (London: Longmans, Green and Co., 1909), pp. 285–86. See also Ian Ker, *John Henry Newman: A Biography* (Oxford: Oxford University Press, 1988), pp. 466–68.

Bishop Challoner continued to revise his own text through new editions, the sixth edition being published in 1777, twenty-eight years after the first. His willingness to amend his text throughout his lifetime encouraged others to do the same, and so derivative editions appeared at regular intervals: Dr. Troy's Bible in 1791, Dr. Murray's Bible in 1835, and Dr. MacHale's New Testament in 1846, each of these named after prominent Irish bishops who modified the Challoner text of the New Testament while leaving his Old Testament virtually untouched.

KNOX'S LITERARY APPROACH TO BIBLICAL TRANSLATION

The text read by Catholics when Knox began his translation work in Aldenham in 1939 was consequently in its essence almost two hundred years old, thereby making it as antiquated to Knox and his contemporaries as Martin's Douay-Rheims translation was to Bishop Challoner and his contemporaries. Critics could easily summon up passages that illustrate the Challoner revision's obsolete language, and Knox had frequently to do so himself to explain to tradition-bound Catholics why the hierarchy asked him to produce a new translation and why he had acceded with alacrity to that summons.

But rather than draw attention to archaisms and Latinisms, it may be more to the point to examine just one among many chapters in Scriptures that becomes particularly opaque in the Challoner revision. At the beginning of one of his letters to the Christians of Asia (Eph 1:3–6), Saint Paul launches into a hymn of praise to Christ for redeeming mankind. Because he is a quick thinker, and sometimes rather impulsively changes direction and alters metaphors, he is often rendered obscure by translators seeking literal word-for-word equivalencies. Here is how Challoner, updating Martin, conveys Saint Paul's words of thanksgiving:

> Blessed be the God and Father of our Lord Jesus Christ, who hath blessed us with spiritual blessings in heavenly places, in Christ:
>
> As he chose us in him before the foundation of the world, that we should be holy and unspotted in his sight in charity.

> Who hath predestinated us unto the adoption of children through Jesus Christ unto himself: according to the purpose of his will:
>
> Unto the praise of the glory of his grace, in which he hath graced us, in his beloved son.

The general idea here comes across, but what happens when the reader looks closely at the text? What does being blessed with spiritual blessings in heavenly places mean? What does the string of words "unto the praise of the glory of his grace" mean? A few verses later (Eph 1:11–14), it continues:

> In whom we are also called by lot, being predestinated according to the purpose of him who worketh all things according to the counsel of his will.
>
> That we may be unto the praise of his glory: we who before hoped in Christ:
>
> In whom you also, after you had heard the word of truth (the gospel of your salvation), in whom also believing, you were signed with the holy Spirit of promise.
>
> Who is the pledge of our inheritance, unto the redemption of acquisition, unto the praise of his glory.

The reader must make a strenuous effort to interpret these lines and still will come up empty-handed when confronted with unintelligible phrases like "the redemption of acquisition". No relief will be gained by resorting to the Authorized Version, which translates the same verses as:

> In whom also we have obtained an inheritance, being predestinated according to the purpose of him who worketh all things after the counsel of his own will: That we should be to the praise of his glory, who first trusted in Christ.
>
> In whom ye also trusted, after that ye heard the word of truth, the gospel of your salvation: in whom also after that ye believed, ye were sealed with that holy Spirit of promise,
>
> Which is the earnest of our inheritance until the redemption of the purchased possession, unto the praise of his glory.

Even many late-twentieth-century translations suffer from a penchant for literalism at the expense of clarity. The New American Bible, which is used in Catholic liturgical readings in the United States, still retains the phrase "for the praise of his glory" in verses 12 and 14, as does the New International Bible, an undertaking of conservative Evangelical Protestants. The former translates verses 5 and 6 as: "In love he predestined us for adoption through Jesus Christ, according to the purpose of his will, to the praise of his glorious grace, with which he has blessed us in the Beloved." It cannot be argued that this is much clearer than Challoner's rendering. What does Knox do with the verses? He begins:

> Blessed be that God, that Father of our Lord Jesus Christ, who has blessed us, in Christ, with every spiritual blessing, higher than heaven itself. He has chosen us out, in Christ, before the foundation of the world, to be saints, to be blameless in his sight, for love of him; marking us out beforehand (so his will decreed) to be his adopted children through Jesus Christ. Thus he would manifest the splendour of that grace by which he has taken us into his favour in the person of his beloved Son.

The latter part of Saint Paul's introduction becomes

> In him it was our lot to be called, singled out beforehand to suit his purpose, (for it is he who is at work everywhere, carrying out the designs of his will); we were to manifest his glory, we who were the first to set our hope in Christ; in him you too were called, when you listened to the preaching of the truth, that gospel which is your salvation. In him you too learned to believe, and had the seal set on your faith by the promised gift of the Holy Spirit; a pledge of the inheritance which is ours, to redeem it for us and bring us into possession of it, and so manifest God's glory.

If the respective word counts are tallied, it will be seen that the Knox translation of Ephesians 1:11–14 is 30 percent longer than the Challoner version of Douay-Rheims, and yet it reads far more smoothly because verbal bridges have been built to help the reader follow the Pauline transitions and asides. Knox himself noted, in a reference to the writings of the Old Testament prophets that applies as well to the writings of the Apostle to the Gentiles:

> The transition from one sentence to the next must be made logically clear, even at the cost of introducing words which are not there, but are implicit in the context. Your vocabulary must be chosen, not so much by reference to the use of this or that word elsewhere in the Old Testament, as by reference to the needs of this particular passage—token-words will not do. You must cast your sentences into a form which will preserve not only the meaning but the *rhetoric* of the original, or the flying wrack of imagery will pass you by.[5]

He opts decidedly for a literary, as opposed to a literal, translation of a text. The point of translating is to put a foreign writer's thoughts into language understandable by the reader, and that means employing idiomatic expressions in the reader's tongue, not translating word for word the idioms of the author's tongue. While most people are aware of the pitfalls awaiting the word-for-word translator of living languages (and thus, for example, would avoid rendering "*Quanti anni fa*?" by "How many years do you make?"), the authority of the Bible as the Word of God has left even seasoned linguists hesitant to adopt any but a literal translation:

> Douay was consistent; it translated the Latin word for word, and if you protested that its version sounded rather odd, replied woodenly, "Well, that's what it says." In the eleventh psalm, for instance, you get the words "deceitful lips, they have spoken heart and heart." Even Challoner saw that that would not do, so he pillaged from the Authorized Version and gave us "with a double heart have they spoken." I don't see what a double heart could be except an abnormal anatomical condition, or an obscure kind of convention at bridge; but anyhow it sounds a little more like English. But when the Latin had "renew a right spirit within my bowels," that was what Challoner put; and when the Latin had "Examine, O Lord, my kidneys," Challoner put that down too; only he changed kidneys to the obsolete word "reins," hoping that his readers would not look it up in the dictionary.[6]

[5] Ronald Knox, *Trials of a Translator* (New York: Sheed and Ward, 1949), pp. 33–34. This series of essays occasioned by his work of translation was first published in England under the title *On Englishing the Bible*.

[6] Ibid., p. 8.

Knox had to confront many reflexive biases, both among Catholic and non-Catholic critics, when he began publishing his translations. To Catholics, it had become almost sacrilegious to tamper with Challoner's basic text. The nineteenth-century editions mentioned previously, and others too numerous and too obscure to list, all derived from Challoner; none of them was based on a fresh translation of the Clementine Vulgate. (Only a translation of the four Gospels direct from the Greek by the great historian John Lingard represented a fresh start, and it never caught on.) All these revisions were written in what Knox calls Bible English, a literary form that was distinct even from the idiomatic English language used by prose writers contemporary with Gregory Martin and the forty-seven scholars behind the Authorized Version. Bible English was preternaturally old, and it was often irredeemably dense, since it often departed from common English usage the better to adhere to a Latin syntax.

Even though Catholics notoriously lagged behind Evangelicals in poring over the Bible, the familiarity gained by repeated exposure to selected, largely New Testament, texts from their recurrence in the liturgical cycle made changes all the more jarring to pious ears. To find fault with Challoner was to find fault with a received text. Knox's goal, however, was to produce a translation that would have been intelligible to a seventeenth-century reader, in language that a mid-twentieth-century reader would recognize as contemporary and that a mid-twenty-second-century reader would find comprehensible and not unduly archaic. It is too early to grade him on the last requirement, although early twenty-first-century readers can compare his prose favorably with that of the newest translations. His quest for a timeless English was not as far-fetched as some critics assumed when he proclaimed it over a half century ago. It should be noted, however, that Knox did see a place for a deliberately hieratic language in liturgical texts. Consequently, to view him as a forerunner of liturgists who produced vernacular texts devoid of the majesty inhering in the Latin texts from which they are derived would be to misread him. The Bible is meant to be read at home, and so, a translation that makes the reader comfortable is in order. The liturgy is a public drama and calls for tradition-bound language.

A corollary of Knox's goal as a translator is that the text should read as if it were an original composition. "Any translation", he observes, is a good one in proportion as you can forget, while reading it, that it is a translation at all. Do not be deceived when your friends tell you that they *like* Bible-English. Of course they do, reading or quoting a few sentences; there is a slow-moving thoroughness about it which conveys a sense of dignity—you get the same in an Act of Parliament. But if they would try to read a chapter on end, which they never do, it would rapidly become tedious, and the attention would begin to wander; why? Because they are reading a foreign language disguised in English dress.[7]

CRITICS OF THE KNOX BIBLE

Criticism on the basis of style was not lacking from friends. Both Arnold Lunn and Robert Speaight expressed the wish that instead of embarking on a new translation, Knox should have contented himself with a revision of the Authorized Version of 1611, which they believe would have drawn more Anglicans closer to the Catholic Church. As Lunn observes in typically combative mode:

Why should we Catholics create *unnecessary* obstacles between ourselves and other English Christians? Why must we even have different names for so many Biblical characters? What Catholic mother would ever talk about a Noe's Ark to her children? Why not imitate the robust confidence of the early Church, which boldly appropriated anything it required from classical antiquity, building the columns of pagan temples into Christian churches, adapting her own feats to synchronize with the pagan feasts and incorporating details of pagan ceremonies?[8]

Speaight goes even further, convicting him of turning rhythmic poetry into pedestrian prose with his translation of the Magnificat and even accusing him of not having the proper literary skill to translate a text into contemporary English. "Knox", he says,

had to turn his back on the whole literary idiom of English-speaking Christianity; to forget the accumulated associations of three centuries; and create something in tune with the modern ear—even if it was not in tune with the modern mind. And the trouble

[7] Ibid., pp. 36–37.
[8] Arnold Lunn, *And Yet So New* (New York: Sheed and Ward, 1938), pp. 20–21.

> was that where poetry was in question—and much of the Bible is poetry—Ronald Knox did not really have an ear for modern literary idioms. In that, as in so much else, he was a pre-1914 man. I make bold to say that the Knox Bible would have been a far more exciting literary achievement if it had been written by Father Martindale. Realising perhaps that he was not really a "modern," Knox deliberately tried to write in a style of what he called "timeless" English—a kind of back-kneed genuflection to the enduring spell of the Authorised Version, which, try as he might, he could not quite conjure away. Where the translation fails—and again I speak only from the literary standpoint—it fails for this reason. The trouble is not in the least that it is modern, but that it is not modern enough; that here, for once, Ronald Knox is not playing his own literary game.[9]

On the other hand, Protestant and secular critics have belabored him not for his abandonment of venerable phraseology but chiefly for his adherence to the Latin Vulgate as the basis for his English text. Solange Dayras, a linguistics expert at the University of Paris, claims that "he did not benefit from the privilege granted to his American counterparts of being able to consult the original", which led him to adopt translations that tilted the texts toward official Catholic teaching. She instances his use of the phrase "do penance" instead of "repent" in Matthew 12:41 in light of the Vulgate "*poenitentiam agere*" whereas the Greek *metanoein* suggests the less confessional (in both senses of the word) term. She also faults him for retaining Mark 16:9–20 and several other verses that are part of the Vulgate text but do not appear in the best Greek manuscripts. And she characterizes as an egregious instance of showing "concern for doctrine rather than for science" his footnote commentary on Matthew 1:25, which in the Knox translation reads, "and he had not known her when she bore a son", and which Knox, after saying that even though the Hebrew should be more literally translated "till she bore a son", then asserts that this does not impugn the perpetual virginity of Mary. Of his Old Testament, she remarks that his style "weakens what is strong and direct" in such poetic works as the Song of Songs. She contrasts his translation

[9] Robert Speaight, *Ronald Knox: The Writer* (New York, Sheed and Ward, 1965), pp. 212–13.

unfavorably with that of Moffatt, whose "sensual lyricism" is preferable to Knox's "rather affected elegance".[10]

Appreciation of style is subjective, and F. F. Bruce, who has other bones to pick with Knox over translation, proclaims that in comparison with other translations, and in particular with Moffatt's, "the Song of Songs has probably never been rendered into such beautiful English as in Knox's version." Bruce, a renowned Protestant exegete, nevertheless holds that viewed in its entirety, "Knox's version inevitably suffers from the limitations inherent in the fact that it is a secondary version—a translation of a translation." Although he marvels at the skill Knox employed to overcome the restriction of adhering to the Latin text, he avers that "no one will go to his version for help in determining the precise sense of the original".[11] In addition to noting his inclusion of those verses absent from the Greek, he disputes Knox's rendering of some key words. For example, he faults Knox for underplaying the doctrine of justification by faith in Saint Paul's Epistle to the Romans. As is well known, the Authorized Version has a strong predilection for the word *righteousness*; Knox would use *virtue* or *holiness* in its stead: "Where justification is in view—God's pronouncing the verdict of Not Guilty on the sinner and conferring a righteous status on him—the introduction of such words as 'holiness' and 'virtue' tends to confuse the issue."[12]

But here it is Bruce who is sacrificing accuracy for theological one-upmanship. The word at issue in Hebrew and in Greek has multiple meanings, according to Knox, depending on the context:

> . . . when used of a man, innocence, or honesty, or uprightness, or charitableness, or dutifulness, or (very commonly) the fact of being in God's good books. Used of God, it can mean the justice which punishes the sinner, or, quite as often, the faithfulness which protects the good; it can mean, also, the approval with which God looks upon those who are in his good books. Only a meaningless

[10] Solange Dayras, "The Knox Version, or the Trials of a Translator: Translation or Transgression?" in David Jasper, ed., *Translating Religious Texts: Translation, Transgression and Interpretation* (New York: St. Martin's Press, 1993), pp. 44–59. The issue of the term *until* is addressed later in this chapter.

[11] Bruce, *English Bible*, p. 208.

[12] Ibid., p. 212.

token-word, like righteousness, can pretend to cover all these meanings.[13]

TEXTUAL MATTERS

It is somewhat surprising that critics such as Bruce, whose book on English translations of the Bible appeared first in 1961 and in revised form in 1970, and Dayras, whose essay appeared in a 1993 book on translations of religious texts, neglected to consult the three volumes of commentary on the New Testament that Knox published between 1952 and 1956. These volumes show the mind of the translator at work. Why, with many variants in the Latin and in the Greek, does he light on a given phrase or word to complete a sentence? Why pick a different English word to translate a single Latin or Greek word in two different sentences? Where are the places the ancient copyists must have slipped up, because a phrase necessary for logical continuity is missing? What happens when the Vulgate gives one sense and the Greek gives another? No critic who has not combed through these commentaries thoroughly can claim competence to judge Knox as a translator, whatever be that person's reputation in exegesis or linguistics. The Biblical texts, for all the great care and attention bestowed on them by saints and scholars, remain somewhat fluid. There is in fact no received text that is entirely free of corruption—whether through omissions, additions, juxtapositions, or other defects resulting from their transmission through the ages. That is not to say that one can legitimately craft a translation simply to suit one's preconceived ideas about what the Bible ought to say. Scholars no doubt have arrived at a percentage, whether upwards of 95 percent or a higher number, of the words in the original texts that are indisputable, and no great import attaches to many of the disputed ones. The critic and the translator, however, are aided in their task of choosing the more probable of variant readings by the fact that the Gospels and the Epistles especially are documents that emerged from an already existing community, the Church, which handed on her beliefs through Tradition. Granted, words used in the written text, such as *grace* and *sin* and *redemption*, and *bishop* and *deacon*, had not yet been solidified in their meaning because they

[13] Knox, *Trials of a Translator*, p. 14.

were being appropriated to a new situation, one that the Greek-speaking world prior to the appearance of Jesus could hardly have formulated in the same sense as the Christians now did. Knox freely admitted parting company with those scholars of the Bible who treated the documents much as a geologist would treat strata of rocks, layer upon immobile layer to be mechanically assigned a degree of priority based on scientific laws. Rather, he saw their writers as living men of the first century, the impress of whose thought is discernible not only in the writings they left behind, often enough in a language that was not their native tongue, but also in the living community that handed on their faith in Jesus Christ to succeeding generations through an oral and living Tradition.[14]

[14] As the distinguished French theologian Yves Congar put it: "Tradition does not age, for to grow old is to change. It is the transmission through time, time which alters all things, of a deposit of faith; but, above and beyond the successive transmissions of this deposit, Christ the Incarnate Word, reigning as Lord above time, in giving the Church its very life, assures too the continuing identity of the truth possessed by the Church. 'Jesus Christ is the same yesterday and today and for ever' (Heb 13.8). We must go even further than this. Tradition is not the simple impermanence of a structure, but a continual renewal and fertility *within* this given structure, which is guaranteed by a living and unchanging principle of identity."

And citing a specific example of the role of tradition, Congar observes: "[T]here was infinitely more in the reality of the Eucharist celebrated by Christ than there is in the accounts given of the sacrament and its institution by the New Testament writings. The New Testament witness is contained in about forty verses: their great richness has not yet been exhausted by commentary, but they still only constitute a testimony, whereas the Church *possesses* the reality to which they witness. The Church was present and communicated at the celebrations of the apostles, who had in turn been with and communicated from the hands of Christ. When, on the days after Pentecost, the faithful devoted themselves to the breaking of bread (Acts 2.42, 46), there as yet existed no written charter for the Eucharist, and when that was drawn up later it would merely report the facts, and express the Church's faith, without further details. While the Old Testament described in great detail the rites for the paschal and sacrificial celebrations, the New Testament lays down nothing; there was a living model to be followed, handed on together with the very reality it celebrated. The Eucharist was thus celebrated for about thirty years before any text existed to make mention of it: it was *par excellence* an object of 'tradition.'" See Yves M.-J. Congar, *Tradition and Traditions: An Historical Essay and a Theological Essay* (New York: Macmillan Company, 1967), pp. 264–65 and pp. 350–51. This is a comprehensive and irenic study of the meaning of tradition, which nevertheless has to condemn the exclusion of the Church from her role as guarantor of the sacred deposit of the faith in the writings of such Protestant theologians as Oscar Cullmann and Karl Barth.

An excellent overview of the relations between Scripture and tradition by a Biblical scholar can be found in Bruce Vawter, C.M., *The Bible in the Church* (New York: Sheed and Ward, 1959), especially pp. 40–73. And yet the same author, in a later volume, *This*

The guardian of that Tradition was the Church centered in Rome, which exercised a maternal custody over the Bible as a record of her own beginnings and her prehistory in the Jewish people. The Church used the Scriptures from the beginning of her existence—the early Epistles being read and reread, and passed from Christians in one city to those in another. As the centuries passed, it devolved on the Church to determine which books ought to comprise the Bible and to establish an official version for use in the liturgy and for reading. Hence the Vulgate produced by Saint Jerome and updated in the late sixteenth century during the papacies of Sixtus V and Clement VIII. Ronald Knox had been commissioned to update the then-current English version of that Vulgate, not because the hierarchy wanted to impose intellectual blinders on him, but because the Vulgate remained the official Roman Catholic text. Knox and other Catholic scholars were well aware of its divergences on several points from the best Greek manuscripts, and even mistranslations of minor words, but if his translation were to be true to his commission and bear the approbation of the English hierarchy, it had to be done from the Church's official text.

Contemporaneous with his labors, a team of scholars under the general editorship of Cuthbert Lattey, S.J., was publishing the Westminster Version of the Bible, each book being issued individually, based on the original languages, for a Catholic audience. But this effort, the first volume of which appeared in 1913, with the New Testament being completed in 1936, was a private scholarly enterprise. It certainly was not frowned on by the hierarchy: its roll call of contributors included many of the foremost Catholic Biblical experts of the day, including a bishop. But it was not meant for use in English missals,

---

Man Jesus (New York: Doubleday, 1975), often falls into the trap of a rigid adherence to the canons of a form criticism slanted by liberal Protestant presuppositions. Aidan Nichols, in a critical analysis of Alfred Loisy's approach to Scripture, Church history, and theology, has put the issue very succinctly when he says: "[T]he possession of dogmatic faith should be regarded not as a disadvantage, but as an enabling advantage for the historian or exegete, precisely in their own work. Dogmatic faith does not make it more difficult to practise the historical study of Christian origins; it makes such study easier, by giving one clearer light in which to see one's subject." Nichols, *From Newman to Congar: The Idea of Doctrinal Development from the Victorians to the Second Vatican Council* (Edinburgh: T and T Clark, 1989), p. 111.

which still carried the old Challoner Douay-Rheims translation opposite the Vulgate text. That is where the Knox version would supervene, so the laity could follow along as the Gospel and Epistle readings were proclaimed at Mass and finally hear the texts in a language no longer too stilted to comprehend. Then perhaps they would be inclined to continue their Bible reading at home and delve into texts that were not included in the yearly liturgical cycle.

KNOX'S BIBLE COMMENTARIES

Gospels

The commentaries provide the rationale underlying Knox's choice of words and phrases and even his inclusion of contested verses, some of which were cited by critics as indications of shortcomings in his translation. It is instructive then to look first at several of the textual decisions he made, which occasioned their displeasure. His inclusion of Mark 16:9–20 at the end of the Gospel of Mark is certainly one of the major points of dispute with a number of exegetes. He readily admits their absence from the earliest manuscripts, and notes Saint Jerome's doubts about their authenticity,[15] as well as the evident change of style from the rest of Mark beginning with verse 9, and the awkward reintroduction of Mary Magdalen. Knox dismisses as implausible the notion advanced by some exegetes that it is based on Luke's Gospel, surmising instead that it might be "the rough notes of a catechist's instructions, on the lines of I Corinthians 15:3–8, which may have been pressed into service to fill a gap, although the reference to the Magdalen betrayed it as belonging to a different context".[16] The text is very old, and Saint Irenaeus, who lived at the end of the second century, attributed it to Mark. So Knox concludes that it might have been "an aide-memoire on the Resurrection known to have been used by the Evangelist" brought in by an editor to fill the gap left by the truncation of the original text. In any case, it is canonical, accepted by the

[15] For a good discussion of St. Jerome's approach to translating, see the essay by Louis Hartmann, "St. Jerome as an Exegete", in *A Monument to St. Jerome*, ed. Francis X. Murphy (New York: Sheed and Ward, 1952), pp. 35–81.

[16] Ronald Knox, *A Commentary on the Gospels* (New York: Sheed and Ward, 1952), p. 116.

Church, and worthy of inclusion as part of the sacred writings. His discussion of this controversial text illustrates the fact that he was quite conversant with the variations in the ancient manuscripts and with the opinions of Biblical scholars. But the Vulgate represented the official approved text, so issues of how much weight is to be accorded the manuscripts, although fully aired and considered, ultimately yield in his plan of translation to the authority of the one text carrying the Church's sanction.

As for the allegedly biased footnote accompanying Matthew 1:25, there is a fuller explanation in the commentary, where he cites passages in Hebrew and Greek to show the inadequacy of the English word *until* in that context.

> It is misleading to translate, in verse 25, "he did not know her until she bore a son," the word "until" having a force in our language which is unknown to its Hebrew equivalent. In I Mach. 5.54 (to quote a single instance out of many) it would be absurd to render "none of them had fallen until they all returned safe and sound." The Greeks, too, had this usage; "they sent away the envoys before hearing them" (Thucydides 2.12). No argument, therefore, can be derived from this turn of speech against the doctrine of our Lady's perpetual virginity. Nor does the phrase "her first-born" imply, in this context, that she had other sons afterwards; it is evidently meant to inform us that she had had no sons before, and was therefore under the obligations mentioned in Luke 2.22–24.[17]

Another illustration of the care he uses in examining the aptness of a particular word arises early in the Fourth Gospel. When Jesus answers Nicodemus' question about being born again, John 3:8 employs an analogy that seems weak: "The wind breathes where it will, and thou canst hear the sound of it, but knowest nothing of the way it came or the way it goes; so it is when a man is born by the breath of the Spirit." A footnote cites the opinion of Maldonatus that Jesus is speaking of the breath of life, but again the commentary is far more illuminating:

> But does "the wind" really give a good sense here? No wholly satisfactory answer has been found to St. Augustine's objection; viz.,

[17] Ibid., p. 2.

> that almost the only thing we *do* know about the wind is whence it comes and whither it goes. So far as Greek is concerned, the wind is mentioned some thirty times in the New Testament, and not once by the word here used. But the essential difficulty lies deeper. Our Lord appears to be saying that the behaviour of persons acted upon by the Holy Spirit is as unpredictable as the wind; has this really anything to do with the context? The point to be established is that spiritual regeneration is a fact, no less than natural birth. The activities proper to spiritual regeneration are not in question; and if they were, they should be illustrated by the activities proper to natural birth, not by atmospheric conditions. Verse 8, thus interpreted, is a loose leaf in the argument.
>
> A suggestion which deserves far more attention than it has received is that of Maldonatus, that "breath" here simply means "breath"—the breath of life, as in Matthew 27.50 and Apoc. 11.11. The mysterious phenomenon of animal life appears capriciously, granted to man or horse, denied to tree or stone. You can verify its presence, most obviously, by that expulsion of the breath which produces animal sounds, but you cannot tell how it comes (Ezech. 37.10) or how it goes (Ps. 145.4). So it is with the spiritual re-birth; it is granted, you cannot tell why, to one man, not to another. This interpretation seems to satisfy the requirements of the context, without doing violence to the language or forcing the thought of the sentence.[18]

Indeed, footnotes to a modern Bible must be brief, unlike in the sixteenth century, when translators used them to carry on verbal warfare with their theological opponents. When Knox appends a footnote to Matthew 11:11, in which Jesus says that the least in the kingdom of heaven is greater than John the Baptist, he simply draws attention to the forerunner as the last figure of the old dispensation, who did not enjoy the blessings available to the least among people under the new dispensation. The commentary offers a richer interpretation of the text:

> The words "least" and "greater" read strangely nowadays, because we are accustomed to think of "greatness" as the description of a man's inner character. But by Hebrew usage "greater than he" is equivalent to the phrase "more highly privileged than he;" and in

[18] Ibid., p. 211.

> this sense it is not difficult to understand the comparison made. The two following verses seem to allege the reason for it. Under the new Dispensation the kingdom of heaven is open to all comers, you can jostle your way in as you will, whereas up to, and including, the ministry of St. John the Baptist, the world was still under the old Dispensation—the kingdom of heaven was something prophesied in the future, not something to be realized here and now.[19]

Often enough, obscure texts involve probable corruptions of the original, corruptions that have appeared even in the earliest extant manuscripts. When Jesus exhorts his disciples to let the light of their faith shine on lampstands rather than remain hidden, he adjures them in a phrase that appears somewhat circular in its reasoning, if Luke 11:36 is to be accepted exactly as the Greek text is written:

> This verse is not necessarily part of what our Lord said; it may be only an explanatory note by the author, to bring out our Lord's meaning. If so, it has failed of its purpose; few verses have been so much discussed, and with so little profit. The literal sense of the Greek is: "If therefore thy whole body is lightsome, having no part darksome, thy whole body will be lightsome, as when the lamp lightens thee with its flashing." The tautology is obvious, nor can we really get rid of it by underlining one phrase in the first part of the sentence and another in the second, by way of marking a different emphasis. Suspicion has arisen, therefore, about the genuineness of the text. If we are to alter the text, we can perhaps do so with least disturbance if we suppose that Luke did not write the word "lightsome" twice over, but used two different words, only distinguished from one another by a single letter. One ought to mean "made of light," the other "full of light." The sense would thus be, "If thy whole body is *photinon*, made of light—that is, connatural to the light and sympathetic to its influence—the whole of it will be *photeinon*, full of light—actually lighted up by the presence of the lamp without." The sentence is better rounded off, if we suppose that by some error of reduplication our text reads "as when" instead of a plain "when." Only in so far as it is capable of absorbing the light does a body become luminous.[20]

[19] Ibid., p. 19.
[20] Ibid., pp. 156–57.

Where a comparison of the recounting of incidents common to the Synoptic Gospels shows a discrepancy, he attacks the problem with the same precision he devotes to the construction of an elaborate detective story, with its interlocking embedded clues calculated to be deciphered by a logician of similar temperament. In Matthew 24:36, Jesus is quoted as saying that the day and the hour of the end of the world are known only to the Father. The comparable verse in Mark 13:32 adds the phrase "not even to the Son". Apparently Saint Jerome puzzled over whether the phrase should be added to Matthew but decided against it, even though many early manuscripts included it. Knox observes that the phrase does not tell against the divinity of Jesus, since, even though it does not refer to his human knowledge (for otherwise Mark would have used Son of Man instead of Son), it merely indicates that it represented knowledge that was not to be communicated to mankind. But which text has priority, that with or that without the phrase that could lead to confusion?

> They may be an insertion, based on Mark. On the assumption that Matthew, when he wrote, had Mark's text before him, that will mean that he omitted the words as likely to give rise to a theological misunderstanding. On the assumption that Mark, when he wrote, had Matthew's text before him, it will mean that Mark restored the full form of the utterance from private sources of knowledge. But the probability, in view of the manuscript evidence, is that Matthew's text did, originally, contain the utterance in its full form; then, in the time of the early Christological controversies, some copyist who was transcribing Matthew's Gospel (but not Mark's) came across the utterance and expunged it, as of doubtful theological tendency. Whatever may be said about the theory of interpolation in general, in this particular passage it lacks plausibility. Suppose a copyist anxious to ensure that Matthew agreed with Mark as closely as possible—why, with all the variations between the two Gospels in front of him, should he hit upon these three words as a suitable subject for interpolation; words which might, and in fact did, give rise to a long tradition of Christological controversy?[21]

Another interesting puzzle is presented by the story related in Mark of the boy possessed by an evil spirit, which caused him to go into

[21] Ibid., p. 106.

convulsions. When Jesus arrives on the scene, he is told that his disciples were unable to cast the spirit out of the tormented youth. After he rescues the boy from his ordeal and the disciples ask why they could not aid him, he replies that such spirits can be cast out only through prayer and fasting. The manuscript record is evenly split between texts including and omitting the words "and fasting". The corresponding account in Matthew includes the phrase, but the whole passage in that Gospel may be a later insertion. Knox adds that some texts have Cornelius in Acts 10:30 fasting and praying, others only praying, and likewise a passage in Saint Paul (1 Cor 7:5). The Vulgate omits mention of fasting in these instances. The following extract, while admittedly lengthy, and perhaps seeming to dwell too much on a discrepancy that might easily be overlooked, serves as an indication of just how thoroughly Knox approached his task as a translator.

> It can hardly be doubted that there has been, at some very early date, a systematic interference with the sacred text. Was it the influence of some Encratite sect, which was determined to ensure, even by forgery, a greater prominence for fasting in the New Testament? Or did some opponent of the same tendency delete, no less reprehensibly, a series of allusions which seemed to put fasting too much in the limelight? Three reasons may be adduced for suggesting that an omission in the text is, on the whole, more likely than an insertion.
>
> (i) The evidence for an omission is strong in the Gospel passage, slight in the Acts and in the epistle. That is what we should expect. In the earliest times, many copies of the Gospels must have been in circulation; many people must have known the Gospels almost by heart. If some designing person mutilated the sacred text, there would be every chance that the fraud would be discovered by means of cross-reference. Whereas in the Acts or in the epistles the omission of a single word might easily pass unnoticed. (Contrariwise, if a fraudulent *insertion* had been made it would have passed muster in the Apostolic writings more easily than in Mark.)
>
> (ii) Be the manuscript evidence what it may, antecedent probabilities must count. What is our Lord likely to have said, in discussing the difficulties of this particular exorcism? "There is no way of casting out such spirits as this, except by prayer" is a sentence curiously devoid of rhetoric. Had the Apostles, then, not prayed at all? Are there some evil spirits so easily expelled, that prayer is unnecessary? Obviously what our Lord means is that there are some spirits

too powerful to deal with by ordinary rule of thumb; you must have recourse to heroic measures. "Prayer" does not suggest heroic measures; "prayer and fasting" does, if you take it for a proverbial phrase, like "might and main," "tooth and nail," etc. (In Acts 10, it is perfectly natural that a Gentile proselyte in spiritual difficulties should have been fasting, though he need not necessarily have done so. In I Cor. 7 it is at least arguable that the mention of fasting improves the sense of the passage.)

(iii) If, with the majority of critics, we cut out Matthew 17.20 (17.21 in the Greek text) as a copyist's insertion, derived from Mark, then that insertion must have been made very early indeed. It is much the oldest criterion we have for determining the true state of the text in Mark. And the manuscripts which give Matthew 17:20 at all give it in the full form, "prayer and fasting."

At the same time, it may be questioned whether Matthew 17:20 itself has not suffered from tendentious correction, like Mark, Acts and Corinthians. The two principal manuscripts which omit "and fasting" in Mark 9 omit the whole of Matthew 17:20. It is difficult to believe that an interpolator would not be content with falsifying the text of Mark; tampering with Matthew as well would invite detection. Whereas a copyist anxious to obscure the notion of fasting might well strike out the whole sentence in Matthew 17, where the sense is complete without it, and the obnoxious word in Mark 9, where the omission of the sentence would have left an obvious gap.[22]

There are times when even the manuscript evidence itself cannot be given undue weight. When the disciples, as recorded in Luke 9:51–56, return from a trip to a Samaritan village indignant at the residents' refusal to welcome them, James and John ask Jesus whether the inhabitants should be punished with fire from heaven. The best early texts tersely combine two verses, but Knox is not convinced.

The suggestion that verses 55 and 56 ought to run simply "But he turned and rebuked them; and so they passed on to another village" is grotesque. Literary considerations here are decisive; the anecdote, so read, is not an anecdote; if there had been no record of what our Lord *said*, the story would not have been told at all. At some very early period, there must have been some tear in a manuscript, some accidental omission; and it might have been necessary, for all time,

[22] Ibid., pp. 94–95.

> to print three dots at the end of verse 54, in apology for the obvious lacuna. But fortunately the missing reply was preserved, probably not in Greek but in a translation, and it begins to reappear in important manuscripts of the ninth and tenth centuries. "He said, You do not understand whose spirit it is (people like) you share. (For) the Son of Man has come to save (men's) lives, not to destroy them"—the bracketed words occur in one manuscript, not in another, because the sentence has had to be retranslated. But there is no doubt about the sentiment, and it carries its own warrant of authenticity with it. There has been no borrowing from other passages, and the words have been accepted, for centuries, as worthy of Christ. The best manuscript tradition can be wrong. Very likely the words "But he turned and rebuked them" were not written by Luke; they may have been inserted, as a rather clumsy makeshift, to fill up the gap left by the omission.[23]

It is interesting to see how Knox posits the interrelationship between the Synoptic Gospels. He believes that Matthew, as traditionally held, was the first to be written but that a compilation of important sayings of Jesus followed, on which both Mark and Luke leaned for some of their narratives. Such an order of composition resolves the major Synoptic problems. On the other hand, the notion that Mark wrote first, followed by Matthew translating some of Mark into Aramaic, with a translator then putting Matthew into Greek, is difficult to reconcile with the close similarity in the Greek employed by the two Gospels. Putting Matthew first chronologically simplifies issues:

> It would explain all the really puzzling features of Synoptic criticism. It would explain (i) why Luke regularly follows Mark, not Matthew, in the incidents which he relates and in the order of his relating them; he followed Mark because he had no access to Matthew. It would explain (ii) why Luke so often disagrees with Matthew about the context of a saying, although the wording of it hardly varies at all; the document in his possession was based on Matthew's text, but was not at pains to give the various sayings in their historical order. It would explain (iii) why we so often get the impression, in these cases, that Matthew, not Luke, has given us our Lord's words in their true setting; Matthew depended on memories, or on

[23] Ibid., pp. 150–51.

a tradition, which recorded them in their historical context, whereas Luke had to fit them into his narrative as best he could.[24]

The traditional attribution of the Fourth Gospel to Saint John, the son of Zebedee, attested as far back as Papias, has withstood all the ingenious attempts to associate it with a second-century exponent of one of the then-current philosophical movements. To Knox, the Gospel text has the earmarks

> of a very old man, who has an old man's tricks of narration. He will recall, as if conjuring them up with difficulty, details about names and places and relationships which have nothing much to do with the story. He will give us little footnotes, as if to make sure that we are following; often unnecessary, often delayed instead of being put in their proper place. He will remember fragments of a conversation, passing on from this utterance to that by mere association of memory, instead of giving us a reasoned *précis* of the whole. He will alternately assume that we know the story already, and narrate it in meticulous detail. He will pass from one scene to another without giving us warning of the change. It is this atmosphere of detached reminiscence that gives the Gospel its literary character.[25]

There are rare occasions when Knox's explications of difficult texts are less than satisfactory. One verse that has caused headaches for commentators trying to square texts with consistent Church teaching is Matthew 19:9, where Jesus, after affirming the indissoluble nature of marriage, appears to offer an exception to the rule. It should be noted first that in a similar verse (Mt 5:32), where Jesus says that "the man who puts away his wife (setting aside the matter of unfaithfulness) makes an adulteress of her", the difficulty is readily disposed of when

[24] Ibid., p. xii. Knox acknowledges his debt to the abbot of Downside for insights into the ordering of the sequence of the Gospels. See Dom John Chapman, *The Four Gospels* (New York: Sheed and Ward, 1944), for a posthumously published series of lectures Chapman gave summarizing the available evidence on their authenticity and ordering. Dom John Chapman (1865–1933) was the son of an Anglican clergyman and was destined for orders himself until he converted to Catholicism in 1890. Eventually he joined the Benedictines and was ordained in 1895. A formidable linguist and patristics expert, he wrote many scholarly articles, some of which were collected in *Studies in the Early Papacy* (London: Sheed and Ward, 1928). A brief biography can be found in *The Spiritual Letters of Dom John Chapman, O.S.B.*, ed. Dom Roger Hudleston (London: Sheed and Ward, 1944), pp. 1–30.

[25] Knox, *Commentary on the Gospels*, p. xvi.

it is understood, as Knox comments, that the words "setting aside" are more accurately translated as "in addition to" or "over and above", so the reference is to the fact of the man becoming an adulterer by remarrying, and then the first woman following suit if she marries again. One wonders, then, why he did not simply translate the words thus, in accordance with his stated philosophy of rendering words, even from the Vulgate, by paraphrase to ensure the accuracy of the sense of a sentence. For Matthew 19:9, his translation runs: "[H]e who puts away his wife, not for any unfaithfulness of hers, and so marries another, commits adultery." Again the ordinary interpretation of the words suggests that if the woman is unfaithful, then the man does not commit adultery by divorcing her and marrying again. But Knox believes a more accurate rendering of the text would replace the words between the commas with "when it is not on account of unfaithfulness". Then the clause would simply be emphasizing the wife's innocence. But leaving aside the question why he did not use the latter phrase to minimize misinterpretation, it is certainly possible that the scholars who produced the Jerusalem Bible catch the real meaning of what Jesus said, when they translate the verse as follows: "[T]he man who divorces his wife—I am not speaking of fornication—and marries another, is guilty of adultery." The interpretation favored by some modern commentators is that Jesus is distinguishing between lawfully married people, for whom another marriage would constitute adultery, and people living together without benefit of matrimony, who could separate and marry others. The Samaritan woman at the well may perhaps be representative of a fairly widespread disdain for marriage as a social institution, then as now in human history.

Pauline Epistles

When he comes to Saint Paul, Knox is at his best, both as a translator and as a commentator. He recognizes that the task of the latter "is to discover, not so much what he said as what was on his mind when he said it".[26] Saint Paul wrote, or dictated, with some urgency and often

[26] Ronald Knox, *A New Testament Commentary for English Readers*, vol. 2: *The Acts of the Apostles; St. Paul's Letters to the Churches* (London: Burns, Oates and Washbourne, 1954), p. 70.

is not at pains to spell out his thoughts in deference to his readers. Consequently, he has been tragically misinterpreted throughout the ages. In fortifying the fledgling Christian community, Saint Paul warned against two major temptations of the age: the Judaizers, who would tie them to the confines of the old legalistic prescriptions, and the antinomians, who would twist Christianity into a license to dispense with the moral law.

It is against the former that he warns his readers in the third and fourth chapters of his Letter to the Romans. Protestant controversialists have sought to dismiss the Catholic understanding of the importance of good works as contrary to the thought of the apostle by quoting these verses, but they have simply misunderstood what he means when he employs the term *works*.

> The word "works" in [Ch. 4] verse 2 takes us back to 3.20 where the full phrase is given: "The works of the Law"—that is, fulfillment of the Law's obligations, circumcision included. In his earlier epistle to the Galatians, St Paul is careful to write "the works of the Law" throughout; by the time he wrote to the Romans, he took his theological vocabulary more for granted, and he is apt to use the shorter formula. But we must not be betrayed into the notion that he is referring to meritorious actions in general; the sense of compliance with the Law's demands, moral and ceremonial, is always present to his mind.[27]

Knox continues his examination of this section of Romans by noting the amount of wasted ink employed by theologians on both sides of the Reformation debates over whether the rest of Chapter 4 is to be interpreted to signify that justification occurs in response to the individual's merits or whether it is a gratuitous covering over of sins. In actuality, Saint Paul is talking only about Abraham, who obtained God's approval not through circumcision but by believing in God. In addition, when he continues to rail against the Law, it is not in the sense that the Law itself induces sin but that sin is compounded by also being a transgression against a positive Law, thereby further burdening people, inducing them to despair of fulfilling all its commands.

The role of the Law is amplified in Galatians 3:23–29, where Saint Paul uses the analogy of a childhood tutor to represent its formative

[27] Ibid., p. 82.

influence on the people chosen by God. Knox's summary well explains the thread of the argument.

> The human race, from Abraham's time to our Lord's, was (so to speak) in its minority; the promises are compared to an inheritance which is in trust, so that the heir cannot touch the revenues of it till he comes of age. The giving of the Law is not a coming of age; the Law is only like a tutor who is appointed, when the child reaches boyhood, to give him the instruction he will need when he grows up to manhood. The Law cannot justify us, any more than such a tutor can empower the heir to draw on the family revenues. It is only with Christ that the world comes of age, assumes the freedom of full sonship. If, having once tasted that freedom, we go back to the observance of the Mosaic Law, we are in exactly the same position as a grown-up man who should go back to the schoolroom and start his sums again.[28]

With the Corinthians, Christian inhabitants of a city notorious for its license, the predominant temptation was to succumb to the message of liberty, of independence from the moral law:

> [T]hey held themselves free, in Christ, not only from the ceremonial observances of the Old Law, but from its moral precepts as well. The Christian was a law to himself; it was his faith, not his actions, that made a Christian of him. We know from Romans 3.8 that St Paul himself was accused, by his detractors, of holding such views. And it seems quite possible that the words "I am free to do what I will," used here and repeated in 9.1, are a quotation from St Paul's own teaching, a "slogan" of his which referred to the controversy over circumcision and the other ordinances of Judaism. It has been caught up by the Corinthians in a wrong sense, and understood as covering the whole extent of the moral law, with disastrous results. St Paul, therefore, is at pains to correct the false impression; but it is characteristic of him (and perhaps deserves the attention of modern teachers) that he does not dwell on the sanctity of the moral law, but on the sanctity of the human body, redeemed by grace and destined for a glorious resurrection.[29]

Many puzzling Pauline phrases are brought into clearer focus by the commentaries. For instance, what precisely does he mean in

[28] Ibid., pp. 226–27.
[29] Ibid., p. 142.

Ephesians 1:23 when he refers to the Church as "the completion of him [Christ] who everywhere and in all things is complete"?

> A man's use of language is often unconsciously influenced by early associations; and it is perhaps worth noticing that St Paul, who had done his studies at the seaport town of Tarsus, must have been familiar with the nautical use of the word rendered "completion"—it meant a ship's crew or (as we say) "complement".... And he may well have thought of the Mystical Body as the essential complement of the Incarnation; if our Lord had not communicated the power of his risen life to a Church, the Incarnation would have remained somehow incomplete—like a head that has no limbs to derive life from it, a boat that has no crew to sail in it. Then, pulling himself up short, St Paul reflects that he has said too much; our Lord's humanity would have been complete in any case. So he adds the saving clause, paradoxical in form, "of him who is utterly, every way complete." [30]

He thoroughly airs the various attempts to explain what Saint Paul meant when, in writing to the Colossians, he spoke of helping to pay off the debt still left after Christ's afflictions. Those theologians who claim that he was merely trying to set an example with his fortitude do an injustice to the text. So do those who argue that Saint Paul was referring to the sufferings Christ endures through the Mystical Body. The language of the text does not support either assertion.

> If we attend closely to the language of the original, the sufferings of Christ are represented as a transaction in the past which has left a debt outstanding, and St Paul is making an "answering" contribution, doing something on his own part in return for something done by somebody else. And that can only mean that the meritorious sufferings of Jesus Christ have in some sense left a gap to be filled, and St Paul must help to do this in return for what has been done for him.[31]

There are so many important Christological passages in the Pauline writings, but one more quote on this topic will suffice to indicate Knox's ability to draw out their meaning with great clarity. In Philippians 2:6 he translates Saint Paul's statement about Christ as follows:

[30] Ibid., p. 246.
[31] Ibid., p. 285.

"His nature is, from the first, divine, and yet he did not see, in the rank of Godhead, a prize to be coveted." First, Knox notes that the commonly rendered phrase "being in the form of God" is inaccurate, since the Greek word usually translated as "form" had by then acquired a new meaning, more like "nature". Likewise, the word *being* should really be translated as "being already" or some such phrase implying prior possession of the attribute it refers to.

> What St Paul says is that our Lord, in coming to earth, did not think of his divine splendour as something which must be clung to at all costs; he laid it aside. He had the opportunity of impressing the world by appearing in majesty, but he did not grasp it. Just so, St Paul at Philippi had the opportunity of exercising his rights as a Roman citizen, but he did not grasp it. And the Philippians, if and when they get the opportunity of asserting themselves at the expense of their neighbours, are not to grasp it either.[32]

Finally, Knox offers a very convincing explanation of what Saint Paul meant in Second Corinthians 12:6 about "a sting to distress my outward nature, an angel of Satan sent to rebuff me". The common presumption is that he was either beset by a temptation of the flesh or (following a number of the early Fathers) some physical ailment. But Knox observes that in his cataloguing of travails endured while preaching the Gospel, he never alludes to any diseases or other bodily infirmities. He logged thousands of miles in Europe and Asia Minor and could hardly have done so had he not enjoyed robust health. As is often the case, Knox finds himself in agreement with one of the great Greek Fathers of the Church, Saint John Chrysostom, who asserted that the trial he was enduring was persecution. Knox narrows the sense further, to the persecution by his own people, the Jews. He cites as more than coincidental the use of the same term in the Book of Numbers to describe the Canaanites in relation to the Israelites, and in Ezekiel to describe what Tyre would be to the Israelites were it not vanquished.

> Is it not probable that St Paul had these two quotations, or one of them, in mind? In both of them, the "thorn in the side" meant a set of people; a set of people living close at hand, and belonging to

[32] Ibid., p. 268.

an older tradition. It was not an inappropriate description of his own Jewish fellow-countrymen, always at his side, always in opposition to him. "Flesh" is substituted for the "eyes" and "side" of the Book of Numbers, but perhaps with some hint of the word's Pauline usage. In Rom. 11.14 he refers to his fellow-Israelites as "my flesh," that is, his own flesh and blood; he was a Jew, with natural Jewish sympathies, and the hatred of his fellow-Jews was an affliction to his "flesh," to the natural man in him.[33]

John's Epistles and Apocalypse

The First Letter of Saint John is replete with verses inviting elaboration. Knox observes that it was likely not a single letter but rather a composite of several documents, since it does not begin with salutations to a particular community and contains many abrupt transitions. There is no doubt, however, of the identity of its author with the author of the Fourth Gospel. John was concerned lest some early Christians fall prey to Docetism, a heresy claiming that Jesus was not God made man but was only overshadowed by God between his baptism and his death, or equally dangerously, that they would be enticed by Gnosticism, the eclectic religion positing a hierarchy of divine beings mediating wisdom to initiates. In First John 4:2–3, the apostle succinctly distinguishes the true from the false prophets: "[E]very spirit which acknowledges Jesus Christ as having come to us in human flesh has God for its author; and no spirit which would disunite Jesus comes from God." The last clause, literally translated from the Vulgate, means "unfasten Jesus" and is not in the earliest Greek manuscripts, although it is cited by Saint Irenaeus and by Origen early in the third century. The Greek texts simply say "no spirit which does not confess Jesus". Knox argues that this difference represents yet one more instance where the Vulgate seems to have preserved the authentic saying, while the surviving Greek manuscripts contain a "corrected" version. The argument he marshals for opting for the priority of the Latin, and consequently supposedly later, text is yet another classic specimen of that combination of pure logic and psychological insight that is manifest throughout his commentaries:

[33] Ibid., p. 205.

> Commonly, "unfasten Jesus" is regarded as a gloss; that is, an explanatory note at the side, which somehow crept into the text and displaced the true reading. But is it thinkable that so ordinary a form of words as "does not confess Jesus" could need to be explained? Or that it could need to be explained by so obscure a form of words as "unfastens Jesus"? No, if the Greek tradition represents the words John wrote, the Latin tradition represents an attempt made by some orthodox person, early in the second century, to discredit the Christological heresies of his age by falsifying the text of John. But this view involves a difficulty which has not been sufficiently observed. If he wanted to emphasize the doctrine of the hypostatic union, why did he not talk about "dividing Jesus Christ," or "splitting up Jesus Christ," or "distinguishing between Jesus and Christ," instead of presenting us with this extraordinary locution, unheard of till his time, "unfastening Jesus"? Once the phrase had been coined, and passed as Scripture, it is obvious that it would be used against the Gnostics, the Docetists, the Nestorians, and so on. But is it the phrase which anyone would coin for this purpose? Is it not much more like the poetical expression of an inspired mystic, than the calculated formula of a scheming theologian?
>
> Whereas, if John wrote "which unfastens Jesus," the substitution of "which does not confess Jesus" would be, on critical grounds, understandable enough. The copyist, caught up by now in the rhythm of John's thought, expects the second half of the sentence to be the exact obverse of the first. But what is this? Instead of the "does not confess" which he has been waiting for, here is a word which looks like "unfastens;" unfastens Jesus? That would not mean anything. So he substitutes the phrase which he expected to find there; the phrase which is actually to be found in II John 7, where Antichrist is defined as one who does not confess Jesus Christ "coming in the flesh." Perhaps, if he is very conscientious, he writes the word "unfastens" in the margin, where it goes unnoticed.[34]

It should not be presumed that Knox was going out of his way to validate the Vulgate simply because it was the official version of the Church. For in First John 5:6, where again the Vulgate diverges from the Greek manuscripts, the lack of support in the form of quotations from the Fathers using the phraseology of the Vulgate is telling

[34] Ronald Knox, *A New Testament Commentary for English Readers*, vol. 3: *The Later Epistles; The Apocalypse* (London: Burns, Oates and Washbourne, 1956), p. 164.

evidence against its antiquity. It is likewise suspect because the version it gives, unlike in First John 4:2 above, is one that a copyist would hardly tamper with to make it more comprehensible.

But the Vulgate ought not to be dispensed with offhandedly. This entire section of First John 5, from verse 6 to verse 8, is anything but straightforward. In the Vulgate, there is a citation of Trinitarian witnesses followed by a second grouping of three witnesses on earth. Here is how Knox translates the three verses: "He it is, Jesus Christ, whose coming has been made known to us by water and blood; water and blood as well, not water only; and we have the Spirit's witness that Christ is the truth. Thus we have a threefold warrant in heaven, the Father, the Word, and the Holy Ghost, three who are yet one; and we have a threefold warrant on earth, the Spirit, the water, and the blood, three witnesses that conspire in one." The middle part of this passage is absent from the Greek manuscripts. Why did these words show up in the Vulgate? Knox suggests a possible explanation for the discrepancies that helps to untangle the obscurities of the selection:

> Namely, that what John wrote was the Greek text as we have it, but without the words "the Spirit and the water and the blood" in verse 8. In the first six verses of the chapter, John has been talking about God, and about Christ, the Son of God, the Two Witnesses of John 8.18. At the end of verse 6 he adds rather awkwardly, as if conscious of an omission, "And the Spirit—the Spirit is the Witness *par excellence*" (John 15:26). Then he adds that there are three masculine Subjects which bear witness; and these three are "into the one thing;" their witness is unanimous. He assumes that his readers will understand what he means; it is an explicitly Trinitarian formula. And so he goes on "if we accept the evidence of men, the evidence borne by God is still more cogent." But some copyist, yielding to the common temptation of inserting explanatory phrases in this epistle, sees the three words, water, blood and spirit, all contained in verse 6, and inserts them, regardless of their neuter gender, after "there are three that bear witness"—to the mystification of posterity. Somewhere in the West, where the unaltered text has survived, a more happily inspired copyist inserts "the Father, the Word, and the Holy Spirit" in the same place. A fresh copyist, with two manuscripts before him, one of either tradition, conflates the reading by copying in both; but he cannot resist toning down the sharpness of the contrast by adding "in heaven" and "on earth" at the appropriate

> points. This becomes the tradition in the West, though it is only a thin stream; in all the Greek and some of the Latin editions the old text, with the fatal gloss incorporated, holds the field.[35]

Given the keen insights into the meaning of texts that Knox displays throughout his analysis of the Gospels and Epistles, his examination of the Apocalypse comes as somewhat of a disappointment. The book, which he accepts as having been written by the apostle John, begs for commentary, not only on what it says, but on what it all means. Alas, Knox chooses to stick to the former and leave the latter to other commentators, among which he particularly recommends one written by C. C. Martindale.[36] In doing so, of course, he is maintaining the approach he has adopted throughout the three volumes, but the Apocalypse is a book unto itself, at least among New Testament books. An unraveling of a Pauline sentence reveals his thought, whereas an unraveling of a sentence in the Apocalypse only invites further questions. If the beast is the Roman Empire, what is its effigy? What cataclysm is alluded to with the sounding of the trumpets? How to explain the events surrounding the woman and the child of Chapter 12? Knox supposes that the Apocalypse is built up from multiple visions and that John wrote them down without any concern for their logical ordering. Therefore, any attempt to find a single key to unlock fully the symbolism contained within is futile. Observing the parallels and borrowings from Ezekiel is helpful, and Knox does try to mesh some of the prophecies with what John would have seen firsthand under the emperors Vespasian and Domitian. And yet one leaves this section of the commentary still somewhat uncertain about whole swaths of John's text.

Critics have left the impression that Ronald Knox was too conservative in his approach to the Bible. They point to his reluctance to deviate from the Vulgate text in his translation as evidence of his unquestioning adherence to authority. However, as the foregoing survey of his commentaries has shown, he paid close attention to the Greek and pre-Vulgate Latin texts of the New Testament, with their

[35] Ibid., p. 172.

[36] See C. C. Martindale, "The Apocalypse", in *A Catholic Commentary on Holy Scripture*, ed. Bernard Orchard et al. (New York: Thomas Nelson and Sons, 1953), pp. 1193–1208.

many variant readings, and he was not averse to offering ingenious reconstructions to explain how a word or verse arrived at its present place in the canonical text. As for his translation, if the Jerusalem Bible has the advantage of giving the reader the best attested translation of the Greek and Hebrew texts, Knox arguably still outshines all others in his presentation of the Pauline Epistles. His is no longer the authorized text in any English-speaking country, but it has perdured for sixty years as a most readable, if not yet "timeless", English version of the Scriptures.

Knox had set out to liberate the English Bible from encrusted archaisms. He was successful in doing so. In 1949 he predicted that "it is doubtful whether we shall ever again allow ourselves to fall under the spell of a single, uniform text, consecrated by its authority."[37] Now that prediction seems to be merely a forecast of the inevitable, but at the time it was not. Taken together with his New Testament commentaries, Knox's Bible represents a monument of scholarship and grace accomplished in the service of the Word of God.

[37] Knox, *Trials of a Translator*, p. v.

CHAPTER TWELVE

SERMONS AND RETREATS: NO MAN BUT JESUS ONLY

EUCHARISTIC SERMONS

In 1926 Knox was invited by Father James Kearney to preach on the Feast of Corpus Christi in the church of that name in Maiden Lane, a busy commercial district of London. He used the occasion to focus on the meaning of that central doctrine of Catholic theology and practice, the doctrine stating that Jesus Christ becomes physically present under the appearances of bread and wine at the consecration during Mass. The doctrine is almost two thousand years old, and saints and spiritual writers of every generation have often meditated on this mystery, which the Church uses the word *transubstantiation* to define as best language can. Knox followed their lead and over time elaborated a many-faceted commentary on the Blessed Sacrament, the initial invitation being renewed annually not only by Father Kearney but also by his successors, for the duration of his life. There exists, therefore, a collection of some thirty or so carefully crafted sermons on the Eucharist. The first nine were printed in a 1935 book titled *Heaven and Charing Cross.*[1] Seventeen new sermons joined three from the earlier volume in a 1956 compilation called *The Window in the Wall.*

[1] Ronald Knox, *Heaven and Charing Cross: Sermons on the Holy Eucharist* (London: Burns, Oates and Washbourne, 1935). The title comes from "The Kingdom of God", an unfinished work by the poet Francis Thompson, who, despite a life of frequent dereliction, was yet mystically attuned to God's presence all about him. The relevant verses are:

> But (when so sad thou canst not sadden)
> Cry;—and upon thy so sore loss
> Shall shine the traffic of Jacob's ladder
> Pitched betwixt Heaven and Charing Cross.

The congregation in Maiden Lane could anticipate each feast day a distinctive and profound glimpse into the inexhaustible mystery of God's compact with mankind from Knox, whose priestly life (so report all who knew him) centered around the celebration of Mass. He brought to his sermons not only the Scripture scholar's command of texts that foreshadow, and those that explicitly refer to, the Eucharist but also a sure knowledge of the mystical tradition in religious literature.

Lover at the Window

Take, for example, the sermon that lends its name to the second volume. Originally titled "Behind the Wall" but modified for the newer collection, it is a masterful evocation of the pursuit of a soul by Christ, educed from the story in the Old Testament where a lover calls out to his beloved, a captive in King Solomon's harem, to flee with him back to their own land. He appears at a window, and she recognizes him, and must choose between him and the worldly riches of a king's entourage.

The story, of course, is from the Song of Songs, whose presence in the Bible as a frankly secular hymn of love has frequently been cited by critics of Christianity as evidence of a lack of divine inspiration for the Scriptures: "No part of the Old Testament gives rise more easily to outraged astonishment, to pharisaical scandal, when it comes into the hands of the profane: that *this* should be reckoned as sacred literature. No part of the Old Testament, I suppose, has more endeared itself to the greatest friends of Christ; they would have spared all the rest to save this."[2] The squeamishness is born of Puritanism gone sour, Puritanism that is suspicious of creation and that soured when it jettisoned belief in the spiritual end of human life so that human love becomes an occasion for vapid sentiment or in its stead for smirking.

Yea, in the night, my Soul, my daughter,
Cry,—clinging Heaven by the hems;
And lo, Christ walking on the water
Not of Gennesareth, but Thames.

For the complete poem and Thompson's other works, see *The Works of Francis Thompson*, 3 vols. (New York: Scribner's, 1912). On his life, see Paul van Kuykendall Thomson, *Francis Thompson: A Critical Biography* (New York: Thomas Nelson and Sons, 1961).

[2] Knox, *Heaven and Charing Cross*, pp. 32–33.

One of the key ideas, however, that Knox is forever trying to get across to his hearers is that the realities of earth are pale imitations of deeper realities in the spiritual realm. As he puts it in one of his sermons, "the whole of this visible creation is but a thin plank between us and eternity".[3] Thus, he says, the water that gives life to mankind on earth is only a dim echo of the "living water" of which Jesus speaks to the woman at the well, and the bread fashioned from wheat is not an archetype but rather was given by God because it would be a useful image of the Bread of Life. So the cynics who deride the mystical writers for overlooking the overt sensual tone of the Song of Songs or for covering it over with religious symbolism as if merely to submerge its open endorsement of the love of man and woman are missing the point entirely. The allegorical approach can be taken too far, the analogies sometimes strained, but in Knox's hands the story becomes a powerful symbol of the appeal of Christ to the wayward sinner. The wall separating the lovers is constructed of spiritual dullness, layered over with sins:

> ... the wall of our corrupt nature, which shuts us off from breathing, as man breathed in the days of his innocency, the airs of heaven; the wall of sense, which cheats us when we try even to imagine eternity; the wall of immortified affection, which shuts us in with creatures and allows them to dominate our desires; the wall of pride, which makes us feel, except when death or tragedy is very close to us, so independent and self-sufficient. Our wall—we raised it against God, not he against us; we raised it, when Adam sinned, and when each of us took up again, by deliberate choice, that legacy of sinfulness in his own life. And through that wall the Incarnation and the Passion of Jesus Christ have made a great window; St Paul tells us so; "he made both one, breaking down the middle wall of partition," as the Temple veil was torn in two on the day when he suffered. He "made both one;" made our world of sin and sight and sense one with the spiritual world; made a breach in our citadel, let light into our prison.[4]

Knox is reminded of the symbolism of the window when he looks at the monstrance with the white Host elevated in the silence of a

[3] Ronald Knox, *The Window in the Wall* (New York: Sheed and Ward, 1956), p. 82.
[4] Ibid, pp. 2–3.

church, "a chink through which, just for a moment, the light of the other world shines through", while, outside, the bustle of people and traffic heralds the pursuit of the ephemeral.[5] Of course, the light is veiled because mortal eyes could no more encompass God in their sight than Moses could when he conversed with him on Mount Sinai. Now it is the mystery of transubstantiation that veils God from mankind, hides him by leaving the appearances of ordinary things, bread and wine, for the senses to behold, while he has left assurance that he is there present:

> Burn all the candles you will in front of it, call to your aid all the resources of science, and flood it with a light stronger than human eye can bear to look upon, still that white Disc will be nothing better than a dark veil, hiding the ineffable light of glory which shines in and through the substance of Christ's ascended Body. A veil, that is what we look at, a curtain drawn over the window, as you may curtain the windows of a sick-room, because the patient's eyes are not strong enough to face the full glare of daylight. But behind that curtain, all the time, is the window which lets our world communicate with the world of the supernatural. As the angels ascended and descended on Jacob's ladder, so here our prayers go out into the unseen, so here grace comes flooding through, like a rushing mighty wind, into the stagnant air of our earthly experience.[6]

And from that window Jesus beckons all to follow him just as the young man called to his betrothed:

> . . . calling us away from the ointments and the spikenard of Solomon's court, that stupefy and enchain our senses, to the gardens and the vineyards, to the fields and the villages, to the pure airs of eternity. Arise (he says), make haste and come. Come away from the blind pursuit of creatures, from all the plans your busy brain revolves for your present and future pleasures, from the frivolous distractions it clings to. Come away from the pettiness and the meanness of your everyday life, from the grudges, the jealousies, the unhealed enmities that set your imagination throbbing. Come away from the cares and solicitudes about the morrow that seem so urgent, your heavy anxieties about the world's future and your own, so short either of

[5] Knox, *Heaven and Charing Cross*, p. 14.
[6] Knox, *Window in the Wall*, p. 4.

them and so uncertain. Come away into the wilderness of prayer, where my love will follow you and my hand hold you; learn to live, with the innermost part of your soul, with all your secret aspirations, with all the centre of your hopes and cares, in that supernatural world which can be yours now, which must be yours hereafter.[7]

In its elegantly composed drawing out of the imagery of a text, its compelling presentment of God's relations with his creatures, and its restrained yet almost palpable fervor, this sermon of only some two thousand words is a remarkable essay in homiletics. Conciseness was Knox's forte; no wearisome digressions tempt the listener's mind to wander. The language is clear and precise, the logical development ineluctable. These, of course, are the staples of his preaching and what makes a collection of his sermons stand out as a literary achievement rather than take on the drab coloration of a theological tome or a polemical tract.[8]

Scriptural Lights on Communion

Astute insights appear so frequently in the pages of these sermons. Who, for instance, has not wondered about the parable of the invitation sent out for the wedding feast? Not the main part of the story, the parallels of which are fairly straightforward—the troubling part is about the guest who declines the wedding garment and is cast outside. Whom does he represent? Knox has a suggestion:

I don't know if it is just a fancy, but the explanation which I always suspect is that there was one man among our Lord's audience to whose conscience he wished to make a special and a last appeal. Judas Iscariot, although he had not yet betaken himself to the chief priests and made his infamous bargain, was, it may well be, already a traitor in heart; at least his future treachery was already known to him who knew all things. In a few days, he was to sit at the supper-table with the Master he was pledged to betray; most probably he was actually to receive, with that black purpose in his heart, that

[7] Ibid., pp. 4–5.

[8] Even as committed a non-Christian as George Bernard Shaw enjoyed listening to Knox preach when he was in Westminster Cathedral, as St. John Ervine notes in *Bernard Shaw: His Life, Work and Friends* (New York: William Morrow and Company, 1956), p. 556.

> very Body and Blood which he had sold for thirty pieces of silver. Called by grace not only to be a member, but to be an Apostle of the Church, he had already lost, or was soon to lose, the wedding-garment of charity which the Bridegroom's own hands had given him. A last warning, to bring him to his knees, if he will, before it is too late—surely that is how Judas must have heard the story. "Confess, Judas! Confess now, while there is still time! He has seen your heart already; he is only waiting for your confidence." That is the voice which Judas hears, and hearing does not heed.[9]

On another Corpus Christi, the parishioners hear the story of Ruth and Boaz offered as a type of the Blessed Sacrament. Knox modestly gives credit for the idea to a French book of meditations he has been reading, but the verbal brushstrokes are characteristically his. The daughters-in-law of Naomi stand for the worldly minded person (Orpha) who returns to her own people, and the faithful person (Ruth) who renounces the world to follow the law of Christ. It will be recalled that, in the story, Ruth must gather grain for the impoverished household by picking up the gleanings from behind the reapers of Boaz's fields. Now, Boaz can be seen as a figure of Christ, sowing the seed and producing a plentiful harvest of food. The reapers would be the saints, those who gather grace by the armful and have their fill of spiritual nourishment. It is left for the rest of mankind to be in the position of Ruth, collecting only stray crumbs of grace because of distractedness and the attraction of other fields that seem to promise more. Where have you gleaned today? is then asked. Do any other fields offer what our Lord does?

> Wherever we turn, whatever field of activity we choose for ourselves, you and I will only be gleaners still. Are we ambitious? Then see how few posts there are in the world by which ambition can really be gratified; others will reap the reward, we shall only be allowed to glean as best we may in their track. Do we desire knowledge, would we wrest from Nature yet more of her secrets? Then see, how many have been in the field before us; how they have swept it bare, and only left to us a few undistinguished avenues of research. Or would we fall back on the vulgar pursuit of riches? Here, too, we are too late in the field; others have been beforehand

[9] Knox, *Heaven and Charing Cross*, pp. 77–78.

> with us, have scraped up all the prizes, and left only the gleanings of their harvest for us who follow them. Would we live for mere pleasures? Why, this is a more pathetic fallacy than the rest! For who that ever asked for pleasure, found that he could fill his bosom with its grudging sheaves? No, pleasures themselves are only the stray pickings of life to be gleaned by the wayside; there is no satisfying yourself with them. Daughter, do not go to glean, for thou canst do no more than glean, in any other field but mine![10]

Boaz is aware of Ruth's predicament and ensures that a generous amount of grain is left in the wake of his farmhands.

> What other householder would so have instructed his servants? And who but our Blessed Lord would have left to us, his indevout worshippers, gleanings so rich from his all-sufficing harvest? Those wayward thoughts of ours, those wandering prayers—what sort of blessing could we expect that they would call down from above? We are not worthy of the least of his mercies, and he gives us—himself! In that Host which was carried round St Peter's this morning, with Princes of the Church for its escort, with multitudes adoring on every side, there was not more of Christ than in the Host which this morning the priest laid upon your tongue.[11]

In yet another parable, the hired servants play a more ignoble role. In the story of the prodigal son, it is the realization that the servants never go in need of their daily bread that brings the repentant son back to his father's household. The prodigal son had his real-life successors in the great-sinners-turned-great-saints who have acutely known what it is to live cut off from God. But the servants who have never strayed run the risk of taking their good fortune for granted.

> We act like hired servants, if we take pains to do no more for God than bare duty demands of us, jealously watching, as it were, the terms of our contract with him. The priest gets up and goes back to the sacristy, and we are on our feet before he can reach the door. We act like hired servants, if we think of our Communions only as they affect ourselves. "I go once a month," you say, "and really I

[10] Ibid., pp. 47–48.

[11] Ibid., pp. 48–49. The text suggests that this sermon was not preached during Mass but rather in conjunction with the Forty Hours' devotion Fr. Kearney held in his parish church.

don't seem to need more than that; there is very little to mention, as a rule, when confession-time comes round." Is that all the Body and Blood of Christ means to you, a kind of talisman to keep down the number of your sins? Or you say, "I'm not unhappy about my Communions; because when I make them and just after I've made them I always have such a wonderful sense of peace, of consolation." Is that all the Body and Blood of Christ means to you, a kind of spiritual treat you can indulge in now and again? When we go to Communion, you and I, we should aim at nothing less than making the life of Jesus Christ ours; immolating ourselves to God, annihilating ourselves before God, in him and through him and in union with his Sacrifice, so that we can say, "It is no longer I that live; it is Christ lives in me." Until we aim at that, the Bread of our Master's house is being wasted on us; we are hired servants, asking, and receiving, nothing better than a pittance for our livelihood.[12]

How Communion Should Influence Our Lives

There is a wealth of positive theology as well in these sermons. In a commentary on the Epistle to the Hebrews, where Christ is presented as saying "thou hast endowed me, instead, with a body", Knox associates the Eucharistic words *Hoc est corpus meum* (This is my body) with three stages in human life: birth, marriage, and death. These are times when individual Christians can offer their bodies in sacrifice to God in virtue of the merits obtained for them by God-become-man in Jesus:

He wore that Body in its state of infancy, humiliated, annihilated for our sakes.... This is my Body, for you, my Mother, to feed and tend; this is my Body, for you, my Foster-Father, to support and protect. He wore it in its state of maturity, espoused to poverty and hardship for our sakes; ... This is my Body, life-giving and life-bringing, stinted of food and sleep, traveling mile upon mile over weary roads, to claim that Church which is my destined Bride. He wore it in its state of death, drained of sweat and blood for our sakes; ... This is my Body, so torn with scourges and buffeting that it can scarcely be recognized; for you, with the nails, to crucify, for you, with the spear, to pierce, for you, Joseph, to bury, for you,

[12] Knox, *Window in the Wall*, pp. 18–19.

> Magdalen, to embalm. *Hoc est corpus meum*, the Body of a Man, belonging to me, who am God; here it is, helpless, here it is, overspent, here it is, pale in death.[13]

And then Knox proceeds to show how each Communion should be a recapitulation of those three stages: a preparation like the watching of the shepherds at Bethlehem, a reception affording an undivided union with God, and a thanksgiving modeled on the veneration the holy women showed his body when they came with precious burial ointments. And yet the Christ worshipped in the Eucharist is not dead. The Church has never doubted that it is the living Christ, body and soul, who is present in the sacred species:

> [T]he sacrifice of the Mass is a mystery, and perhaps its relation to the sacrifice on the Cross is the most mysterious thing about it. Only this is certain, that the Victim who is there presented to the Eternal Father for our sakes is the dying Christ; it is in that posture that he pleaded, and pleads, for our salvation, atoned, and atones, for the sins of the world. We herald that death in the holy Mass, not as something which happened long ago, but as something which is mystically renewed whenever the words of consecration are uttered. From the moment of his death on Calvary until the time when he comes in glory, the dying Christ is continually at work, is continually available. It is in this posture of death that he pleads for us, when the Mass is offered. And it is in this posture of death that he comes to you and me when he comes to us, the living Christ, in Holy Communion.[14]

Nor was Knox content to preach a theology of the Eucharist that concentrated solely on the relationship between the individual communicant and God. Several of these sermons were given while World War II raged, and even if Nazi Germany was imbued with a fundamentally anti-Christian philosophy, to be sure there were devout soldiers and civilians, fellow believers, caught on either side of the conflict. Knox could extol the bond of unity because a higher order than the political assured him of its existence:

> War has sundered the nations—yes, it can interrupt the exchange of commerce, of ideas, of diplomatic courtesies. It cannot interrupt

[13] Ibid., p. 56.
[14] Ibid., p. 97.

> the current of sacramental fellowship which unites us with all Christians, even with our enemies, when we and they partake of the same heavenly banquet. Only an unworthy reception, on their side or on ours, can interrupt that. The bread and wine which the priest will be offering a moment from now are gifts of unity and of peace, making us one with all our fellow Catholics, in Poland, in France, yes, in Italy and Germany too. Years may have to elapse before the external conditions of free intercourse are re-established between us. But by the greatest of all titles, as children round our Father's table, we are already at one. The Blessed Sacrament, the Jerusalem of our souls, stands apart from and above all the ebb and flow of world-politics, its citizenship a common fellowship between us and those who are estranged from us, those who at the moment are our enemies. Our friends yesterday, our friends tomorrow—in the timeless existence to which that altar introduces us, they are our friends today.[15]

In another sermon, he places it in a more homely context, one that may require less studied resolution to accept as theologically true but perhaps more charity to put into practice:

> [T]he Mass is essentially a corporate affair, a family affair, in which the priest is meant to stand out against a background of faithful laity; in which the laity ought to have the sense of sharing God's mercies with all the people round them, even with the woman who has taken their favourite seat, even with the man who looks as if he had come to rob the poor-box. The Mass is not just me worshipping; I am part of a crowd, the crowd of *circumstantes* [people standing around], who are making, by their concerted action, a joint offering to Almighty God.[16]

Father Philip Caraman, in his introduction to the volume of pastoral sermons in which these two books of Eucharistic sermons can also be found, rightly refers to them as a "modern treatise on the Blessed Sacrament", equivalent in their profundity to the work of any spiritual writer. It is quite a tribute to Knox's homiletic skill in treating this topic, that what were designed to be thirty separate talks given over thirty years could read as a single literary composition. And more

[15] Ibid., pp. 11–12.
[16] Ibid., p. 88.

so, in that they were written for oral delivery rather than for private reading. As Knox himself noted, the author of the printed sermon has a distinct advantage over his reader, but it is an ambiguous one: "To him, as he rereads it, every inflexion of voice, every unexpected piece of emphasis, every impressive pause recurs automatically; the words will not, for him, lie flat on the page. Association reawakes the emotions which he felt, and tried to inspire. And then he remembers other people's published sermons, and how terribly like dried seaweed they look."[17] Perhaps the desiccation is more pronounced when reliance is placed on oratorical flourishes to ensure the text's initial favorable response in the pews. Of course, there was none of that in Knox's mien: he was too diffident, and he detested showmanship at the altar or in the pulpit. His texts were meticulously crafted and were read to the congregation without embellishment.

PASTORAL SERMONS

Parables of Jesus

Another collection of sermons called *The Mystery of the Kingdom* comprises two series of talks, the first being twelve sermons on the parables of Jesus, and the second being reflections on the five separate futures awaiting the seed scattered in the parable of the sower. Knox adduces compelling arguments to show that in the parables, Jesus was preparing his hearers for the establishment of the visible organized Church on earth; indeed, the phrase "kingdom of God" is to be understood as "the Catholic Church". Not a very fashionable thesis among modern exegetes, and indeed not very fashionable in the 1920s either, but then the "Sadducee of to-day, like the Pharisee of our Lord's time, goes wrong because he skims lightly over the parables, and accepts their moral lessons without penetrating the theological mysteries which underlie them."[18] To be sure, there have also been some profound

[17] Ronald Knox, *The Mystery of the Kingdom* (London: Sheed and Ward, 1928), p. v.

[18] Ibid., p. 5. A short work by Wilfrid Harrington, O.P., purporting to get to the root of the parables in their original setting, *A Key to the Parables* (New York: Paulist Press Deus Books, 1964), signally fails to see the equivalence of the kingdom with the Church and is otherwise rather pedestrian in its insights, perhaps because of his admitted heavy reliance on the work of Protestant Scripture scholars. Knox, however, is not alone in asserting the

scholars, such as Henri de Lubac, who would dispute the identity of the phrases as they have been evoked in patristic and theological commentary, but Knox makes a compelling case as far as the parables themselves are concerned.[19]

It is important to recall that they were addressed to people who were encumbered with a predisposition to look for a political Messiah who would immediately establish a triumphant Jewish kingdom and destroy the Gentile hegemony. The parables are designed to disabuse them of those ideas, but the Pharisees and others closed their minds to the startling new message: seeing they see not, and hearing they hear not, neither do they understand—

> what a terrible irony there is in the situation of those Pharisees! The Messias has come, the kingdom is at hand; prophets and kings desired it long and died before the sight; these men have attained the privilege denied to their forefathers, to be the contemporaries on earth of the Son of God. He announces in a series of allegories the programme of his kingdom; and that is just what they want to hear him do. Want to hear it in order that they may trip him up in his talk and have material for accusing him and condemning him to death. They rub their eyes and cannot see; strain their ears and still cannot hear. "Now, what of that last parable? Surely we might make something out of that.... No, no, you can't go to the people with evidence of that sort. We must have proof, not vague insinuations and suspicions of double meaning." And all the time, under their very eyes, the death-warrant of the Old Covenant is being signed,

identity. In a book of short reflections first published in 1930, Bede Jarrett notes: "It is a curious thing that Our Lord usually uses the word Heaven when He is talking of the earth. It figures in such an expression as the 'Kingdom of Heaven,' and this means almost always the Church which He came to found here below." See Bede Jarrett, *The Space of Life Between* (New York: Sheed and Ward, 1945), p. 146.

Bede Jarrett (1881–1934) was an Oxford-trained historian who served as provincial of the English Dominicans from 1916 to 1932. Among his many administrative achievements was the establishment of the Oxford Blackfriars in 1929, the first priory in Oxford since the Reformation. Despite many years spent in governance and in near-constant travel to various Dominican outposts on three continents, he managed to leave behind an impressive array of historical and devotional writings. His life has been somewhat sketchily told in Kenneth Wykeham-George, O.P., and Gervase Mathew, O.P., *Bede Jarrett of the Order of Preachers* (London: Blackfriars Publications, 1952), but he deserves a new biographer.

[19] See Henri de Lubac, *Catholicism: Christ and the Common Destiny of Man* (1950; reprint, San Francisco: Ignatius Press, 1988), especially pp. 67–76.

> in words which those faithful auditors, the Apostles and disciples, will never forget. The Pharisees listen to the hated Prophet, and he says exactly what they want him to say, and yet God's Providence shuts those vigilant eyes, stops those attentive ears, and, to them, the message is lost. What irony! Surely, even if it were a mere human story, our pulses would thrill to read it![20]

Slowly but progressively, Jesus outlines a different future, its features discernible to a sympathetic hearer but eluding the grasp of the hardened of heart.

One reads in this light the story of the Good Samaritan. It has its obvious moral about charity to neighbors, but its theological significance is deeper. Of course the Good Samaritan is Jesus "on his journey"—come to earth—and the wounded man represents sinners, but how rarely are congregations told that the inn to which he is taken is the Church, and the innkeeper the successor of Saint Peter? The Church too is the leaven in the dough that energizes the society in which she acts; the treasure in the field that is alone worth the purchase price of Christ's sacrificial death; the mustard seed that grows slowly over time. When Jesus says that many are called but few are chosen, he is not revealing any ratio between the number of saved and the number of reprobate but rather distinguishing between the ecclesia (the called) and the saved (the chosen). He is thereby undercutting a basic tenet of early Protestantism that the Church is composed solely of the elect. Not all those who profess to hold the Creed are thereby saved: all must run the race to the end, as Saint Paul warns.

The parable of the wheat and the tares not only reinforces this point, since the two crops may be hard to distinguish before the harvest; it also signals a lengthy duration for the Church, since the man sowing the seed is described as rising and sleeping for many days. It is another hint to the Jewish listeners to reorient their expectations of how God will act:

> The Jews, then, think of the kingdom as the time when God will awake from sleep. Our Lord tells them that the kingdom will be as if God awoke only to sow fresh seed in his field, and then slept again. The husbandman in the parable rises from sleep each day; that may mean that God will from time to time interfere providentially

[20] Knox, *Mystery of the Kingdom*, p. 7.

> in the world's history; but in general our lesson is that God will still leave us to ourselves, still allow each man to act in his own way unrebuked, without thereby sanctioning or approving his action. So it will go on until the harvest.[21]

Not all the parables, however, are occasioned by the desire of Jesus to explain what the Church is. Some, like the parable of the wise and foolish virgins, are explicable as warnings to members of the new Church on earth to be vigilant, especially in the exercise of charity, signified in the story by the oil in the lamps. The end of each person's probationary period

> will find some of us ready to spring up and greet their Lord, but only those who are in a state of habitual grace, who have bought for themselves the oil of charity before it is too late. When once the terrible moment of decision has passed, not all the prayers of paradise will avail us: as the tree falls it will lie. "That, as he believed and hoped in thee," so run the words of the burial prayer. It is right that we should commend the faithful in a special way to the mercy of the God in whose presence they have eaten and drunk, who has taught in their streets; but it is possible to have kept the faith, to know where to turn in hours of spiritual need, and yet to find the door shut and the sentence pronounced, *I know you not whence you are.*[22]

And while the story of the laborers in the vineyard has obvious relevance to the tension that might erupt between the followers of the Law who accepted Jesus and the late-coming Gentiles whose lives up to the eleventh hour appeared reprobate in the eyes of the Jewish converts, it speaks to all ages about the danger of comparing merits accrued in human scales. But Knox descries another image too that can be searing to a sense of complacency and yet hopeful to those who retain enough of the oil of charity to be able to greet their Master at the end of life's journey, however little they may seem to have accomplished. It is of those would-be laborers not yet chosen by the master, who are biding their time in the marketplace:

> You have, perhaps, passed such loiterers in the streets with mixed feelings of pity and contempt, marked how they seemed to converse

[21] Ibid., p. 58–59.
[22] Ibid., p. 72.

> but rarely, puffed at empty pipes, gazed vacantly at the stream of busy life that passed them by; and you have wondered how existence could be tolerable with so little of apparent purpose. And yet, look at your own record as you would look at it if you were told that the story of it was to close to-morrow: how much of it has more value for eternity than if your lot had been cast at the street-corner? So much of misdirected effort, of aimless drifting, of unreflective self-indulgence, of unworthy solicitude! And then remember that when Christ our Lord came to earth he came not only to the souls that awaited and welcomed his advent, but to those who, till then, had lived without the thought of God: remember that as he hung upon the Cross he had words not only for those two who watched him so faithfully, but for the unwilling spectator of the Passion who had come out to die defiantly, with no anxiety for his soul's case, yet, on the impulse of a moment, yielded to the pursuit of those nailed Feet, the beckoning of those motionless hands. It is not too late to devote what remains of life, though it be but the spent ashes of a life, to all outward seeming, in service of God's vineyard. That service will not be reckoned by length of days, but by the whole-heartedness of the final surrender. "Because no man hath hired us"—no man? Here is an Employer who values the evening as if it were the morning sacrifice; let the lifting up of your hands be your evening sacrifice now. "Son, go and work to-day in my vineyard"—it is never too soon. "To-day thou shalt be with me in Paradise"—it is never too late.[23]

The parable of the sower and the seed is so suffused with details suitable for meditation that, as was mentioned above, Knox devoted a whole series of talks to its elucidation. One may presume that none of his auditors or readers would be in a position to identify with the seed that fell by the trammeled wayside, which had no chance to grow, typified by Pontius Pilate, so dismissive of truth. Nor with the seed that fell on stony ground, which shot up quickly but withered for lack of roots and represents those Christians who easily give up their faith at the first crisis provoked by the pressure of worldly influences.[24] But perhaps the seed that fell among thorns

[23] Ibid., pp. 125–26.

[24] In another sermon, he paints a thumbnail sketch of the convert who succumbs after an initial burst of devotion: "How impatient they were at the beginning, those souls, always wanting to hurry on their reception, saying, 'Yes, yes,' before the priest had time to explain

offers a warning that everyone may well need to heed. Judas, alas, is the archetype of all the souls who have let the thorns choke the emerging growth:

> We think with horror of the double life Judas must have lived all those years, a thief and a miser in the service of the Prophet that had not where to lay his head. But have we really to look farther than our own souls to find the key to his psychology? In theory we sanctify our pleasures by offering them to God; in theory we cast our care upon him and submit it to his will. But in practice, are we not conscious of a dual control in our souls, two principles fighting for the mastery? The echoes, the anticipations of our worries and our enjoyments pursue us into the moments we think we are dedicating to the service of God—for all the world like Judas, listening to the Sermon on the Mount and fingering his keys. Please God, we are only like Judas in his early stages. But it may give us cause to pray more earnestly. *Lead us not into temptation.*[25]

The test to be administered to determine whether the thorns have the upper hand is not an easy one:

> Examine yourself to find, not the sin you most often commit, but the thing in your life which counts for most next to your religion, the thing which is more likely than anything else to count for even more than your religion. And then imagine to yourself what would happen if a strong temptation came across your path in that very matter. You are always thinking about money—what would happen if you suddenly lost all you had, or if you had the opportunity to increase your possessions unjustly? You are anxious about health—what would you do

---

the doctrine they were discussing! How they roped themselves with medals, in those days of first enthusiasm, and knew what Mass was being performed at which church next Sunday, and were in two minds about a religious vocation! And then the sun got up, not perhaps the fierce, burning sun of persecution which has tested Catholics in other ages, but the glaring sun of the world's cynicism, the wicked old world, with its cocked eyebrow and its shrugged shoulder. There was trouble, perhaps, about a mixed marriage, or they found family opposition was a more serious business than they had reckoned with, or it may have been simply that they came up against everyday realities: in any case, the blade that shot up so green in the pale light of early morning, under the shadow of the sheltering hedge, drooped and died in the glare of the common day." Ronald A. Knox, *University and Anglican Sermons of Ronald A. Knox*, ed. Philip Caraman, S.J. (New York: Sheed and Ward, 1963), p. 334.

[25] Knox, *Mystery of the Kingdom*, p. 156.

> if you became a permanent invalid? You are promoting some good work—what attitude would you adopt if legitimate authority were suddenly to suppress the object of your devotion? Imagine the worst that could happen, and then tell God that, happen what may, he comes first.[26]

If one learns from one's faults and infirmities, as the apostles did after dispersing when Jesus was arrested, tried, and crucified, the opportunity for thirtyfold growth awaits. And through the mystery of God's providential care, even the succumbing to temptation, and even the tempter, albeit unwillingly, are turned to good effect:

> It was only after the humiliation of Good Friday, after the penitential tears and the experience of forgiveness, that the disciples learned, as it seems, all in a moment, the fortitude which enabled them to stand against kings and princes and to carry their Master's name to the utmost ends of the earth. Satan, our Lord told them, had desired to have St Peter that he might sift him as wheat, and God allowed it; allowed him to blow away the chaff, the bluster and the brag and the self-confidence, that were the last obstacles to his sanctity; but the good seed remained, ready to be ground in the mill of persecution and give life to the Body of the Church.[27]

The corresponding trials in most people's lives may be less dramatic, but no less real and no less critical to the achievement of sanctity:

> There are few souls, I suppose, that have not felt at some time the humiliation of defeat. We thought we had counted the cost, prepared ourselves for the worst that could happen, worked ourselves up to an unshakable resolution. We had practised with our swords, slashing about in front of the looking-glass, as it were, and felt that we knew all the strokes. And then we went out and did manfully, and found ourselves following our Master in his Passion, albeit at a distance; it may be, where others failed. Come what might, we would not lose sight of him. And then, astonished at our own courage, we began to play with fire: we allowed ourselves some little indulgence—what if it were a remote occasion of sin? We had faced worse, and come out of it unharmed. And then we began to parley with temptation, and failed, somehow, to give it a straight answer.

[26] Ibid., pp. 158–59.
[27] Ibid., pp. 165–66.

> And then suddenly, without giving us time to remember all our good resolutions and our admirable array of motives to the contrary, Satan made a violent assault on us, and we consented. And still we would not be warned, and, partly with the feeling that it did not matter much now, partly ashamed to draw back from a position once adopted, we remained where we were exposed to the temptation, and this time the consent was deliberate, final, inexcusable. Only then did we awake, as the cock-crow awakes a man from sleep, from the lethargy of a disordered conscience; only then did we see, in a single glimpse, the Face of Christ suffering for our sins. And, please God, we wrenched ourselves free, and the night we fled into opened up to us the flood-gates of contrition.[28]

With contrition comes humility, and a recognition of dependence on God's grace; prudence, so that future occasions of sin are avoided; and love for God, who will even use weaknesses to draw the sinner ultimately to himself.

The Old Law and the New

Some reflections published in the late 1920s offer a refreshing perspective on the cadenced contrasts between the demands of the old and of the new law, which Jesus proclaimed in the Sermon on the Mount. As recorded by Saint Matthew, Jesus frames each statement dramatically with the opening clauses, "You have heard that it was said ... But I say to you ..." And since then, the legalistic and the scrupulous have been diffracting their meaning and rendering them more obscure to the average reader. What, for example, does Jesus mean when he tells his listeners not to swear but simply to say yes or no? The Fundamentalist preacher will assert that he is denouncing cursing, the Quaker that he is invalidating oaths of loyalty to country. But, as Knox points out, in reality he is trying to impress on his listeners that a truthful person has no need to be bound by oaths.

> If you make a statement, it ought naturally to be a true statement, whether you swear to it or not. If you declare the intention of doing a thing, then, as a matter of course, you will do the thing, whether you have bound your conscience by oaths or not. The

[28] Ibid., pp. 166–67.

> disciple of the Sermon on the Mount will (because he loves God) have a natural sincerity about him which will never trouble itself about perjury, because it will shrink from the mere suggestion of untruth.[29]

And when Jesus compares the old law's proscription of murder with the new law's proscription of anger, with its consequent liability for judgment, he does not intend to equate the two. Rather, he is crafting

> a kind of satire on the legalistic way in which the Jews regarded their religion; on the legalistic way in which you and I sometimes regard our religion, when we forget what Master it is we serve. The point is, not that an angry word is as culpable as a mortal blow, but that the source of either is a disposition of the human heart; and such a disposition as ought not to be found at all in the Christian heart, or if it finds a harbour there, should be harboured only for a moment.[30]

There will in all likelihood be innumerable occasions in all people's lives when they will experience anger. What then should be their response in the light of the Sermon on the Mount?

> [I]f sudden irritation does get the better of us for a moment, and we say something we regret afterwards, we are to make it right as soon as possible. If you are offering your gift at the altar, and remember that your brother has some cause of offence against you, run back and be reconciled to him before you offer your gift. Do we remember that as often as we should, when we bring to the altar of the Christian sacrifice the poor gift of our unworthy devotion? We are careful to make our peace with God by confession; are we equally careful to make sure that we are at peace with our fellow men? That does not mean that we should always be going about apologizing to one another; a person who is always apologizing is very often a nuisance. But tell me, when you've "had words" with somebody, isn't there usually a chance, before the next time you go to confession, of saying some kind word, doing some trifling service,

[29] Ronald A. Knox, *The Pastoral Sermons of Ronald A. Knox*, ed. Philip Caraman, S.J. (New York: Sheed and Ward, 1960), p. 54.

[30] Ibid., p. 58.

> which will obliterate the memory of your quarrel without the need of referring to it?[31]

In this advice there is nothing beyond man's capabilities, but it entails an attitude that will be ingrained only after countless efforts at amendment.

The admonition against divorce and remarriage struck the contemporaries of Jesus as unduly harsh, given the Mosaic abrogation of the bond in certain cases, and modern society too raises a jaded eyebrow in feigned disbelief that marriage vows can be irrevocable. But Knox reminds his readers that Jesus has bound himself to his Church despite the shortcomings of her members and that the obligation of fidelity ceases to be an encumbrance when it is actuated by love, not a sentimental love, but a love that unites the married couple with God and remains cognizant of the nature of the vocation being lived.

> We Catholics have a touching habit of making the profession of a nun into a sort of parody of a wedding service: the preacher is expected to address the novice as if she were a bride just waiting for the nuptial blessing. One of these days, I would like to reverse that process, and preach a wedding sermon in which I should address the bride and bridegroom as two souls who were about to take their solemn vows in some enclosed order of religion. A little enclosed order of two, with an object of its own and a spirit of its own—the oldest of all the religious orders, because it was founded by Adam and Eve.[32]

Paradox of the Christian Life

The Lenten season in 1928 also provided the setting for six Wednesday sermons on the paradoxical situation confronting Christians that Saint Paul catalogued in his Second Letter to the Corinthians. The enemies of the Church will charge her adherents with being deceivers when they are in fact truthful, poor yet rich, dying yet alive, and so forth. The expectation the earliest Christians held about the imminence of the Second Coming and the dissolution of the world surely,

[31] Ibid., p. 59.
[32] Ibid., p. 64.

in the eyes of the critics, betokened a dying sect. It is likewise with its emphasis on virginity.

> The most valued and the most treasured among her children, men and women devoted to religion, have died without offspring: even her ordinary workaday priests are pledged to a life of celibacy—and yet the Catholic type is perpetuated, the Catholic body grows and flourishes. When persecution arises, she defies all maxims of prudence, and plunges the most devoted of her servants into a hopeless struggle, which leads to nothing but their imprisonment and death. And still, on the ruin of those types, fresh edifices of faith have been built up, fresh ramparts to defend her from her assailants. "As dying"—a hundred times the world has prophesied our imminent dissolution—"as dying, and behold we live." [33]

Another seeming tension exists between the joy the Christian professes while also experiencing sorrow. To the world it is incomprehensible, but the world has an impoverished notion of what joy is:

> There is a joy which is mere thoughtlessness, the world's privilege; you may be light-hearted, because the sorrows of others and the sins of others strike no responsive chord in your being. But there is also a sorrow which is mere melancholy; which finds in suffering only material for pessimism, which finds in sin only the occasion for disgust. Not such is the sorrow, not such the joy, of God's saints. They have felt, with a sensitiveness of which you and I can only form a dim idea, man's impiety towards God, man's cruelty towards his fellow man, and have pitied, too, all the suffering they saw around them, itself the fruit and the expiation of sin. They have wept and scourged themselves, and spent long nights in an agony of prayer. Yet they have rejoiced, too, because they saw, as we do not see clearly, the beautiful and harmonious working of God's will for men, the perfectness of his dealings, the justification of his revealed message. The sentiments of pity, of horror, of indignation which were provoked in them had no power to dislodge from their hearts that abiding happiness which comes only from a perfect conformity to God's will. They shared the seven sorrows of our blessed Lady, but they shared her joys too. They agonized with their Master, yet, even while they agonized, they rejoiced with him.[34]

[33] Ibid., p. 200.
[34] Ibid., p. 190.

Saints

The feast days of saints and invitations to preach in churches dedicated to a particular saint provided yet another opportunity to gather together sermons with a common theme, focusing on some features—not always the most apparent ones—of the saint in question that might inspire emulation as much as admiration. Knox was especially keen that his listeners not think of the saints as figures of another age whose actions and motivations are unintelligible to the modern mind, such as the heroes of the Bible were presented to him in his Evangelical youth:

> The patriarchs as you knew them when you were quite small, whether from picture-books or from the confirmatory evidence supplied by stained-glass windows, were old gentlemen with beards who had their clothes, mostly in rather dowdy purples and browns, hitched up round them in an inconvenient sort of way, and always carried a large stick in one hand and a thurible in the other when, apparently, they were just going out for a walk. Heavy, lifeless figures they seemed, against a flat, conventional background of palm-trees, and you felt it was impossible that they should ever mean anything to you or carry any living message.[35]

By dint of the occasions giving cause for these sermons, most of his subjects were English or were founders of orders or societies (Saints Benedict, Dominic, Ignatius Loyola, Philip Neri) that had a profound effect on English Catholicism. Twenty of these panegyrics were collected in a 1941 book called *Captive Flames*, which takes its title from a poem by Henry Vaughan:

> If a star were confined into a tomb,
> Her captive flames must needs burn there;
> But when the hand that locked her up gives room,
> She'll shine through all the sphere.[36]

[35] Ronald A. Knox, *The Occasional Sermons of Ronald A. Knox*, ed. Philip Caraman, S.J. (New York: Sheed and Ward, 1960), p. 57.

[36] The poem is titled "They Are All Gone into the World of Light" and expresses Vaughan's desire to join the souls of the blessed in heaven. For a larger selection of his religious and secular poems, see L. C. Martin, ed., *Henry Vaughan: Poetry and Selected Prose* (London: Oxford University Press, 1963).

The intense interior life of the person enjoying communion with God cannot be immured within the precincts of corporeal individuality. It radiates outward with the profligacy of God's love for all creatures. The image is especially apposite in the case of Saint Thérèse of Lisieux, whom Knox commemorates in two sermons preached eighteen years apart. A young nun closed off from the outside world in a Carmelite convent nevertheless could serve in the divine economy as a spiritual engine for missionary activity throughout the world and could do so without performing any seemingly extraordinary actions within her lifetime. Yet after her death in 1897, because the graces she had won by her obedience to God's will radiated unfettered across the globe, this obscure nun would become one of the best-known saints in the twentieth century.

Of course, sanctity is usually attained by people who have no thought of gaining fame in the world, and often every probability of being ignored—or worse, trampled on—by the fashionable of the times. Nowhere is this more evident than in the case of the English martyrs. Saint Thomas More and Saint John Fisher could so easily be portrayed by contemporary molders of public opinion as quibblers over a trivial detail in the preamble to the oath they refused to take. Even many adherents of the Catholic faith could chide them for going too far in antagonizing a king who still held to 90 percent of what the Pope believed.

> How lonely, then, must have been the position of that handful of men who laid down their lives as martyrs in the first persecution! How little hope was there (it must have seemed) that posterity would ever ratify and applaud their solitary protest! But they endured, as seeing him who is invisible; these men had that confidence in God which sees behind the shifting panorama of politics, and rests in eternal truth. They were approved by the testimony of faith, laying down their lives in a hopeless cause, and leaving the promise of better times to posterity.[37]

It took only a few decades to vindicate their prescience about the road down which England was heading with the Henrician impetus. But the knowledge that the first martyrs were right brought little

[37] Knox, *Occasional Sermons*, p. 105.

comfort to the generation of young men who had to go abroad to be ordained priests and then return by stealth to their native land to attempt to rekindle the embers of the faith that was proscribed by the Elizabethan regime. Life on the mission in England meant almost certain capture and death within a few years of arrival, death surrounded by the opprobrium reserved for traitors.

> These priests, then, these seminary priests who slunk about the town in their disguises, must have seemed to Englishmen of the day part of a dead world, like ghosts from the old graveyards which housed the bones of their Catholic ancestors. And yet there must have been old-fashioned people about the town, with their families, who had never accepted the new religion; had conformed to it outwardly, perhaps, through fear of consequences, but had never come to believe in the claims of the usurping ministers who occupied the parish pulpits. And to them, these seminary priests were an odour of life; they brought back memories of the old days when Mass was said at St Alkmund's, when the figures, the emblems of our Lady and the saints were to be seen everywhere, in a brighter and a freer England. In this dead world of Protestantism the sight of Father Garlick or Father Ludham, passing by them without recognition in the street, was like a ray of sunshine piercing through fog. For these men brought with them that Bread of Life which had been interdicted to a starving England these thirty years. An odour of life unto life.[38]

In a less dramatic way, Newman and Manning and Benson and Knox himself had to face the decision of throwing in one's lot with the side that bore no earthly chance of gaining the adherence of the majority of their fellow citizens.[39] If martyrdom be interpreted as a witnessing,

[38] Ibid., p. 133. Two classic works that give an excellent account of the trials and tribulations of the missionary priest are John Gerard, *Autobiography of a Hunted Priest* (New York: Doubleday, 1962), and Philip Caraman, S.J., *Henry Garnet 1555–1606 and the Gunpowder Plot* (New York: Farrar, Straus and Company, 1964). Still unsurpassed as a history of the religious upheaval in England in the sixteenth century is the three-volume study by Philip Hughes, the relevant volume for the Elizabethan times being *The Reformation in England*, vol. 3: *True Religion Now Established* (New York: Macmillan Company, 1954). An excellent and vivid history of the English mission from Campion to Garnet can be found in Alice Hogge, *God's Secret Agents* (New York: Harper Collins, 2005).

[39] Reference has already been made to the biographies of Newman by Ker, Benson by Martindale, and of course Knox by Waugh. It remains to mention the fine study by Robert Gray, *Cardinal Manning: A Biography* (New York: St. Martin's Press, 1985), which supersedes an earlier biography by Knox's friend Shane Leslie, written in 1921.

they could at least claim some fellowship with the generations that chose as they did but paid for the choice with their lives. So Knox can be excused for inserting a personal reflection in one of his sermons extolling the Elizabethan confessors of the faith:

> To have been brought up among the busts of portly gentlemen in semi-classical costume who became Lord Chancellors and Poets Laureate and what not, people who started as boys with your hopes, your ambitions, and succeeded, one way and another, in scrambling up the difficult slopes of fame, among portraits of bishops with puffy sleeves and lawyers in important wigs; and then to find yourself in a place where the most treasured roll of school successes is a long list of names the world has never heard of, men who died convicted as traitors to their country—that should be, to anybody, a sufficiently impressive sermon on the rewards to be sought in this world and in the next. I was taught where, we are assured on good authority, the battle of Waterloo was won. I am teaching where the battle of Tyburn was won, and I thank God for it.[40]

The modern ecumenically minded Christian may wince at the commemoration of the heroic vanguard of the Catholic reformation, but to do so would certainly be to miss Knox's point about these saints. He is not simply writing with the zeal of a convert, eager to show that the exemplars of the faith he now embraces were greater than those of the Anglicanism he has left. The glory of Edmund Campion and Cuthbert Mayne and the other martyrs is not just in their loyalty to the Roman communion but also in their unflinching steadfastness to that faith in the teeth of a totalitarian society. Writing in 1949, long after he had eschewed controversial literature, Knox could see the uncanny parallel between the twentieth century and the England Queen Elizabeth ruled:

> It is one of the few satisfactions you get out of living in times like these, that they help you to understand history. The emergence of the modern gangster-State has made it much easier for you and me to realize what it was like, living in the golden days of Good Queen Bess; the spies, the informers, the agents provocateurs, the search-warrants, the faked accusations of conspiracy, the crushing fines, the

[40] Knox, *Occasional Sermons*, pp. 112–13. Tyburn was the scene of execution of Catholics during the Elizabethan era.

> rack and thumbscrew, the scheming of unscrupulous men at the head of affairs, the sudden rise and fall of favourites—it is all happening now. In Elizabethan England, as in so many parts of the world today, a new gang had worked their way to the top, and they meant to stay there. The old religion could not be tolerated, because it was part of the old order, on whose ruin their hopes depended. Catholicism might be allowed to die out, if it cared to, by a slow process of decent inanition. But to give it artificial respiration, to perpetuate its orders and its sacraments—that would not do. If the Government had really been frightened of foreign plots, their remedy was simple, they could have allowed the old hierarchy of Queen Mary's reign to go on ordaining. But no, that would have been no better than foreign seminaries; it would have been a link with the past.[41]

The twentieth century, he knew, would count at least as many martyrs as the sixteenth, only posterity may never have the opportunity for extolling them because the newer regimes became more efficient in obliterating their memory.

As was previously mentioned, many of the sermons are about saints who had a tangible effect on England's religious history. One such person, who was both a king and a saint, was Edward the Confessor. Knox notes the irony of his having constructed Westminster Abbey, and yet his mortal remains are consigned to a rather unheralded spot while monuments to great statesmen and poets beckon the modern tourist through "that strange mausoleum of nine hundred years of English history which is neither church nor cathedral, because it is too proud to be either". Edward was a political failure and apparently a rather unprepossessing figure to boot, but he was a holy man who was beloved by the poor, to whom he was most generous. So the contrast between his tomb and the tombs of the immortals suggests the rhetorical question to Knox:

> Ask yourself which you would rather have been, in life, of all those great dead who lie in Westminster Abbey, and you will find it a difficult question to answer: there is so much that dazzles, so much that captivates the imagination. Would you rather have written this, have painted that, have built that, have discovered that, have won

[41] Ibid., p. 137.

> this triumph or have carried that enactment?—You can hardly say. But ask yourself which of those great dead you would rather be now, your body there, your soul far away—is there any Christian who would not ask to change places with the Confessor; who would not choose his resting-place, there to wait for the opening of the great Doomsday Book, in which nothing is recorded of men but whether they meant good or evil, whether they loved or neglected God?[42]

Knox had a particular devotion to Saint Philip Neri, manifested in the three separate sermons preached at various Oratories, which Father Caraman has included in his volume. The saint's sense of humor obviously attracts Knox, and the lack of airs, the matter-of-fact interest in all human souls, and the freedom from excessive regulations and organization that he sees as the hallmark of Oratorian spirituality. But the genius of Saint Philip derives of course from an intimate communion with God, which must perforce place all human activity in the proper perspective. The following lengthy quote from one of those sermons summarizes well the saint-in-the-making's vantage point:

> Now, the saint who has been with God, who has familiarized himself with the thought of God's greatness and the heavenly scale of values—what must he think when he comes back to the unreal pomps, the sordid competition, the pretentious would-be wisdom of the world's citizens? Must not he see man as a coxcomb, strutting about in borrowed plumes, and making himself ridiculous afresh with every fresh air he puts on of proprietorship or of self-assertion? Must not he see the world's mad competition as a fond striving for prizes not worth the dust of conflict, and only capable of deluding us because we never rest satisfied with their attainment, but press on at once after others no less transitory? Oh, yes, I grant you, the cynic equally gets that point of view, but the cynic has only found the moral from the record of his own disappointments, and his heart is soured and warped, so that he may scourge the world with satire, but cannot save it from itself. But the saint, the man whose heart is all on fire with desire for the salvation of his fellow men, yet reads in the world about him the pathetic story of their misdirected effort: who sees the mockery of man's boasting, the futility of his striving, yet knows that man, so ridiculous in his

[42] Ibid., pp. 24, 26.

> parade of earthly circumstance, is really a prince, if he but knew it, only not here—will not he be privileged to greet man's follies with the kindly laughter which has in it an echo of heaven and, with the infectiousness of that laughter, teach man to know his present littleness, and through his littleness the greatness that might be his?[43]

With that realization of the proper ordering of desires, the path to sanctity can be mapped out.

RETREAT MEDITATIONS

Practicing the Presence of God

Whether the five books of retreat meditations authored by Knox (two of them posthumously compiled) constitute a genre distinct enough from other published sermons to warrant special attention is perhaps debatable. But viewed together, they offer the reader the fruit of a judicious spiritual director's considerations on how a person, situated either in the lay or in the clerical state, can live a life that is continually reflective of the presence of God.

Knox was himself steeped in the literature of ascetic and spiritual writers, and from that treasury of wisdom, he invokes Brother Lawrence's *The Practice of the Presence of God* and Père de Caussade's *Sacrament of the Present Moment* almost as often as *The Imitation of Christ* in his retreat talks. But what exactly does he mean by putting oneself in God's presence? It is sobering to recall mankind's anomalous position in creation:

> A whole universe attentive at every moment to God's voice, at every moment alive to God, all of it except us, his children. Let us put it to ourselves more forcibly, by reminding ourselves that even *that* is only true where our conscious wills are concerned. Our bodies—they are alive to God all right. If you yawn in church, that may mean that your mind is not being attentive, but your body is being attentive to the Divine will; each muscle reacts as God tells it to react. And I suppose the same is true, when you come to think of it, of our unconscious minds. If some memory intrudes itself upon your thoughts, a dangerous memory, which he allows to tempt you, a gracious memory, which he sends to inspire you, what exactly is

[43] Ibid., pp. 69–70.

happening inside you? This: that your unconscious memory, alive to God's voice, has been searching about in its lumber-room for the exact thing he wanted it to find. Only later, only when your *conscious* mind comes into play, does the temptation become a test at which you fail, the inspiration a grace with which you, somehow, do not correspond. Could anything be more humiliating to us than this spectacle of a listening universe in which we, and we only, are deaf to the Divine call?[44]

And yet Knox is all too aware of the humanness of human beings, of the tendency to be distracted in prayer, to be carried away by mundane tasks or to while away idle moments in pointless pastimes, to suggest that people can focus their thoughts on God throughout the day. Instead, he recommends a less direct approach, whereby

[44] Ronald Knox, *A Retreat for Lay People* (New York: Sheed and Ward, 1955), p. 15.

Br. Lawrence was the religious name of Nicholas Herman, a lay Carmelite brother in seventeenth-century Paris renowned for his saintly simplicity. The classic account of his spiritual life is a very short work, taking up only sixty-four pages in one modern printing, equally divided between recollections of his conversations and fifteen of his letters of spiritual direction. His writing is succinct, unadorned, and suffused with humility. For example, speaking of himself in the third person, he writes: "If sometimes he is a little too much absent from that divine presence, God presently makes Himself to be felt in his soul to recall him, which often happens when he is most engaged in his outward business. He answers with exact fidelity to these inward drawings, either by an elevation of his heart toward God, or by a meek and fond regard to Him; or by such words as love forms upon these occasions, as, for instance, *My God, here I am all devoted to Thee. Lord, make me according to Thy heart.* And then it seems to him (as in effect he feels it) that this God of love, satisfied with such few words, reposes again, and rests in the fund and center of his soul. The experience of these things gives him such an assurance that God is always in the fund or bottom of his soul that it renders him incapable of doubting it upon any account whatever." See Br. Lawrence, *The Practice of the Presence of God* (Westwood, N.J.: Fleming H. Revell Company, 1958), p. 43.

The retreat talks of Jean-Pierre de Caussade, S.J. (1675–1751), to a French convent of Nuns of the Visitation were transcribed and copied over by many hands until they were first published in a somewhat altered form in 1860. The original text only appeared in French in 1966 and was translated into English by Kitty Muggeridge. The essence of Père de Caussade's approach is to invite the aspirant to holiness to realize that perfection is not to be sought in great actions or laborious meditations or in contemplative ecstasies but rather in humble acquiescence to God's will in each and every moment of one's life: "To discover God in the smallest and most ordinary things, as well as in the greatest, is to possess a rare and sublime faith. To find contentment in the present moment is to relish and adore the divine will in the succession of all the things to be done and suffered which make up the duty to the present moment." See Jean-Pierre de Caussade, *The Sacrament of the Present Moment* (Glasgow: William Collins Sons and Co., 1981), p. 84.

> the thought of God is at the very apex of our unconscious minds all the time, overflowing all the time into our conscious thoughts, our conscious acts. It is like a taste in the mouth, a perfume in the nostrils, that conditions for the time being the whole of your experience, without your noticing that it is there. Not God in the very centre of the picture; that is not possible in this life, even for the Saints; but God only just out of the very centre of the picture, so that he dominates the grouping of the whole. Alive to God, every thought of yours haunted—let us not be afraid to use that word for it—haunted by the Divine presence.[45]

Earthbound as we men are, we can only hope to approach the thought of God circuitously, through his creatures. Knox gives an example of how even a supposed distraction at Mass can be turned into a meditation:

> For instance, your eyes are caught by the flowers on the altar, and you say to yourself, "Good gracious, here am I with only a few minutes to spend in church, and I start thinking about flowers!" No, don't say that; think about the flowers and let them take you to God. That one on the left is drooping rather; they'll all be drooping soon—what a short time flowers last! Flowers? So do we, for that matter; what was it the Greek poet said when he sent a wreath to the girl he was in love with? "Girl and garland, both must bloom and both die." And then your mind travels back to yourself a part of this impermanent world, and then it travels off again outwards, and sees as the background, as the obverse of all this impermanence, that eternal being which is God's. Eternal God, brought near to me in the sight of a flower on the altar—you have not really been wasting your time. Your mind has only been like an aeroplane, taxiing before it can be airborne.[46]

Love of God

Now, this consciousness of God ought to generate a loving response on the part of his creatures. And the failure to "feel" that love is another scruple that hinders a confident growth in the spiritual life.

[45] Knox, *Retreat for Lay People*, p. 19.

[46] Ronald Knox, *The Layman and His Conscience: A Retreat* (New York: Sheed and Ward, 1961), pp. 49–50. Similarly, Gerald Vann describes how contemplation of a candle at Mass can lead to deep insights. See Gerald Vann, O.P., *The Divine Pity* (London: Collins, 1960), pp. 149–50.

While the great saints could have a premonition of God's limitless love that could in turn elicit from them an almost romantic response, for the vast majority love will seem artificial and a tepid imitation of the love exhibited toward fellow people. Knox, however, will remind his auditors of the danger of gauging love by emotional pitch—his lifelong study of enthusiastic movements stands as a warning of emotion's illusory appeal in religious practice. If someone wills to love God, to the degree one tries to love him, one is doing so and should not worry about any lack of feeling that love.

Excessive preoccupation with measuring one's love of God just retards the individual's growth in love. The following analogy (which may not exactly embody the latest in speech therapy techniques) gets the point across:

> Have you ever noticed how people who stammer always get their symptoms wrong? They will tell you, for instance, "I find it quite easy to talk about my b-breakfast, and my lunch, and my t-t-tea, but I find it almost impossible to talk about my d-d-d-d-d-d-dinner, because for some reason I seem quite incapable of pronouncing the letter d-d-d-d-d-d-d-dee." The obvious comment on that is, "So far from being incapable of pronouncing the letter D, you've just pronounced it about seventeen times in my hearing." They *can* pronounce the letter D, but because they think they can't, they never manage to get on with the next vowel. And they think they can't love God, never get on to the next thing—which is giving up their lives and their wills to him.[47]

And Knox warns:

> If the devil can make you think that you aren't loving God, it's his best hope of persuading you to stop loving God; he has no weapon like despair. It doesn't matter how little enjoyment you get out of your religion, it doesn't matter how little progress you seem to be making in the affairs of your soul; it may all be like dragging a log uphill, every Hail Mary wrenched from you with an effort, but you *are* loving God.[48]

By the same token, self-analysis to discover and root out sinful practices can be an exercise in futility. The purpose of a retreat (whether

[47] Knox, *Retreat for Lay People*, pp. 77–78.
[48] Knox, *Layman and His Conscience*, p. 38.

experienced in a retreat house under a director's guidance or just in an armchair with one of Knox's retreat books at hand) is simply to open one's heart and one's will to God and thereby let the Holy Spirit work unimpeded in one's life. As Knox notes, "[T]here is a whole world of minute mental happenings which, but for his watchful care, may turn to poison for us. We are asking him to guide us, not only in the momentous choices which seem to us important, but in every tiny decision of our wills, because the effects, even of such a decision, may have results beyond our knowing." [49] The person who cultivates this awareness of God's presence will more easily recognize that the ordinary tasks of daily life—seemingly routine jobs or interactions with family and friends and acquaintances—are those very opportunities ordained by God for fulfilling his designs. To do that work as he would have it done is to be on the pathway to sainthood. Invariably, sacramentalizing the present moment also breeds a healthy optimism about the future: if tomorrow is left in God's hands, accomplishing the work of today will not be held hostage to paralyzing worries about foreseen difficulties. And it also renders us far less beholden to others' opinions of us: God alone sees into hearts, and reads motives more truly than even the individual can, so it is to him only that we look for judgment.

Dealing with Sin

Knox is well aware that achieving this state of spiritual equanimity is no easy feat, because fallen nature inclines people to so many shortcomings and vices that impede their progress. His retreat talks are replete with shrewd insights into the more common vices dragging us down and recommendations for overcoming them, recommendations the surface simplicity of which belies a profound understanding of human psychology.

> When we do try to look at our sins coolly, honestly, and see them as they are, what gets us down sometimes is not the greatness of them so much as the littleness of them; they are so paltry, so mean. We aren't the sort of rollicking medieval Christian who killed a

[49] Ibid., p. 59–60. A truly profound and moving series of meditations on the impermanence of worldly achievements in the journey of life can be found in Bede Jarrett, *No Abiding City* (London: Burns, Oates and Washbourne, 1934).

> man and then went off on a pilgrimage to the Holy Land and spent the rest of his life in sackcloth and ashes. We seem to pass our time like coral-insects, laboriously building up for themselves a great mountain of purgatory out of tiny little peccadilloes; a harsh word here, an uncharitable criticism there, petty dishonesties, almost imperceptible self-indulgence. It humiliates us somehow, to feel that we are such mediocre people, even about our sins. It's not, of course, that we would like to be more sinful than we are; only we have the feeling we might repent better if we had more to repent of. "Though your sins be as scarlet," Isaias says, "they shall be white as snow"—yes, that is splendid; but what is ever going to rid us of this prevailing tinge of pink?[50]

In *A Retreat for Priests*, the only volume of talks that were actually given on a single occasion, Knox ties in each meditation with an Old Testament personage or event. The flight from Egyptian bondage is a suitable type of the Christian's renunciation of allegiance to the world. But the weakness shown by the Israelites mirrors our attachment to sin:

> [Y]ou could not but carry away with you, something of the world you had left behind. Just a keepsake, just a souvenir, of the world you had left behind. There was some passion or some curiosity still unmortified, there was some ambitious spirit still unconquered, there was some dependence on worldly comforts or consolations, which still went with you; you found room for it, at the last moment, in your knapsack. That keepsake, that souvenir, is your danger; will grow up into a golden calf if you are not on your guard about it.[51]

Knox devotes a whole meditation to the corrosive trait of murmuring, which betrays a lack of gratitude to God by finding fault with one's circumstances rather than accepting them and inflicts damage on others' reputations. How much better we would be if we could turn those occasions when we would like nothing better than to carp about someone's shortcomings into occasions to exercise patience with fellow creatures. After all, are we really any better than the people we so glibly criticize?

> Most of us have some unlovable qualities which we can't help; most of us do and say the wrong thing, without meaning to; and besides

[50] Ronald Knox, *Retreat for Beginners* (New York: Sheed and Ward, 1960), p. 93.

[51] Ronald Knox, *A Retreat for Priests* (1946; reprint, London: Sheed and Ward, 1959), pp. 68–69.

> that, there are our faults. Part of the reason why God put you into the world was to exercise the patience of others by your defects; think of that sometimes when you are going to bed. It is a salutary thought. . . . Your bad temper, your excessive cheerfulness, your tiresomeness in conversation; he chose the right person, didn't he? Well, if other people are being so admirably exercised in patience by you, it seems a pity you shouldn't be exercised by them now and again in your turn; that's only fair. The offering of patience which you can make to God; the little things you have to put up with—and that offering is to be made in silence. How it spoils that offering if you make any comment on it in the presence of other people! You must offer it to him like a casket of myrrh, not wasting the scent by opening the lid before it gets to him.[52]

To curb an allied sin, that of quarreling, Knox advises his hearers to imagine themselves a third party to the intemperate words they intend to use to someone's face; that onlooker views such a display of anger with acute embarrassment. That should impress on anyone tempted to use vitriolic language that verbal assaults are not a very effective way of resolving disputes.

This attention to repairing faults ought not to render us paralyzed at the magnitude of the task, as if God were demanding the impossible of us.

> We mustn't conceive the mount of the beatitudes as if it were a new Sinai, covered all over with notice-boards, only more of them. Sinai, I mean saying, "Thou shalt not kill, thou shalt not steal, thou shalt not covet," and then a whole fresh lot of boards put up saying, "Thou shalt not be angry," "Thou shalt not call people Raca," "Thou shalt not say Thou fool." Our Lord did say that his yoke was easy, that his burden was light, and he means it. So that when he says, "Your justice must give fuller measure than the justice of the scribes and Pharisees" the point is not that we should feel bound to do a whole lot of things the scribes and Pharisees didn't. The point is that we should go about the business of living as God wants us to live in a spirit which the scribes and the Pharisees never dreamed of.[53]

[52] Ronald Knox, *The Priestly Life* (New York: Sheed and Ward, 1958), pp. 66–67.
[53] Knox, *Layman and His Conscience*, p. 129.

Prayer

But above all, Knox returns to the advice that is the overarching theme of all his retreat talks: if we would only remember that we are in the presence of God, our attachment to sins would diminish and we would find the practice of virtue easier. Prayer too becomes a more natural act the more it is recognized as placing oneself at the disposal of God's communications to us rather than as the completion of a set of formulaic texts. Knox clearly does not denigrate the recital of prayers, especially of the Rosary, about which he gives several illuminating meditations. There are times too when mental distractions are such that the only act of worship accomplished is that of the body kneeling and the voice uttering familiar prayers. Only the scrupulous would deny any efficacy to such efforts at prayer, even when the context is the Mass and the prayers are primarily those listened to as the priest recites them.

Indeed Knox recalls, at the time of the Eucharistic Congress in Dublin, observing an Eastern Rite prelate celebrating Mass using the Mozarabic liturgy in front of a congregation composed primarily of elderly Irish women who were concentrating solely on their Rosary beads. At the risk of offending liturgists, he saw this as an example of diversity in unity in the worship of God. Long priestly experience brought him to a realization that one of the chief obstacles to efficacious prayer in people's lives is this notion that formulas above all count with God, whereas in fact,

> we must go to him as a Father, who understands us, not treat him as if we were trying to put across a difficult message to somebody who was rather deaf and rather stupid.... Since God knows every thought which passes through our minds, the use of words in our prayer is designed for our sakes, not for his; it's just because we want to be sure that such and such a consecrated formula has been repeated in full.... To keep quiet in his presence, letting our hearts go out to him in utter confidence, in appealing love, in a tender sense of our own unworthiness—that, no less than any formula of words, and perhaps more than any formula of words, is what is really meant by prayer.[54]

[54] Knox, *Retreat for Lay People*, pp. 227–28.

Last Things

Death is a subject that cannot be shirked in any retreat program, uncongenial as the thought of it is to almost everyone, Knox included. Theologically, he reminds the retreatant, it should be looked forward to with anticipation as the end of a life of struggle to serve an invisible God, the moment when shadows give way to reality and we finally see God face to face. But the dissociation of soul and body it necessarily entails for even the most saintly of people, coupled with fear of the unknown, combine to create a natural revulsion in us. This transitory existence we are accustomed to affords many creature comforts and loves and friendships to which we would fain hold on, and so would bypass the opportunity for the fuller life Jesus has promised us. A common occurrence affords an example:

> I'm sure you must have had the experience before now of being asked out to something or other and really rather wanting to go, knowing that it will be rather fun when you get there, and yet—yet at the last moment, when the time comes to start, you begin to hang back and wonder why on earth you accepted that invitation. There is the effort of going there; there is the almost equal effort of leaving off whatever it is you are doing at the moment. . . . Why on earth was I such a fool, you ask yourself, as to accept that invitation, when I might have been staying quietly at home? In the end you go, simply because you have said you'd go; at least, I hope you are not one of those appalling people who ring up at the last moment and plead an important subsequent engagement. And when you do get there, of course you enjoy yourself thoroughly, as you knew you would. I wonder, isn't that rather the position we are all in about leaving earth for heaven? We know that we shall be happy there; and yet the silly spell which our earthly occupations and ambitions exercise over us is so strong that we should never summon up the energy to take the journey, if it rested with ourselves whether we should take it or not.[55]

So death comes to us all, at a time not of our choosing (since we would be inclined to defer it indefinitely). In one meditation, titled "Death as a Friend", Knox draws attention to the release from

[55] Knox, *Retreat for Beginners*, pp. 190–91.

worries it entails. We offer up unfinished projects to God's providential management, then old grudges no longer weigh on us, and especially the fear that damnation awaits us melts away, overcome by the virtue of hope and a clearer realization of Christ's infinite mercy. "Trust in God, which meant such a difficult struggle even in our best moments hitherto, has now become part of the atmosphere we breathe. Even during the interval—if there *is* an interval—between death and judgment, we shall be so conditioned by that atmosphere of trust that there will be no sense of insecurity, though we are still unjudged." [56]

Of course, that is not to say that damnation is not an option for a person to choose, but the final impenitence required to seal it suggests that it will not come as a surprise to those who experience it.

> We have to say, then, that in spite of that love with which God regards every creature he has made, it is possible for a human soul, by misusing his graces, by neglecting his warnings, by defying his will, obstinately, to the last, to bring itself to perdition; to a state in which it no longer responds to the love of God, the love of God no longer acts upon it, any more than a magnet would act upon a piece of wood. By its own fault, it has shut out God's mercies and made for itself a godless universe. While it still lived on earth, the effect of that was not manifest. The sun gave its light and warmth, the earth ministered food, life offered its comforts, to that rebellious soul as much as to any other. And on the other side, that soul felt no need of God; for, in this world in which we walk by faith and not by sight, it is possible to lose sight of God without any sense of deprivation, because we can still huddle creatures closer to us and content ourselves with them instead.
>
> But when death comes, the soul cannot do without God any longer. Creatures vanish from its grasp; it is thrown back on its need for God—and God is not there.[57]

C. S. Lewis, in the imaginative short novel *The Great Divorce*, depicted hell as an enormous bleak city populated by irritating and irritable people who chose to reside there because they clung tenaciously to the vices they cultivated on earth, even when given the opportunity

[56] Knox, *Priestly Life*, p. 166.
[57] Knox, *Retreat for Beginners*, pp. 210–11.

to go to heaven if only they would purge themselves of their extreme self-centeredness.[58] Knox paints a similar picture:

> Do you know what it is to start the day in a thoroughly bad temper, put out of humour by some misadventure at the beginning of it? You have missed an important train, perhaps, or you have got into a temper unreasonably, and it has ruffled you; a bad omen to begin your day's work with. Unless you have unusually steady nerves, you will know the effect of such an experience on your peace of mind; how you find fresh food for disgust in everything you come across. Each little petty annoyance, knocking your head against something or sitting in a draught or having somebody next you who whistles to himself, becomes so intolerable an annoyance that you feel you want to scream with rage. Why is that? Because you are not at peace in yourself; and to the man who is not at peace in himself there can be no peace in his surroundings either; the world is at war with him. Now, if you multiply that experience to the scale of eternity you will catch some glimpse of what hell must be like. The sufferings of sense are only the echo, as it were, of that deep-rooted discomfort which pervades our whole being. As we saw, so long as his earthly life lasted the unhappy man could call upon the creatures around him for their services like the rest of us, and they obeyed him. There was nothing to warn him that he was an outlaw in God's universe. But now, now it is all different. A soul made for God, which finds itself in eternity cut off from God, is a complete misfit; we are at war with ourselves, and therefore our whole environment is at war with us. We cannot, with our limited imaginations, form any very accurate picture about what our environment will be like in a future existence. But we can be quite certain that, to the lost soul, that environment will be utterly hostile. Put it in this way—if a lost soul entered heaven by mistake, the music of heaven would seem to it like a series of hideous discords. It carries the seeds of its own misery in itself.[59]

[58] C. S. Lewis, *The Great Divorce* (New York: Macmillan Company, 1946).

[59] Knox, *Retreat for Lay People*, pp. 56–57. Bede Jarrett had put it thus in a book written forty years earlier for a similar audience: "It is as though in a flash we had at last understood what everything in life was for, discovered the meaning of everything that had befallen us, found the solution to all the perplexities that had worried us—and then realized that our own previous ideas, and the practice that had followed them, had resulted in our complete inability to make use of life; a perfect nightmare in which one knew the use of everything, but could use nothing to its purpose. This torment, then, can come only to

The choice of avoiding that bleak fate is at hand to everyone, and no more inspiring example of how easily, how directly, we can respond to grace and turn away from the path to perdition is given than by the Penitent Thief.

> We have no evidence in scripture that this man had ever harboured a generous sentiment, or possessed a redeeming virtue; even on the cross, his repentance is an afterthought. Of such, you would have said, the devil reaps his harvest of souls. Yet at the last moment, it may be, in which the gift of speech was granted him, he spoke a few words to his guiltless fellow-sufferer; and from that Heart, busy with all the tragedies of a universe, came to this one suppliant his sentence of reprieve, "Amen I say to thee, to-day thou shalt be with me in Paradise."[60]

The Penitent Thief seized the opportunity at the last minute, when it was presented to him. If we seize that moment now, and continuously hereafter, we will be able to offer ourselves to God in a way parallel to the offering Jesus makes at each consecration during Mass.

> The crucial moment in the holy Mass is when the priest says, *Hoc est corpus meum*. And in our sacrifice the crucial moment is that of death, when we too say, *Hoc est corpus meum*. "This is my body, Lord, the body thou gavest me, and art now taking away from me, the body in which I have suffered, and sinned. Come, holy oils, and seal these gateways of sense, the points of contact in me between body and soul; seal them well, this is a secret present from me to my God." And if death is the moment of consecration, we, as we look forward to it now, are making our offertory; we are holding out our bodies on the paten, ready against the moment when they will be caught away from us in the consummation of the sacrifice. In a fallen world, sacrifice means the destruction, the annihilation, as far as possible, of the thing offered. It is God's merciful decree that death should not be a complete annihilation. But this separating of soul and body is the nearest thing to

---

those who have died in revolt against God—not those who seemingly die in sin, for in the last ebb of consciousness who knows what mercies God has in store? But if any such pass out from here hating God, in revolt against Him—then, flung out as they are into eternity (an unchanging Now), they must remain for ever hating and losing, and conscious of their incalculable loss." See Bede Jarrett, *Meditations for Layfolk* (1915; reprint, London: Catholic Truth Society, 1941), pp. 74–75.

[60] Knox, *Retreat for Lay People*, p. 30.

> annihilation which it is ours to give. Let us look forward, then, to death, as the moment at which we shall make to God the supreme confession of our creatureliness; when we shall immolate, in honour of his eternity, this transitory existence of ours; offer him this candle, to be blown out. The dearer a thing life seems to you, the harder it seems to relinquish, the more motive for generosity in offering it. So little, the real value of the sacrifice we make, when we give our souls into his hands; all the better, then, if (by a kind of sentimental value) it means much to us, who make it.[61]

And what are we to think of heaven? Here it must suffice simply to accept Saint Paul's breathless exclamation that eye has not seen nor ear heard what God has in store for us. But perhaps a glimmer of that felicity descends on us on those occasions when we are transported by a pure joy, one we instinctively share with our fellow men:

> so we picture it as part of those heavenly joys which we shall share one day, please God, with those whom we loved on earth, with the saints who are bathed in it, glowing with it, according to the more perfect measure of their receptivity. No, don't let us try to imagine heaven; we shall get nowhere. Let us only try to see our present happiness—a mere slice of experience, outlined for us by contrast with the dull level of ordinary life—against a background of essential happiness to which, somehow, it belongs.[62]

Only Jesus

There is a timeless appeal in these retreat talks, so carefully directed to the individual reader as well as the contemporary listener. *The Layman and His Conscience* begins with a reflection on the scene where Jesus singles out the blind man Bartimaeus from a crowd and summons him to himself. Each of us is being called likewise, uniquely, for a conference with Jesus on our current progress in the spiritual life:

> He is interested in everything about you, even the things that bore other people, your health, your foibles, your scruples. He cares as much for you individually as if you were the only soul he had ever created; God doesn't do things—can't do things—by halves. He

[61] Ibid., pp. 41–42.
[62] Knox, *Layman and His Conscience*, p. 210.

> arranged to meet you here; arranged that you should go into retreat just now, with this particular background of worries and problems which you brought in with you. You, on your side, had almost given up the struggle to preserve your own identity; were prepared to treat yourself as just an average Christian, taking your cue from the rest, looking round to see what they did and falling into line with them. You would be one of a crowd, and sooner or later, please God, you would rush the barriers into heaven as one of a crowd, while nobody was looking. "You didn't really think that?" he says. "When a soul reaches its heaven, it is always a separate event; its course has been mapped out for it beforehand, and it achieves its destiny just so, and not anyhow else. We had a plan, hadn't we, for your life? And I have come to see how it is getting on. Not very brilliantly, I expect; never mind—*animaequior esto*, be calm about it."[63]

Knox would not exacerbate scruples or fears of damnation. Nor would he countenance the depiction of God as a policeman out to trap careless transgressors of the law. It is actually the post-Transfiguration Jesus upon whom Knox wants his readers to be focused as they emerge from retreat, not shining brilliantly while flanked by the prophets of the old dispensation, but

> "Jesus only with them;" better that you should go away with the sense of a Divine Friend, always at your side to check, to console, to encourage you; a Friend whose presence you make your own whenever you will turn to him, amidst the press of secular occupations, in a devout moment of recollection.
>
> No man any more, but Jesus only—yes, you will meet the people you are accustomed to meet; but if only you would learn in meeting them to see Jesus in them! Is there some face that tempts you with memories of unholy desires in the past? You will see behind it

[63] Ibid., pp. 5–6. As Dom John Chapman observes: "We all have one unpleasant person to live with, whom we can't get away from—ourselves. Put up with yourself, and take your own hated imperfection and weakness as an unpleasantness you have to bear with. It is very hard, but it is really a very perfect act of love to God." See *The Spiritual Letters of Dom John Chapman, O.S.B.*, ed. Dom Roger Hudleston (London: Sheed and Ward, 1944), p. 156. Chapman wrote far more extensively of contemplative prayer than Knox ever did, and his letters make clear his debt to St. John of the Cross and Père de Caussade for his insights into the abandonment of the will to God in prayer. A useful discussion of his contribution to spirituality is the chapter by B. C. Butler in *English Spiritual Writers*, ed. Charles Davis (New York: Sheed and Ward, 1961), pp. 182–202.

a soul which Jesus loves, a soul in which Jesus desires to express his own image. Is there someone whose conversation bores you, whose importunity wearies you, whose outward manners offend you? Here too you will see Jesus only—the Crucified appealing to you out of those human souls, that need your care, your forbearance, your compassion. Jesus with you, not an abstract idea, not a historical memory, not enthroned in the terrors of Judgment, but a Friend, human and divine, constantly at your side, sharing your burdens, understanding your difficulties, sympathizing with your work.[64]

[64] Knox, *Layman and His Conscience*, pp. 217–18.

INDEX